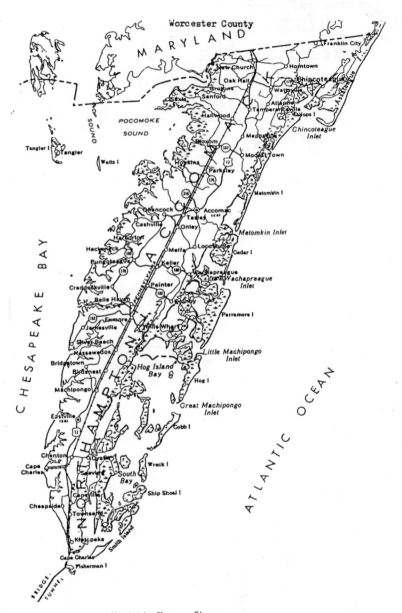

Virginia's Eastern Shore

Marriage Records of Accomack County, Virginia 1776-1854 Recorded in Bonds, Licenses and Ministers' Returns

by

Nora Miller Turman, M.A., C.G.E.

HERITAGE BOOKS, INC.

Other Heritage Books by
Nora Miller Turman:

The Eastern Shore of Virginia, 1606-1964

The map used as a frontispiece was created by
A. Hughlett Mason, Ph.D. 1905-1974

Published 1994 by

HERITAGE BOOKS, INC.
1540-E Pointer Ridge Place,
Bowie, Maryland 20716
(301) 390-7709

ISBN 0-7884-0135-1

A Complete Catalog Listing Hundreds of Titles
on Genealogy, History, and Americana
Available Free on Request

TABLE OF CONTENTS

FOREWORD

Marriage Records of Accomack County, Virginia, 1776-1854: Records in Bonds, Licenses, and Ministers' Returns is a major contribution to Virginia genealogy and history. Nora M. Turman has collected all extant marriage bonds, 1776-1850, on file in the Accomack County Clerk's Office, Accomac, and in the Virginia State Library, Richmond. She has also included bonds for the years 1831-1841 and 1847-1850 which were abstracted by earlier genealogists from records which have since disappeared.

Moreover, she has augmented the bonds with marriages recorded only in the Ministers' Returns, 1805-1850 and 1850-53. Also included are the eighteen surviving Accomack County marriage records from the colonial period.

Marriage Records of Accomack County, Virginia, 1776-1854 is a worthy companion to Jean M. Mihalyka's _Marriages, Northampton County, Virginia, 1660/1-1854_ (Bowie, MD, 1991) and the capstone of a distinguished genealogical career.

Brooks Miles Barnes
Onancock, Virginia
October, 1994

ACKNOWLEDGEMENTS

Thanks are due to the personnel, both past and present, of the office of the Accomack County Clerk of Court and of the Eastern Shore Public Library. The Virginia State Library, the Drummondtown Branch of the Association for the Preservation of Virginia Antiquities (APVA), and the Eastern Shore Chapter of the Daughters of the American Revolution (DAR) had a part in preserving the original marriage bonds. Grateful thanks to these and other organizations and individuals who have helped save Accomack County marriage records.

Those who have been most helpful in collecting and editing these marriage records receive special thanks. Samuel L. Cooper, Clerk of Court, and Cloretta Harris, Assistant Clerk, helped in rescuing the badly faded Ministers' Returns and in other ways. Brooks Miles Barnes and associates at the Eastern Shore Public Library helped in more ways than can be listed in this space. Elizabeth Mason gave permission to use the map. Mary Frances Carey located and abstracted some marriage bonds and provided the list of alternate names for women. Jean M. Mihalyka provided the challenge for this undertaking by producing a similar volume for Northampton County. Jane Corson Lassiter and Brooke Tompkins entered the 6,000 records and other text into the computer. Gladys Lee Hamilton ably proofread the manuscript.

To these and others goes my sincere appreciation

Nora Miller Turman
Certified Genealogist
Emeritus
Onancock, Virginia
October 1994

SOURCES

Accomack County Clerk's Office, Accomac

Marriage Bonds, 1857-1850
Marriage Licenses, 1850-1854
Marriage Register No. I, 1805-1850
Marriage Register No. ii, 1850-1854

Eastern Shore Public Library, Accomac

Marriage Bonds, 1800-1831 (microfilm of originals in the Virginia State Library, Richmond)
Typescript Abstracts:
  Accomack Marriage Bonds, 1800-1805, by Mary Frances Carey
  Accomack Marriage Bonds, 1805-1831, by Mark C. Lewis
  Accomack Marriage Bonds, 1832-1841, by Nora M. Turman
  Accomack Marriage Bonds, 1847-1850, by Nora M. Turman
  Accomack Marriage Licenses, 1850-1854, by Mary Frances Carey
The Marriage License Bonds of Accomack County, Virginia, 1660/1-1854, compiled by Stratton Nottingham (Onancock, VA, 1927)
Map of the Eastern Shore of Virginia by A. Hughlett Mason, Ph.D. (1905-1974).

Examples of bonds and a summary of Virginia marriage laws are found in Jean M. Mihalyka, Marriages, Northampton County, Virginia, 1660/1-1854, (Bowie, MD, Heritage Books, Inc. 1991).

FEMALE NAMES WITH ALTERNATE FORMS

A name used for either a man or a woman can sometimes cause a problem for the researcher, as can different spellings. We find "Francis" and "Frances." for example, used for both men and women in the records. However, greater problems are found with the various versions of a given name that are used interchangeably in the records. Therefore, a list of these variants, compiled by Mary Frances Carey, C.G., and arranged by their modern spellings, follows.

Adaline	Addie
Amelia	Milla, Milly
Ann	Anna, Annie, Nan, Nancy
Caroline	Carrie, Lina
Catherine	Cattie, Caty
Charlotte	Lottie
Clarissa	Clarsie, Clarsey
Damara	Damy, Daisey
Eleanor,	Ellen, Nell, Nelly, Nora
Elizabeth	Ellen, Eliza, Betty, Betsy, Lib, Lizzie
Esther, Hester	Essie, Hessy, Hetty
Euphemia	Uphamia, Famey
Frances	Fanny
Gertrude	Gatty, Girty, Trudy
Harriet	Hattie, Hetty
Henrietta	Henny, Hetty, Ritter
Isabelle,Isabella	Belle
Leticia, Letitia	Lettice, Letty
Lucretia	Critty, Luky
Mariah	Annamariah, Ritter
Margaret	Margie, Peggy
Martha	Matty, Patty, Patsy
Mary	Manie, Molly, Polly
Matilda	Tilly, Tinny
Mildred	Millie, Milly
Rebecca	Becky
Sarah	Sally, Sadie, Sary
Susan, Susanna	Suky, Sue
Tabitha, Tabithia	Tabby. Biddy, Bithy
Trephenia	Tippy, Treppy
Zipporah	Zippy

INTRODUCTION

When Virginia became a commonwealth in 1776 the only change in the colonial marriage law requiring the reading of banns or a bond by the groom was that the bonds were now given to the governor. In 1780 the General Assembly enacted a law giving Methodist, Presbyterian, and other ordained ministers the right to officiate at marriages. Only minor changes were made in the marriage laws until 1848.

Banns

The minister of the church (or churches) where the couple resided read at three divine services as follows:

> I publish the banns of marriage between (name of groom) and (name of bride) of (name of parish). If any of you know just cause why they may not be joined together in holy matrimony, you are bidden to declare it. This is the first (or second or third) time of asking.

Bonds

Virginia law stated that the Clerk of Court of the county where the bride resided should take bond with good security for the sum of fifty dollars or more to the Governor of Virginia with the condition that there was no lawful cause to obstruct the marriage for which the license was desired. The bond was signed by the groom and his security. Incidentally, these signatures are helpful in identifying different people with the same name. An Act of the General Assembly in 1848 repealed the law permitting marriage by reading banns. Bonds were discontinued in 1850.

Licenses

Licenses were issued by the Accomack County Clerk of Court from 1850. They usually contained the name of the mother or guardian of the bride if the bride was under eighteen years of age. Licenses with Ministers' Returns are recorded in Marriage Register No. II, 1850-1854.

An Act of the General Assembly passed 11 April 1853 stated:

From 1 January 1854 the Clerk of Court of every county shall keep three books to be called respectively Register of Marriages, Register of Births, and Register of Deaths. Every person solemnizing a marriage shall return a duly signed copy of the license which contains the date and place of marriage, full names and ages of both parties, whether single or widowed, place of birth and residence, names of their parents and occupation of the husband. The Clerk of Court shall put a summary of each marriage in the Marriage Register and index it.

A license could be secured only in the county or city where the woman lived. After World War II the law was amended so a license could be obtained in the county or city where either the man or woman was resident.

Ministers' Returns

Ministers' Returns, 1805-1850 and 1850-1853, are bound together. Some 1849 marriages are recorded in 1850. Dates have been standardized to day-month-year when complete information is given. Some ministers only listed the year, and one have those marriages "between June 1825 and September 1837." Some ministers did not file reports. Unless a bond exists, there is no record of many marriages before 1854 and of some thereafter.

Maryland Marriages

Some couples got licenses in Snow Hill, seat of Worcester County, Maryland, for convenience or to avoid giving bond or having banns read. Snow Hill was nearer than Accomac and accessible by boat for those living in upper Accomack County. Couples married in Virginia with Maryland licenses are listed in both states. Between 1795 and 1865 many couples were married in Worcester County.

Alternate Spellings

Family names may have a number of spellings. For example, Adkinson may appear as Atkinson, Bailey as Bayly, Benson as Bentson, Bird as Byrd, Dalby as Dolby, Medcalf as Metcalf, Nickson as Nixon, Pewsey as Pusey, Somers as Sumers, Starling as Sterling, Tailor as Taylor, Wescoat as Wescott, Vessells as Wessells, Truitt as Trewett (and five other variations), and Winder as Window.

Importance of Marriage Records

Accomack County has no birth or death records before 1854. Records from 1854 through 1896 include only those given to the Commissioner of Revenue along with tax assessment. Modern vital statistics did not begin until 1912. Bible records are reliable only if entries were made as births or deaths occurred. Few gravestones before 1854 have survived, and some of those existing were erected years after a death and have incorrect dates. Census entries are sometimes approximate. Although Eastern Shore court records are continuous from 1632, specific information must often be gleaned from a variety of sources. Marriage records are among the most reliable sources for family histories.

African American Marriages

African Americans are identified by FN (Free Negro), although five different terms were used in the bonds and licenses. No marriages by banns were found for African Americans.

Arrangement of Marriage Records

Marriages are arranged alphabetically by surnames of the grooms followed by the name of the bride and the security, if from a bond, and the dates which were taken from the bonds, even if ministers' returns were available. Some ministers gave actual dates of ceremonies, while others grouped them by year or years. The date of a bond might be a day, a week or a month earlier than the ceremony. Dates on the court records may even differ by a few days from those that appear in a family Bible. A marriage by banns is not on record if the minister failed to file the return with the Clerk of Court.

Index of Brides

A list of brides, alphabetical by family and given names, follows the grooms list.

```
Abbott, George H.          Mary White                      2 Jun 1814
     Severn H. Dukes and T. Henry Copes, sec.

Abbott, John               Leah Abbott                    10 Dec 1785
     Thomas Parker, sec.

Abbott, John               Bridget Barnes                 16 Jan 1775
                           of Susanna
     William Black Bunting, sec.

Abbott, Martin             Mahala Collins                 14 Jan 1833
     FN                    FN of Southy
     James Martin and Sewell Martin, sec.

Abbott, Samuel             Mary Ann Savage                 7 Feb 1828
     of Tommy              of Robert
     John Savage of R. and William Watts, sec.

Abbott, William            Nancy Cowley                   23 Feb 1828
     of Thomas             of William
     Richard Bloxom and James James, sec.

Abdale, Joseph             Elizabeth Ward                  5 Jan 1803
     John Bonwell of James, sec.

Abdale, Revel              Nancy Minson                   25 Apr 1808
     George Miles, sec.

Abdel, Abel                Sally Custis                   26 Jul 1833
     J. Poulson, sec.

Abram FN                   Bethamia Pewitt FN             25 May 1825
     freed by Crippen
     Molly Pewitt, sec.

Adair, George             Mrs. Francis E. Kellam          15 May 1852
                           (wid of Francis Kellam)

Adair, John W.            Margaret S. Savage               5 Mar 1851
                           of Mary Rowley

Adair, Theodore W.         Mary Watson                    28 Feb 1820
                           of Ephraim
     James W. Parker, sec. and Ephraim Watson, consent

Adams, David               Comfort Ewell                  21 Jan 1806
     Obed Adams, sec.

Adams, James C. (wdr)      Mary Powell of Seth            22 Jan 1850
     John R. Drummond, sec.
```

```
Adams, James C.          Susan K. Rayfield        20 Dec 1839
     Edward C. Adams, sec.

Adams, John              Milcah Ann Parks         13 Oct 1829
     of Obed                 of Arthur
     Obed Adams and Arthur Parks, sec.

Adams, Leonard H.        Virginia S. Joynes        8 Apr 1857
                         of Edward

Adams, Obed              Sally Silverthorn         5 Nov 1798
     Robert Taylor, sec.

Adams, Stephen           Betsy Lurton             27 Aug 1798
     Thomas Jenkins, sec.

Adams, Thomas B.         Maria Rayfield of Wm.    25 Jan 1830
     Thomas J. White, sec.

Adams, Thomas B.         Elizabeth B. Lewis        9 May 1838
                         of Robert
          William W. Adams, sec.

Adams, Thomas            Mary Wilson              15 Jul 1831
          John Gladding, sec.

Adams, William           Mary Lewis               17 Dec 1835

Addir, John B.           Joice Ames of Joseph     23 Feb 1829
     Joseph S. Hill, sec.

Addison, Arthur          Elizabeth Evans          30 Dec 1811
                         (wid John)
          William Roley, sec.

Addison, George          Eliza Selby              27 Dec 1820
                         (wid Harvey)
          Arthur Addison, sec.

Addison, George          Elizabeth Selvy          28 Dec 1820

Addison, Isaac FN        Phyllis Revell            3 Jun 1820

Addison, James H.        Ann R. Scarburgh         11 Feb 1834
                         of George
          Robert W. Williams, sec.

Addison, James H.        Ann R. Scarburgh         13 Apr 1834

Addison, John            Ann Small                15 Nov 1820
     of Arthur              of Levi Addison
```

Arthur Addison and John S. Johnson, sec.

Addison, John   Susanna Kellam   10 Oct 1786
    William Leatherbury, sec.

Addison, Kendall   Miss Jane O. Coward   13 Sep 1819
    Samuel Coward and Richard D. Bayley, sec.

Addison, Levi   Dority Aimes   22 Dec 1800
    Benjamin Ames, sec.

Addison, Richard   Matilda Sharpley   16 Jan 1821
    of Arthur   of John
    Ralph B. Corbin, sec., John Addison consent

Addison, Richard   Seymour Bunting   26 Feb 1810
    Ayres Taylor, sec.

Addison, William (wdr)   Caroline J. Bayly   23 Jul 1844

Addison, WIlliam B.   Euphamia Bowman   13 Nov 1806
    Isaac Outten, sec.

Addison, Willilam   Nancy Milby (wid John)   23 Aug 1806
    Shadrack Ames, sec.

Ague, William   Sussey James   10 Jan 1801

Ailworth, James   Elizabeth Lillaston   18 Nov 1806
    John Dix, sec.

Ailworth, James J.   Sarah Parramore   12 Mar 1846

Ailworth, John B. (wdr)   Ellen A. Bagwell   7 Oct 1847
                           of Augustus W. Bagwell
    John W. Gillit, sec.

Ailworth, John B.   Jane C. Conquest   10 Oct 1839
    Edmund R. Allen and Thomas R. Joynes, sec.

Ailworth, William   Nancy Duncan   2 Sep 1805
    Major Bird, sec.

Alexander, Peter T.   Henny Sharpley   2 Nov 1827

Alexander, Thomas   Mary Kellam   1 Jan 1812
    Ezekiel Kellam, sec.

Allen, Daniel FN   Esther Goliah FN   6 Apr 1808
    Levin Godfree, sec.

Allen, Edmund R.   Mary R. Custis of Wm.   22 Oct 1840
     H. B. Custis and James J. Ailworth, sec.

Allen, John   Margaret Arbuckle   11 Nov 1785
     Edward Arbuckle, sec.

Allen, John   Euphamia Milburn (wid)   17 Dec 1810
     Stephen McCready, sec.

Allen, John (wdr)   Lovey Maddox of John   5 Mar 1822
     John Maddox, sec.

Allen, Joseph   Hannah Hutson   2 Jun 1794

Allen, Joseph   Rachel Dickerson   27 Dec 1791

Allen, Robert FN   Jane Rosser   26 Jan 1844

Allen, Thomas (wdr)   Nancy Hatheway   20 Aug 1835
     James and Robert Taylor, sec.

Allen, Thomas   Nancy Marshall   27 Nov 1826
     of Zodac   of Thomas
     Frederick Conner and David Broadwater, sec.

Allen, Thomas   Sally Massey   8 Oct 1819
     of Moses   (wid James)
     James Duncan and Samuel Walston, sec.

Allen, Thomas   Hepsey Evans   30 Aug 1803
     John Marshall, sec.

Ames, Benjamin   Elizabeth Pearce   17 Jul 1802
     Robert Snead, sec.

Ames, Benjamin   Betsy Rayfield   6 Jan 1801
     Thomas Scarburgh, sec.

Ames, Benjamin   Nancy Hyslop   21 Oct 1805
     John Ames, sec.

Ames, Churchel   Leah Kellam of Sacker   17 Oct 1825
     John Hutchinson, sec.

Ames, Churchill   Mary Scott   25 Jan 1808
         Shadrock Ames, sec.

Ames, Edward T   Sarah Hopkins of Stephen   9 Mar 1846
     John B. Ailworth, sec.

Ames, Edward H.   Ann Kellam of Adah   18 Jan 1831

Wm. M. Ames and John Hyslop, sec.

Ames, Edward D.	Ann Heath of Joseph	23 Dec 1851
Ames, Edward T.	Sarah Hopkins	10 Mar 1847
Ames, James S.	Margaret Doughty	21 Nov 1849
Ames, James (wdr)	Catherine Savage of Littleton	16 Aug 1858
Ames, James H. of Molly East	Belle S. Purnell of Issac L.	3 Jan 1853
Ames, James S.	Margaret Dowty (wid of Jeptha Dowty)	20 Nov. 1849

Benjamin D. Wise, sec.

Ames, Jesse W.	Mahala C. Milby of Jno., dec'd.	14 Jan 1817

Richard Ames, sec.

Ames, Jesse	Tamar Harmon	7 Apr 1829

Thomas H. Ames and Littleton P. Henderson, sec.

Ames, Jesse	Mahala Milby	10 Jan 1817
Ames, John	Margaret Lingo	28 Sep 1814

Thomas Bradford, sec.

Ames, John	Coty Ames	25 Mar 1812

Luther Mears, sec.

Ames, John C.	Susan Stewart of James, dec'd., ward of John S. Walker	18 Apr 1822

John S. Walker, sec.

Ames, John S.	Leah Harrison of Wm.	29 Oct 1824

Arthur McLain, sec.

Ames, John A. of Jesse	Molly G. Floyd of Benjamin	26 Feb 1816

James Harrison, sec.

Ames, John A.	Adelaide Hack	22 Nov 1831

Richard P. Read, sec.

Ames, John E.	Margaret F. James	25 Sep 1839
Ames, John	Caty Mers	14 May 1804

Richard Mers, sec.

Ames, John E.	Margaret S. James of Levin	23 Sep 1834

John T. Ward and John J. Blackstone, sec.

Ames, John A.	Molly G. Floyd	nd 1816
Ames, John	Phillis Garrison	4 Oct 1786

Littleton Addison, sec.

Ames, Joseph F.	Nancy Bradford	8 Nov 1844
Ames, Joseph F.	Sarah Hyslop	14 Oct 1840
Ames, Joseph	Molly Williams	29 Jun 1809
Ames, Joseph F.	Sarah Hyslop of Smith	28 Sep 1840

Edward H. Ames and Richard P. Read, sec.

Ames, Joseph	Tinney Snead	19 Oct 1795
Ames, Leir	Sally A. Mears of Richard of John	4 Dec 1815

Agrippa Bell, sec.

Ames, Levi (wdr)	Adah Kelly of Chas.	19 Mar 1816

John Ames, sec.

Ames, Levin	Comfort Scott	30 Dec 1805

Richard Bloxom, sec.

Ames, Levin S.	Ann P. Hornsby orphan of Eli	28 May 1827

George H. Hack, sec.

Ames, Nathaniel of Caleb	Molly Kellam of Howson	21 Dec 1824

Shepherd Ames, sec.

Ames, Richard T.	Louisa Taylor	6 Sep 1842

Isaac Phillips, sec.

Ames, Richard W.	Susan Chandler of Geo.	9 Jan 1849

Semel H. Shiela and William Mister, sec.

Ames, Richard	Margaret Ames (wid)	23 Nov 1812

Avery Melvin, sec.

Ames, Richard	Leah Seymour	30 Aug 1802

```
Ames, Samuel W.          Sarah Smith              21 Oct 1824
    of Joseph            (wid Charles)
    George K. Taylor, sec.

Ames, Shadrock Jr.       Eliza Hornsby            24 Sep 1810
    Jesse Ames, sec.

Ames, Shepherd           Nancy Vere               22 Feb 1819
    of Cabel             of Thomas
    Jesse Ames, sec.

Ames, Smith              Sarah Phillips            6 Apr 1848
    Peter Turlington, sec.

Ames, Sturgis            Rachel Peusey            25 Feb 1822
                         of Willam, dec'd.
    John C. Ames, sec.

Ames, Thomas H.          Sally W. Hornsby          1 Dec 1819
    of Jesse             of Betty Ames
    Shadrock N. Ames and Betsy Ames, sec.

Ames, Thomas             Elizabeth S. Wise        26 Apr 1852
                         of Solomon Wise

Ames, William            Margaret J. Elliot       13 Jan 1849
    of Stringer          of Eliza Elliot
    Napoleon N. White and Edmond R. Allen, sec.

Ames, William C.         Joice Doughty            13 Dec 1837

Ames, William            Esther Darby             18 Nov 1811
    John F. Mears, sec.

Ames, William C.         Joice Doughty            27 Nov 1837
                         of Jeptha
    Edward M. Colonna, sec.

Ames, Zadock             Sally Wright             22 Apr 1839
    William S. Sturgis, sec.

Ames, Zadock             Sarah Snead               6 Jan 1835
    Joseph B. Roberts, sec.

Ames,Thomas              Sukey Wise               31 Mar 1794

Anderton, Edward         Elizabeth White          24 Apr 1848
                         of Henry White
    William Stant and George H. Ewell, sec.

Andrews, Alfred (wdr)    Catherine Lucas          27 Dec 1856
```

(wid of Elijah)

Andrews, Alfred   Elizabeth Fisher   8 Dec 1851
                     of Henry Fisher

Andrews, Benjamin   Ellen Wessells   19 Jan 1858
                     ward of James Mason

Andrews, Eleanoh   Hetty Taylor   11 Jan 1810
     William Thornton, sec.

Andrews, Isaac   Nancy Harmon   5 May 1809
                     of Priscilla
     William S. Watson, sec.

Andrews, Jacob   Anne Porter   16 Dec 1801
     William Andrews, sec.

Andrews, James   Nancy Fisher   25 Mar 1829
     of Jacob   of Fairfax
     James Kelly and Robert Taylor, sec.

Andrews, Joseph   Nancy R. Cherrix   24 Apr 1854
                     of Mary Watson

Andrews, Nordicia   Nancy Daisey   23 Jan 1826
     William Sharpley, sec.

Andrews, Robert   Catherine Bundick   26 Dec 1831
                     of Abbot
     David Mears and Littleton A. Hinman, sec.

Andrews, Samuel   Elizabeth Russell   24 Dec 1838
     James P. Gibbons, sec.

Andrews, William   Emiline Rew   24 Dec 1841

Andrews, William   Mary Mason   22 Jan 1850
                     of Randal
     Kendal B. Stokley and David Steelman, sec.

Annis, Custis   Euphamia West (wid)   25 Apr 1808
     Thomas Justice, sec.

Annis, Custis   Elizabeth Trehearn   18 Sep 1820
     (wdr)   of James
     Isaac Henderson, sec.

Annis, George W.   Catherine B. Finney   10 Jun 1818
     Henry F. Finney, sec.

Annis, James   Elizabeth Clayton   4 Jan 1849
                      of Thomas R. Clayton
      Robert S. Taylor, sec.

Annis, Levi   Tabetha Bundick   28 Feb 1831
      William Taylor, sec.

Annis, Major   Miss Polly Shrieves   30 Jan 1832
                      orphan John
      Robert Russell Jr., sec.,

Annis, Micagu   Sarah Clark   4 Sep 1809
      Joshua Riggs, sec.

Anno, Joseph   Molly Williams   30 Jun 1806
      Levin Bloxom, sec.

Anothony, Abel   Nanny Thompson   9 Dec 1802
      Stephen Charnock, sec.

Anthony, Abel FN   Rachel Sample FN   27 Nov 1837
      Joshua B. Wyatt, sec.

Arbuckle, George W.   Ann C. Cropper   27 Sep 1831
      David D. Abbott, sec.

Arbuckle, James   Sally Henderson   28 Dec 1812
                      of Lemuel Sr.
      Lemuel Henderson Sr. and Samuel Henderson, sec.

Ardis, Daniel   Tabitha Mason   10 Nov 1798

Ardis, Daniel   Polly Jaques   19 Ap 1806
      Thomas Wise, sec.

Arlington, John   Mary Susan Bull   13 Dec 1853
                      of Thomas S. Bull

Arlington, John   Rosey Bagwell   5 Apr 1786
      William Mears, sec.

Armitrader, Archibald Mary Duncan   27 Dec 1827
      Robert Twiford, sec.

Armstrong, Benjamin H.   Margaret A. C. Chandler 26 Nov 1851
      of Baltimore Co., MD   of Major Chandler

Armstrong, George   Ann W. Golland (wid)   26 Nov 1834
      Charles Tatham, sec.

Arthur FN   Arey FN   29 May 1826

Samuel Henderson, sec.

Ashby, Albert G.   Elizabeth F. Nottingham   10 Dec 1833
                      of David
    Albert C. Ashby and Joseph S. Hill, sec.

Ashby, Albert G.   Ester B. Nottingham   15 Jul 1842

Ashby, Benjamin   Margaret Edmunds   11 Nov 1834
                      (wid)
    William Ashby and James B. Ailworth, sec.

Ashby, Branson FN   Sussan Upshur FN   27 Mar 1838
                      of Mary
    Jacob Bell, sec.

Ashby, Charles   Mary Floyd   27 Dec 1852
                      of Elizabeth Floyd

Ashby, David   Ada Feltcher   30 Jun 1834
                      ward of said David Ashby
    Ezekiel Ashby, sec.

Ashby, George Sr.   Elizabeth Major   25 Sep 1826
                      (wid William)
    George Smith, sec.

Ashby, George (wdr)   Ann Bagg of Wm.   30 Sep 1816
    William Ashby, sec.

Ashby, George   Margaret Taylor   11 Nov 1819
    (wdr)   of Batholmew
    Hutchinson Kellam, sec.

Ashby, James   Matilda Custis   23 Jun 1794

Ashby, James   Elizabeth Joynes   10 Apr 1821
    (wdr)   of Reuben, dec'd.
    Alexander McCollom, sec.

Ashby, James   Sarah Ann Garrison   19 Oct 1837
                      of Abel
    John H. Langsdale, sec.

Ashby, James   Jane Garrison   25 Jan 1848

Ashby, Robert   Sally Poulson   29 Oct 1816
                      (wid William)
    William R. Custis, sec.

Ashby, Smith   Hannah Garrison   16 Dec 1816

```
of John              of Sally
Joshua Garrison and William Wallis, sec.
```

Ashby, William (wdr)   Margaret Edmunds of Jno. 16 Dec 1816
    Thomas Ashby, sec.

Ashby, William   Rosey Bayly of Major   11 May 1831
    John Wrlborn, sec.

Ashby, William   Mary Bech   9 Mar 1818
    of John   of Ezekiel
    Joshua Burton, sec.

Ashby, William   Polly Shield   2 Oct 1804
    Ismay Shield sec.

Ashmead, James R.   Elizabeth Jacob   20 Nov 1813
                       (wid Teackle)
    Thomas R. Joynes, sec.

Ashmead, James R.   Nancy Monson   10 Jul 1822
    Severn Kellam, sec.

Ashon(?), William   Hessy Pruitt(?)   27 Jan 1804
    George Nelson, sec.

Augustus, William FN   Sary Davis FN   27 Jan 1806
    Isaac Holland, sec.

Aydelott, James   Ann W. Baker   30 Nov 1826
    of Benjamin   of David K.
    D.K. Baker, sec.

Aydelott, William J.   Eleanor F. Marshall   14 Mar 1839
                       of Solomon
    Solomon Marshall, sec.

Aydlott, Benjamin   Mary Walburn   6 May 1822
    of William   of Drummond
    Sebastian Cropper and Oliver Logan, sec.

Ayres (Aires), Levin   Sinah Baker   3 Dec 1805
    Ezekiel Baker sec.

Ayres, Edmund B.   Elizabeth Twiford   26 Dec 1822   6
Edmund   of Revell
Edmund Ayres and Revell Twiford, sec.

Ayres, Elisha   Agnes Nock   16 Mar 1821
    of Levin   of William, dec'd.
    Zorobabel West and John Custis, sec.

```
Ayres, Elisha              Sally Ann Davis of Wm.   21 Feb 1832
    John Davis and James J. Allworth, sec.

Ayres, Francis             Margaret Rodgers         27 Oct 1785
    Laban Chandler, sec.

Ayres,  Francis            Susannah Crowson         23 Feb 1818
                             of Levin
    Levin Crowson, sec.

Ayres, Francis J.          Mary A. Burton           20 Oct 1850

Ayres, Henry of Tho.       Polly Simpson of Geo.    11 Nov 1825
    Samuel Walston, sec.

Ayres, Henry               Sally Lankford           19 Sep 1809
    John Snead, sec.

Ayres, James               Polly Galdding           25 Dec 1837
                             of Jesse
    Samuel C. Ahball and James K. Duncan, sec.

Ayres, John J.             Margaret Peusey          14 Dec 1829
                             of Stephen
        Stephen Peusey, sec.

Ayres, Levin R.            Ellen Mason              12 Mar 1839

Ayres, Levin R. (wdr)      Lucretia Gray of Tho.    25 Nov 1850

Ayres, Levin R. Jr.        Susan Jane Guntor        25 Oct 1853
    of Francis R.            of Agnes


Ayres, Littleton           Rachel Hurt (Hurst?)     28 Dec 1829
                             of Thomas
        James Lewis, sec.

Ayres, John                Margaret Colonna         24 Dec 1841

Ayres, Thomas              Betty Chandler            8 Sep 1787
    John Custis, sec.

Ayres, Thomas Littleton    Margaret Bull             7 Apr 1846

Ayres, Thomas              Nancy Thorns             27 Feb 1815
    John Custis, sec.

Ayres, William             Rachel Justice           18 Jan 1786
    John Riggs sec.
```

Ayres, William FN   Elizabeth Taylor FN   25 Dec 1854

Bacon, James   Fanny Johnson of Wm.   25 Dec 1826
     Henry Silverthorne, sec.

Badger, Abel   Nanny Mason   1 Feb 1811
     Jacob Mason, sec.

Badger, Burwell B.   Mary Jane Savage   27 Mar 1848
     (wdr)   of James K.
     James K. Savage, sec.

Badger, Eldred B.   Margaret Kellam   17 Feb 1839
                        of Samuel
     John Arlington, sec.

Badger, James G.   Charlotte James   17 Aug 1839

Badger, John   Sally Underhill   1 Aug 1798
     John Edmunds sec.

Badger, Nathaniel   Mary Robins   15 Dec 1806
     Thomas Edmunds, sec.

Badger, Nathaniel Sr.   Sally Martin   7 Apr 1832
     (wdr)   (wid Smith)
     Irma Wyatt, sec.

Badger, Nathaniel Jr.   Margaret J. Kellam   19 Dec 1838
     John Window, sec.

Badger, Robert   Mary P. Poulson of Jno.   2 Dec 1829
     Charles Belote, sec.

Bagwell, Charles   Nancy Grinalds   25 Jan 1791

Bagwell, Charles   Elizabeth Taylor   14 Sug 1820
     of Charles, dec'd. of Southy
     Southy Taylor, sec.

Bagwell, George P.   Peggy Dix   5 Jun 1799

Bagwell, Heely   Elizabeth P. Bloxom   22 Dec 1819
                        of Anderson
     Anderson P. Bloxom, sec.

Bagwell, Heely P.   Sarah Ann Edmunds   17 Oct 1843

Bagwell, Heely D.   Elizabeth Kellam   22 Oct 1838
                        (wid of Esaw)
     James J. Ailworth, sec.

Bagwell, Henry   Catherine Burton   24 May 1843

Bagwell, Henry   Sarah Drummond   26 Apr 1821
                            (wid George)
        Littleton P. Henderson, sec.

Bagwell, Isacah   Christine Newton   2 Jan 1790

Bagwell, Isaiah N.   Rosey S. Russell   15 Dec 1840
                            of James Russell
        Edmund J. Poulson and William Walston,sec.

Bagwell, John   Rosey G. Dix   18 May 1814
                            (wid John)
        James W. Twiford, sec.

Bagwell, John   Anne Young   25 Jan 1786
        Edmund Scarbrough sec.

Bagwell, John FN   Violet Guy FN   17 Jan 1857

Bagwell, Josiah N.   Leah Finney   10 Jan 1854
        (wdr)   of William Finney, dec'd.

Bagwell, Moses FN   Eveline Bundick FN   1 Sep 1841
        Isaac West, sec.

Bagwell, Moses FN   Sabre White FN   26 Jul 1858

Bagwell, Moses FN   Elvina Bundick   7 Sep 1841
                            of Elijah

Bagwell, Thomas   Sarah H. Wise   25 Sep 1828

Bagwell, Thomas P.   Miss Sarah H. Wise   28 Feb 1828
                            of Tully, dec'd.
        D. Bowman, sec.

Bagwell, William   Margaret G. Teackle   9 Dec 1811
        William Parramore Jr., sec.

Baines, John   Nancy Baines   1 Sep 1790

Baker, Aron   Betsy Onions   1 Jan 1811
        Richard Young, sec.

Baker, Asa (wdr)   Tabitha Bloxom   18 Nov 1841
                            (wid Elijah)

Baker, Asa   Elizabeth Mears   11 Nov 1835
        John Baker, sec.

Baker, Daniel   Nancy Copes   12 Jan 1799

Levin Copes sec.

Baker, Daniel James White sec.	Peggy Copes	31 Jul 1804
Baker, David John R. Slocomb, sec.	Betsy Slocomb	12 Oct 1805
Baker, David John R. Slocomb, sec.	Betsy Slocomb	12 Oct 1805
Baker, Edmund of Solomon Willliam Baker, sec.	Sally Powell of Isaac	2 Mar 1819
Baker, Ezekiel	Nancy Ganet	30 Sep 1799
Baker, George John Baker, sec.	Sinah Bishop	25 Jan 1836
Baker, George of Samuel George S. Fisher, sec.	Polly Rodgers of Labin	27 Nov 1820
Baker, Hezekiah William Gibb sec.	Jamimah Hennaford	25 May 1787
Baker, Hezekiah Ezekiel Baker, sec.	Tabitha Baker of Rich.	7 Jun 1816
Baker, James	Susan Bloxom of Dennis	13 Nov 1844
Baker, Preeson Ezekel Baker, sec.	Elizabeth Young of Wm.	10 Sep 1810
Baker, Samuel of Edmund	Hester Wright orphan of Edith	14 Jan 1858
Baker, Samuel of Hezekiah William Baker, sec.	Henny Baker of John	9 Feb 1819
Baker, Shadrack	Nancy Sterling	10 Jan 1798
Baker, Shepherd	Mary Littleton	12 Mar 1838
Baker, Stephen Solomon Baker sec.	Hepsy Baker	2 Feb 1802
Baley, Custis FN	Susan Sample FN	3 Aug 1849

```
Ball, James              Hannah Ball           18 Nov 1816
    of Samuel            (wid Levi)
    Levin Wilderson and William H. Hickman, sec.

Ball, John shoemaker     Sally Darby of Owen   26 Oct 1818
    Geroge S. Fisher and Zorobabel Kellam, sec.

Ball, Levi               Livey Slocumb         31 Dec 1803
    John Slocumb, sec.

Ball, Levi               Henrietta Riley       17 Feb 1830

Ballard, James FN        Esther Roberts FN     23 Feb 1813
    William R. Taylor and William Beavens, sec.

Bancker, Charles Nicholas  Sarah Upshur Teackle  25 Jan 1805
    John Teackle Sr., sec.


Bandy, Kendall           Rachel Penn            5 Jul 1804
    James Morris sec.

Bandy, Kendall           Rosey Bunting         26 Oct 1799
    Mark Ewell sec.

Barker, George           Sophea Scott          12 May 1804
    William Budd, sec.

Barnes, Abel             Rachel Chandler        8 Jan 1807
    William R. Custis, sec.

Barnes, Archibald        Elizabeth Tatham      19 Jan 1842

Barnes, Arthur           Ann Ayres             23 Nov 1835
                         of Littleton Ayres
        Littleton Ayres, sec.

Barnes, Arthur           Euphamia Lewis         2 Feb 1803
    William Lewis, sec.

Barnes, George           Eveline Justice       28 Feb 1855
    of John (of A)       of William (of B)

Barnes, James of John    Betsy Johnson of John  25 Aug 1806
    John Barnes and Levin Matthews, sec.

Barnes, James            Agnes Taylor          26 Oct 1807
                         (wid Ephraim)
        John Barnes, sec.

Barnes, John             Susanna Lillaston     12 Jul 1806
                         (wid Jacob Lillaston)
```

Barnes, John	Sally Johnson of Isaiah	3 Oct 1832
Thomas Johnsson, sec.		

Barnes, John P.	Sally W. Gibbons (wid)	13 Jan 1858
Barnes, John	Mary Parker Copes	18 Feb 1809
Spencer Barnes, sec.		

Barnes, John	Susannah Lilliston (wid Jacob)	12 Jul 1806
Edmond Lilliston, sec.		

Barnes, Louis, (wdr)	Virginia Clayton of George	6 Feb 1852

Barnes, Parker of John	Rosey Outten of Joseph	29 Jan 1821
William Shrieves, sec.		

Barnes, Robert (wdr)	Rita Bundick (wid Richard)	27 Mar 1826
William Taylor, sec.		

Barnes, Samuel	Nancy Dee	24 Jan 1804
Isaac Dix sec.		

Barnes, Samuel of Robert	Lydia Lewis of Elizabeth	25 Dec 1841

Barnes, Spencer	Margaret Hinman	c. 1798 (badly damaged)

Barnes, Thomas	Frances Killmon	22 Feb 1812
Samuel Killmon, sec.		

Barnes, Willliam	Bridget Barnes	1 Jan 1811
John S. Bundick, sec.		

Barnes, Wm. of Arthur	Elizabeth Garrison of John	13 Dec 1827
James H. Bell, of Arthur, sec.		

Bayly, Custis FN	Eliza Beckett FN	31 Jul 1835
William Ames, sec.		

Bayly, Custis FN	Susey Sample FN	28 Feb 1849
William S. Sturgis and Samuel Lilliston, sec.		

Bayly, Edward	Sally Gardiner of William Gardiner	30 Dec 1854

Bayly, Elijah	Susanna Mason	6 Sep 1803
Henry Trader, sec.		

Bayly, Erastus B.   Sally Ewell   17 Mar 1847
                           of Charles

Bayly, Esme   Elizabeth D.Kellam   30 Dec 1805
     George Kellam sec.

Bayly, John   Esther Bradford   21 Jan 1775
     Edmund Bayly sec.

Bayly, John T.   Nancy P. Johnson   28 Nov 1849
                           of Ann P. Sparrow
     Charles C. Willett, sec.

Bayly, Levin   Hepsey Cord   6 Feb 1799
     Thomas Bayly sec.

Bayly, Levin   Leticah Smith   30 Jul 1855
                           of Valentine Smith

Bayly, Peter FN   Sarah Wise FN   6 Nov 1854

Bayly, Richard   Elizabeth Wright   31 Mar 1840
                           of John
     Richard Sparrow, sec.

Bayly, Thomas M.   Margaret Pettit Cropper 31 Mar 1802
                           of John Cropper
          Edmund Bayly sec.

Bayly, William P., Esq. Elizabeth C. Parramore   2 Dec 1847
     Thomas T. Cropper, sec.

Bayly, Zadock   Nelly Lucas   13 Jan 1790

Bayne, Calmore T.   Eliza A.R. Harmonson   30 Nov 1825
                           orphan of Matthew
     John W. Cropper, sec.

Bayne, John F.   Ann C. Bayly   30 Sep 1817
     George W. Arbuckle and Richard D. Bayly, sec.

Bayne, Walter D., Esq.   Harriet E. R. Joynes   23 Dec 1823
     Calmore L. Bayne and Edward L. Snead, sec.

Beach, Abel of Reuben   Elizabeth Ashby of Tho.   7 Jun 1820
     Thomas Ashby, sec.

Beach, Able J.   Sarah A. E. Ames   12 Feb 1851

Beach, George   Rosey Nock of Solomon   14 Dec 1813
     Garrison Burton, sec.

```
Beach, John of Kendall    Betsy Edmunds of James    30 Sep 1816
    James Edmunds, sec.

Beach, Joseph             Elizabeth Blen of Anna    12 Dec 1807
    William Coulburn, sec.

Beach, William            Mary Glassby              28 Jul 1839

Beach, William            Tabitha Finney            31 Oct 1825
    of Kendall            orphan of William
    John S. Beach, sec.

Beasley, Henry, jailor    Margaret Johnson of Sam.  14 Mar 1818
    Major Bird, sec.

Beasley, John             Leanah East                8 Jun 1835
                          of Steven East

Beasley, John             Susan Watson              27 May 1850
    (wdr)                 of Cathy Watson
    William J. Belote, sec.

Beasley, John             Leannna East              10 Jun 1835

Beasley, Perry            Susan Onions              30 Aug 1841
                          ward of Perry
    William Shreves, sec.

Beasley, Smith            Fanney Damblin            10 Sep 1810
    Isaac Powell, sec.

Beasley, Tully            Caty Hickman of Peggy     22 Feb 1813
    Edward Bell Jr., sec.

Beasley, William          Nancy Rayfield            16 Apr 1839
                          (wid of Levi)
    George Bull of B. and Edward Mears, sec.

Beasy, Micajah            Betsey Warrington         26 Aug 1805
    Skinner Marshall sec.

Beauchamp, Elijah         Polly Shankland           30 Jan 1808
    George Marshall, sec.

Beavans, Henry FN         Athy Seymour FN           19 Jul 1837
    William D. Seymour, sec.

Beavans, John W.          Henrietta Taylor           8 Mar 1856
    of Joshua             of Bundick Taylor, dec'd.

Beavans, Joshua           Patsy Silverthorne        31 Jan 1804
    Samuel Johnson, sec.
```

```
Beavans, Joshua of Wm.    Sally Broadwater of Jno.   2 Oct 1815
     Smithy Broadwater, sec.

Beavans, Major           Cathy Becket                30 Apr 1832
     Rosey Becket, sec.

Beavans, Ralph           Mary Martin                 25 Jan 1830
                         ward of John Martin
     John Martin and James Kellam of A., sec.
Beavans, Robert FN       Mary Evans FN               24 Dec 1845

Beavans, Rowland         Ann Finney (wid)            24 Mar 1811
     Zadak Selby, sec.

Beavans, Walter          Hannah Peck                  2 Jul 1804
     Mathias Outten sec.

Beavans, William M.      Anna Gillett                31 Jan 1804
     Joshua Beavans, sec.

Beavans, William         Martha Brodwater             9 Jul 1790

Beavans, William H.      Betsy M. Core                8 Feb 1800
     George P. Bagwell sec.

Becket, Lewis FN         Harriet Roane FN            27 Aug 1855

Becket, Peter            Ariena Nutt                 10 Jan 1800
                         of Adah Nutt
     Babel Major sec.

Becket, Peter FN         Polly Becket FN             27 Sep 1858

Becket, Peter FN         Rosey Beavans FN            27 Dec 1831
     Jonathan W. Richardson, sec.

Becket, Peter FN         Candis Sample FN            26 Oct 1835
     John B. Bradford, sec.

Becket, Samuel FN        Tiny Holt FN                 8 Oct 1832
     Samuel Parker, sec.

Becket, Samuel FN        Charity Sample FN           30 Dec 1816
                         of Betty
     Daniel Roam, sec.

Becket, William FN       Harriet Rone FN             15 Jan 1852

Beckett, Arnistead FN    Eliza Bayly FN              31 Jul 1835
     William Ames, sec.

Beckett, John FN         Susan Evans FN              28 Mar 1854
```

Beckett, Sam FN   Sally Roans   21 Jan 1840
                      of David FN
    George S. Rogers, sec.

Beech, Ezekiel   Anne Spiers   26 Nov 1785
    John Spers sec.

Beesly, Smith   Betty Bennett   -- Jun 1795
    James Bennett sec.   (badly damaged)

Beeson, Henry   Mary Budd   20 Nov 1849

Bell, Agrippa of Wm.   Elizabeth Roberts   13 Nov 1816
                      (wid William)
    Felix Bell, sec.

Bell, Agrippa   Mary Smith of George 24 Nov 1812
    Smith Stringer, ssec.

Bell, Anthony (wdr)   Katurah Glenn (wid) 18 Oct 1848
    George H. Bell, sec.

Bell, Anthony   Ann Tignall   18 Dec 1813
    William E. Bradford, sec.

Bell, Anthony   Retuny Glenn   17 Oct 1847

Bell, Edmund (wdr)   Elizabeth Hinman   14 Nov 1831
                      of Moses
    William Laws and Levin Core, sec.

Bell, Edward   Nancy Guy   6 Apr 1806
    Willam Budd sec.

Bell, Edward J.   May A. Bell   28 Apr 1852

Bell, Edward   Alicia White (wid)   1 Jan 1808
    James Bell, sec.

Bell, Edward, Jr.   Mary A. Bell   26   Apr   1852
                      of Charlotte Bell

Bell, Elias   Polly Adams of Obed 7 Mar 1831
    Obed Adams, sec.

Bell, Felix   Sarah Green of George 31 Aug 1827
    Thomas Edmunds, sec.

Bell, Geodiah   Leah Hannaford   26 Jun 1813
                      (wid William)
    John W. Garrison, sec.

```
Bell, Geodiah            Barbour Harmon            6 May 1812
     John Garrison, sec.

Bell, George             Tabby Clayton            15 Feb 1804
     Dennis Clayton, sec.

Bell, George W.          Elizabeth Beach           2 Dec 1848
                         of John S. Beach
     George W. Bell and Abel J. Bird, sec.


Bell, George             Nancy Hall               13 Jul 1805
     Geodiah Bell, sec.

Bell, George             Margaret Williams        15 Sep 1818
     (wdr), bricklayer   of Jehu
     Solomon Marshall, sec.

Bell, George             Margaret R. Weoch        19 Dec 1821
     of Geodiah          of William
     William Bell, sec.

Bell, Isaac              Kessy Heath of Joseph    21 Mar 1817
     Henry Walker and James Walker, sec.

Bell, Jacob of John      Margaret B. Elliott       7 Oct 1818
                         of William
     Henry Stewart, sec.

Bell, Jacob (wdr)        Sally Mears of Levin     28 Nov 1825
     George H. Bell, sec.

Bell, Jacob (wdr)        Nancy Kelly               6 Jul 1837
     Jacob Bell and Zorobabel Willis, sec.

Bell, Jacob of Geodiah   Margaret Mears of Abel   16 Mar 1827
     John T. Elliott, sec.

Bell, James H.           Charlotte Garrison        8 Jan 1827
     of Geodiah          orphan of John
     William H. Bell, sec.

Bell, James R.           Mariah Drummond          25 Aug 1839

Bell, James S.           Elizabeth Mears          22 Dec 1844

Bell, John H. of Edward  Sarah Melson of James    22 Feb 1826
     William Budd and James Melson, sec.

Bell, Joseph L.          Caroline Clegg           23 Jan 1836
```

Bell, Lorenzo D.
  of Edward
    George H. Bell, sec.
	Alice Ann Stewart
	orphan Levin
		4 Oct 1831

Bell, Lorenzo D.	Margaret Mapp	17 Sep 1850
Bell, Rohn	Sarah Kellam	7 Jan 1846

Bell, Seth
  of Thomas
    John G. Joynes, sec.
	Frances B. Outten
	orphan John
		28 Nov 1825

Bell, Thomas H.	Margaret Bell	17 Dec 1844
Bell, Thoroughgood	Cathy Lilliston	17 Oct 1839
Bell, Victor John Custis of John, sec.	Margaret Taylor of Ezekiel	24 Nov 1829
Bell, William Levi Small, sec.	Nicey Kelley	13 Jan 1800
Bell, William Jacob Bird, sec.	Sally Smith of Levin	28 Nov 1808

Bell, William T.
  of Jacob
    Jacob Bell and Richard J. Ayres, sec.
	Emily Smith	30 Dec 1839

Bell, William H. Henry Walker, sec.	Margaret West orphan Abel	19 Dec 1823
Bell, William F.	Emily Smith	25 Jan 1840
Bell, William John Bell sec.	Rachel Bradford	3 Oct 1800
Beloate, James H. of W. H.	Eliza B. Kellam of Charles Kellam	16 Feb 1853
Beloate, William	Eliza Jones (wid)	4 Jul 1849
Belote, Caleb Zorobabel Edwards sec.	Euphamy Edwards	26 Aug 1805
Belote, Charles Joseph Gunter, sec.	Betsy Martin	26 Dec 1810
Belote, Charles	Hessy Poulson of John, dec'd.	18 Jun 1828

William Belote, sec.

Belote, George M.   Elizabeth Heath   2 Dec 1823
                           of Joseph, dec'd.
     Henry Walker and Jms. W. Twiford, sec.

Belote, George M. (wdr) Patience Fisher of Geo. 27 Dec 1826
     John A. Coleburn, sec.

Belote, George   Peggy Michom   1 Jan 1802
     John Savage of Abel sec.

Belote, Hancock   Catherine Watson   28 Dec 1809
                          of Frederick
     William Damerald, sec.

Belote, Jesse   Nancy Lewis of Thomas   28 May 1808
     James Belote, sec.

Belote, John   Rachel Mears   11 May 1800
     John Savage sec.

Belote, John   Elizabeth Heath   29 Dec 1823

Belote, John   Sarah Hawley   14 May 1800
     John Savage sec.

Belote, John   Polly Taylor   9 Sep 1839
     of Charles
Charles Belote and George W. Mason, sec.

Belote, John Jr.   Sally Mears   15 Dec 1801
     William Heath sec.

Belote, Laban   Elizabeth Tatham   3 Dec 1807
     Obediah Thornton, sec.

Belote, Leven B   Nancy Savage   20 Dec 1837
     George T. East, sec.

Belote, Levin   Sally Warrington   29 Mar 1844

Belote, Levin   Nancy Savage   21 Dec 1837

Belote, Lewis   Mary Mears   25 Jun 1827
     orphan James   orphan Arthur
     Charles Belote and James Mears of Arthur, sec.

Belote, Noah   Elizabeth Wise   2 Feb 1775
     John Wise, sec.

Belote, William   Kezuah B. Dunton   18 Jun 1828

of James of H., dec'd.   of Richard, dec'd.
Charles Belote, sec.

Belote, William   Sally Phillips   20 Dec 1832
                           of William
     Thomas C. Mason, sec.

Belote, William H.   Elizabeth James   4 July 1849
     (wdr)   (wid of Levin)
     John N. A. Elliott, sec.

Bennet, James H.   Margaret Mister   15 Mar 1852
                           (wid of Thomas Mister)

Bennett, Coventon (wdr)   Margaret Carnthers   29 Aug 1825
                           of James
     James Carnthers, sec.

Bennett, Coventon   Sally Parker   nd 1815

Bennett, Coventon   Molly Lang   6 Dec 1804

Bennett, Covington   Sally Parker   5 Jan 1815
     James Ames, sec.

Bennett, James H.   Margaret Mister (wid)   18 Mar 1852

Bennett, James   Sally Garret   24 Jan 1798

Benson, Edward   Patsy Firchett   5 Jul 1839

Benson, James   Fanny Marriner   28 Dec 1812
     Daniel Benson, sec.

Benson, Jonah   Betsey Core   17 Jun 1794

Benson, Joseph E.   Catherine A. B. Dix   27 Nov 1851
     (wdr)   (wid of Julius J. Dix)

Benson, Joseph   Ann Warrington   23 Aug 1805
                          of Teackle and Ester Warrington
     Southy Warrington, sec.

Benson, Robert   Charlotte Ann Bell   20 Dec 1851
     (wdr)   (wid of James A. Bell)

Benston, Daniel   Betsy Taylor   23 Sep 1800
     Isaac Duncan, sec.

Benston, James   Catherine Mears   22 Nov 1843

Benston, John   Polly White (wid)   9 Oct 1801

John Turner, sec.

Benston, McKenney	Vianna Kelley	29 Sep 1801
Benston, Zadock	Nancy Taylor	8 Dec 1789
Benton, Joshus Sr. John Wharton, sec.	Margaret Floyd of Wm.	15 Feb 1819
Berry, Charles Major Lewis, sec.	Margaret Lewis orphan William	31 Jan 1831
Berry, George John Gardner, sec.	Henrietta Bishop	29 Dec 1809
Berry, Henry P. David Mears and Nathaniel Bird, sec.	Mahala Bundick of Abbott	26 Nov 1832
Berry, James of John Woney Rew, sec.	Catherine Rew of Woney	18 Jan 1818
Berry, William Peter Delastatious and Peter Blades, sec.	Margaret T. Bayly	12 Dec 1830
Berry, William J. (wdr)	Sally S. Russell	28 Jan 1852
Berry, William P. Cosiah Taylor and William Beavans, sec.	Mary R. Hall of Dixon	7 Jan 1829
Beswick, William	Leah Watson	7 Jan 1841
Bibbins, Thomas Peter Bibbins, sec.	Arena Becket	2 Aug 1800
Binston, George T.W.	Susan Kelley	12 May 1832
Birch, Daniel	Embery Cunigan	15 Mar 1849
Birch, George William Davis, sec.	Patience Cherix	9 Sep 1811
Birch, George (wdr) John Marshall of Moneas and James P. Dunton, sec.	Hetty Blades of Jms.	27 Mar 1827
Birch, George	Elizabeth Scott	10 Aug 1837
Birch, John	Margaret Chapman	15 Jan 1844
Birch, John of John	Sally Jones	12 Aug 1843

Birch, Joseph (wdr)   Sally Lingo (wid)   20 Jun 1837
    Samuel S. Carey and James J. Ailworth, sec.

Birch, Joseph (wid)   Polly Ferguson (wid)   15 Jul 1842

Birch, Thomas of Wm.   Sally Melson of Bagwell   9 May 1817
    James Conner and Isaac Henderson, sec.

Birch, Thomas Lingo   Ann Hill   6 Jan 1847

Birch, Thomas   Mary Crippen Conner   18 Jan 1833
    of Daniel   of Grover
    David Watts and John B. Ailworth, sec.

Birch, William   Mary Fassit (wid)
    of Joseph

Birch, William   Nancy R. Michael   15 Jan 1833

Birch, William   Nancy Read   24 Dec 1832
                           of Marshall Read
        David Watts and William A. Mathews, sec.

Bird, Bennet M.   Henny Bird of Major   29 Nov 1819
    of Natheniel
    George Northern and William Mason, sec.

Bird, Colmore of Selby   Hetty Taylor of Teackle   1 Feb 1820
    Custis Bird, sec.

Bird, Daniel T.   Tenny Gillispie   21 Jan 1811
    William Gillispie, sec.

Bird, Daniel T.   Rhodah Riggen of Nathan 17 Oct 1815
    Obediah Riggen, sec.

Bird, David   Rachel Mason   16 Jul 1834
                           of S. Midleton
        Thomas Bird, sec.

Bird, Denjamin W. T.   Ann Northam   24 Jan 1848
                           of Southy Northam
        Samuel J. Gladding, sec.

Bird, Ebern   Ann Lewis of Nanny   12 Nov 1821
    James Kelly of Muddy Creek and William Coard, sec.

Bird, Ebern   Peggy Bunting   3 Jan 1801
    Jacob Bird, sec.

```
Bird, Ebern                Henrietta Savage          31 Dec 1833
                           of William
     Major Savage, sec.

Bird, Ebon                 Maria Wyatt               28 Mar 1836
     George Scott, sec.

Bird, Eburn                Maria Wyatt                7 Apr 1834

Bird, George T.            Mary Mears                31 Dec 1849
     (wdr)                 of Thomas Mears
     William S. Fletcher and Rilchard T. Savage, sec.

Bird, George P.            Dameriah Bird             22 Nov 1839
                           of Daniel
     John W. Bird and John P. Drummond, sec.

Bird, Jacob                Elizabeth Lucas           27 Apr 1829
                           of William Zadock
     Zadock Bayly, sec.


Bird, Jacob                Rebecca Northam           11 Nov 1815
     of Nathaniel          of Leah Vessel
     Daniel Bird, sec.

Bird, Jacob                Henrietta Savage          18 Jan 1834

Bird, Johannes (wdr)       Laney Coke of Richard     17 Sep 1816
     Major Bird, sec.

Bird, Johannes             Peggy Kelly               10 Sep 1802

Bird, John Jr.             Elizabeth Poulson of Wm.  29 May 1809
     Daniel Bird, sec.

Bird, John                 Esther Ross                7 Jun 1790
     William S---, sec.

Bird, Levi FN              Ada Laylor FN              6 Apr 1835

Bird, Levin FN             Adah Taylor FN            30 Mar 1835
     Mitchel Chandler and Thomas Scarburgh, sec.

Bird, Littleton T.         Mary F. Bird              27 May 1850
                           of Johannas Bird
     John H. Custis, sec.

Bird, Nathaniel            Tabitha Justice of Tho.   10 Mar 1828
     Bennet M. Bird, sec.
```

Bird, Obed S.	Hetty C. Mears of Tho. Mears	17 Dec 1850
Bird, Parker Ezekiel Bloxom, sec.	Kesiah Gilaspee	4 Feb 1800
Bird, Parkes Martin R. Kelley and Thomas A. Northam, sec.	Mary Trader of Teackle Trader	4 Feb 1850
Bird, Richard	Nancy J. Parks	1 Oct 1843
Bird, Richard	Nancy J. Parks	1 Oct 1843
Bird, Samuel R. William S. Bird and H. L. Wessells, sec.	Mary E. Bird (wid)	27 Dec 1847
Bird, Selby of Parker Spencer Drummond and Nathaniel W. Bird, sec.	Amanda Kelly of Thomas	26 Feb 1838
Bird, Seymour John Snead, sec.	Eliza Henderson	29 Aug 1811
Bird, Thomas of Jacob Middleton Mason and John Mister, sec.	Susan Mason of Middleton	8 May 1828
Bird, Thomas	Susan Mason	btw 1835-1837
Bird, Thomas H. William J. Bird and Jeremiah Taylor, sec.	Mary Ann Wheatley	8 Jan 1849
Bird, William of Ebern Abel Mears, sec.	Hessy Mears of Abel	3 Apr 1816
Bird, William	Caziah Hinman	7 Jan 1792
Bishop, Henry George Bundick, sec.	Elizabeth Bundick	29 Oct 1830
Bishop, Jacob (wdr) John B. Hickman, sec.	Tenny B. Hickman of John Bishop	1 Aug 1821
Biswick, Nathaniel Robert Russell of Joshua, sec.	Peggy Turlington (wid Charles)	10 Nov 1813
Blackstone, Bowman	Kessy Salisbury	13 Dec 1847
Blackstone, John	Margaret Gillett	Jan 1841

Blackstone, John J.   Margaret D. Gillett   6 Jan 1841
                             ward of William Parramore
        William Parramore, sec.

Blackstone, William B.   Elizabeth Bundick   11 Mar 1816
                             of Justice
        John Custis and William P. Custis, sec.

Blades, James   Nelly Grey   5 Dec 1786
        Thomas Guy, sec.

Blades, James   Mary Sharpley   21 Dec 1843

Blades, Moses of James   Rosey Wright of Jacob   29 Dec 1819
        Levin Hyslop, sec.

Blake, Joshua FN   Agnes Church FN   14 Dec 1832
        George Jenkins and Caleb Duncan, sec.

Blake, Major FN   Sene Davis FN   25 Sep 1807
        William Vernelson, sec.

Blake, Nehemiah   Sophia Melvin   16 Mar 1804
        John Davis, sec.

Blake, Wesley   Triphany Taylor   22 Apr 1847
                             of Jabez
        Robert Marshall and John T. Custis, sec.

Blake, William FN   Esther Bagwell FN (wid)   24 Sep 1822
        Major Blake, sec.

Blake, William   Rachel Taylor   11 Feb 1788

Bloxom, Argil   Lucretia Evans   28 Sep 1795

Bloxom, David   Lucretia Miles of Jesse   28 Aug 1825
        George Bloxom, sec.

Bloxom, Dennis   Henrietta Garett   16 Jan 1809
        William Powell, sec.

Bloxom, Dennis   Henney Baker   27 Feb 1837
                            (wid of Samuel)
        James T. Gibbons and John Turlington, sec.

Bloxom, Eli   Molly Abbott   27 Mar 1820
        of Nicholas   (wid George)
        Littleton Bloxom, sec.

Bloxom, Elijah   Tabitha Tatham   10 Jan 1835

Ezekiel Tatham, sec.

Bloxom, Elijah R.   Elizabeth S. Drummond   24 Oct 1833

Bloxom, Ezekiel   Sally Wimbrough   27 Dec 1798
     Thomas Justice, sec.

Bloxom, Francis Asbury   Anna Bunting   9 Dec 1826
                         (wid William)
     James Millener, sec.

Bloxom, George   Polly Belote   27 May 1815
     Thomas Chandler, sec.

Bloxom, George   Narcissa Bloxom   3 Sep 1828
     of George   orphan Major
     William Bloxom, sec.

Bloxom, George Sr.   Esther Gillispie   15 Dec 1828
     (wdr)   (wid James)
     Joseph P. godwin, sec.

Bloxom, George   Betsey White   12 Feb 1834
                         of George
     Thomas Hinman, sec.

Bloxom, Jacob   Nancy Tylor   9 Mar 1806
     William W. Burton, sec.

Bloxom, James   Molly Hinman   10 Jan 1807
     William Davis, sec.

Bloxom, Levin   Elizabeth Litchfield   18 Jan 1825
     of Levin (wdr)   of Southy
     Levin Shrieves and Levin Core, sec.

Bloxom, Levin   Catherine Bishop   31 May 1819
     orphan Levin   of Southy
     William Powell and William Nock of E., sec.

Bloxom, Major   Betsey Hope   10 Feb 1799

Bloxom, Nicholas   Nancy Holloway   8 Dec 1798
     William Stephens, sec.

Bloxom, Perry   Burnetta T. Bloxom   2 Aug 1853
     of George   of David Bloxom, dec'd.

Bloxom, Rich. of Argil   Rosey Bull of Custis   27 Dec 1817
     John Snead, sec.

Bloxom, Richard Jr.   Henny Walker of Wm.   2 Jan 1822

Robert P. Broadwater, sec.

Bloxom, Richard Sr.	Jinney Fletcher	29 Jul 1805
Bloxom, Richard	Betsy Giddens	3 Nov 1801
Bloxom, Robert Handcock Belote, sec.	Nanny Belote	10 Mar 1787
Bloxom, Sam., shoemaker Southy W. Bull and James Bull, sec.	Elizabeth Barrett	12 Jun 1829
Bloxom, Severn William S. Matthews, sec.	Polly McMath (wid Zadock)	16 Jul 1811
Bloxom, Severn	Catherine Kellam	24 Feb 1794 (badly damaged)
Bloxom, Simpson Jr.	Tabitha Bull	29 Oct 1799
Bloxom, Southy John Abbott Bundick, sec.	Susanna Kellum	5 May 1804
Bloxom, Stephen	Betsy Williams	21 Sep 1806
Bloxom, Stephen Stephen Brimer, sec.	Nancy Brimer	6 Jan 1834
Bloxom, Thomas Nathaniel Hall, sec.	Polly Copes	24 May 1808
Bloxom, Thomas H.	Margaret Justice	11 Dec 1844
Bloxom Thomas H. (wdr)	Phebe Elizabeth Bull of Thomas Bull	3 Jan 1855
Bloxom, Walter of Richard Andrew Lee, sec.	Rosy Trader of George Ward	27 Mar 1819
Bloxom, William C. shoemaker Revell Parker, sec.	Eliza A. Coleburn of Richard	30 Apr 1827
Bloxom, William D. of George George Bloxom, sec.	Hetty Bloxom of Major	22 Nov 1824
Bloxom, William	Mary Wessells of John, dec'd.	31 Dec 1855

Bloxom, William	Tabitha Bloxom	11 Jun 1834
Bloxom, Woodman	Nancy Matthews	8 Jan 1798
Bloxxom, Woodman Elisha Wheelton, sec.	Miss Nancy Wheelton	28 Jan 1812
Boggs, Elijah William Finney, sec.	Miss Ann Riley	24 Dec 1811
Boggs, Francis Thomas Underhill, sec.	Elizabeth D. Underhill	20 Jun 1811
Boggs, Francis Teackle Justice, sec.	Ann Marshall	30 Dec 1833
Boggs, Francis Joseph Boggs, sec.	Agnes Crowson	4 Mar 1802
Boggs, Henry	Nancy Harper orphan John, ward of Richard Addison Richard Addison and Samuel Nock, sec.	27 Dec 1824
Boggs, Henry J.	Elizabeth Rodgers	22 Jan 1843
Boggs, Henry	Nancy Harper	31 Dec 1822
Boggs, James Thomas W. Finney, sec.	Elizabeth Rodgers of Levi	28 Jun 1819
Boggs, John R. of Elijah Elijah boggs, sec.	Leah Boggs of Francis	10 Jun 1833
Boggs, John R. of Elijah	Leah Boggs of Francis	17 Jun 1833
Boggs, Joseph of Francis Samuel S. Nock, John Downing and James Chesser, sec.	Margaret Downing of William	1 Mar 1823
Boggs, Joseph P. WIlliam C. Boggs, sec.	Susan E. Underhill	14 Feb 1832
Boggs, Levi R. of James	Hester A. Mapp of George S.	26 Dec 1853
Boggs, Thomas D.	Susan A. Chandler	20 Feb 1844
Boggs, Thomas D.	Susan Chandler	24 Jan 1844

Boggs, William C.   Elizabeth Sturgis   29 Sep 1834
                           (wid of Nathaniel)
     Thomas Sturgis, sec.

Boisnard, John   Sarah Teakle   25 Ape 1783
     William Gibb, sec.

Bonewell, George   Bridget Bull   14 Sep 1789
     Isaiah Evans, sec.

Bonewell, Southy   Mary Snead   27 Mar 1787
     Skinner Wallop, sec.

Boniwell, Heely   Elizabeth Warington   28 Nov 1831
                           ward Heely Boniwell
     Robert J. Poulson, sec.

Bonnewell, Elijah   Sally Metcalf   18 Jul 1840
                           of Jesse
     Jesse Metcalf, sec.

Bonnewell, Jesse   Nancy Fox   6 Oct 1835
     Thomas R. Joynes, sec.

Bonnewell, McKul (wdr)   Susan Jester   20 Apr 1835
                           (wid of Joseph)
     William Finney, sec.

Bonnewell, Thomas   Elizabeth Colonna   5 Jan 1836
                           of William
     Levin S. Ames, sec.

Bonnwell, Clement   Rachel Russell   18 Feb 1804
     William White, sec.

Bonwell, Elijah   Leah Wise   3 Jan 1809
     McKeel, sec.

Bonwell, George   Polly Rodgers   17 Dec 1800
     George Salisbury, sec.

Bonwell, Jesse   Peggy Dix   4 Dec 1806
     Reuben Rogers, sec.

Bonwell, John   Elizabeth Custis   10 Sep 1807
                           of Revel
     John Joynes, sec.

Bonwell, John   Catherine Kellam   26 Apr 1806
                           of Dolly
     Thomas Snead, sec.

Bonwell, Levi FN   Peggy Jubilee FN   2 Dec 1815
     Simon Parks FN, sec.

Bonwell, McKeel Sr.   Margaret Salisbury   30 Jul 1808
     John Bonwell, sec.

Bonwell, McKeel Sr.   Margaret Russel   16 Feb 1820
     (wdr)   of Abe
     John Watson of John, sec.

Bonwell, McKeel Jr.   Sarah Bull of Richard   5 Jan 1803
     McKell Budd, sec.

Bonwell, Peter of Geo.   Eliza Hall of Henry   5 Dec 1817
     William Holland and John Custis, sec.

Bonwell, Stephen   Peggy Topping   21 May 1796
     George Topping, sec.

Bonwell, Thomas   Betsy Taylor   3 Oct 1807
     Ralph B. Corbin, sec.

Bonwell, William   Elizabeth Willet   7 Apr 1828
     of John   of Waitman
     William Parramore Jr. and Levin Core, sec.

Bool, James R.   Susanna R. Chandler   27 Sep 1848

Bool, Luther T.   Sarah F. Johnson   18 Jul 1848

Booth, Charles   Leah Barnes   29 Dec 1807
     William Thornmen, sec.

Booth, Charles   Elizabeth Lewis   13 Feb 1850
                        of Nancy
     Isaiah Johnson, Jr. and Edward N. Taylor of B., sec.

Booth, Crippen   Peggy Tarr   8 Apr 1803
                        of Aephaniah
     David Watts, sec.

Booth, James   Mareah Jones   7 Apr 18834
                        of John Jones
     Eris Boston and Levia Core, sec.

Booth, John   Esther Birch   9 Jan 1801
     John Birch, sec.

Booth, Joseph   Martha Spalding   25 Jul 1797

Booth, William   Salley Henderson   1 Mar 1825

```
of Crippen            of William H.
John Knox and James Melvin, sec.

Booth, William        Elizabeth Bowdoin        1 Aug 1853
    of Coventon       of Elizabeth Carpenter

Boston, Daniel        Ignatia Bird            27 Apr 1818
    of Daniel         orphan Selby
    Colmore Bird and Walter Wessells, sec.

Bottimer, Thomas      Lizzie E. B. Floyd       1 Jan 1851

Bowden, Caleb         Chanty Russell          19 May 1830
                      of John

Bowden, Crippen       Nancy Carpenter         17 Dec 1835

Bowdin, William       Anne Hickman            25 Mar 1805

Bowdoin, Edward       Elizabeth Bloxom        11 Feb 1797

Bowdoin, James        Ziporah Simpson         26 Feb 1812
    Charles Carpenter, sec.

Bowman, Edmund T.     Matilda Taylor          18 Dec 1829
    Levin Rogers, sec.

Bowman, Egbert G.     Margaret Scarborough    14 Feb 1831
                      of Thomas
    Willliam N. Ames, sec.

Bowman, H. Bayly      Ann Cord (wid)          30 Mar 1808
    James Poulson, sec.

Bowman, H. Bayly      Euphamia Rew (wid Jno.) 13 Feb 1810
    Thomas M. Bayly, sec.
Bowman, Henry B.      Henny Bull of Custis    21 Dec 1831
    Bowman H. Bayly, sec.

Bowman, John of Levin Matilda Mason           15 Jun 1825
                      (wid Bennett)
    Reuben Rew, sec.

Bowman, John J.       Sarah Sturgis of Tho.   25 Dec 1815
    Levin Laylor, sec.

Bowman, John of Robt. Betsy Watson of Wm.     20 Nov 1815
    Abbott Trader, sec.

Bowman, Littleton Ed. Christabel Rodger       30 Apr 1828
    of Richard        of Peter
        Zeldy J. Coloney, sec.
```

Bowman, Robert FN   Keziah Stephens FN   15 Jan 1828
                           of Thomas
       Thomas Stephens FN, sec.

Bowman, Robert   Polly Townsend   27 Jul 1807
       Henry Thornton, sec.

Bowman, Upshur   Betsy Smart   3 Jan 1812
       Nathaniel Taylor, sec.

Bradford, Abel   Nancy West of Abel   26 Dec 1815
       James Walker, sec.

Bradford, Arthur   Elvira Heath of Major   27 Feb 1832
       Tabam Bradford, sec.

Bradford, Arthur   Caty Bell   2 Dec 1833
                           of William
       Arthur and Laban Bradford, sec.

Bradford, Benjamin   Miss Catherine Bell   24 Mar 1832
       of Jacob   ward Torenyo D. Bell
       T.L. Kellam, sec.

Bradford, Charles   Catherine Martin of Jno.   27 Dec 1806
       George Russell, sec.

Bradford, Charles B.   Salley Pratt   30 Dec 1811
       William E. Wise, sec.

Bradford, Charles   Elizabeth Sharply   12 Aug 1847

Bradford, Charles   Sally Lingo   18 Sep 1803
       William Lewis, sec.

Bradford, Edward D.   Sally Wright   24 Jul 1833
       of John B.
       Samuel H. Scarburgh and John Arlington, sec.

Bradford, Ezra   Rachel C. Coleburn   26 Mar 1855
                           of John Coleburn

Bradford, Fisher   Ann B. Walter   25 Dec 1848
                           of Solomon Walter
       Nathaniel B. LeCato, sec.

Bradford, Jacob   Margaret Bell   29 Apr 1806
       Benston Bradford, sec.

Bradford, John W.   Nancy Nock   8 Dec 1841

Bradford, John W.   Catharine Garrison   29 Apr 1839
    James H. Bell, sec.

Bradford, Laban   Leah Tigner   28 Sep 1835
    Arthur Bradford, sec.

Bradford, Littleton   Nancy Harmon   2 Feb 1902
    William Elliott, sec.

Bradford, Nathaniel   Margaret Beach   2 Mar 1825
    of Richard   of Molly
    John S. Beach, sec.

Bradford, Thomas J.   Ann D. Watson   18 Feb 1833
                             of William
    John Z. Johnson, sec.

Bradford, Thomas   Alsey P. Bradford   12 Oct 1786
    George Hyslop, sec.

Bradford, William   Nancy Mears of Wm.   17 Feb 1831
    Joshua Turner, sec.

Bradley, Benjamin FN   Margaret Bagwell FN   13 Jan 1821
                              of George
    Nock Riley, sec.

Bratcher, Aaron   Mary Parks of Chas.   7 Aug 1821
    George Blake, sec.

Brewington, William   Mary Waterfield   10 Mar 1805

Brickhouse, Joseph B.   Louisa B. Bradford   8 Jun 1850
                               of Margaret Bradford

Briggs, Joseph H.   Ann S. Warrington   20 Dec. 1825
                           of Stephen
    James Eihelberger, sec.
Brimer, Caleb   Rachel Marriner   3 Jul 1800
    Stephen Bloxom, sec.

Brimer, Joseph   Polly Bishop   4 Feb 1803
    Caleb Brimer, sec.

Britcher, William   Nancy Miles   29 Jan 1843

Britches FN   Betty Nidab FN   19 Mar 1803
    Joshua Broadwater, sec.

Brittingham, James   Henrietta Massey   25 Mar 1822
    John S. Melvin, sec.

- 39 -

```
Brittingham, John          Nancy Taylor                30 Aug 1813
     Arthur Cord and William W. Hickman, sec.

Brittingham, John          Esther A. Tull               5 Jun 1852
     (wdr)                 (wid of John W.)

Brittingham, John          Mary S. Marshall            18 Aug 1848
                              of Solomon
     Solomon Marshall, sec.

Brittingham, Levi          Polly Holt                  10 Feb 1802
     John Holt, sec.

Brittingham, Thomas        May A. Waterfield            7 Mar 1838

Brittingham, William       Charlotte Bunting           22 Jan 1850
                              of Sheppard
      Purnell B. and Smith Chesser, sec.

Broadwater, Ames           Mary Taylor                 27 Nov 1854
                              of William Taylor

Broadwater, Cabel          Elizabeth Corbin            22 Dec 1824
     of Elias              (wid Ralph)
        David Broadwater and John Custis, sec.

Broadwater, Christopher  Elizabeth Collins             14 Jun 1813
     Ralph B. Corbin, sec.

Broadwater, David          Ann White of James          20 Dec 1823
     Caleb Broadwater and Samuel Walston, sec.

Broadwater, Edward         Euphanica Taylor            27 Dec 1809
                              of Southy
        George Bonwell, sec.

Broadwater, Edward         Polly Case                  30 Nov 1799
     David Mills, sec.

Broadwater, Elias          Polly Jones                 23 Mar 1813
                           (wid Edward)
        David Miles, sec.

Broadwater, Elijah         Mary Holland                29 Apr 1834
     James Duncan and William P. Mood, sec.

Broadwater, Elijah         Mary Holland                 4 May 1834

Broadwater, Henry          Rachel Taylor               29 Aug 1825
       Thompson Holmes and Nehemiah Stockley, sec.
```

Broadwater, Henry   Sophia R. Powell   12 Apr 1802
    Jacob Burton, sec.

Broadwater, Henry   Euphany Hill   11 Feb 1804
    of William
    Hillary Sherwood, sec.

Broadwater, Israel FN   Sarah Laws FN   4 Nov 1852

Broadwater, Jacob   Mary James   5 Oct 1789

Broadwater, James FN   Comfort Planter FN   5 Apr 1854

Broadwater, John   Nancy May   28 Apr 1807
    William Smulling (?) and William R. Taylor, sec.

Broadwater, Joseph   Mary Massey   29 Jul 1816
                           (wid John)
    Michael Robbins and William Jenkins, sec.

Broadwater, Joseph   Sarah Broadwater   26 Jan 1790

Broadwater, Joshua FN   Barshaba Crippin FN   10 Dec 1803
    Thomas Crippin, sec.

Broadwater, Joshua   Lydia Holden   3 Feb 1820

Broadwater, Robert   Betsy Riggs   8 Jun 1807
    Thomas Hope, sec.

Broadwater, Robert   Sarah Nock   25 Dec 1807
    Edwin Bell, sec.

Broadwater, Savage   Nancy Broadwater   28 Apr 1806
    David Miles, sec.

Broadwater, Savage   Betsy Fedderman   21 Mar 1804
    Elias Broadtwater, sec.

Broadwater, Southy   Polly Benston   3 Aug 1820
    (wdr)
    Savage Broadwater and George D. Chandler, sec.
Broadwater, Southy   Euphanica Massey   10 Aug 1831
    (wdr)   (wid Cabel)
    Thomas C. Delastatious and William E. Beavans, sec.

Broadwater, Southy   Nancy Garrett   27 May 1823
    John Custis and Walter D. Bayne, sec.

Broadwater, Southy   Esther Hill   19 Oct 1791

Broadwater, Southy   Atta Broadwater   29 Dec 1806

Major Hinman, sec.

Broadwater, William   Fiske Williams   13 Jun 1807
    William Murrah, sec.

Broadwater, William   Nancy Miles   27 Jan 1834
    (wdr)   (wid of George)
    William J. Matthews, sec.

Broadwater, William   Catherine Russell   21 Apr 1840
    (wdr)   (wid of Colmore Sr.)
    Thomas A Gibbons and William Parramore, sec.

Broadwater, William FN   Sarah Williams FN   23 Jan 1839
    Jesse Broadwater FN and David Mears, sec.

Brockshaw, Jacob   Levinear Evans   30 Jul 1800
                     of Richard Evans
    Severn Tyler, sec.

Brosdwater, George T.   Louissa Crippen   8 Dec 1851
    FN   FN of James Crippen FN

Broughton, William   Margaret Taylor   7 Nov 1831
    William J. Matthews and John W. Holland, sec.

Brown, Dudley P.   Tabitha Garret   10 Sep 1810
    Tommy Abbott, sec.

Brown, Levi FN   Sarah FN   12 Feb 1813
    Richard D. Bayly, sec.

Brown, William   Silvia Mathews   9 Mar 1801
    Levin Godfrey, sec.

Brown, William FN   Jenney --- FN   6 Jul 1802

Brown, William FN   Nancy Griffin FN   27 Dec 1804
    Levin Godfree, sec.

Browne, Peter Dr.   Sally C. Bayly   11 Nov 1839
    Thomas H. Bayly, sec.

Budd, John   Sally Scott   24 Jan 1803
    William Budd, sec.

Budd, John   Polly Annis   28 Feb 1848
                     (wid of Custis Major)
    Southy Budd Jr., sec.

Budd, Major   Nancy Mason   12 Jan 1830

```
                        (wid Thomas)
     Edward Gunter, sec.

Budd, McKeel               Margaret Taylor          29 Jan 1841
Budd, McKeel (wid)         Jane Parks               27 Feb 1843

Budd, McKeel               Eliza Salisbury          12 Jun 1845

Budd, McKul (wdr)          Jane Parker              25 Feb 1833
                           of Arthur
     Arthur Parks, sec.

Budd, McKul Jr.            Margaret Taylor           7 Jul 1841
     James H. East, sec.

Budd, Thomas               Sally Wright             29 Dec 1842

Budd, William              Betsy Parker             10 Jun 1806
     William Foster, sec.

Budd, William S.          Mary Fosset               7 Jun 1838

Budd, William             Betsy Young              13 Apr 1802
     Robinson Scott, sec.

Budd, William             Betsey Parker            10 Jun 1806

Budd, William S.          Sarah Bull               14 Nov 1838
                          of John Bull Sr.
     John Bull Sr., sec.

Bull, Custis              Margaret Melson          24 Jul 1839

Bull, Daniel              Molly Chambers           31 Jul 1807
     Southy Bull, sec.

Bull, Daniel              Betty Giddens            25 Nov 1789
                                                   (badly damaged)

Bull, Edward S.          Susan Kellam              26 Oct 1843

Bull, Edward S.          Susan Kellam              26 Oct 1840

Bull, Eli                Nancy Fitzgerald          24 Dec 1785
     Elijah Fitzgerald, sec.
Bull, Elijah             Nancy White               13 Feb 1809
     John Bull of John Church, sec.

Bull, Elisha             Esther Custis              3 Jul 1832
     John Bull, sec.

Bull, Ezekiel            Susanna Colloney          25 Feb 1796
```

Bull, George John A. Bundick, sec.	Hetty Bull of Major	5 Jul 1815

Bull, George
    of Benjamin
    George T. Gibb, sec.
	Ann Bonwell
	(wid Stephen)
		6 Jun 1810

Bull, George	Hetty Bull	6 Jul 1815
Bull, James of Bagwell William Grinnalds, sec.	Polly Grinnalds of Wm.	6 Nov 1816

Bull, James R.
    of James Bull Jr.
    James R. and Francis A Bell, sec.
	Susanna R. Chandler
	of Mitchell Chandler
		27 Feb 1848

Bull, James
    (wdr)
    Smith Cutler and John E. Wise, sec.
	Henrietta Bayly
	of Zadoch Bayly, dec.
		28 Jan 1850

Bull, John Matthias Phillips Jr., sec.	Jane Phillips of Matthias	10 Aug 1814
Bull, John Jr. Daniel Bull, sec.	Harriet Chambers	31 Jul 1810
Bull, John Jr.	Nancy Turnel	30 Jan 1796
Bull, John T. of Thomas Bull	Tabitha Hancock	23 Jan 1854
Bull, John FN John Poulson, sec.	Mary Keller FN	24 Dec 18847
Bull, John R.	Susan Chandler	27 Sep 1848
Bull, John Preeson Snead, sec.	Sarah Russell	29 Jul 1774
Bull, John R.	Juliet Carmine	7 Oct 1840
Bull, Joseph T.	Harriet E. Phillips of Smith Phillips	7 Jan 1852
Bull, Luther T.	Sarah F Johnson	18 Jul 1848
Bull, Major of Wm. Charles C. Willet, sec.	Hessy Gray of Solomon	30 Dec 1818
Bull, Major	Leah Lilliston	31 Dec 1845
Bull, Richard	Katherine Hargis	13 Jun 1806

James White, sec.

Bull, Richard	Caty Hargis	13 Jun 1796
Bull, Richard Richard Bull and Richard Killey, sec.	Leah Melson	30 Aug 1836
Bull, Souhty Charles Snead, sec.	Susanna Fitzgerald	7 Jul 1785
Bull, Southy Benjamin Prewitt, sec.	Susanna Fitzgerald	3 Apr 1810
Bull, Southy Jr. George West, sec.	Mary N. West of George	6 Nov 1836
Bull, Southy W.	Polly Mason	21 Mar 1838
Bull, Southy Edward Gunter, sec.	Anne West	30 May 1803
Bull, Southy Jr.	Mary A. West	9 Jan 1836
Bull, Spencer of Wm. John S. Bundick, sec.	Nancy Moore of Laban	4 Jun 1817
Bull, Thomas John B. Ailworth, sec.	Sally Bundick	19 Oct 1830
Bull, Thomas George Mapp, sec.	Polly Mapp of George	9 Jan 1829
Bull, Thomas Samuel Kellam, sec.	Rachel Floyd	15 Feb 1815
Bull, Thomas (wdr) William Parramore Jr., sec.	Anne Elliott (wid Thomas)	12 May 1825
Bull, Thomas W.	Elizabeth M Neely	5 Nov 1851
Bull, William of William Spencer Bull, sec.	Salley Baker of Hezekiah	6 Nov 1818
Bull, William Southy Bull, sec.	Sukey Bull	23 Dec 1811
Bull, William Levin Crowson, sec.	Katherine Evans	1 Jan 1808
Bull, William	Catherine	3 Jan 1808

Bull, William	Mary A. Mears	7 Jun 1847
Bull, William H.	Sally Hickman	11 Jan 1843
Bull, William James Mears, sec.	Mary Ann Mears	5 Jun 1848
Bull, William	Sukey Bull	23 Dec 1817
Bull, Willaim Thorowgood Bell, sec.	Nancy Drummond	20 Sep 1799
Bullman, S.C.	Elizabeth H. Mapp of Robins H. Mapp	3 May 1853
Bundick, Abbott Isaac Taylor, sec.	Betsy Taylor	11 Sep 1791
Bundick, David of Rich. Richard Bundick and Henry Bagwell, sec.	Elizabeth Beauchamp	19 Feb 1830
Bundick, Edward Topping James W. Custis, sec.	Keziah Mears ward of J. W. Custis	28 Jan 1839
Bundick, Elijah FN John A. Bundick, sec.	Peggy Harmon FN	3 Apr 1804
Bundick, George Sr. Stephen Hickman and Richard D. Bayly, sec.	Milly Hickman	15 Dec 1815
Bundick, George W. Levi Dix, sec.	Elizabeth Hickman of Richard	25 Oct 1816
Bundick, George Jr. Tommy Abbott, sec.	Nancy Holt	28 Jun 1811
Bundick, George Sr. Evande Cameron, sec.	Elizabeth Kellam	11 Jun 1811
Bundick, George Thomas (wdr)	Drucilla H. Miles Sally Miles	31 Oct 1854
Bundick, George Caleb Broadwater, sec.	Betty Laws	25 Aug 1785
Bundick, George T.	Sarah A. Hickman	28 Dec 1842
Bundick, George George Taylor, sec.	Rachel Mason	23 Mar 1802

```
Bundick, Jabez            Tabitha Taylor            7 Jan 1819
    of Abbott            of Charles
    Abbott Bundick, sec.

Bundick, James           Nancy Selby              23 Dec 1806
    Mack Crippen, sec.

Bundick, James FN        Mary FN                  24 Jun 1812

Bundick, John            Jane Taylor               8 Dec 1808
    of Long (?)          (wid George)
    Littleton Lecato, sec.

Bundick, John A.         Elizabeth Twiford        24 May 1806
    Robert Twiford, sec.

Bundick, John            Sally Nock               27 Dec 1798
    William Baker, sec.

Bundick, John B.         Margaret E. Floyd         8 Apr 1846

Bundick, John R.         Jane Tyler

Bundick, John            Tabitha Taylor           10 Jan 1819
    of Abbott

Bundick, John A.         Elizabeth Hannaford 13 Sep 1802
    Edmund Bayly, sec.

Bundick, John            Mary Nelson              29 Dec 1846

Bundick, Joseph          Margaret Bloxom           7 Feb 1831
    George Bundick, sec.

Bundick, Joseph          Molly Baker              24 Feb 1808
    William Baker, sec.

Bundick, Joshua          Sally Cropper            16 Feb 1816

Bundick, Joshus FN       Ibby Crippen FN           3 Feb 1816
    Levi Bundick, sec.

Bundick, Lewis FN        Sally Moses FN           24 Dec 1816
                         of Phellis
        Joshua Bundick FN, sec.

Bundick, Richard         Molly Lewis               8 Nov 1825
    (wdr)                (wid William)
    Sacker Scott, sec.


Bundick, Richard         Rachel Fosque             4 Feb 1829
```

```
(wdr)                    (wid John)
     Custis Hargis, sec.

Bundick, Richard A.       Ritta Annis of Levin      11 Jul 1821
     Custis Annis, sec.

Bundick, Richard          Lany Nelson                4 Dec 1804

Bundick, Richard          Nancy Hickman              5 Oct 1838
     (wdr)                (wid of Joseph)
     John L. Snead, sec.

Bundick, Richard          Nancy Onley                4 Jan 1848
     of Richard
     John W. Berry and George Hichman, sec.

Bundick, Samuel C.        Sally Bunting             14 Dec 1836
                          of Solomon
          Samuel Bundick and Walter Lewis, sec.

Bundick, Severn           Caroline Thornton         14 Jan 1856
                          of John

Bundick, Thomas E.        Mary A. Lewis             20 Dec 1858

Bundick, William          Polly Prescott             8 May 1827
     of George            of Thomas
     George Bundick and Richard DC. Bayly, sec.

Bundick, William          Polly Davis               23 Jun 1814
     of George            of Henry
     James Taylor, sec.

Bundick, William          Polly Parks               28 Oct 1809
     Elijah Parks, sec.

Bundick, William          Atta Bunting              22 Jul 1806
     William Bunting, sec.

Bundick, William H.       Margaret L. Taylor (wid)  15 Sep 1842

Bundick, William          Ann Hinman                10 Dec 1834

Bundick, William J.       Elizabeth Seymour Baker   14 Dec 1853
     of William           of Asa Baker

Bunting, Colmore (wid)    Ann Davis (wid)            8 Feb 1843

Bunting, Eliza            Rosey Johnson of Sam.     22 Jan 1823
     David Miles and George Croswell, sec.

Bunting, George S.        Rose Ann Fitchett          2 Jul 1843
```

Bunting, George   Polly Taylor   31 Mar 1819
    of John   of James Seul
    Robert P. Broadwater, sec.

Bunting, George   Elizabeth Gladding   29 Sep 1836
                              ward of said George Bunting
        Samuel C. Abbott, sec.

Bunting, George   Sally Ramsey (wid)   26 Sep 1806
        George W. Burton, sec.

Bunting, George S.   Rose Ann Fitchett

Bunting, Henry   Mary L. Landing   21 Dec 1843

Bunting, Isma of Isma   Elizabeth Waterfield   29 Jul 1816
                              (wid)
        Samuel Henderson and Robert White, sec.

Bunting, Jacob   Mary Custis   16 May 1856
                              of Margaret

Bunting, James   Hannah Reggins   21 Feb 1814
                              (wid Levin)
        Spencer Drummond and William W. Burton, sec.

Bunting, James S.   Sally S. Hope   16 Nov 1852
                              of James Hope, dec'd.

Bunting, John   Rebecca Merrill   23 Feb 1829
        James McCready, sec.

Bunting, John   Rebecca Merrill (wid)   15 Feb 1829

Bunting, Jonathan   Elizabeth Jones   30 Jun 1807
        James Jenkins, sec.

Bunting, Luther   Rosey Mason of Henry   27 Nov 1809
        George Smith, sec.

Bunting, Luther   Elizabeth Lewis   4 Mar 1812
        Andrew Tunnell, sec.

Bunting, Smith   Maria Bunting of Zeler   27 Dec 1806
        George S. Fisher, sec.

Bunting, Smith   Nanny Rodgers   5 Dec 1805
        John Phillips, sec.

Bunting, Solomon   Catherine T. Elliott   17 Aug 1831
        John T. Elliott, sec.

Bunting, Solomon Jacob Bradford, sec.	Susanna C. Bradford	6 Nov 1810
Bunting, Solomon George Fosque, sec.	Leah Mayson	16 Aug 1803
Bunting, Thomas S. Edmund Garrison, sec.	Lorea Elliott (wid Thomas)	31 Jul 1831
Bunting, Thomas C. M. P. Jacob Bell, sec.	Juliet L. Smith of George Smith	10 Nov 1834
Bunting, Thomas	Rose Evans	c. 1800 (badly damaged)
Bunting, William Black Presson Snead, sec.	Sally Cropper	15 Sep 1785
Bunting, Thomas C. (wdr) Thomas Floyd, sec.	Maria G. Floyd ward of Thomas Floyd	19 Mar 1841
Bunting, Thomas Jonathan Bunting, sec.	Susannah Bayey	22 Dec 1785
Bunting, Thomas	Sukey Bunting	29 Jan 1841
Bunting, Thomas (wdr)	Harriet Kellam	28 Nov 1853
Bunting, William William Kellam, sec.	Rachel Samage of Susy East	31 May 1830
Bunting, William R.	Agnes Bloxom (wid Custis)	3 Mar 1810
Bunting, William R. John Nelson Jr. and Sacker Scott, sec.	Betsy Fox (wid Thomas)	29 Jan 1827
Bunting, William R. ward of Golden F. Fox	Ann P. Shield of James Shield	31 Dec 1849
Burbage, Capt. Peter	Margaret Watts	3 Jun 1827
Burbage, Capt. Peter	Ann Hinman	14 Dec 1832
Burbage, Peter L. (wdr) Isaac K. Hopkins and John Ewell, sec.	Ann Hinman	12 Nov 1832
Burch, Joseph	Betsy Cherricks of Arthur	16 Jun 1806

Arthur Cherricks, sec.

Burch, William   Phebe Thoirnton   25 Jan 1854
    (wdr)   of John Thornton, B.D.
Burchett, John   Scarburgh Northam   2 Jul 1789

Burdett, Thomas   Tabitha Wallop   20 Jan 1792

Burlidge, Peter L.   Margaret W. Watts of Wm.   2 Jan 1828
    William Watts and Jenkins Bowen, sec.

Burton, Garrison   Sally Elliott   9 May 1804
    Parker Copes, sec.

Burton, George T. W.   Susan Kelly   8 May 1847
    of John W. Burton
    Jackson D. Tunnell, sec.

Burton, George   Ann J. Rowly   1 Nov 1834
    Walter Broadwater and George P. Scarburgh, sec.

Burton, John B.   Sarah P. Bagwell   30 Mar 109
    George P. Bagwell, sec.

Burton, John W.L.   Charlotte Bloxom   18 May 1830
                        of Nancy
    Peter Delastatues and Levin Core, sec.

Burton, John (of John) Maria Whealton   13 Aug 1833

Burton, John J. R.   Sarah M Ashby   28 Oct 1851
    of Joshua Burton   of Smith Ashby and Hannah B. Ward
                                           (formerly Ashby)

Burton, Joshua   Polly Bradford of Tho.   29 Apr 1822
    William Parramore, sec.

Burton, Joshua Sr.   Margaret Floyd   18 Feb 1819

Burton, Joshua   Polly Bradford   29 Apr 1822

Burton, Samuel B.   Elizabeth Copes   29 Dec 1835
                        of John C. Copes
        Thomas Cropper, sec.

Burton, William W.   Ann D. Groton   6 Apr 1807
    William R. Custis, sec.

Burton, William   Nancy Rew   22 Jan 1850
    of Betsy   of John Rew Jr.
    Wiliam Rew Jr. and Kendall B. Stokley, sec.

Butman, John   Hessey Bayly   8 Apr 1803
  Major Hastings, sec.

Byrd, Colwell P.   Elizabeth A. Trader 16 Sep 1854
  of Johannas Byrd, dec'd. of William Trader

Byrd, George W.   Elizabeth Wessells 20 Dec 1852
         of Capt. John Wesells

Byrd, Riley F.   Sally Wessells   25 Oct 1852
         of Walter Wessells, Jr.

Byrd, Samuel   Mary E. Byrd (wid) 30 Dec 1847

Byrd, William T.   Hetty N. Fisher   22 Feb 1853
         of Henry Fisher

Callahan, James   Caroline Gladding   31 Dec 1835
                         of John Gladding
          John Gladding and John B. Ailworth, sec.

Cammell, John   Leah Davis   28 Jan 1799
          Nehemiah Bratton, sec.

Caple, Isaiah   Elizabeth Phillips

Cares, John   Elizabeth Stakes   16 Feb 1790

Carlile, Alexander   Milly Parker   19 Feb 1785
          Jacob Savage, sec.

Carmar, Gilbert   Mary Ann Watson   29 Oct 1833
          Temathy Hill, sec.

Carmine, James   Dinah Bennett   17 Mar 1795
          John Bradford, sec.

Carmine, Samuel J.   Hetty Watson   16 Aug 1849

Carmine, Samuel J.   Hetty Watson   16 Aug 1850
                         of Susan Watson
          John H. Snead, sec.

Carmine, Thomas   Sarah G. Tunnell   21 Dec 1847
                         ward of William J. Churn
          Thomas Carmine and William J. Churn, sec.

Carmine, Tully R.   Sarah A. Nock   11 May 1853
          of William   of Elijah W.

Carpenter, Jacob   Elizabeth Holloway   13 --- 1805
          James Conner, sec.   (badly damaged)

Carpenter, Lewis C.   Anatha M. Ames   5 Dec 1838
                         ward of Levin S. Ames
          John C. Mapp, sec.

Carpenter, Revel   Elizabeth Bowen   25 Oct 1834

Carter, Daniel FN   Rachel Robins FN   11 Jan 1817
          Thomas H. Bayly, sec.

Carter, Edmund   Fanny Drummond   1 Sep 1812

Caruthers, James   Rosa Lewis   15 Sep 1839

Caruthers, William   Elizabeth Ann D. Smith   12 Jun 1826
          of James   orphan William W.
          Severn East and Margaret Smith, sec.

Case, Charles FN   Nancy Gardener FN   29 Oct
     Richard Ames, sec.

Case, Charles FN   Rachel Jubilee (wid) FN   18 Dec 1849
     Thoroughgood T. R. Mears, sec.

Case, Major   Betsey Riggs   12 Jan 1799
     Jacob Andrews, sec.

Casey, Patrick   Charity Smith   7 Mar 1786
     William Smith, sec.

Chambers, Edmund   Mary Wise   5 Jun 1785
     Kelly Wise, sec.

Chambers, Edward   Rebecca Wise   25 Nov 1818
     of Edward   of Levin, dec,d.
     Daniel Bull, sec.

Chambers, Elijah   Peggy Nelson   8 Feb 1786
     Rufus Huntley, sec.

Chambers, John   Sally Bloxom of Arzil   24 Dec 1831
     Edward Chandler, sec.

Chambers, Levin   Ann F. Lilliston   17 May 1831
                           (wid Elijah)
     Edward Chandler, sec.

Chambers, Major   Elizabeth Guy   23 May 1784
     William Leatherbury, sec.

Chance, Elijah   Peggy Wharton   15 Jan 1813

Chance, Elijah   Leah Spiers   16 Jan 1809
     John Wise, sec.

Chance, Elijah   Elizabeth Beach   26 Jan 1847

Chance, James   Mary Ann Haley   26 Dec 1853
     of William   of Benjamin and Elizabeth

Chance, William   Anna J. Beach of Jos.   26 Feb 1831
     John H. Harmon and James Glen, sec.

Chandler, Bagwell   Nancy Ward of John   27 Feb 1832
     Joseph Crockett, sec.

Chandler, Edmund   Mary Stanley   2 Nov 1828

Chandler, Elisha   Amy Chandler   7 Aug 1805

Mitchell Chandler, sec.

Chandler, James	Nancy Annis	30 Aug 1850
Chandler, James	Peggy Burton Phillips	25 Nov 1801
Chandler, John H.	Catharine Smith	2 Sep 1843
Chandler, John W.	Elizabeth Fosque	20 Mar 1837
Chandler, John B.	Sally Ann Ayres (wid)	27 Jun 1844
Chandler, John R.	Margaret Phillips	27 May 1835
Chandler, John H.	Catherine I. Smith of Thomas H.	31 Aug 1834

Thomas H. Smith, sec.

Chandler, John K.	Elizabeth Chandler	7 Oct 1837
Chandler, John K.	Elizabeth Scarburgh	7 Oct 1837

Walter J. Kellam and John H. Wise, sec.

Chandler, John M.   Elizabeth Fosque   16 Mar 1839
Edward Glen and Jacob jester, sec.

Chandler, John R.   Margaret Phillips   25 May 1835
ward of Mitchell Chandler   ward of Edward Phillips
Mitchell Chandler and Edward Phillips, sec.

Chandler, Laban   Esther Singleton   20 Dec 1815
     (wid Richard)
Mitchell Chandler, sec.

Chandler, Laban   Margaret Rolly   18 Jul 1822
     (wid Ray)
Levin Ayres, sec.

Chandler, Laban   Polly Bull of Bagwell   24 Feb 1810
William Scott, sec.

Chandler, Littleton   Sarrey Melson of Jno.   9 Mar 1815
James Mister, sec.

Chandler, Mitchell   Susanna Laylor   7 May 1803
Thomas Chandler, sec.

Chandler, Mitchell   Sarah Bonwell (wid)   12 Sep 1826
Levin Taylor, sec.

Chandler, Mitchell   Keziah Laylor   3 May 1802
Arthur Laylor, sec.

Chandler, Mitchell   Susan Bird of Ebern   4 Mar 1817
    William Bird, sec.

Chandler, Sylvester R.   Mary A. Kellam   20 Mar 1844

Chandler, Thomas   Juliet Elliott   1 Dec 1845

Chandler, Thomas   Nancy Smith   28 Jan 1812
                          (wid Robert)
    Shadrack Ames, sec.

Chandler, Thomas B.   Sarah A. Gunter   10 Jan 1848
                          of Edward Gunter
    Levin R. Ayres, sec.

Chandler, William D.   Margaret Wise of Geo.   22 May 1816
    William E. Wise, sec.

Chandler, William   Leah Kellam (wid)   22 Jan 1810
    James Ironmonger, sec.

Chandler, William   Phamey Ironmonger   5 May 1801
    Edward Ironmonger, sec.

Chandler, Zorobabel   Sally Moore   7 Dec 1824
    William E. Wise sec.

Chapman, William   Jane Evans   27 Apr 1802
    Charles Stockly, sec.

Charles FN   Elizabeth Stevens FN   24   Jul   1806
    freed by Drummond
    William, freed by Drummond, sec.

Charnock, Abel   Atha Turner   10 Jun 1785
    Williams Gibbs, sec.

Charnock, Edward   Polly Shores   13 Mar 1819   6
George   of Solomon
Edward Glenn, sec.

Charnock, Edward   Sally Simpson   12 Mar 1839
    Jacob Lurton, sec.

Charnock, Eli   Margaret Charnock   28 Dec 1825
    of John   of Owen
    Owen Charnock, sec.

Charnock, Henry   Anna Ewell   15 Dec 1825
    of Robert   of William, dec'd.
    John Johnson of Thomas, sec.

```
Charnock, James            Mary Charnock            15 Sep 1844

Charnock, Richard          Lovey C. Scott (wid)     27 Dec 1847
    David B. Northam and Bernard C. Scarborough, sec.

Charnock, William          Peggy Mason              13 Feb 1809
    Owen Charnock, sec.

Charnock, William (wdr)  Sally Charnick (wid)       28 Aug 1849
    William Charnock and Richard T. Ames, sec.

Charnock, William          Sally Charnock           29 Aug 1849

Chase, Alsander            Sarah Davis              29 Sep 1856
                           of Henry

Chase, Rev. Moses B.       Sarah C. James            2 Apr 1824

Chase, Robert              Nancy Lewis              22 Dec 1826
                           of Capt. Raymond
        Charles Smith and Capt. Kendall Silverthorne, sec.

Cherricks, Arthur          Caroline Hall             9 Nov 1846

Cherricks, James           Ann Kelly                22 Jun 1848

Cherricks, William         Betsy Whealton of Josh.  16 Jun 1807
    Arthur Cherricks and Joseph Burch, sec.

Cherrix, John              Amy Burch                26 Oct 1812
    John Conner, sec.

Chesher, Ephraim           Lusey Marshall           13 Oct 1798
    George Wilson, sec.

Cheshire, Custis           Sally Butler             18 May 1810
    Elias Shreives, sec.

Cheshire, Eli              Anne Chace               14 Oct 1806
    Ephraim Outten, sec.

Cheshire, John             Comfort Tyler of Jabez    2 Dec 1815
    Ephrain Tyler, sec.

Cheshire, Purnell          Lane Trader              21 Sep 1804
    Shadrack Warrington, sec.

Cheshire, Thomas           Susan Moore              14 Aug 1806
                           of Bratcher
        Jacob Andrews, sec.

Chesser, Eli               Lucinda Lucas of Wm.      6 Apr 1829
```

Jacob Bird of Nathaniel, sec.

Chesser, Elisha   Sally Boggs   12 Dec 1832
 William E. Wise, William P. Custis, William Parramore, sec.

Chesser, Gillet   Ann Hinman   9 Jun 1842

Chesser, Henry   Margaret Taylor   28 Mar 1839
 Samuel C. Abbott, sec.

Chesser, John   Comfort Tyler   4 Dec 1815

Chesser, John   Susanna Northam   10 Feb 1858
         of Elizabeth

Chesser, John   Mariah Marshall   8 Mar 1834
         of Robert
 James Mister, sec.

Chesser, Purnell   Ann Baker of Wm. 21 Nov 1849
 Henry Chesser, sec.

Chesser, Shadrock   Eliza Chesser   31 Dec 1832
 ward of Solomon Ewell of Nancy Chesser Lewis
 Solomon Ewell and Nancy Lewis, sec.

Chesser, Smith   Margaret Brittingham 29 May 1840
         of James
 Henry Chesser, sec.

Chesser, William   Sally Small   26 Jul 1825
         gdn. of James David
 James Chesser and Purnell Chesser, sec.

Chessire, Erastus   Harriet Brittingham 16 Jun 1851
         of James

Chessire, James   Elizabeth Trader 16 Aug 1822
 of William   of Staton
 John & Samuel Lewis, sec.

Chessire, Robert   Elizabeth Duncan 26 Jan 1832
         of Jesse
 Gilbert Northan, sec.

Chisher, William   Leah Marshall   7 Aug 1797

Christiam, George S. Elizabeth Henderson 10 May 1834
         of Zorobabel
 James M. Savage, sec.

Christiam, William Elizabeth Seymore 30 Oct 1810

Litt. Hammell, sec.

Christopher, Delight   Tenny Ayres of Levin   30 Dec 1822
   Ezekiel Baker, sec.

Christopher, Delighty   Mary Taylor   20 Apr 1833
                    (wid of William)
     William W. Dix, sec.

Christopher, George   Mrs. Ann Hope   29 Mar 1828
   Henry Walker, sec.

Christopher, George   Susanna Fisher   29 Jun 1795

Christopher, Levin P.   Nancy Trader   28 Feb 1853
                    of William

Christopher, Williamson Leah Wilson   4 Jun 1789

Christopher, Wm.   Betsy Miles   28 Jun 1815
   Abbott Trader, sec.

Church, Littleton FN   Bridget Case   29 Jan 1850

Church, Solomon FN   Susanna Poulson FN   24 Jul 1809
   Harry Becket, sec.

Church, Stephen   Rachel Anthony   9 Dec 1802
   Abel Anthony, sec.

Churn, Henry K.   Serenia J. Onions   13 Feb 1850
                    of William, dec'd.
   James Waples of Thomas, sec.

Churn, Henry K. of Thom. Sarah Russell of Betty   27 Nov 1820
   Joseph Riggs, sec.

Churn, John   Elizabeth Abdill   23 Dec 1831
                    of Joseph
   Joshua B. Wyatt, sec.

Churn, John   Sally Pritiloae   31 Jan 1820
                    ward of John Robins
   John Robins, sec.

Churn, Thomas   Sally Cottril   11 Nov 1822
   Isaac D. Robins, sec.

Churn, William   Nancy Harrison   24 Dec 1791

Churn, William   Margaret Taylor   10 Dec 1810
                    (wid Shady)

John Mears of Wm., sec.

Clark, Tiner W.	Margaret S. Winder	8 Sep 1851
Clark, William P.	Rachel Mister	10 Oct 1842
Clavill, William B. O.N. Knox and James D. McAllen, sec.	Ann W. Mears of Geo.	27 Oct 1847
Clawill, George	Lydia Hill of Timothy	7 Apr 1846
Clayton, Dennis Charles Bagwell, sec.	Susanna Riley	12 Feb 1800
Clayton, George Jr.	Hannah S. Young	19 Dec 1840
Clayton, George Thorgood Taylor, sec.	Ann K. Bagwell of Chas.	27 Jan 1817

Clayton, John
   of Dennis
   Samuel Andrews and William T. Joynes, sec.
	Hannah Young
	of William
		19 Dec 1840

Claywell, George (wdr) Edward Taylor, sec.	Mary Turlington	20 Aug 1832
Cluff, Benjamin Parker Coard, sec.	Leah Dennis	8 Apr 1803
Cluff, Littleton	Nancy Sharpley	23 Dec 1838
Cluff, Robert Hancock Shrieves and Zadoc Selby, sec.	Elizabeth Tunnel	14 Jan 1817
Coard, George S.	Harriet Ann West of George, Sr.	7 Jan 1851
Coard, James	Maria Taylor (wid)	24 Apr 1854
Coard, John W.	Nancy Chandler	10 Sep 1845
Coard, John James Taylor, sec.	Anne Ayres	27 Jun 1803
Coard, Parker George Thomas, sec.	Polly Abbott	23 Jun 1806
Coard, William Jr. Edward Taylor, sec.	Mary Collins	28 Aug 1834
Coard, William Parker Coard and James, Taylor sec.	Anne Morris	13 Apr 1808

```
Cobb, James              Leah Stevens              16 Feb 1843

Cobb, William            Molly Phillips            15 Apr 1807
     John Turlington, sec.

Coke, Richard            Leney Taylor              11 Jan 1792

Colburn, John C.         Christabella Bailey       29 Dec 1834
                         (wid of Littleton)
        Isaac Moore, sec.

Cole, John               Elizabeth Bloxom          21 Dec 1827
     tailor, (wdr)       (wid Stephen)
     Richard Gillaspie and Gorah Taylor, sec.

Cole, John               Elizabeth Savage          28 Dec 1808
                         (wid Richard R.)
        John Roswell, sec.

Coleburn, George         Julie Downing             10 Apr 1854
                         of Francis

Coleburn, James          Betsy Taylor              18 Dec 1833
     John M. Colburn, sec.

Coleburn, James          Nervilla E. Ames           6 Nov 1852
     (wdr)               of Leadock, dec'd.

Coleburn, James          Sally Taylor              28 Apr 1791

Coleburn, James          Betsy Taylor              19 Dec 1833

Coleburn, John A.        Elizabeth J. Trader       23 Apr 1825
                         of Littleton
        John W. Hancock, sec.

Coleburn, John (wdr)     Elizabeth Bloxom (wid)     8 May 1836

Coleburn, John N.        Elizabeth R. Bloxom        6 May 1836
     (wdr)               (wid of Samuel)
     Samuel Jenkins and Joseph W. Gibb, sec.

Coleburn, John C. (wdr)  Christabell Bayly         29 Dec 1834
Coleburn, Revel          Peggy Polk                 7 Sep 1785
        William Polk, sec.

Coleburn, Robert         Mary Fosque               22 Nov 1813
        George Beach, sec.

Coleburn, Samuel         Eliza Heath                6 Dec 1837
                         of Mary A. Heath
        Joshua W. Elliot, sec.
```

```
Coleburn, Samuel          Dorinide V. Hutchinson    6 Feb 1832
    George W. Parker, sec.

Coleburn, Thomas          Taby Phillips           28 Dec 1825
    of George             alias Gileous
    Severn East, sec.

Collings, John            Diademia Cherix           5 Sep 1806
                          of Jesse
      George Marshall, sec.

Collins, Edward           Harriet Wilson            9 Feb 1837
    John H. Bunting, sec.

Collins, George           Polly Wise              28 Dec 1791

Collins, George           Esther Merrill          25 Mar 1811
    of Philby             (wid)
    Daniel J. Marshall, sec.

Collins, James            Fanney Marshall         16 Mar 1801
                          (wid)
        William Johnson, sec.

Collins, John             Nancy Holt              21 Feb 1804
    Thomas Collins, sec.

Collins, John             Nancy Welch             26 Nov 1810
    Warrington Staton, sec.

Collins, John             Sally Thornton          12 Aug 1799
    John Watson, sec.

Collins, John             Susan Waters             3 Feb 1815
                          (wid James)
        Nathaniel Benson and Thomas R. Jaynes, sec.

Collins, John             Tabitha Carmine         24 Nov 1853
    of John               of John

Collins, Skinner          Rebecca Taylor          21 Jul 1806
    George Marshall, sec.

Collins, Skinner          Reba Taylor             23 Jul 1806

Collins, Southy           Annis Watson            10 Sep 1814
                          (wid Joshua FN)
        Edmund Nutts, sec.

Collins, Thomas           Elizabeth Taylor         4 Apr 1833
                          of Joseph
      John Taylor, sec.
```

```
Collins, Timothy of Wm.  Eliza Matthews of Issac  19   Sep    1813
    Levin Wilkerson, sec.

Collins, William         Elizabeth Gaskins          26 Jun 1845

Collins, William         Rebecca Owen               17 Aug 1788

Collins, William         Marcy Richardson           29 Dec 1813
                           (wid Edward)
          Isaac Ayres, sec.

Collins, William         Molly Bentson              30 Jan 1788

Collins, William (wdr)   Nancy Davis (wid)          28 Apr 1834
    Meshack Duncan and Thomas Ross, sec.

Colmore, John A.         Elizabeth Trader           24 Apr 1825

Colny, James             Elizabeth Stephens         22 Feb 1806

Colona, John W.          Sarah Ann Boggs            28 Nov 1836
                           of Elizabeth
          Lewis L. Snead, sec.

Colona, Thomas T. of Wm. Eliza D. Tunnell           19 Apr 1821
    John W. Watson and Thomas M. Bayly, sec.

Coloney, George          Sarah Walker                7 Dec 1798
    Robert Davis, sec.

Coloney, James           Leah Melson                 6 Nov 1833
    (wdr)                  of Jonathon
    Smith Melson, sec.

Coloney, John of Elijah  Susan Parks of Edmund  29   Mar    1823
    Edward Parks, sec.

Colonna, Benjamin S.     Mary C. Powell              6 Jan 1848

Colonna, Edward M.       Elizabeth Ann Darby        27 Nov 1837
    William C. Ames, sec.

Colonna, Edward P.       Ann B. Mears of Wm.         5 Jun 1826
    John R. Parker, sec.

Colonna, Elijah          Sally Hinman (wid)         13 Dec 1852

Colonna, Henry           Catherine Hickman           3 Jan 1827
    of Kendall             of Bridget
    Walter Wright and George Littleton, sec.

Colonna, James T.        Ann Bennett                28 Mar 1846
```

(Colony, Colona)

Colonna, James   Charlotte Parker   4 Jan 1839
    Daniel Lewis, sec.   of Arthur

Colonna, John   Margaret Ayres   29 Dec 1847
    Thomas D. Lewis, sec.

Colonna, John W.   Sarah Ann Boggs   30 Nov 1836

Colonna, John   Elizabeth Windon   12 Jan 1848
    William H. Arbuckle and Lonis C.H. Finney, sec.

Colonna, John   Elizabeth Window   20 Jan 1848

Colonna, Labby J.   Elizabeth Colonna   13 Sep 1833
                of Major Colonna
    Charles Tatham and Levin Core, sec.

Colonna, Major D.   Sally Beach of Geo. 22 Feb 1841
    Edward A. Revell, sec.

Colonna, Major D.   Sally Beach   20 Feb 1843

Colonna, Samuel W.   Anna M. Parker   10 Dec 1823
                (wid Thomas J.)
    T.W. Adair, sec.

Colonna, Samuel W.(wdr) Brunetta Parks   6 Feb 1833
    Patrick Colonna, sec.

Colonna, William   Sally Scott   18 Feb 1843

Colonna, William   Sally Scott of Major 16 Feb 1841
    Major Scott, sec.

Colonna, William   Mary Berry of Chas. 28 Jan 1856

Colonna, William   Louia Walter of Abel 16 Jan 1837
    Lorenzo D. Mears, sec.

Colony, Benjamin   Betsy Beach   26 Jul 1802
    Reuben Beach, sec.

Colony, Ebern of Major Mary Lawson of Robert 18 Jan 1816
    Henry Wise, son of Solomon, sec.

Colony, Elijah   Sarah Evans   23 Aug 1792

Colony, James of Elijah Sinah Simpson of Chas. 28 May 1817
    John Colony, sec.

```
Colony, John            Elizabeth Smith         22 Dec 1774
    William Colony, sec.

Colony, Kendall         Tabitha Right           23 Jan 1796

Colony, Upshur          Anne Darby               7 Mat 1775
    John Colony, sec.

Colony, Watson          Rose Folio              31 Dec 1810
    Benjamin Colony, sec.

Colony, Watson          Rosey Bayly             18 Feb 1806
    Walter Mears, sec.

Colony, William         Elizabeth Watson        11 Feb 1795
    Robert Twiford, sec.

Conner, Cabel R.        Eleanor R. Lilliston    25 Mar 1822
    Issac Smith, sec.

Conner, Calen           Sarah Pitts of John     26 Mar 1827
    William P. Moore, sec.

Conner, Frederick       Mary Tunnell            30 Apr 1836
    (wdr)               (wid of William)
    David Broadwater and Levin Core, sec.

Conner, Frederick (wdr) Mary Tunnell (wid)      20 Apr 1836

Conner, George          Margaret Shepherd        1 Apr 1811
    Charles Carpenter, sec.

Conner, George          Susanna Doughty         17 May 1819
    (wdr)               of Josiah
    Thomas D. Welburn and John S. Melvin, sec.

Conner, James           Elizabeth Whealton       1 Apr 1811
                        of Joshua
    Charles Carpenter, sec.

Conner, Jesse FN        Ann Stevens FN          23 Jan 1854
                        of Rica FN

Conner, Joseph (FN)

Conners, Joseph FN      Mariah Griffin FN       28 Dec 1847
    Joseph S. Fedderman, sec.

Connoway, William       Elizabeth Reid           3 Feb 1786
    Levin Rodges, sec.
```

Conquest, Alfred   Deliah Thornton (wid)   31 Mar 1856

Conquest, Edward H.   Mary Ann Broadwater   20 Nov 1838
                      of Joseph
    Jacob J. Staton and William W. Coleburn, sec.

Conquest, Edward H.   Mary Ann Bowden   22 Nov 1839

Conquest, Joseph   Serena Ewell   28 May 1839
    Joseph Staton and Henry Townsend, sec.

Conquest, Nathaniel   Ann Burton   4 Nov 1842

Conquest, Richard   Ann Lilliston   20 Nov 1833

Conquest, Richard   Harriet Lilliston   15 Nov 1833
    William L. Matthews, sec.

Conquest, William   Nancy Drummond   3 Jan 1797

Conquest, William   Euphania Marshall   6 Apr 1811
    Thomas M. Bayly, sec.

Conquest, William J.   Hetty Conquest   15 May 1821
    of James   of Joseph
    William D. Conquest and James Conquest, sec.

Copeland, Samuel   Anne Hall   12 Jan 1801

Copes, Beverly   Nancy Moore   7 Feb 1812
    George Marshall, sec.

Copes, Charles S.   Nancy Hickman   5 Jun 1818
    of Thomas   (wid Rick)
    Daniel Baker, sec.

Copes, Henry   Lovey White   14 Dec 1838
    Thomas Crowson, sec.

Copes, Henry S.   Ann T. Colebarn of Jms. 24 Jan 1816
    William R. Custis, sec.

Copes, Isaac L.   Elizabeth Phillips   26 Dec 1815
                      of William
    William Phillips, sec.

Copes, James   Eliza Ardis   7 May 1832
    Peter Copes and Victor Bell, sec.

Copes, John   Margaret H. Dix of Isaac 22 Jun 1827
    Southy W. Bull, sec., Isaac Dix, consent

```
Copes, John                Margaret Andrews          13 Dec 1854
    (wdr)                   of Rober, dec'd.

Copes, John C.             Ann Outten                 6 Jul 1813
    Henry S. Copes, sec.

Copes, John Henry          Nancy Russell              3 Jan 1849
                           of Elijah
    Jacob Warner and John E. Gibbons, sec.

Copes, John C. (wdr)       Henrietta Wright of Geo.   3 Jun 1820
    Levi Dix and James Watson, sec.

Copes, Levin               Salley Metcalf            12 Sep 1787
    Souhty Simpson, sec.

Copes, Levin FN            Cibell Garrison FN         3 Jun 1826
    Jingo Johnson FN, sec.

Copes, Nathaniel           Peggy C. Hutchinson       11 Oct 1820
                           of William
    William Hutchinson, sec.

Copes, Parker              Polly Joynes of Wm.        8 Jan 1817
    John Watson, sec.

Copes, Parker              Tabitha Edmunds            4 Oct 1787
    Levin Copes, sec.

Copes, Peter               Rebecca Broadwater        23 Oct 1807
    Jesse Gladding, sec.

Copes, Peter Parker        Sophia Hall               26 Jan 1829
    Garrison Burton and James, Shields sec.

Copes, Peter Parker        Peggy Elliott             18 Dec 1809
                           (wid Teackle)
    John Arlington, sec.

Copes, Peter               Rachel Broadwater         21 Sep 1831
                           (wid Henry)
    Robert White, sec.

Copes, Revell              Rebeccah Jones of Ed.     15 Apr 1816
    Solomon Marshall, sec.

Copes, Savage              Elizabeth White           21 Feb 1844

Copes, Solomon (wdr)       Sally Porter of James     11 Feb 1839

Copes, Solomon             Sally Garrett             11 Feb 1804
    Richard P. Savage, sec.
```

Copes, Solomon   Hennetha Scott   10 Dec 1828
                      (wid Thomas)
    David Broadwater and Samuel Henderson, sec.

Copes, Southy   Euphemy Ironmonger   2 May 1785
    Southy Simpson, sec.

Copes, Thomas P.   Ann P. Shield   7 Jan 1834
    Peter B. Savage, sec.

Copes, William   Sophia White   14 Dec 1829
                      of Solomon
    Solomon White, sec.

Copes, William   Sarah Metcalf   17 Sep 1803
    Raymond Taylor, sec.

Copes, Wlliam   Polly Metcalf   6 Aug 1803
    Isaac Dix, sec.

Corbin, Capt. Stephen   Mary Miles   23 Feb 1844

Corbin, Coventon   Sally Drummond   31 Dec 1807
    Richard Dix, sec.

Corbin, Edmond   Elizabeth Tunnell   19 Dec 1832
                      of Josiah
    Josiah Tunnell, sec.

Corbin, Edward L.   Ann Conner   30 Nov 1835
                      of Frederick
    William Ewell and william M. Dix, sec.

Corbin, George   Nancy Sterling   17 Sep 1796

Corbin, James S.   Mary Adair   28 Oct 1830
                      (wid Theodore)
    George W. Arbuckle and Jno. B. Ailworth, sec.

Corbin, John B.   Sarah Jane Hack   25 Jul 1848
                      of John W.
    Ephriam K. Wilson and Charles B. Duffield, sec.

Corbin, Littleton D.   Mary L. Hinman   13 Jul 1842

Corbin, Peter D.   Charlotte Milligan   19 Nov 1828
                      of John
    George Jenkins and Caleb Broadwater, sec.

Corbin, Peter D.   Charlotte Milligan   20 Oct 1818

```
Corbin, Robert              Betsy Tunnell              18 Feb 1809
     Robert Marshall and Jesse Duncan, sec.

Corbin, William H.          Ann Lilliston of Edward    23 Feb 1832
     Isaac W. Lilliston and Gilbert, Ewell sec.

Corbin, William             Peggy A. Metthews          29 Apr 1807
     Ralph B. Corbin, sec.

Cord, Arthur of John        Patsy Collins              23 Feb 1813
     William W. Hickman and James, Gibbons sec.

Cord, William               Elizabeth Rew of Chas.      9 Nov 1824
                            ward of Richard Rew
     Richard Rew, sec.

Core, Caleb                 Ann Abdell                 24 Apr 1826
     (wdr)                  (wid Revell)
     Edmund Watson, sec.

Core, Edward                Adah Ann Cropper           27 Jan 1834
                            of Orseymous
     Simthy W. East, sec.

Core, John of Levin         Comfort Fitchett of Jno.   27 Mar 1819
     Gale Henman and Walter, Mason sec.

Core, John W.               Amey G. Bunting             5 Nov 1851
     of Levi                of William, dec'd.

Core, Levi                  Elizabeth Cowley of Wm.    29 Sep 1829
     Levin Core, sec.

Core, Levi of Levin         Sally Russell of Joshua    12 Jan 1819
     William Laws and Thomas Russell, sec.

Core, Levin                 Susan C. Moore of          13 Dec 1826
                            of Joseph
     Alexander McCollum, sec.

Core, Levin                 Sarah A. Savage             2 May 1837
     (wdr)                  (wid of Sylvester)
     William W. Dix, sec.

Core, William T.            Mary C. Warner              3 May 1843

Core, William               Margaret Bunting           11 Dec 1809
     George Bunting, sec.

Core, William               Mary Collins               31 Aug 1834
```

Corton, John   Nancy Massey   13 Apr 1810
    John Aydelott, sec.

Costen, Wilsson FN   Rachel Crippin   14 Aug 1849

Costin, Ezekiel   Sinah Clemmons   8 Aug 1785
    Bennett Mason, sec.

Cotton, William   Salley Garrett   6 Dec 1798
    William Pettett, sec.

Coulling, David   Annie Wharton Parker   7 Jul 1855
                            of George

Counes(?)   George   Mrs. Hetty James   27 Mar 1832
    (wdr)   (wid Thomas)
    James S. Dunton and Litt. P. Henderson, sec.

Coventon, Joseph L.   Ann Massey   16 Jan 1817
    William R. Drummond, sec.

Cox, James   Elizabeth Wise Bayly   25 Jun 1774
    James Broughton, sec.

Coxon, William H.   Peggy Bull   28 Dec 1802
    John Cropper Jr., sec.

Cozen, William H.   Nancy Taylor of James   13 Jun 1834
    Thomas H. Bayly, sec.

Crack, John   Ann Richison   9 Jan 1811
    William Jones, sec.

Crawford, Henry   Margaret J. Silverthorn   7 Mar 1853

Creckmore, William W.   Sarah A. Leatherbury   23 Nov 1835
    James Eichelberger, sec.

Creekmore, William   Sarah A. Leatherbury   24 Nov 1835

Crippen, Branson FN   Comfort Crippen FN   25 May 1840
    Henry J. K. and Edmund T. Russell, sec.

Crippen, John P.   Rosanna Lipincott   4 Apr 1826
    of Savage   of Samuel, gdn of Wm. E. Wise
    Whittington P. Pool and Jon C. Russell, sec.

Crippen, Mark FN   Sarah Heating FN   28 May 1812
    John Drummond, sec.

Crippen, Samuel   Elizabeth Wise   6 Apr 1806
    John Wise Jr., sec.

```
Crippen, Stephen FN      Sarah Harmon FN           14 Sep 1807
     Esau Guthry (black woman), sec.

Crippen, Thomas          Susanna Custis             3 Sep 1783
     Richard Mears, sec.

Crippin, Edward FN       Eveline Bayly FN          18 Mar 1856

Crippin, Thomas FN       Sirrah Crippin FN         16 Dec 1803
     Joshua Broadwater, sec.

Crocket, Elisha          Cathy Crocket             15 Dec 1812
     John Crocket, sec.

Crocket, Hukey           Judah Parks               28 May 1832
     Reuben Parks, sec.

Crocket, Lewis           Mary Crocket               5 Sep 1832
     (wdr)                of Henry
     Henry Crockett and Edward R. Allen, sec.

Crocket, Lewis           Nelly Crockett             5 Aug 1832
                         of Henry
     John Thomas, sec.

Crockett, Annanias       Polly Mason               21 Jan 1820
                         of Middleton
     Thomas Crockett, sec.

Crockett, Asa            Susan E. Turner           28 Feb 1844

Crockett, Asa of Thos.   Catherine Moore of Ste.   18 Jan 1820
     John Moore, sec.

Crockett, Capt. Tho.H.   Nancy Smith               12 Apr 1842

Crockett, David          Emiline Crockett          19 May 1836
     Levin Crockett, sec.

Crockett, George of Jno. Sinah Evans of Geo.       21 Jan 1825
     Josiah Crockett, Tyler Crockett and Richard D. Bayly, sec.

Crockett, Henry          Sally Thomas of Ben.      26 Jun 1812
     Elisha Crocket and Joseph Crockett, sec.

Crockett, John           Sarah Paul              btw 1835-1837

Crockett, John           Ellen Crockett of Tho.    29 Dec 1856

Crockett, John Jr.       Sarah Pail                 9 Mae 1827
                         of Zorobabel
     Tyler Crockett, sec.
```

```
Crockett, Joseph          Zepora Parks of Job       18 Sep 1816
     Amaniar Crockett, sec.

Crockett, Josiah          Elizabeth Parks           25 May 1827
     of Zachariah           of Job
     James H. Stokes and Richard D. Bayly, sec.

Crockett, Josiah          Sally Shepherd            3 Jan 1821
     of Zachariah           of Major
     William Lee Jr., sec.

Crockett, Lewis           Mary Crockett             9 Nov 1837

Crockett, Peter           Mary Abet of Lely         9 Jan 1834
     John Thomas, William R. Custis and Levin Core, sec.

Crockett, Peter           Mary Abdel                btw 1835-1837

Crockett, Planner         Polly Crockett            21 Feb 1827
     William Prewitt and Thomas, Crockett sec.

Crockett, Severn          Cleo Parks                29 Jan 1835
     Joseph Crockett and Levin Core, sec.

Crockett, Severn          Eleamor Pruitt of Geo.    6 Jun 1839
     William Lee and George Pruitt, sec.

Crockett, Severn          Cleo Parks                29 Jan 1835

Crockett, Southy     Elizabeth Moore               8 Dec 1840
     John R. Boggs, sec.

Crockett, Southy          Elizabeth Stone           9 Dec 1840

Crockett, Thomas of Jno. Mary Ann Evans of Geo.    28 Dec 1827
     Tyler Crockett, sec.

Crockett, Tyler           Coty Doughty              23 Sep 1812
     William Doughty, sec.

Crockett, Tyler of Tom   Euphamin Evans of Rich.    10 Jan 1820
     David Evans and Trivis, Crockett sec.

Crockett, William         Rhoda Parks               2 Jan 1817
     of Jno.                of Job
     Annanias Crockett and John Thomas, sec.

Cropper, Coventon H.      Leah B. Seymour           14 Jun 1837
     Joseph Gibb, sec.

Cropper, Coventon H.      Sarah T. Gellett          10 Aug 1841
     (wdr)
```

John J. Blackstone, sec.

Cropper, Dr. John W.	Mary A. Savage	15 Sep 1832
Cropper, George W.	Melinda M.H. Bayne of Colmore, dec'd.	22 May 1828

John W. Custis, sec.

Cropper, John P.	Rosanna Lippincott	5 Apr 1827
Cropper, John W.	Mary Ann Savage of John	1 Sep 1832

Thomas H. Bayly, sec.

Cropper, John S.   Tabitha Bull of Betsy   1 Mar 1826
    Thomas Bull, sec., John Snead, guardian, consent

Cropper, John Henry   Sarah Ann Haly   7 Jan 1846

Cropper, Orseymeous   Mary Nock   19 Jun 1828
    (wdr)   (wid Samuel)
    Elijah Nock, sec.

Cropper, Orseymeous   Lacey Savage   18 Feb 1823
    (wdr)   (wid Nathaniel)
    Richard W. East, sec.

Cropper, Orseymous   Sally Hargis   18 Aug 1843

Cropper, Reuben   Nancy Taylor   24 Jan 1824
                        of Shadrock
    Edward Taylor and Shadrock Taylor, sec.

Cropper, William D.   Susan C. Welburn of Wm. 27 Aug 1827
    John Marshall of Thomas and Alexander McCollom, sec.

Cropper, William D.   Maria Peck   18 Feb 1815
    Sebastian Cropper and Henry S. Copes, sec.

Crosby, Samuel   Mary J. Kilman   6 Aug 1850
                        of Edward

Crosby, Thomas   Mary Killnom of Wm.   5 Dec 1849
    Edmund J. Poulson and James T. Melson, sec.

Crosville, Hance   Keziah Laws   13 Jun 18388
    George Howard and Isaiah Bagwell, sec.

Croswell, George   Susanna Corbin   c. 1785
    Richard Drummond, sec.   (not dated)

Croswell, John H.   Arinthia Johnson   9 Jan 1854
                        ward of Samuel C. Johnson

Crowly, George   Bridget Mason   5 Jun 1803
     Clement Bonwell, sec.

Crowson, James   Sarah Melson   8 Jan 1856
                             of James, dec'd.

Crowson, John   Nancy Kelly   7 Jan 1801
     Benjamin Pruit, sec.

Crowson, John   Sally Cobb   18 Jun 1831
     John Hargis, sec.

Crowson, John (wdr)   Hessy Scott of Severn   12 Mar 1822
     Thomas Hargis, sec.

Crowson, John (wdr)   Esther Lewis of Thomas   27 Mar 1820
     William R. Custis, sec.

Crowson, Levin   Demeriah Annis   4 Jan 1843

Crowson, Levin   Amey Powell   2 Jan 1795
     Edmund Only, sec.

Crowson, Major   Nancy Bull   2 Aug 1800
     Levin Crowson, sec.

Crowson, Thomas   Nancy Melson   31 Jan 1831
                             orphan George
     George West, sec.

Crowson, Thomas   Mary Fosque   12 Jan 1836
     (wdr)   of Rachel Bundick
     Richard and Rachel Bundick, sec.

Crowson, Thomas   Sally Lee   23 Jan 1838
     (wdr)   of Andrew
     Andrew Lee and James White, sec.

Crowson, William   Polly Watson   27 Dec 1798
     William Wise, sec.

Cully, William   Sally Edwards of Jacob   13 Oct 1829
     George Elliott, sec.

Curby, Henry   Polly Taylor   4 Jun 1803
     Thomas Bonwell, sec.

Custis, Henry B,   Elizabeth Fletcher   10 May 1829
     Thomas Edmunds, sec.

Custis, Henry   Tabitha West of John   23 Sep 1813
      John West, sec.

Custis, Henry Sr.   Betsy Fletcher   30 May 1816

Custis, Henry   Susanna Slocomb   9 Apr 1787
      Southy Simpson, sec.

Custis, James   Margaret D. Bayly   27 Oct 1840
      Robert J. Poulson, sec.

Custis, John H.   Harriet Eshom   20 Jan 1841
      of Henry
      Henry P. Parker and James J. Ailworth, sec.

Custis, John   Tabitha Gillett   21 Jun 1803
      John K. Evans, sec.

Custis, John H.   Harriet Esham   11 Jan 1843

Custis, John of John   Margaret Ward   20 Feb 1824

Custis, John Sr.   Sarah Selby   25 Feb 1823
                       (wid William)
      Richard D. Bayly, sec.

Custis, Lewis FN   Sally Allen of Esther   1 Jan 1819
      Edmund Custis, Robert Meada and Richard D. Bayly, sec.

Custis, Luther   Ada Grinnalds   31 Aug 1857
      of John H.   of Parker, dec'd.

Custis, Revel, Jr.   Sarah Custis   20 Dec 1784
      Revel Custis Sr., sec.

Custis, Revell   Peggy Smart Stringer   23 Jan 1795
                                               (badly damaged)

Custis, Robinson   Frances Yearby West   30 Nov 1775
      Edmund Custis, sec.

Custis Tho. B. of Jno. Elizabeth Joynes   23 Jan 1829

Custis, Thomas, Jr.   Nancy Dix   28 Dec 1805
      George Twiford, sec.

Custis, Thomas W.   Mary Parker   15 Mar 1843

Custis, Thomas of John of Only   22 Jan 1829
      Isma Nock, sec.

Custis, Thomas B.   Elizabeth C. Joynes   23 Jun 1829

Custis, Thomas   Margaret Coleburn   20 Jun 1834
            of Richard
  William Custis of Thomas and James Fosque, sec.

Custis, Thomas B.   Mary B. Parramore   16 Sep 1829
  William Parramore, sec.

Custis, Thomas   Elizabeth P. Scarburgh 7 Dec 1829
  of Jno.   orphan William M.
  Jesse Kellam, sec.

Custis, Thomas   Elizabeth Joynes   22 Jun 1829
  of Jno. (only)
  Isma Wyatt Jr., sec.

Custis, Walter Mason   Nancy Riggin of Stephen 5 Jul 1821
  Covington Mason, sec.

Custis, William Smith   Bridget Pennock   2 Jan 1787
  George Oldham, sec.

Custis, William Stan   Virginia L. Potter   18 Mar 1847
           of Ann M. Smith, formerly Potter
  John W. Gillett, sec.

Custis, William   Leah Parker   25 Oct 1833
  of Henry   (wid of John)
  Joseph Turlington, sec.

Custis, William of Only Susanna Gunter of Levin 16 Jan 1810
  Galin Conner, sec.

Custis, William Stran   Virginia Potter   18 May 1847

Custis, William of Wm. Elizabeth Stran   2 Nov 1814

Custis, William H. B.   Emeline U. S. Conquest 19 Oct 1840
  James H. Dix, sec.

Custis, William H.   Elizabeth Boggs of Wm. 2 Dec 1815
  James Boggs, sec.

Custis, William R.   Elizabeth Custis   21 Sep 1819
           (wid H.B.)
  Richard D. Bayly and Henry S. Copes, sec.

Custis, William   Melinda Byrd   27 Mar 1820
  of Henry   John G. Joynes guardian
  Thomas R. Joynes, sec., John G. Joynes, consent

Custis, William R.   Elizabeth Custis   27 Jun 1814

Henry S. Copes, sec.

Custis, William P.   Elizabeth Fisher   16 Apr 1816
    Richard D. Bayly, sec.

Cutler, George   Delia Thornton   2 Jan 1836

Cutler, George W.   Mary Ann Robins   23 Mar 1846

Cutler, George P.   Susan A. Ames (wid)   24 Sep 1828
    Richard W. Guest and Elisha H. Davis, sec.

Cutler, George P.   Deliah Thornton   25 Dec 1837
    Smith Cutler and Spencer Drummond, sec.

Cutler, Smith   Hetty Bird   15 Feb 1832
                           of Johannes
        Selby Bird, sec.

Cutler, Smith   Molly Justice   14 May 1806
    John Custis, sec.

Cutler, Smith   Sabra Coleburn   29 Aug 1792

Cutler, William W.   Anne M. Scarborough   20 Dec 1825
                           of Thomas
    Levin Rodgers,

Cyrus FN   Elija Morris   10   Aug   1821
                           of George FN
        William R. Custis, sec.

Dagan, Thomas   Tabitha Lewis   27 Jul 1811
     Sally Lewis, sec.

Daisey, James   Nellie Curtis   12 Jul 1839

Daisey, John   Peggy Booth   20 Jul 1834

Daisey, Parker T.   Elizabeth Melvin   6 Dec 1837

Daisey, William   Margaret Andrews   4 Mar 1850
                         of Mordici
          Thomas T. Cropper, sec.

Daisey, William   Margaret Andrews   12 Mar 1849

Dalby, James   Joyce Benson   4 Feb 1809
     James Benson (Beniston), sec.

Dameral. William   Sukey Porter (wid Geo)   2 Aug 1813
     James Parker, sec.

Damlin, William   Sally Scott   26 Mar 1839
     George Bull, sec.

Dan, Silas   Peggy Kellam   20 Feb 1816
     of Selick   of Reuben
     William Unerhill, sec.

Darby, Benjamin F.   Sarah T. Rowley (wid)   1 Mar 1851

Darby, Custis   Peggy Martin   20 Jun 1803
     Isaac Martin, sec.

Darby, James L. (wdr)   Leah B. Watson of Wm.   13 Apr 1826
     James W. Twiford, sec.

Darby, James L.   Susannah Snead   26 Feb 1816
                         of Bowdoin
          Bowdoin Snead, sec.

Darby, James L.   Peggy Ames   12 Feb 1820
     (wdr)   of Churchill
     Thomas Pewsey, sec.

Darby, John   Ann Belote   29 Jan 1927
     of William   orphan George
     Samuel Follio, sec.

Darby, Shadrach   Kessy Rodgers   29 Nov 1809
     Wm. Mears of Wm., sec.

Darby, Shadrach   Charlotte Kellam   17   Apr   1823
    (wdr)   of Robert
    Thomas W. Mears, sec.

Darby, William G.   Anne Kelly of Stephen   29 Dec 1829
    Samuel Kelly, sec.

Darby, William   Margaret Walker   28 May 1838
    (wdr)   of Henry
    John Window, sec.

Darby, William G.   Elizabeth Edmunds   20 Jul 1848
    (wdr)   of William
    Bennet C. Scarborough, sec.

Darby, William   Mary Colonna   16 Sep 1840
    (wdr)   of William
    Thomas A. Hack and Levin Joynes, sec.

Davis, Alfred T.   Emaline J. Duncan   8 Feb 1853
    of Noah   of Meshack

Davis, David   Mary Wallop   24 Dec 1810
    David Watts, sec.

Davis, Elisha H.   Susanna Joynes of Wm.   24 Dec 1817
    Matthias Outten, sec.

Davis, Elisha J.   Anna Coard of Parker   5 Jun 1828
    Thomas D. Welburn, sec.

Davis, George M.   Margaret Merrill   27 Jan 1841

Davis, George W.   Margaret B. Sterling   28 Aug 1848
    (wdr)   of Henry, dec'd.
    Peter D. Corbin and James H. Fletcher, sec.

Davis, George W. (wid)   Mary A.B. Sterling   29 Aug 1848

Davis, Henry   Damey Lillaston   16 Dec 1792
         David Davis, sec.

Davis, Henry of Wm.   Hetty Jester   31 Jan 1831
    David Mears and Litt A. Hennean, sec.

Davis, Henry   Hetty Trader   2 Mar 1836
    William Trader, sec.

Davis, Henry   Leah A. Mapp   29 Mar 1841
    George T. Mapp, sec.

```
Davis, Isaac P.          Mary S. Gillett          8 Mar 1812
    Caleb Duncan and Lemuel Henderson Jr., sec.

Davis, James of Henry   Nancy West of Alex.      31 May 1819
    Isaac West of Alex., sec.

Davis, James            Esther Sterling           9 Mar 1809
    Levi Small, sec.

Davis, James            Nancy Small (wid John)   16 Jun 1809
    Levi Small, sec.

Davis, James            Nancy West               19 May 1819

Davis, John             Catherine White          30 Sep 1815
                        of Bridget
    Peter Martin, sec.

Davis, John             Catherine White          30 Sep 1814

Davis, John             Maria Collins            12 Sep 1827
    of Major            of Skinner
    Thomas D. Welburn and Levin Core, sec.

Davis, Joseph           Nelly Crippen             8 Sep 1806
                        of Zipporah Davis
    George Marshall, sec.

Davis, Joshua           Mary Owen                25 Feb 1806
    Batholomew Mears, sec.

Davis, Major            Nancy Wooldup             1 Nov 1803
        James Melvin, sec.

Davis, Noah of Jms.     Milcah Kelly of Jesse    22 Aug 1826
    Jesse Kelly, sec.

Davis, Savage           Peggy Mapp                5 Sep 1803
    Custis Willis, sec.

Davis, Thomas S.        Sally Townsend           25 Jul 1839

Davis, Thomas           Elizabeth Pitt of Robt.  26 Jun 1830
    James P. Duncan and George P. Scarburgh, sec.

Davis, William          Susanna Fitchett         12 Apr 1806
    Reuben Rew, sec.

Davis, William          Comfort Fisher           10 Dec 1810
    Luther Bunting, sec.

Davis, William (wdr)    Sally Hickman (wid)      25 Dec 1844
```

```
Davis, William (wdr)        Polly Lucas (wid Major)  18 Jun 1823
     Thomas Johnson, sec.


Davis, William             Nancy Whealton of Mary   29 May 1812
     James Conner, sec.

Davis, William             Rebecca Russell          19 Dec 1808
     Selby Lewis, sec.

Davis, William             Betsey Gillett           28 Jan 1806
     Levin Taylor, sec.

Davis, Zadoch              Sally Owens              15 Mar 1804
     Drummond Williams, sec.

Davis, Zadock             Sarah Delastatious       13   Feb    1827
     (wdr)                 (wid James)
     Purnel Chesser and Samuel Nock, sec.

Davis, Zadock (wdr)       Ann Downing (wid John)    3   Feb    1827
     Wm. Davis of Samuel and Samuel Walston, sec.

Davison, Derry FN         Amy FN                    4 Jan 1792

Deeble, William H.        Eliza K. Scarborough     18 Dec 1807
     Henry Scarborough, sec.

Deharo, Carla             Lucy James               31 Mar 1829
     Levin Rogers, sec.

Delastatius, James        Sally Harper (wid Jms.)  28 Feb 1814
     James Justice and Jesse Duncan, sec.

Delastatius, Peter        Susan Fisher             12 Oct 1836
     (wdr)                 of Riley
     William B. Savage and John D. Parks, sec.

Delastatius, Peter        Mary Dickerson           12 Jan 1786
     Ezekiel Delastatus, sec.

Delastatius, Peter        Narcissa Taylor          22 Jun 1831
                          ward Solomon Marshall
     John D. Welburn and Wes. Ellis, sec.

Delastatius, Samuel       Eliza Hill (wid)         30 Aug 1836
                          of John
     Samuel S. Carey and James McCollum, sec.

Delastatius, Sebastian    Peggy Pratt               1 Oct 1790

Delastatius, Selby        Elizabeth Jester         22 Apr 1786
```

of Rachel
John Sharlock, sec.

Delastatius, Thomas Crippen   Sarah Mathews (wid) 13 May 1806
    Selby Delastatius, sec.

Delastatius, William   Mariah Tunnall   21 Aug 1811
    Zadoch Selby, sec.

Delastatius, William   Ann Russell of Robert   6 May 1815
    William S. Tunnell, sec.

Dennis, Jesse FN   Sabra Rosary   30 Aug 1810
    William Outten and John Bull, sec.

Dennis, Lemuel   Sally Dunton   15 Jul 1842

Dennis, Shadrock   Nancy Cutler   5 May 1824

Derry FN   Sarah FN   16   Jan   1811
    William R. Drummond, sec.

Dewer, Joshua R.   Sarah A. Cropper   22 Feb 1840
                        of Orseymous
    John D. Fletcher, sec.

Dickerson, Edward   Nancy Taylor   29 Nov 1791

Dickerson, Jesse   Margaret Stockley   9 May 1814
    Nathaniel Stockley, sec.

Dickerson, Jesse   Sally Bloxom   13 Jan 1817
    (wdr)   of Azariah
    Jacob Warner, sec.

Dickerson, Jesse Jr.   Susanna Byrd   8 Apr 1856
    of Jesse   of John W.

Dickerson, John T.   Lydia Nock   1 Oct 1805
        Ayres Tatham, sec.

Dickerson, Michael   Rebecca Taylor   27 Dec 1787

Dickerson, Thomas   Hetty Gaskins   14 Dec 1832
    George Jenkins and Caleb Duncan, sec.

Dien, Isaac S.   Elizabeth Shous   4 Aug 1834
    William Killman, sec.

Dies, Daniel   Esther Psrks   26 Dec 1806
    George Prewitt and Fieldy Dies, sec.

```
Dies, Isaac H.           Polly Ann Dies          30 Sep 1847
    (wdr)                of Daniel
    Stephen Dies, sec.

Dies, Issac (wid)        Elizabeth Shores          6 Aug 1834

Dies, Issas S.           Polly Ann Dies            7 Aug 1847

Dies, William            Betty Hutson            29 Dec 1830
                         orphan John
    John Evans, sec.

Dise, John S.            Sally H. Scarburgh       18 May 1843

Dix, Asa                 Betsey Fletcher         16 Nov 1802

Dix, Asa                 Patty Fletcher          14 Mar 1804
    John A. Bundick, sec.

Dix, Caleb               Elizabeth Taylor        30 Dec 1803
    Hancock Simpson, sec.

Dix, George M.           Catherine Berry         14 Dec 1853
    of George            of James, dec'd.

Dix, George (wdr)        Sally Marhsall of Tho.   7 Mar 1816
    Richard Dix, sec.

Dix, George              Sally Marshall           9 Feb 1816

Dix, George              Betsy White             30 Oct 1811
                         (wid Levin)
    Thomas Turnal, sec.

Dix, Isaac               Nancy Taylor            17 Sep 1822
    (wdr)                (wid Raymond)
    William Parramore, sec.

Dix, Isaac               Polly Metcalf            6 Aug 1803
    William Copes, sec.

Dix, James (wid)         Catherine Savage         3 Dec 1814

Dix, James H.            Margaret Watson         10 Jun 1822
                         of Ephraim
    Samuel W. Colonna and John Y. Bagwell, sec.
    Ephraim Watson consent

Dix, James H.            Catharine T.C. Scarburgh  2 Dec 1834
    Samuel Melson, sec.

Dix, John S.             Sally H. Scarburgh       18 May 1843
```

Dix, Julues P.   Catherine A. Henderson   18 Feb 1831
                        of William
        Augustus W. Bagwell, sec.

Dix, Levi   Sukey Copes   23 Dec 1806
        John S. Bundick, sec.

Dix, Levin   Barshaby Sturges   3 Dec 1774
        John Dix, sec.

Dix, Preeson   Polly Johnson   4 Sep 1808
        George Wright, sec.

Dix, Revel   Nancy Taylor   31 Dec 1855
                        of Justice B.

Dix, Revel   Nancy Bull   29 Apr 1808
        Thomas West, sec.

Dix, Richard   Elizabeth Outten   24 Feb 1806
        John Wset B.S., sec.

Dix, Richard   Tabitha Parks   24 Jul 1792

Dix, Thorogood (wdr)   Julianna Taylor (wid)   25 Jul 1843

Dix, Thorogood of Geo. Nancy Vessels   13 Mar 1830
        John West of Benjamin and James W.Twiford, sec.

Dix, William C. (wdr)   Hetty Bloxom (wid)   6 Oct 1847
        Edward Gillespie and David Broadwater, sec.

Dix, William H.   Susan Rayfield   28 Oct 1825
                        of Major
        Major Rayfield Sr., sec.

Dix, William   Sally Watson   31 Mar 1806
        Richard Bloxom, sec.

Dix, William C.   Sally Willett   31 Mar 1825
                        of Waitman, ward Richard J. Ayres
        James Taylor, sec.

Dix, William W.   Sarah Ann J. Parker   1 Dec 1825
        of Isaac   of John
        Levin Core, sec.

Doffield, Charles B.   Sarah E. Joynes

Dolby, John C.   Mary Saunders   21 Oct 1845

Dolby, Nathaniel   Ellen Riley   22 Sep 1830

Dolley, William B.   Mary Edward   10 Jan 1824
    of Branson   of Laban
  John Jester, sec.

Dorman, Matthew   Atalanta Barnes   9 Oct 1802
    Joseph Leonard, sec.

Doughty, James   Margaret Ashly   11 Dec 1838
    James Ashly and James J. Ailworth, sec.

Doughty, James C.   Elizabeth Wright   24 Dec 1838
                            of Isaac
      Thomas J. Doughty, sec.

Doughty, Jeptha   Margaret Colony   22 May 1804
    William Doughty, sec.

Doughty, John   Molly Folluo   26 Nov 1832
                            of Upshur
      Samuel Folluo, sec.

Doughty, Thomas J.   Margaret R. Folluo   19 Dec 1836
                            of Joyce
      Samuel Folluo, sec.

Doughty, Thomas S.   Sally Townsend (wid)   15 Jul 1839
    James A. Doughty and Raymond Riley, sec.

Douglas, James   Scarbrough Broadwater   30 Jan 1786
    John Joynes, sec.

Douglas, Walter   Margaret Henderson   11 Dec 1809

Douglas, William FN (wdr)   Eliza Church FN   11 Jan 1839

Douglass, Walter FN   Mary Blake FN   3 Jan 1831
    George Mathews and John C. Stevenson, sec.

Downing, Arthur   Catherine Howard   13 Mar 1789

Downing, Arthur   Zillah Turner   17 Feb 1785
    John Michael, sec.

Downing, Dr. Arthur W.   Mary P. Bayly   7 Nov 1837
    Thomas B. Custis and John J. R. Joynes, sec.

Downing, Edmund FN   Emily Bayly FN   22 Dec 1852
                            of Custis, Jr. FN

Downing, Edward T.   Anna E. Twyford   24 Jul 1858
                            of Obed P.

Downing, George FN   Ann Arnstrong FN   30 Jan 1854

Downing, George FN   Charlotte Drummond FN   29 Aug 1853

Downing, George FN   Sarah Case FN   29 Apr 1854

Downing, George D.   Ara Lucas of William   30 Mar 1829
     John Gladding Jr., sec.

Downing, Henry FN   Susan Becket   20 Mar 1853

Downing, Henry FN   Leah Harman FN   26 Nov 1828
                            of Scarburgh
          Esau Gutty, sec.

Downing, James   Margaret Bell   23 Dec 1844

Downing, John B.   Sally Grinalds   4 Dec 1823
                            (wid William)
          Sebastian Cropper and John Waters Cropper, sec.

Downing, John   Nancy Warrington   20 Dec 1825
     of William   of Shadrach
     Peter Copes, sec.

Downing, John   Elizabeth Chesser   1 Mar 1823
     of Arthur   of Purnel
     Samuel S. Nock, James Chesser and Joseph Boggs, sec.

Downing, John of John   Sally Taylor of Geo.   25 Dec 1822
     John Bundick, sec.

Downing, John   Mary Mears of John   11 Dec 1827
     John Bundick of Jno, sec.

Downing, Joshua FN   Nancy Wheaton FN   31 Dec 1813
     William Fortune, sec.

Downing, Samuel   Mrs. Agnes D. Ker (wid)   4 Dec 1806
     James Poulson, sec.

Downing, Samuel   Elizabeth Bayly of Major   1 May 1815
     Richard D. Bayly, sec.

Downing, Solomon FN   Nancy Scarburgh FN   25 Jan 1803
     Francis Downing, sec.

Downing, Solomon FN   Bridget Downing FN   26 Sep 1839

Downing, William F.   Betsy Broadwater   24 Jun 1844

Downing, William FN	Sarah Bayly FN	27 Dec 1851
Downing, William FN	Sarah Bayly FN of Custis, Jr. FN	22 Dec 1852
Downing, William	Elizabeth Drummond (wid of Richard) nee Riley	26 Feb 1801
Downng, John David Bowman, sec.	Esther Mapp	25 Feb 1799
Dowty, Edward Edward and Major Dowty, sec.	Sally Conner of Caleb	18 Jan 1841
Dowty, John Charles Joynes, sec.	Mary Howell of Sarah Howell	14 Aug 1775
Dowty, Major R. Samuel Folluo, sec.	Eliza S. Ames of Wm.	13 Dec 1833
Dowty, Major R. Edward Dowty, sec.	Susan R. Dowty	22 Jun 1840
Dowty, Thomas Sr. Hutchinson Kellam, sec.	Betsy Milby (wid Gilbert)	19 Sep 1818
Dowty, William John Savage, sec.	Tabitha Heath	16 Oct 1799
Drewer, Joshua R.	Sarah A. Cropper	24 Feb 1840
Drummond, Capt. David S.	Lavinia Slocum	15 Jan 1847
Drummond, Constantine	Susan Chesser	12 Jul 1857
Drummond, Ezekiel Josial Speight and Daniel Drummond, sec.	Tinny Grinnalds	9 Oct 1811
Drummond, Henry Robert Drummond, sec.	Sophia Rodgers	23 Nov 1785
Drummond, Henry William D. Chandler, sec.	Mary R. Dunton of Carvey	24 Nov 1828
Drummond, Henry FN	Ann Downing FN	31 Oct 1853
Drummond, James	Harriet Kellam ward of James Drummond	24 Nov 1828

William D. Chandler, sec.

Drummond, James   Ruth P. Taylor   7 Mar 1850
   (wdr)   of James, dec'd.
George K. Turner, sec.

Drummond, John R.   Elisha Fletcher   10 Apr 1844

Drummond, John   Phany Miles   15 Jun 1803
   Joshua Boggs, sec.

Drummond, John C.   Ann T. Drummond   6 Jun 1823
   Noah Drummond and Thomas R. Riley, sec.

Drummond, John P.   Nancy Warner of Isaac   27 Dec 1815
   Richard D. Bayly, sec.

Drummond, Levin FN   Nancy Holt FN, of Wm.   13 May 1815
   William Holt, sec.

Drummond, Noah   Catherine S. Drummond   29 Jun 1818
   of Charles   of William
William S. Drummond, sec.

Drummond, Richard   Nancy Fletcher   11 Jan 1801
   Edmund Bayly, sec.

Drummond, Richard   Esther Snead   22 Oct 1785
   Edmund Custis, sec.

Drummond, Richard   Elizabeth Riley   31 Jan 1784
   Edmund Custis, sec.

Drummond, Richard T.   Susan T. Custis   19 Dec 1851
                   of William C.

Drummond, Robert   Sarah Ann Drummond   12 Jun 1810
   Michael Higgins, sec.

Drummond, Robert   Peggy Drummond   5 Nov 1801
   Richard Drummond, sec.

Drummond, Robinson   Belinda Spence   16 Jul 1851
                    (wid of Wesley)

Drummond, Spencer   Susanna Fletcher   20 Jan 1808
   Walter Wessells, sec.

Drummond, Stephen   Catherine Trader   6 May 1794

Drummond, William T.   Harriet J. Watson   26 Oct 1847
                    of William C.

George L. Powell, sec.

Drummond, William Jr.   Anne Robinson Riley   14 Apr 1786
    William Gibb, sec.

Drummond, William   Ann Delastatius   3 Jan 1814
    William Only, sec.

Drummond, William   Mary Coleburn   21 Dec 1798
    George Coleburn, sec.

Drummond, William Jr.   Anne Robinson Smith   4 Jan 1775
                          of William R.
    Tully Robinson Wise, sec.

Drummond, William R.   Ann S. Watts   19 Feb 1811
    Samuel Downing, sec.

Drummond, William   Mary Parker   3 Mar 1824

Drummond, William   Rebecca Corbin   19 Jan 1848

Duffy, Major FN   Agnes FN   16 Jan 1813
    Daniel Gustine FN, sec.

Duncan, Caleb   Elizabeth Hargis   29 Mar 1813
    Lemuel Henderson and George D. Wise, sec.

Duncan, Edmund   Sarah Bird of Major   25 Aug 1810
    Daniel T. Bird, sec.

Duncan, Edmund   Sally Coah   8 Jun 1812
    William Duncan, sec.

Duncan, James   Parmelia A. Mason   26 Nov 1821
    orphan Jesse   orphan Bennet
    Thorowgood Taylor and Isoial Johnson, sec.

Duncan, James Jr.   Attalanta Delastatious   20 Jan 1812
    Joshua Thornton, sec.

Duncan, James   Elizabeth Garrison   12 Nov 1834
                          ward of John J. Ayres
    John J. Ayres, sec.

Duncan, James   Ann Burton   29 Sep 1823
    (wdr), of Eli   (wid William)
    Henry Harvey and William Whittington, sec.

Duncan, James   Nancy Dix   12 Oct 1799
    John A. Bundick, sec.

- 89 -

```
Duncan, James (wdr)        Anne Moor (wid)           18 Dec 1790
     Southy Bull, sec.                               (badly damaged)

Duncan, Jesse Sr.          Elizabeth Jenkins         19 Aug 1817
                           (wid Custis)
     William Duncan and William P. Custis, sec.

Duncan, Jesse             Peggy Bloxom               26 Feb 1816
     of Jesse             (wid Azariah)
     William Ailworth, sec.

Duncan, John R.           Thealy Ann Byrd            23 Dec 1856
     of Meshack           of Eborn

Duncan, John T.           Margaret S. Taylor         23 Jan 1854
     of James S., dec'd.     of Henry W.

Duncan, Meshack           Critty Northam              4 Mar 1825
                          of Southy
     William Mason, sec., Southy Northam consent


Duncan, Noah G.           Louisa H. Milligan          4 Nov 1840
                          (wid of John)
     James K. Duncan and James H. Fletcher, sec.

Duncan, William Sr.       Elizabeth Bunting          26 Dec 1827
                          (wid George)
     Caleb Duncan, sec.

Duncan, William           Evelyn Kellam              24 Mar 1853

Duncan, William T.        Evaline C.J. Kellam        13 Mar 1853
                          of Margaret W.

Duncan, William (wdr)     Elizabeth Bunting (wid)     7 May 1834
     John H. C. Bunting, sec.

Dunston, John             Cassey Coard of Wm.        27 Oct 1847
     John B. Stevenson and Isaac K. Stevenson, sec.

Dunston, John             Rebecca Bloxom             18 Dec 1806
     Arthur Whittington, sec.

Dunston, John             Cassey Coard               27 Oct 1847

Dunston, Levin            Milly Johnson of Wm.       11 Dec 1807
     William Gascome, sec.

Dunton, Custis M.         Elizabeth C. Willis         8 Nov 1852
     (wdr)                of Littleton
```

Dunton, Duke   Molly Floyd   20 Feb 1804
    Benjamin Potter, sec.

Dunton, George R.   Margaret Bradford   25 Feb 1835

Dunton, George R.   Margaret Bradford   2 May 1834
    Augustus J. F. Kellam, sec.

Dunton, George   Sarah Leatherbury   8 Jun 1808
    John Burton Esq., sec.

Dunton, James   Margaret Watts   16 Aug 1841
    John P. Stevenson, sec.

Dunton, Thomas R.   Emaline Fitchett   10 Oct 1832

Dyes, Feldy   Levice Evans   16 Dec 1807
    George Prewitt, sec.

East, Charles   Tabitha Bunting   17 Jul 1812
    Jesse Powell, sec.

East, Edward Littleton   Mary Ann Keaton   7 Nov 1851
                             of William, dec'd.

East, George   Margaret East of James   19 Oct 1830
    Levin White, sec.

East, George   Margaret East   20 Sep 1830

East, George (wdr)   Tempy Pickett   23 May 1836
    John Beasley and John S. Gibb, sec.

East, George   Sarah Savage   5 Jun 1837
    Edward Turlington, sec.

East, George S.   Molly Ames   13 Nov 1849
    (wdr)   (wid of Nathaniel Ames)
    John B. Ailworth, sec.

East, James H.   Sarah Ann Lewis of John   24 Mar 1832
    Major Rayfield, sec.

East, James H.   Margaret Melson   9 Mar 1842

East, John   Ann Henderson of Polly   6 Dec 1843

East, John W.   Margaret A. Bullman   14 Feb 1848
    Thomas H. James, sec.

East, John W.   Patricia K. Mason   10 Sep 1845

East, John W.   Patricia K. Mason   10 Sep 1845

East, John   Margaret A. Bell   16 Feb 1847

East, John   Susanna Savage   22 Mar 1816
    of John   of Littleton
    Zorobabel Richardson, sec.

East, Major   Margaret Justice of Tho.   11 Oct 1830
    Southy W. Bull sec.

East, Nathaniel   Mary Trader   28 Feb 1831
                             (wid Teackle)
    Levin White, sec.

East, Parker   Mary Fisher (wid John)   23 Nov 1815
    John Kellam of Jno, sec.

East, Richard   Elizabeth M. Bonwell   5 Jun 1821

```
of Severn              of Clement, Francis Boggs, guard.
  Smith Carmine, sec.

East, Richard          Rachel Taylor          23 Jan 1837
  of Severn              of James
  Thorogood Dix, sec.

East, Severn           Peggy Holsten          18 Oct 1814

East, Willliam         Nancy Crowson          21 Dec 1832
                         of Levin
       William Rolly, sec.

Edmonds, John          Tabitha Nock           24 Jul 1844

Edmonds, Thomas        Nancy Green            23 Dec 18

Edmunds, John W.       Sarah Ann Floud        26 Nov 1832
                         of Benjamin
       Benjamin Floyd, sec.

Edmunds, Thomas of Wm. Nancy Green of George. 16 Dec 1814
       Henry Stewart, sec.

Edmunds, Thomas        Ann Teackle            28 Feb 1811

Edmunds, William       Peggy Satchell Wyatt    7 Jul 1799
       John Edmunds, sec.

Edward, Doughty        Sally Cowan            20 Jan 1843

Edwards, Bagwell       Eliza Levi Groten       3 Jan 1822
                         of Severn
       James Taylor of Pungoteague, sec.

Edwards, John B.       Mrs. Nancy Willett     29 Jul 1816
                         (wid George)
       Jacob Edwards, sec.

Edwards, John          Alice Poulson          27 Jun 1837
    William B. Kellam, sec.

Edwards, John A.       Ann Arlington          22 Feb 1827
                         of John, dec'd.
       John S. Gibbs, sec.

Edwards, Major         Sally Badger           23 Apr 1812
                         (wid John)
       Abel Edwards, sec.

Edwards, William       Peggy Mason            29 Feb 1808
       William Badger, sec.
```

Edwards, William   Sarah Mister of Wm.   25 Jul 1827
    John G. Joynes, sec.

Edwards, Zorobable   Jenny Hanniford   19 Dec 1805
    Nathaniel Badger, sec.

Eichelberger, James   Susan Finney   28 May 1806
                          of Euphemy Finney
        William White Burton, sec.

Eichelberger, James   Hennetta Twiford   6 May 1816
    John J. Wise, sec.

Eichelberger, James   Euphamen Rodgers   22 Dec 1819
    (wdr)   (wid Levi)
    William Cockle, sec.

Eichelberger, William D. Denera Scarburgh   1 Mar 1837

Eichelberger, William   Demary S. Scarburgh   27 Feb 1837
                          (wid of Samuel)
        James H. Dix, sec.

Elliot, George   Ann Lewis   26 Feb 1838
                          of Zadock
        Zadock Lewis, sec.

Elliot, George (of Chas.)   Nancy Edwards   12 May 1824

Elliott, Abel R.   Lovea Savage of Jacob   29 Dec 1828
    Henry Walker, sec.

Elliott, Caleb   Esther Kelley   13 Mar 1833
        J. B. Ailworth and C. P. Scarburgh, sec.

Elliott, Charles   Margaret Matthews   4 Jan 1822
    of Charles   of Anthony
    George Scott, sec.

Elliott, George   Ann Lewis   27 Feb 1838

Elliott, James (wdr)   Elizabeth Parker   12 Feb 1827
                          of Robert
        Charles Elliott of John, sec.

Elliott, James   Sally Roders   21 Sep 1815
                          (wid Ayres)
        Joseph Turlington, sec.

Elliott, Jesse   Margaret Bagwell   18 Mar 1817
                          (wid Thomas)

James Stewart, sec.

Elliott, John Thomas of Thomas	Caroline Parker of Thomas	6 Jan 1855
Elliott, John George Elliott, sec.	Nancy Caruthers	26 May 1834
Elliott, John W. A. Garrison Burton, sec.	Elizabeth G. Burton of Garrison	5 Apr 1836
Elliott, Teackle	Lavinia Garrison	23 Nov 1847
Elliott, Thomas Joshua Burton, sec.	Ann Trader	30 Mar 1811
Elliott, Thomas Thomas Zadoch Lewis, sec.	Lovena Lewis of Zadoch	12 Dec 1825 6
Elliott, Thomas of James John Elliott, sec.	Catherine Phillips of Thomas	29 Dec 1828
Elliott, William tailor John W. Custis, sec.	Elizabeth W. Robins of Thomas	19 Dec 1825
Elliott, William Phillip Fisher, sec.	Elizabeth Fisher	18 Mar 1806
Elliott, William of Teackle William Parramore, sec.	Alice T. Bradford of Thomas A.	4 Apr 1821
Elliott, William James Floyd, sec.	Susan G, Mears	27 Dec 1824
Elliott, William	Elizabeth Robins	20 Dec 1825
Ellis, John John Welburn, sec.	Nancy Rowley	4 Nov 1802
Ellis, William H.S.	Hannah H. Taylor	22 Jun 1843
Emerson, Robert FN Levin Godfree, sec.	Agnes Hill FN	26 Dec 1809
Emerson, Robin FN	Bridget Guffin FN	12 Mar 1813

of Mary
Peter Poulson FN and John Nock, sec.

Eson, George   Sally Hall   30 Dec 1801
    John Hall, sec.

Evans, Arthur   Jenny Handy   11 Sep 1798
    George Matthews, sec.

Evans, Capt. Revell   Christiana Joynes   22 May 1848

Evans, Crippen   Scarbrough Davis   7 Nov 1805
    William Ardis, sec.

Evans, David of Geo.   Rachel Parks of Job   10 Jan 1826
    Tyler Crocket and Trivis Crocket, sec.

Evans, Denwood   Sally Parramore   15 Mar 1849
                        of John
        John Parramore and L. J. Bell, sec.

Evans, George   Leah Brumbley   1 Aug 1795

Evans, George FN   Ada Nock FN   8 Dec 1856

Evans, Hamilton   Zippora Tyler   11 Oct 1848
                        of David
        Selby Byrd and Edward D. Trader, sec.

Evans, Henry   Polly Powell (wid)   23 Dec 1800
    James Rooks, sec.

Evans, Jacob   Peggy White   23 Sep 1790

Evans, James   Lavinia Silverthorne   29 Jul 1834
                        (wid)

Evans, James H.   Charlotte Marshall   8 Feb 1853
    of John   of Henry

Evans, James   Lovinia Silverthorne   28 Jul 1834
                        (wid of John Silverthorn)
        Juls Coleburn and James C. Jenkins, sec.

Evans, John   Leah Robins   25 Feb 1793
    George Mathews, sec.

Evans, John   Hester Dix   26 Jul 1839
    William Dix, sec.

Evans, John   Lucretia Watson   23 Jul 1785
    Southy Simpson, sec.

Evans, John (wdr)	Hetty Ewell	5 Jul 1843
Evans, John of Robert Wilson Taylor, sec.	Elizabeth Waterfield	29 Dec 1808
Evans, John of Levin Thomas Hall and Henry Hall, sec.	Margaret West (wid Solomon)	23 Dec 1820
Evans, John Jr. James B. Jacob and Samuel Ewell, sec.	Nancy Waters of William	31 Dec 1827
Evans, John (of John)	Nancy Waters	10 Jan 1827
Evans, John of Crippen Arthur Coard, sec.	Frances Marshall of Solomon	24 Jan 1826
Evans, John of Crippen John Snead, sec.	Nancy Coard of John	29 Jan 1817
Evans, John of Francis Severn Tyler, sec.	Sally Parks	24 Jun 1806
Evans, Levin	Sarah Thomas	31 Aug 1788
Evans, Levin John Derby, sec.	Rebecca Mathews	17 May 1785
Evans, Littleton Edmund Bell, sec.	Rachel Roach	2 Nov 1837
Evans, Littleton	Rachel Roache	5 Jun 1838
Evans, Major William Dyes, sec.	Shady Prewitt	16 Jun 1829
Evans, Pete of Richard Armanias Crocket and William Lee, sec.	Triffena Crocket of Jno.	15 Dec 1818
Evans, Revel Elias D. Joynes, sec.	Christina Joynes	13 May 1848
Evans, Revell of Elijah Job Parks, sec.	Judah Parks of John	31 Jan 1818
Evans, Robert William Drummond Sr., sec.	Katey Daniel	26 Mar 1774

Evans, Teackle of Rich.   Anna Crocket of Jesse   28 Apr 1819
     Asa Crockett and Stephen Parks, sec.

Evans, Thomas Jr.   Sally Marshall   3 Dec 1814
     Revell Lewis and Smith Melson, sec.

Evans, Thomas   Sinah Trickle   30 Dec 1813
     Aaron Shorer, sec.

Evans, Thomas   Sarah Marshall (wid)   20 Jul 1801

Evans, William   Patsy Ann Pruitt   1 May 1845

Evans, William   Jane Powell   28 Feb 1848
                         ward of John W. Chandler
     John R. Boggs, sec.

Evans, William   Jenney Melvin   15 Oct 1799
     Elisha Whealton, sec.

Evans, William   Polly Chambers   28 Nov 1807
     Henry Crocket, sec.

Evans, William   Polly Marshall   19 Jun 1845

Ewart, Robert   Margaret Boggs   15 Feb 1787
     George Smith, sec.

Ewell, Charles   Susan Nelson   25 Nov 1849

Ewell, Charles   Sally Schoolfield   4 Oct 1788

Ewell, Edward   Margaret J. Taylor   30 Sep 1850
                         of Patsy

Ewell, Edward W.   Susan Taylor   1 Feb 1837
                         (wid James)
     John S. Ewell and Samuel White, sec.

Ewell, Edward N.   Susan Taylor (wid)   2 Feb 1831

Ewell, George H.   Nancy Fitchett of Jon'a 23 Jun 1813
     Thorowgood Taylor, sec.

Ewell, George   Elizabeth Vessells   28 Dec 1829
     of Solomon   of Thomas
     Shepherd Young and Thomas Vessells, sec.

Ewell, George Thomas   Elizabeth Young   30 Jan 1840
     of George   of Gellett

James Gray and Nathaniel Revell, sec.

Ewell, George H.   Betsy Melson of Daniel   27 Aug 1806
    Solomon Ewell, sec.

Ewell, George   Amey Bloxom   30 Dec 1805
    Elias Taylor, sec.

Ewell, George FN   Hetty Downing FN   10 Jan 1840
    Charles Tatham and Edward P. Pitts, sec.

Ewell, Gillett   Elizabeth Corbin   1 Jan 1830
                          of Coventon
    Coventon Corbin, sec.

Ewell, Henry F.   Patsy Wessells of Jms.   26 Dec 1825
    George H. Ewell, sec.

Ewell, James   Rachel Parks   2 Oct 1789

Ewell, James   Sally Matthews   25 Apr 1831
                          orphan Jacob
    John Parker Jr., sec.

Ewell, James of Jms.   Margaret Taylor of Chas.   9 May 1823
    Solomon Ewell, sec.

Ewell, James   Hester Walker   26 May 1852
                          of Levin, dec'd.

Ewell, James   Esther Whealton   26 Mar 1788

Ewell, John   Margaret Onley   8 Jul 1840
                          (wid of Francis)
    John Arlington, sec.

Ewell, John   Margaret Only (wid)   10 Jul 1833

Ewell, Samuel B. A.   Noreisa Crippen   24 Jun 1833
    Jackson Tunnell, sec.

Ewell, Seymour B.   Narcissa Crippen   1 Jul 1833

Ewell, Solomon   Margaret Jacob   23 Jun 1806
    William S. Tunnel, sec.

Ewell, Solomon Sr.   Hetty S. White   9 Jan 1826
    William C. White and Littleton R. Henderson, sec.

Ewell, Solomon   Polly Justice   4 Jan 1792

Ewell, Thomas   Elizabeth Evans   7 Feb 1814

                              (wid John)
         Jacob Waterfield, sec.

Ewell, Thomas W.   Ann Taylor of Agnes   1 Dec 1819
         Thomas C. Delastatius, sec., Ayres W. Taylor consent

Ewell, William FN   Sally Dickinson FN   25 Apr 1803
         Robert Jenkins, sec.

Ewell, William   Tilpah Jane Smith   15 Jan 1829
         James B. Jacob and John W. Holland, sec.

Ewell, William Whittington   Anne Mathews   7 Oct 1783
         Charles Ewell, sec.

Ewell, William H.   Cornellia Pool   11 Sep 1841

Fackler, Rev. David M.   Susan S. Satchell   5 Feb 1840
        Leven F. and Thomas R. Joynes, sec.

Farrors, Dr. William H.   Catherine A. Jackson   13 Feb 1833
                          of John
        Isaac Bagwell and John C. Stevenson, sec.

Fatherly, John W.   Nancy Watson   16 Dec 1821
        Jacob Watson, sec.

Fedderman, John W.   Elizabeth White   18 Dec 1831

Fedderman, John   Rachel Matthews   6 Aug 1829
                          of Washburn
        Washburn Matthews and Goral Taylor, sec.

Fedderman, Joseph M.   Sarah Godwin   5 Mar 1850
        (wdr)   of Nicholas T.
        James H. White, sec.

Fedderman, Joseph   Martha Susan Mitchell   22 Jan 1852
                          of Elizabeth S.

Fedderman, Joseph   Elizabeth Mathews   14 Sep 1827

Federman, Major   Grace Marshall   3 Mar 1804
        Cearn Augustin, sec.

Ferguson, James   Patience Jones   5 Feb 1825
        of William   of John
        John Jones and Sebastian Cropper, sec.

Ferguson, Jamess   Polly Showard (wid)   13 Aug 1832
        James B. Thomas and John B. Ailworth, sec.

Fidderman, John W.   Elizabeth D. White   15 Dec 1830
                          of James
        William C. Slocomb and John H. Powell, sec.

Field, John D.   Mary Ann S. Logan   30 Mar 1852
        (wdr)   (wid of Oliver Logan)

Fields, John D.   Elizabeth Ann McMaster 21 Jan 1835
        Francis D. Miller and Henry Bagwell, sec.

Fields, Samuel FN   Winney Marshall FN   4 Aug 1823
                          of Isaac FN
        Isaac Marshall, sec.

Fields, William B.   Mary S. Corbin   26 Sep 1853
        (wdr)   of George W.
        James P. Selby, sec.

```
Filio, Upshur            Joyce Colonna of Major    22 Jun 1813
    William Gillett, sec.

Finnell                  Catherine Moore           31 Dec 1816
    James Eichelberger, sec.

Finney, Andrew G.        Susan C. Bunting           2 Nov 1853
                         of Solomon

Finney, Henry F. of Wm.  Ann W. Parker of Henry    11 Sep 1819
    John Ewell, sec., Agnes Parker (mother), consent

Finney, Henry            Catherine Andrews (wid)

Finney, John             Catherine Bowman           2 Sep 1799
    William Seymour, sec.

Finney, John Jr.         Nancy Broadwater          28 Jul 1794

Finney, Thomas W.        Sarah Fletcher of Tho.    27 Dec 1819
    Spencer Drummond, sec.

Finney, Walter R.        Sally Arlington of John   23 Oct 1819
    Alex. Straham, sec.

Finney, William          Leah Parker               29 Dec 1810
    James Eichelberger, sec.

Finney, William          Margaret Sarah Mapp       16 Jan 1850
    of William             of George S.
    George S. Mapp, sec.

Finney, William          Sally Bundick              5 Oct 1801
    Edmund Bayly, sec.

Finney, William          Rosey Arlington           28 Nov 1814
    Elijah Boggs, sec.

Finney, William          Elizabeth S. Marshall     31 Jan 1787
    Thomas Evans, sec.

Fischer, William         Elizabeth Rodgers          3 Nov 1774
                         (wid)
    John Finney, sec.

Fisher, George S.        Rachel James               8 Dec 1825
    (wdr)                  of Sally Harrison
    John A. Coleburn, sec.

Fisher, George           Kessy Tatham              16 Jun 1823
    (wdr)                  of Rickett
```

Thomas Guy, sec.

Fisher, George Joseph Turlington, sec.	Rachel Turlington	25 Aug 1803
Fisher, Henry F. of Jns'a Teackle Trader, sec.	Elizabeth Trader (wid Archibald)	21 Mar 1816
Fisher, James P.	Hetty Bloxom of Major, dec'd.	29 Dec 1856
Fisher, John R. George Fisher, sec.	Mary Ann Kellam	9 May 1804
Fisher, Kendall W. Osborne J. Bird, sec.	Susan Berry	11 Jan 1841
Fisher, Maddox John Justice, sec.	Leah Mears	15 Jan 1802
Fisher, Major Alexander Lang and Littleton Bloxom, sec.	Sally Bloxom of Nichlous	2 Sep 1817
Fisher, Meshack Edward C. Northam and John W. Bird, sec.	Rachel B. Northam of Southy	7 May 1833
Fisher, Phillip Thomas Lindsey, sec.	Susanna Abdell of Elisha	7 Oct 1815
Fisher, Riley (wdr)	Keziah Bird (wid)	5 Jan 1827
Fisher, Riley Nicholas P. Godwin, sec.	Nancy Godwin	11 Aug 1807
Fisher, Riley	Nancy Godwin	11 Oct 1812
Fisher, Riley (wdr)	Louisa Brown	21 Aug 1855
Fisher, Robert Edward G. Hutchinson, sec.	Nancy Hutchinson of Wm.	30 Sep 1830
Fisher, Teackle	Nancy Johnson	23 May 1792
Fisher Thomas R.	Prudence Jane Wright	13 Apr 1849
Fisher, Thomas H.	Rachel Ann Bird of Johannas	1 Aug 1848

Edward D. Trader, sec.

Fisher, Tully   Nancy Small   4 Aug 1824
   George Christopher, sec., James Davis, father-in-law,
   (stepfather) of Nancy, consent

Fisher, Tully Wise   Hessy Bird   26 Oct 1809
   George Wilson, sec.

Fisher, William F.   Caty Andrews   17 Feb 1841
               (wid of Robert)
   James B. Andrews and Nathaniel Topping, sec.

Fitchett, Denwood   Margaret Leatherbury 23 Aug 1852
               of George P.

Fitchett, John   Joyce Andrews   21 Jan 1786
   Griffin Savage, sec.

Fitchett, Joshua   Patsy Polk   23 Oct 1810
   Thomas Sturgis, sec.

Fitchett, Nathaniel T. Susanna P. Godwin   26 Jan 1820
   Edmund Godwin, sec.

Fitzgerald, Charles   Tabitha Milliner   20 Oct 1829
   of Elisha   of Smith
   Southy Hall and Smith Milliner, sec.

Fitzgerald, Samuel   Louisa Coleburn   14 Nov 1826
               of Richard
   Thomas Lillison, sec.

Fitzgerald, Thomas E. Margaret Ann Hopkins 25 Dec 1837
               of Stephen
   Stephen Hopkins, sec.

Fleharty, George   Catherine Willis   1 Apr 1809
   Daniel Bull, sec.

Fletcher, George L.   Elizabeth B. Drummond 8 Dec 1841

Fletcher, Henry   Mary S. Justice   4 Aug 1810
   Thomas Custis, sec.

Fletcher, James J.   Elizabeth Hope   26 Oct 1848

Fletcher, James T.   Elizabeth Ann Hope   25 Oct 1848
               of Kendal
   Thomas S. White and Edmund R. Allen, sec.

Fletcher, James H.   Elizabeth Ann Broadwater 13 Nov 1844

Fletcher, John R.   Louisa M. Broadwater   19 Mar 1850
                           of David
        Peter Corbin, sec.

Fletcher, John T.   Sarah B. Dickerson   22 May 1845

Fletcher, John   Susanna Lewis   28 Sep 1825
                           of Raymond
        Henry Silverthorne, sec.

Fletcher, Spencer D.   Tabitha Milligan of John 7 May 1827
        Michael Robins and Spencer Drummond, sec.

Fletcher, Stephen   Bekey Wyatt   26 Nov 1804
        William T. Barcraft, sec.

Fletcher, Thomas   Elizabeth Choard   9 Aug 1804
        John Wallop, sec.

Fletcher, Thomas Jr.   Elizabeth S. Wallop   20 Oct 1813
        Henry Silverthorne, sec.

Fletcher, Thomas R.   Elizabeth Hinman   22 Nov 1846
        of Henry

Flewharte, George   Elizabeth Scott   4 Feb 1815
        Raymond Rolly, sec.

Flewharte, John   Comfort Crowson   2 Feb 1815
        John Willet, sec.

Floyd, Benjamin   Sarah Hornsby   8 Jun 1794

Floyd, Benjamin (wdr)   Mary Richardson of Chas. 6   Sep   1821
        Thomas S. Richardson, sec.

Floyd, Benjamin   Elizabeth Bagg of Wm.   12 Jun 1815
        Robins Mapp, sec.

Floyd, Benjamin (wdr)   Mary Powell (wid)   1 Dec 1832
        Joshua K. Roberts, sec.

Floyd, Elijah   Rachel Garrison of Jms.   27 Mar 1816
        Thomas Smith, sec.

Floyd, Frederick   Sarah Bayly   17 Sep 1804
        Jonathan Garrison, sec.

Floyd, Fredrick   Catherine Elliott   8 Jun 1851

Floyd, George   Maria Stewart   28 Dec 1818

of Frederick   (wid Levin G.)
Thomas Smith of Joseph, sec.

Floyd, Izer   Betsy Allen   19 Oct 1816

Floyd, James   Catherine Kellam   23 Dec 1785
    Charles Richardson, sec.

Floyd, James G.   Elizabeth Jane Sturgis   17 Nov 1853
    of Elijah   ward of Lewis L. Snead

Floyd, John   Matilda Walter of Rich. 25 Mar 1822
    Benjamin Stringer, sec., Richard Walters, consent

Floyd, John R.   Louisa J. Roberts   19 Sep 1848
    ward of Thomas S. Richardson   of Lewis S.
    James B. Floyd, sec.

Floyd, Matthew   Elisa Beach   30 Jun 1823
                       (wid Joseph)
        George Floyd, sec.

Floyd, Thomas of Wm.   Sally Ashby of John   26 Apr 1819
    Thomas J. Edmonds and Thomas James, sec.

Folio, Henry   Susan Darby of Wm.   12 Feb 1814
    James L. Darby, sec.

Folio, John   Caty Morgan   7 Nov 1810
    Mitchell S. West, sec.

Folio, William   Mary P. Jones   12 Nov 1845

Follio, Samuel   Malinda Doughty   27 Jan 1823
                       ward Samuel W. Colonna
        Samuel W. Colonna, sec.

Fosque, Daniel FN   Nelly Dennis   24 Jan 1844

Fosque, James   Emma Miles   21 Nov 1850
                       of William

Fosque, John P.W.   Nancy Bull of Ben.   29 Dec 1824
    Thomas Scott, sec.

Fosque, John R.   Ann Carmine   3 Oct 1812
    of John   of Smith R.
    Smith R. Carmine, sec.

Fosque, John   Rachel Bunting   11 May 1816
    of George   of Solomon

John Crowson, sec.

Fosque, John   Margaret Custis   3 Jul 1786
    Francis Savage, sec.

Fosque, John   Sally Ewell   28 Feb 1839
                         ward of James Whealton
        Jacob J. SStaton and William S. Ewell, sec.

Fosque, Nathaniel B.   Ann Scott   4 Jan 1843

Fosque, Nathaniel   Margaret Stephens   30 Mar 1829
                         of Charles
        Samuel Rayfield, sec.

Fosque, Nathaniel   Sally Glen   11 Feb 1809
    Arthur Roberts, sec.

Fosque, William   Leah Dickerson   3 Feb 1786
    Edward Dickerson, sec.

Fosque, William T.   Ann Eliza Savage   23 Jun 1847

Fosque, William T.   Eliza Ann Savage   16 Jun 1847
                         of George
        Elijah N. Nock and George S. Savage, sec.

Foster, Abraham   Charity Bagge   21 Feb 1786
    William Gibb, sec.

Foster, George   Susa Ward   2 Aug 1806
    Custis Darby and Samuel Barnes, sec.

Foster, John   Elicia Powell   17 Feb 1807
    Thomas W. Rodgers, sec.

Foster, Selby   Nancy Foster   14 Jun 1806
    George W. Burton, sec.

Foster, Selby   Tabitha Hopkins   1 Nov 1808
                         of Stephen
        Richard D. Bayly, sec.

Foster, Selby   Nancy Foster   14 Jun 1806

Fox, George G.   Elizabeth Susan Mears   17 Apr 1852
                         of John S.

Fox, Golden F.   Elizabeth Sarah Kelly   3 Feb 1847

Fox, James   Nancy Mears   26 Nov 1821
    of Golden

Zorobabel Mason, sec.

Fox, James	Eleanor Lilliston	15 Dec 1842
Fox, John Golden (wid William B.) William P. Custis, sec.	Mary Ross	23 Aug 1817
Fox, Levin Edward and Thorogood Mears, sec.	Maria Mears	30 Mar 1840
Fox, Levin John B. Wyatt, sec.	Polly Wyatt of Wm.	26 Aug 1822
Fox, Thomas Ezekiel R. Bloxom, sec.	Mary Ashby of Samuel	26 Dec 1836
Fox, Thomas William R. Custis, sec.	Elizabeth Grennalds of William	4 Jul 1815
Fox, William George Dunton, sec.	Polly Dunton	20 Aug 1807
Fox, William	Mary A. James	20 Jun 1835
Freeman, Robert	Esther Carter	12 Oct 1790
Furness, Ephraim Isaac Henderson, sec.	Polly Massey	7 Jan 1799

6

```
Gale, Matthew            Margaret Gordon          6 Mar 1738
   of Somerset Co. MD
   John Leatherbury, trustee

Gardener, Thomas         Mary Bull               26 Jul 1841
   of William             (wid of Southy)
   Levi Gray, sec.

Gardner, Wm. of John     Hetty Bloxom of Levin   17 Apr 1821
   Jacob Bishop, sec.

Gardner, William         Sophia Lewis (wid)      11 Jul 1810
   Thomas Custis Sr. and Jno Snead, sec.

Garner, Griffin          Lucinda Parks           15 Sep 1823

Garnett, Dr. Alex. Y.P.  Mary E. Wise        12 Jun 1848
                          of Henry A.
      John C. Wise, sec.

Garret, Charles          Rosey Chandler           5 Sep 1798
   Edward Ironmonger, sec.

Garrett, John            Salley Taylor           28 Mar 1787
   George Trewet Taylor, sec.

Garrison, Abel           Peggy Kellam             5 May 1812
   Thomas Bagwell and John, Snead sec.

Garrison, Edmund of Wm.  Bridget Ross            25 Dec 1816
   Thomas R. Joynes, sec.

Garrison, Edmund         Adah Fletcher            7 Nov 1806
   Samuel Garrison, sec.

Garrison, George         Elizabeth Peusey        30 Sep 1833
   ward of William B.
   Welburn B. Garrisson and George L. Rogers, sec.

Garrison, Isaiah         Adah Churen              6 Aug 1783
   Berry Floyd, sec.

Garrison, John           Sarah Harman            17 Mar 1810
   William Stockley, sec.

Garrison, Samuel         Elizabeth Groten         2 Aug 1804
   Benjamin Harrison, sec.

Garrison, Thomas         Mary Bull               20 Jul 143

Garrison, William Sr.    Esther Rodgers          19 Apr 1819
   (wdr)                  (wid)
```

William Custis and Isaac Kendall, sec.

Gascoynes, William   Esther Mathews   27 Jun 1796

Gaskins, James   Sally Stant   29 Oct 1832
                        (wid of Samuel)
     Thomas Fletcher and Elijah Miles, sec.

Gaskins, John S.   Letita R.B. Broadwater 10 Feb 1857
                        of Walter

Gaskins, Meshach   Elizabeth Bowen   31 Jan 1831
                        (wid Whittington)
          Michael Robins, sec.

Gaskins, Revell of Wm. Margaret Melson of Geo. 13 Dec 1826
          George Melson Sr. and Zadoc Selby, sec.

Gaskins, Teackle   Mary Riggs   10 Jul 1806

Gaskins, Teackle   Mary Riggs   11 Jul 1806
                        of Joshua Riggs
          Arthur Watson and George Eshon, sec.

Gellispie, John   Fanny Miles   29 Jan 1827
                        orphan George
          Richard Gillispie, sec.

George FN   Billy FN   29 Dec 1806
          Samuel Downing, sec.

George freed by Bagwell Scarburgh Tunnill FN 13 Aug 1800
          Daniel, sec.

German, William D.   Rachel Trader   17 Nov 1851
                        (wid of Whittington Trader)

Giban/Givan, John   Betsy Rodgers   18 Dec 1814
                        (wid Richard)
          Caleb Duncan and Henry S. Copes, sec.

Gibb, John   Zepporah Bonwell of Nanny   8 Jan 1820
          Henry Harvy, sec.

Gibb, Thomas C.   Margaret Taylor   11 Jun 1817
     of William   of Crippen
          Thorowgood Taylor, sec.

Gibbons, James   Catherine Wright   28 Jul 1809
          John Teackle, sec.

Gibbons, James T.   Mary West   26 Nov 1836

orphan of Zorobabel
William W. White, sec.

Gibbons, John E.   Sally Warner   21 Dec 1854
   of Solomon, dec'd.

Gibbs, George Thomas   Comfort Bull   26 Jul 1809
    George Bull, sec.

Giddens, Reuben   Betsy Vessells   20 Dec 1797

Gilchrist, Andrew   Laney Middleton   15 Apr 1805
   Richard D. Bayly, sec.

Gilden, Edward   Mary Eliza Belote   24 Aug 1854
    of George, dec'd.

Gillaspie, James of John Esther Bundick   27 Dec 1816
   Edmund Bell and John, Bull sec.

Gillaspie, Richard G   Mary Hickman   18 Sep 1822
   of Jno.   (wid Kendall)
   Noah Riggins, sec.

Gillespie, Albert   Catherine A. Dix   23 Dec 1857
    ward of William Pettitt

Gillespie, Edward   Susan Jane Bloxom   4 Jan 1844

Gillespie, John L.   Hester Crowson   14 Dec 1843

Gillespie, John W.   Sally A. White   20 Dec 1856
    of William C.

Gillespie, Peter J.   Susan Metcalf   6 Jan 1847

Gillett, John   Mary Wallop   8 Sep 1791

Gillett, Southy W.   Sarah Ann Hargis   24 Mar 1842

Gillett, William   Henrietta Selby   15 Dec 1813
    of Zadock
   Zadock Selby, sec.

Gillispie, Edward J.   Catherine Finney   26 Dec 1848
    Teackle K. Tyler, sec.

Gillispie, William   Rachel Savage   9 Jun 1813
   Isaac Young, sec.

Givans, Gilbert   Sarah Merril of Geo.   29 Nov 1813
   George Merril and Caleb Duncan, sec.

Givens, Henry (wdr)   Lavinia Ames   7 Oct 1841

Gladding, Alfred   Lavinia Ss. Taylor   5 Jan 1853
                             of Ezekiel, dec'd.

Gladding, George W.   Hetty Wheatly   12 May 1828
                             orphan John
          John Addison and Isma Bunting, sec.

Gladding, Jesse   Sally Thornton   16 May 1814
                             (wid John)
          Peter Hack, sec.

Gladding, John   Hepsey Powell   10 Jan 1800
          William Delastatius, sec.

Gladding, John A.   Mary Merrill   16 Dec 1828
     of John   (wid John)
     John Gladding, sec.

Gladding, John   Margaret Jane Johnson   8 Feb 1851
                             of John S.

Gladding, John   Nancy Callaham   15 Dec 1830
                             (wid Joseph)
          Isaac Long, sec.

Gladding, Joseph   Nancy Trehearne   28 Apr 1807
          Spencer Lewis, sec.

Gladding, Samuel T.   Elizabeth Northam (wid)   7 Feb 1848
          William Smullins, sec.

Gladding, Solomon   Sally Small   16 Sep 1826
     of Solomon   of James, dec'd.
          Southy Northam and Samuel Walston, sec.

Gladston, William   Ann Vermillian   26 Nov 1836
          John B. Bradford, sec.

Glass, Andrew   Elizabeth B. Henderson   10 Nov 1820
                            of Isaac
          Bagwell Topping, sec.

Glen, James   Kiturah Garrison   1 Jun 1801
          George Smith, sec.

Glenn, Edward   Nancy Parker   5 Jan 1848
                            (wid of George)
          William P. Smith and William H. Massey, sec.

Godfree, Abel FN   Amy Selby FN   29 Mar 1815
    Drummond Welburn, sec.

Godfree, Parker FN   Tinny Church FN   19 Jul 1806
    Levin Godfree, sec.

Godfrey, John FN   Elizabeth Laws FN   1 Nov 1856

Godfrey, Skinner   Lena Godfrey   28 Jul 1803
    Levin Godfrey, sec.

Godwin, Edmund Jr.   Elizabeth Drummond   28 Dec 1829
                            of Spencer
    Spencer Drummond and Wes. Ellis, sec.

Godwin, Esau   Ann S. West   8 Feb 1802
    Jonathan West, sec.

Godwin, James D.   Elizabeth Ann Conquest   1 Jan 1851

Godwin, Joseph B.   Matilda Fitchett   18 Dec 1820
    of Edmund   of Jon'a
    George H. Ewell, sec.

Godwin, Nicholas P.   Sally Duncan   30 Mar 1805
    John Staton sec.

Godwin, William   Harriet Mason   26 Feb 1827
    of Edmund   of Bennett
    Nathaniel Fitchett and Felix, Bull sec.

Goffigon, William   Margaret L. Bradford   22 Sep 1847

Goffigon, William   Susanna Fenny   28 Jan 1839
                            ward of William Goffigon, Sr.
    Richard Read, sec.

Goffigon, William   Susan A. Finney   30 Jan 1839

Goffigon, William   Margaret S. Bradford   22 Apr 1847
    (wdr)   (wid)
    Abel B. Colonna and Edward l. Bradford, sec.

Gootee, James   Elisha Lewis   27 Jan 1836
                            (wid of William)
    George S. Rew, sec.

Gootee, James   Elisha Lewis   25 Jan 1836

Graham, William   Levinia Teackle   24 Sep 1818
                            of John, dec'd.
    Richard D. Bayly, sec.

Grant, John John Snead, sec.	Agnes Snead of John	29 Dec 1820
Gray, Dennis James Thornton, sec.	Polley Ewell	9 Feb 1814
Gray, James Thomas Gray and Thomas Bunting, sec.	Elizabeth Bunting of Thomas	21 Dec 1847
Gray, Levin (wdr)	Ann White of Richard A.	24 Dec 1851
Gray, Levin Laban J. Gunter, sec.	Elizabeth Gunter (wid of Leven Gunter)	6 Apr 1836
Gray, Levin	Ann White	24 Dec 1851
Gray, Solomon	Betsy Lewis	27 Dec 1791
Gray, Thomas	Margaret Ann Melson	17 Feb 1851
Gray, Thomas (wdr)	Ann East	19 Feb 1846
Green, John	Bekey Wilson	29 Oct 1799
Grey FN Ralph R. Corbin, sec.	Sabrough FN	20 Mar 1806
Grey, James George H. Ewell, sec.	Mahala E. Scott	22 Feb 1830
Grey, Thomas Major Bull, sec.	Nancy Justice	25 Feb 1822
Grey, William Solomon White, sec.	Rosey white of Solomon	18 Dec 1823
Griffin, Abel William W. Burton, sec.	Betsy Quinaway	17 Jul 1806
Griffin, George FN William R. Custis, sec.	Mary Poolman FN	10 May 1825
Grinalds, Harry blacksmith John Dix, sec.	Sally Stephens	30 Jul 1807
Grinalds, John	Mary Colbourn	24 Feb 1834

Grinalds, John   Eliza Jester   30 Apr 1838
                          of James
      Timothy Hill, sec.

Grinalds, John   Eliza Jester   4 May 1838

Grinalds, Richard   Sarah Copes (wid)   20 Jan 1807
      John Cropper Sr., sec.

Grinalds, William   Susanna Twiford   28 Dec 1809
      Samuel Walston, sec.

Grinales, Southy   Sarah Abbot   2 Aug 1786
      Edmund Custis, sec.

Grinnalds, John   Mary Coleburn   24 Feb 1836
      ward of John Bull Sr.   of Richard
      Samuel Fitzgerald and John Bull, sec.

Grinnalds, Parker   Elizabeth Melson of Jms. 7 Aug 1930
      James Melson, sec.

Grinnalds, Southey   Ader West   21 Jan 1806
      Isaac Wright, sec.

Grinnalds, William Sr   Sally Joynes   21 Sep 1814
                          of William, dec'd.
      William White (BS), sec.

Groten, John   Elizabeth Kelly   28 Dec 1829
      James Fox, sec.

Groten, John   Elizabeth Bloxom of Rachel 30 Sep 1822
      Eli Bloxom, sec.

Groten, William D.   Susan Watson of Ephraim 23 Dec 1816
      Henry S. Copes, sec.

Groten, Zorababel   Anne Kellam   29 Aug 1785
      Levin Walker, sec.

Groton, James   Eliza Pane of Wm.   26 Dec 1850

Groton, William T.   Mary Miles   21 Mar 1848
      of William D.
      William D. Groton, sec.

Groton, William D.   Lovey Bull   3 Feb 1839
                          of George B.
      John White and James J. Ailworth, sec.

Groton, William D.(wdr)   Lovey Bull   2 Mar 1839

Guest, Richard W.   Mahala C. Ames   29 Jul 1828
    (wdr)   (wid Jesse)
    Elisha H. Davis and Littleton P. Henderson, sec.

Guest, Richard   Sally Welburn of Wm.   1 Apr 1816
    Sebastian Cropper and Richard McClosky, sec.

Gunter, Edward   Agnes Grant   9 Mar 1830
                          (wid John)
        Americus Scarburg, sec.

Gunter, Edward   Elizabeth Dickerson   5 Mar 1808
                          (wid)
        William Snead, sec.

Gunter, James   Sarah Ann Russell   31 Dec 1846

Gunter, John   Nancy Custis   29 Aug 1803
        Zadoch Kellam, sec.

Gunter, Joseph   Mahala Sturgis of Thos.   14 Mar 1828
        Thomas Sturgis and John J. Bayly, sec.

Gunter, Laban   Isabella Chandler   19 Dec 1833

Gunter, Selby   Rachel Barnes   2 Jun 1811
        William D. Outten, sec.

Guster, Ever FN   Betsy Alline   18 Oct 1816
                         of Daniel and Esther FN
        Stephen Nedad, sec.

Guy, George   Margaret Webb   5 Mar 1834

Guy, Jacob FN   Esther West FN   4 Sep 1851

Guy, John   Ann Parker   10 Sep 1799
        Henry Guy, sec.

Guy, Jonathan   Elizabeth Smith   1 Feb 1811
        Jacob Phillips, sec.

Guy, Major   Sarah Ironmonger   10 Feb 1803
        William Rolly, sec.

Guy, Major   Susan A. Mister   22 Oct 1847

Guy, Major   Rachel Millliner   21 Jun 1783

Thomas Copes, sec.

Guy, Scarburgh (FN)   1 Jun 1806

Guy, Thomas   Catharine Ivy (?)   30 Sep 1833
George S. Rogers, sec.

Guy, Thomas H.   Rebecca Revell   21 Feb 1824
                       of John, dec'd.
James Poulson, sec.

Guy, Thomas Jr.   Nancy Justice   25 Feb 1822

Guy, William of Jno.   Sally Parker of Michael   24 Dec 1810
Jonathan Guy, sec.

Guy, William Jr.   Susanna Lawrence   29 Jan 1827
                       orphan William
William Guy Sr., sec.and consent

Guy, William   Susanna Fletcher   10 Jan 1804
Robinson Savage, sec.

Hack, John W.   Sabra Corbin Cropper   12 Nov 1823
                          of Thomas
        Litt. C. Henderson, sec.

Hack, Peter Thos. W.   Sarah T. Selby   13 Jan 1823
                          of Zadock T. Selby
        Litt. P. Henderson sec. Zadock T. Selby cons.

Hack, Peter   Elizabeth Smith   17 Nov 1774
        of Peter Hack   of John Smith
        Levin Joynes, sec.

Hack, Thomas P.   Margaret H. Scherer   18 Oct 1832
        Severn Kellam, sec.

Haggaman, John   Ann Belote   27 Jul 1812
                          of John
        Elijah Chance, sec.

Haggoman, John   Mary Anne Jameson   18 Jun 1786
        George Ker, sec.

Haines, William   Sarah Migee   2 Jan 1787
        Jacob Taylor, sec.

Haley, Benjamin   Elizabeth Chandler   26 Dec 1825
        William Chandler, sec.

Haley, James P.   Rosetta A. Wood

Haley, Robert   Margaret Turlington   4 Nov 1802
        Revel West, sec.

Haley, William of Wm.   Nancy Grinalds of Wm.   8 Feb 1819
        William Grinalds, sec.

Hall, Anthony   Jane Trader of Nancy   7 Dec 1850

Hall, Asa   Hetty Booth   26 Mar 1814
                          (wid John)
        John Hall, sec.

Hall, Benjamin   Meliah Walston   14 Nov 1814
        Henry S. Copes, sec.

Hall, Charles   Lucretia Moore   1 Mar 1786
        George Young, sec.

Hall, George E.   Sally Drummond Killman 27 Jun 1851
                          of James

Hall, Gilbert   Rachel Chandler   17 Jul 1802

                            - 118 -

Gilbert Hall and James White, sec.

Hall, Henry   Sarah R. Drummond   5 Feb 1811
     George Eshon, sec.

Hall, Henry   Ann Corbin   31 Aug 1818
     of Henry, dec'd.   of George
     Noah Drummond, sec.

Hall, Henry Hammond   Ann Hack Pitt Beard   1 Dec 1818
                               of Matthew
     M. Beard and Alex. McCollum, sec.

Hall, John   Nancy Hickman   25 Jul 1814
     Raymond Taylor and Asa, Hall sec.

Hall, John C.   Catherine C. Bagwell   11 Oct 1848
     (wdr)   (wid of Henry)
     Lonis D. Drummond, sec.

Hall, John C.   Ann B. Ayres of Francis   10 Nov 1830
     William P. Custis, sec.

Hall, John   Henrietta Dison   2 Sep 1801
     Elijah Shay, sec.

Hall, Richard of Rich.   Peggy White of Robert   29 Jul 1816
     Robert White and Samuel Henderson, sec.

Hall, Robert S.   Jane H. Drummond   17 Jan 1837
                               of Spencer
     Charles Drummond, sec.

Hall, Robert   Mary Kellam   18 Jul 1809
     Thomas Turner, sec.

Hall, Robert (wdr)   Elizabeth Waters   7 Apr 1839
     James Brittingham, sec.

Hall, Robert   Kessy Willett   25 Apr 1825
     of Jesse   of Waitman Willet
     John Y. Bagwell, sec.

Hall, Thomas   Mahala Carpenter   14 Mar 1853
                               of Richard

Hall, Thomas J.   Elizabeth H. Martin   20 Dec 1853
     of Robert   of Catherine

Hall, Thomas, Sr.   Sally Northam   2 Mar 1852
     (wdr)   of William, dec'd.

Hall, William	Polly Hinman (wid)	26 Feb 1834

Hall, William
   of Robert
     Robert Hall, sec.
	Sally Kilman
	   of Amy
		4 Nov 1835

Hall, William W.	Elizabeth Bancum	24 Aug 1817
Hallett, John George S. Fisher, sec.	Margaret Leatherbury of Ann	9 Apr 1805
Hammell, Littleton Samuel Trader, sec.	Margaret Seymour (wid)	16 Dec 1807
Hammond, Charles John Burton, sec.	Comfort -----	27 Sep 1787
Hammonds, George FN William R. Drummond, sec.	Hannah Downing FN	26 Jan 1813
Hanaford, William John R. Warrington sec.	Leah Harman	20 Jan 1812

Hancock, James
    William Hargis, sec.
	Polly H. Taylor
	   of Matthew
		28 Dec 1807

Hancock, John (wdr) Samuel Carey, sec.	Sally Ann Sharply	10 Apr 1837

Hancock, John
   William Sharpley Sr. and Levin Core, sec.
	Margaret Knox
	   (wid Robert)
		13 Jan 1830

Hancock, John W.
   of Elijah
  Thomas Pusey, sec. Richard Mears of John cons.
	Nelly Mears
	   of Richard of John
		17 Jan 1820

Hancock, Levin P.	Elerine Smart	24 Sep 1846

Hancock, Mitchell
   of William
  William Hancock, sec.
	Betsy Taylor
	   of Shadrach
		8 Mar 1813

Hancock, Teackle Levi Small, sec.	Rebecca Bloxom	29 Apr 1811
Hancock, Thomas Sacher Trader, sec.	Rebecca Trader	14 Apr 1804

```
Hancock, William (wdr)     Polly Justice of Tho.     16 Sep 1822
     Samuel A. Justice, sec.


Hancock, William          Leah Hope                  16 Feb 1818
     of Thomas            (wid Elijah)
     George Arbuckle, sec.

Hannaford, Wm. Jr.        Ann Window                 10 Aug 1811
     Zorobabel Window, sec.

Hargis, Benjamin          Ann Guy                     8 Feb 1825
     of Levin             of George
     George Floyd, sec.

Hargis, Custis            Pricilla Pearce            13 Jun 1800
     John Pearce and Smith Buntin, sec.

Hargis, George           Ann Trader                   3 Apr 1833
     Levin Core, sec.

Hargis, George           Charlotte Mears            25 Feb 1856
     (wdr)               of Levin

Hargis, John Jr.         Elizabeth J. Ames          15 Mar 1847
     of William          of Molly, (wid of Nathaniel)
     John D. Heath, sec.

Hargis, John Jr.         Sally Bunting of  Smith    20 Dec 1825
     Sacker Scott, sec.

Hargis, John             Elizabeth Ames             17 Mar 1847

Hargis, Levin            Mary Wallis of Daniel       9 Dec 1816
     Isaac Coleburn, sec.

Hargis, Thomas           Polly Scott                13 Feb 1823
                         of Betsy Sterling
Thomas C. Gillett, sec.

Hargis, Thomas           Rachel Hitchens             6 Jun 1850
     (wdr)               of Ezekiel
     George S. East, sec.

Hargis, Thomas W.        Margaret Fletcher          25 Jun 1847

Hargis, Thomas (wdr)     Elizabeth Wallop of Wm.     5 Mar 1821
     Robert Knox, sec.

Hargis, Thomas W.        Margaret W. Fletcher       22 May 1847
     (wdr)               of Elizabeth S., wid of Thomas
```

William H.B. Wallop, sec.

Hargis, Thomas George Corbin, sec.	Wise Marshall	16 Nov 1786
Hargis, William Levin K. Lewis, sec.	Mary Elliott (wid Thomas)	9 Nov 1830
Harman, Henry George Scott, sec.	Ann Doe	25 Dec 1811

Harman, William
  (wdr)
    Henry Walker, sec.
	Ann Stewart
	(wid of Henry)
		24 Feb 1834

Harman, Zorobable Robert Walker, sec.	Sally Watson	5 Jan 1787
Harmanson, John I.	Anne C. Arbuckle	1 Jun 1853
Harmon, Abel H. Abel R. Harmon and William Burton, sec.	Nancy Chance of Elijah	3 Oct 1825
Harmon, Arthur FN	Elizabeth Shepard FN	29 May 1854
Harmon, George of Wm. Lancelot Ward, sec.	Leah East of James	19 Sep 1829
Harmon, Henry Purnel O. Twiford, sec.	Mary Topping	27 Dec 1813
Harmon, John of John Albert R. Heath and Thomas Floyd, sec.	Margaret Nock of Robt.	27 Nov 1826
Harmon, John John Bird, sec.	Mary Bird	30 Jan 1806
Harmon, Kendall Sr. William Badger and Zorobabel, Chandler sec.	Sally Kellam (wid John)	25 Aug 1806
Harmon, Levin John N. Tull and Henry Bagwell, sec.	Caroline Lambden	16 Mar 1847
Harmon, Major FN	Leah Johnson	15 Jun 1843
Harmon, William of John James Walker, sec.	Betsy Kellam of Jms.	20 May 1819

```
Harmon, William W.        Margaret Kellam              5 Jan 1854
     (wdr)                (wid of Charles Kellam)

Harmonson, James R.       Tabitha Snead               10 Jun 1858
                          of Lewis L.

Harmonson, John L.        Ann C. Arbuckle              2 Jun 1853


Harris, Benjamin          Absabeth Lecatte            11 Apr 1809
     William Lecate, sec.

Harris, George            Rachel Shield                8 Sep 1830
                          orphan Asa
Edmund Garrison, sec.

Harris, George B.         Rachel Shield               15 Sep 1830

Harris, George Burton     Elizabeth Shield            18 Apr 1849

Harris, Thomas            Sarah A. Kelley              1 Jun 1836
     Thomas Stockley, sec.

Harris, Thomas G. (wdr)   Betsy Bayly                 13 Sep 1854

Harrison, Abel R.         Ann Harrison                18 Dec 1820

Harrison, Evans           Mary Mears                  24 Nov 1834
     Major Savage Sr., sec.

Harrison, George (FN)     Mary Ewell                  21 Dec 1841

Harrison, James           Peggy Garrison              21 Mar 1808
     Frederick Floyd, sec.

Harrison, James           Catherine Mason             29 Dec 1825
                          orphan John
     Thomas H. Kellam, sec.

Harrison, Major (FN)      Leah Johnson                15 Jun 1843

Harrison, Savage          Euphemy Kellam               8 Jan 1800
     Jacob Kelley, sec.

Harrison, Smith           Rachel Smith                 4 Dec 1834

Harrison, Smith (wdr)     Mary Hitchens               16 May 1853

Harrison, Smith           Mary Hitchens                5 Jun 1853

Harrison, Smith           Rochel Smith                 6 Dec 1834
     William Mason, sec.
```

Harrison, Stephen P.   Peggy Carse   2 Apr 1814
    Arthur Mclain sec.

Harrison, William H.   Rachel Ann Ayres   6 Oct 1852
    of Elizabeth W.

Harrison, William   Betsy Kellam   26 May 1819

Harrison, William   Mary Turlington   6 Jul 1786
    Thomas Snead, sec.

Harrison, William   Ann F. Taylor   31 Dec 1827
    of William   of Major
    George K. Taylor, sec.

Harrison, William Sr.   Molly East   21 Nov 1826
    (wdr)   (wid Parker)
    John A. Coleburn, sec.

Harrison, William H.   Rachel Ann Ayres   7 Oct 1852

Harrison, William   Sally James   21 Dec 1814
    (wid James)
William Dammeral, sec.

Harry FN   Tabitha Bagwell FN   29 Mar 1814
    of Esther
    William Drummond and Henry S. Copes, sec.

Hart, James   Mary Killmon   14 Dec 1826
    of John   of Ezekiel
    William Killman, sec. Ezekiel Killmon cons.

Hart, John Jr.   Elishea Parkes   27 Jan 1834
    John Hart Sr., sec.

Hart, Richard   Nancy Simpson of Revel   11 Aug 1831
    John Harmon, sec.

Harter, John (FN)   Henny Teackel   12 Apr 1831

Harvey, Henry   Patience Chandler   22 May 1806
    Thomas Chandler, sec.

Harvey, William   Sally Jacob of Richard   16 May 1812
    Daniel Baker, sec.

Hastings, Major   Nellie Cottingham   26 Apr 1803
    Richard Townsend, sec.

Hastings, Richard   Sally Wyatt   21 Jun 1811
    William Bird, sec.

```
Hastings, Thomas          Nancy Davis (wid)        5 Jan 1810
     Robert Scott and John, Snead sec.

Hathway, William          Nancy Wimbrough          9 Feb 1840

Hatton, George FN         Molly Parker FN         28 Jan 1833
     Edward L. Bayly, sec.

Hawley, Samuel            Sally Walters of Tho.    21 Jun 1830
     Americus Scarburgh, sec.

Heath, Albert R.          Jane Arlington          26 Mar 1838
     John Nock, sec.

Heath, Albert R.          Sarah R. Watson         13 Dec 1843

Heath, Cornelius C.       Ann Mears of Jesse      19 Dec 1838
     John D. Heath, sec.

Heath, George            Margaret Martin          24 Dec 1833
     Robert R. Lingo, sec.

Heath, John F.           Rosey Giddeons           31 Oct 1825
     Elijah Lillison, sec.

Heath, John F.           Elizabeth Martin         13 May 1835
     Edward Turlington, sec.

Heath, John             Ann Lillaston of Sarah    18 Sep 1813
     John Turlington, sec.

Heath, John Robinson     Mary Gorgan              20 Jan 1807
     Major R. Heath, sec.

Heath, Joseph            Susanna Heath            11 Feb 1786
     Henry Heath, sec.

Heath, Josiah B.         Prissey Phillips          8 Dec 1808
                         of Matthias
     Mattihias Phillips, sec.

Heath, Louis D.          Sarah Ann Core (wid)     27 Sep 1845

Heath, Major             Peggy Harom              27 Jan 1806
     Robert Nock, sec.

Heath, Major R. (wdr)    Margaret Kelly of Isaiah 13 Feb 1826
     George Beach, sec.

Heath, William           Sally Haley of Ben.      16 Aug 1809
     Bennet Mason, sec.
```

Heath, William   Sally Haley   25 Jan 1808
    James Hornsby, sec.

Hellenese, Peter   Sally Williams   27 Apr 1829
                        (wid John)
        David Watts and Thomas Tatham, sec.

Henderson, Edward   Sarah Dunstan   23 Feb 1831
    Drummond Massey and Joseph Henderson, sec.

Henderson, Edward FN   Tamer Gusten FN   18 Oct 1815
    Samuel Henderson, sec.

Henderson, Edward, (wdr) Margaret Johnson   18 Feb 1837
    Bundick Taylor and James Johnson, sec.

Henderson, Isaac (wdr) Mary L. Piper (wid)   8 Dec 1820
    William Kendall, sec.

Henderson, Jacob   Mary C. Taylor   6 Nov 1839
    (wdr)   (wid of George)
    A. M. Powekk, sec.

Henderson, James   Peggy Johnson   19 Oct 1801
    John Johnson, sec.

Henderson, James   Margaret Waterfield 19 Oct 1841

Henderson, John   Martha Boston   16 Oct 1799
    George Bonwell, sec.

Henderson, John   Nancy Downing   29 Dec 1828
    of Brittingham   (wid John)
    Oliver Logan and Charles, Garrett sec.

Henderson, Joseph   Maria Massey   6 Jan 1829
    of Brittingham   of Caleb
    John Slocomb, sec.

Henderson, Lemuel   Catherine Beard   23 Dec 1805
    Zadoc Selby, sec.

Henderson, Littleton P. Elvira W. Bagwell   19 Dec 1822
    Richard D. Bayly, sec.

Henderson, Robert   Polly Gunter   19 Feb 1818
    of Robert   of Laban
    Thomas R. Riley, sec.

Henderson, Samuel   Sarah A. Parker Drummond 8 May 1810
    William Downing, sec.

```
Henderson, Samuel J.      Susan S. Logan            24 Mar 1851
                          of Oliver , dec'd.

Henderson, William        Catherine McKeel          10 Jul 1803
     Thomas Rodgers, sec.

Henderson, William H.     Harriet A. Dunton          7 Jan 1838

Henderson, William        Elizabeth Foster          18 Apr 1834
     Elijah Miles, sec.

Henderson, William A.     Harriet A. Dunton         24 Jan 1838
     Edmund Bayly, sec.


Henderson, William        Sarah Turner (wid)        15 Jan 1828
     Littleton P. Henderson, sec.

Henderson, William        Cassey West               21 Dec 1816
     of Samuel           of Comfort Twiford
     James Eichelberger, sec.

Henderson. Henry          Elizabeth Massey          31 Jul 1803
     William Slocomb, sec.

Hickman, Asa              Elizabeth Bell            25 Apr 1825
     (wdr)               of Esther
     Nathaniel Lang, sec.

Hickman, Arthur           Betsy Parks               16 Apr 1800
     John Dix, sec.

Hickman, Arthur           Betsy Only                 2 Jan 1801

Hickman, Asa              Kessy Lilliston           30 Aug 1817
     of Thomas           of Selby
     Michael Riggins and John Watson, sec.

Hickman, Ayres W.         Molly Dowty of Jeptha     28 Jul 1828
     Samuel Follio, sec.

Hickman, Charles          Ann Young                 25 Apr 1825
     of Edward           (wiw William)
     James Floyd, sec.   Tully Beadey as to ages

Hickman, Dennis           Bridget Dix                2 Apr 1792

Hickman, Edmund           Polly Fitchett            25 Dec 1826
     of Stephen          of William
     Thomas Hickman, sec.

Hickman, Edward           Nancy Bunting             19 May 1834
```

of Smith
John Elliott, sec.

Hickman, Edward   Sally Roberts   14 Apr 1813
    Levi Dix, sec.

Hickman, Edward   Peggy Parker   25 Aug 1787
    Samuel Parker, sec.

Hickman, George   Critty Copes   11 Apr 1825
  of Laban   of William, de'c.d
    Thomas Pewsey, sec.

Hickman, George T.   Elizabeth Bull   13 Feb 1821
  of John   of George, dec'd.
    Revel Dix, sec.

Hickman, George L.   Emily C. Riley   5 Dec 1833
    Jonathan West, sec.

Hickman, Henry   Mary Ann Snead   18 Sep 1832
                         of Elizabeth
    Elizabeth Snead and Thomas Crowson, sec.

Hickman, Henry   Lissa Balye   10 Oct 1780

Hickman, Isaac   Margaret Copes   24 Dec 1831
                         (wid John)
    George Hickman and Thomas P. Bagwell, sec.

Hickman, Isaiah   Mary Long   13 Sep 1803
    William Ardis, sec.

Hickman, Jesse   Tabitha W. Lilliston   30 Mar 1809
    John Lambden, sec.

Hickman, John Jr.   Polly Colony   8 Mar 1806
    James Ailworth, sec.

Hickman, John Berry   Mary Pettitt   13 Feb 1787
    Thomas Hickman, sec.

Hickman, John of Ben.   Henny Pettit of Wm.   3 Jan 1820
    Thomas Pettit, sec.

Hickman, John   Henny Pettit   3 Jan 1820

Hickman, John H.   Elizabeth Moore   19 Dec 1848
                         of William S., dec'd.
    Henry B. Lilliston, sec.

Hickman, Kendall   Mary W. Callier   28 Jul 1817

WIlliam Hickman, sec.

Hickman, Kendall   Elizabeth Bundick of Wm. 18 Dec 1809
    Justice Bundick, sec.

Hickman, Raymond   Polly Dauzey   28 Nov 1821
    (wdr)   (wid William)
    James White, sec.

Hickman, Revel   Hessy Warner   5 May 1808
    William Warner Jr., sec.

Hickman, Richard   Polly Prewit   21 Aug 1829
    William Northam of E. and Henry B. Northam, sec.

Hickman, Richard   Ann Barnes of John   27 Jun 1815
    Jacob Warner and William Riley, sec.

Hickman, Richard   Elizabeth Waterfield   5 Jan 1787
    Selby Hichman, sec.

Hickman, Robert   Rachel Smith (wid)   3 Jan 1833

Hickman, Robert   Ann Starling   18 Apr 1837

Hickman, Robert   Rachel Smith   18 Dec 1832
                        (wid of Ezekiel)
    Levi Moore and George Moore, sec.

Hickman, Robert   Ann Starling   15 Apr 1837
    of Isaiah   of John
    Major Mason, sec.

Hickman, Samuel   Caty Only   14 Feb 1841
    James R. Taylor, sec.

Hickman, Spencer   Peggy Bayly   31 May 1791

Hickman, Stephen   Hessy Satchell   21 Dec 1816
    John Only, sec.

Hickman, Stephen   Esther Dix   15 Oct 1796

Hickman, Thomas of Tho. Tippah Pettitt of Wm.   25 May 1818
    Charles Lewis, sec.

Hickman, Thomas   Dulaney Lillaston   3 Jun 1785
    Willett Lillaston, sec.

Hickman, Thomas   Sally Fitzgerald   29 Sep 1829
    of Stephen   of Elisha

Southy W. Bull and William E. Bevans, sec.

Hickman, William K.   Henrietta Ball   9 Dec 1839
    John Scarburgh and Nathaniel W. Bird, sec.

Hickman, William   Eliza Henderson   21 Sep 1818
    of Hampton   of James
    William Marshall, sec.

Hickman, William   Nancy Melson   18 Jul 1852
                   of Polly

Higgins, Michael H.   Marianna Parramore   22 Jan 1844

Hill, Broadwater   Ann Richison (wid)   2 Jan 1810
    Ralph Richison, sec.

Hill, James   Narcissa Brittingham 13 Jul 1811
                  (wid Elijah)
    John Gladding, sec.

Hill, John   Elizabeth Waters   25 Mar 1823
    of Broadwater   of William
    William A. Marshall, sec. William Waters, consent

Hill, Joseph   Anna Payne   2 Jul 1852
    of Timothy

Hill, Lewis FN   Arisla FN   26 Dec 1820
    Jingo Johnson, sec.

Hill, Robert   Sophia Collins   17 Feb 1809
    Richard D. Bayly, sec.

Hill, Timothy (Capt.)   Rebecca Russell of Jno. 15 May 1822
    David Watts and Richard D. Bayly, sec.

Hill, William Sr.   Polly Brittingham   1 Dec 1818
                  (wid Levin)
    Samuel J. Merrill and Thomas D. Welburn, sec.

Hinman, Argil C.   Ann Gillespie   14 Jun 1836
                   orphan of James
    Henry Berry, sec.

Hinman, Elijah   Nancy Milburn   26 Aug 1816
    of Moses   of Joachim
    James Duncan, sec.

Hinman, Ezekiel   Sally Northam   10 Aug 1819
    of Isaiah   of Custis
    Custis Northam, sec.

```
Hinman, Galen              Caty Andrews              9 May 1812
     Zorobabel West, sec.

Hinman, George             Polly Young               2 Dec 1797

Hinman, James T.           Sally Kilman (wid)        1 Apr 1845

Hinman, John               Elizabeth Ayres          14 Mar 1835
     of Window             of Thomas
     Thomas Ayres and Elizabeth Lewis, sec.

Hinman, Littleton A.       Polly Barns of John      18 Jan 1827
     Richard Hickman and William W. Dix, sec.

Hinman, Littleton          Serena Taylor            16 Jan 1847
     Edward N. Taylor and LGeorge Fletcher, sec.

Hinman, Major              Peggy Bunting            31 Oct 1808
                           (wid John)
     James Gillett, sec.


Hinman, Major              Mrs. Seymour Hickman     26 Dec 1798
                           (wid)

Hinman, Moses Wise         Mary Waterfield           3 Aug 1824
     of Thomas             (wid Jacob)
     Henry Whaley and John Coleburn, sec.

Hinman, Moses              Elizabeth Howard         17 Jun 1799
     Little Walker, sec.

Hinman, Perry              Hetty Warrington of Geo. 28 Dec 1825
     Abbott Warrington, sec.

Hinman, Samuel C.          Elizabeth Young of Tho.  29 Jan 1827
     Ezekiel Hinman and George Christopher, sec.

Hinman, Samuel C.          Elizabeth Hickman         7 Aug 1823
                           of Stephen
     George Precott, sec.

Hinman, Samuel             Mary Watson              15 Feb 1856
     (wdr)                 of Mitchell

Hinman, Stephen            Margaret Ann Lewis       17 Dec 1850
                           of Issac, dec'd.

Hinman, Thomas             Mary Young               20 Oct 1837
     Robert C. Parks, sec.

Hinman, William            Elizabeth Taylor         14 Dec 1839
```

Godiah Bell, sec.

Hinman, William P.   Elizabeth Ewell   25 Dec 1848
                            of Galan
      Richard T. Savage and David Mears, sec.

Hinman, William   Tabitha Bundick   3 Nov 1796

Hinman, William   Elizabeth Riggen   9 Jul 1811
     of Anne   ward of John Teackle Esq.
     George Bell, sec.

Hinman, William   Sarah Warrington   25 Feb 1807
                            (wid George)
      Thomas W. Bayly, sec.

Hitchens, Charles   Ann Harrison   18 Dec 1820
     of Richard   of William
     William Harrison, sec.

Hitchens, Ezekiel (wdr)   Mary Kelly of Wm.   1 Sep 1823
     John Kelly, sec.

Hitchens, James   Sally Ironmonger   1 Jul 1823
Hitchens, John   Elizabeth Harrison   31 May 1823
     of Ezekiel   of William
     James Hitchens, sec.

Hitchens, John   Margaret Pitchet of Jno.   6 Sep 1828
     John Phillips of John, sec.

Hoffman, James   Nancy Lucas   11 May 1803
     George Wilson, sec.

Hoffman, William   Molly Hutson   2 Feb 1800
     George Wilson, sec.

Holden, James FN   Sarah Floyd FN   20 Dec 1839
     John E. Ames and Evin Mathinson, sec.

Holden, James (FN)   Judy Floyd   26 Dec 1839

Holland, Asa   Mary Matthews   28 Nov 1831
                            (wid Atkins)
      Edmund S. Godwin and Shadrach Taylor, sec.

Holland, Capt. Edward   Clara West   14 Sep 1840

Holland, John W.   Ann Smith   15 Feb 1819
     of Benjamin   of John, dec'd.
     James N. Hargis, sec.

```
Holland, John S. D.        Sally Watson              27 Sep 1841

Holland, Richard FN        Delina Taylor             26 Dec 1849

Holland, Samuel H.         Clarissa Russell           4 Jan 1839
                             of James
       James Russell, sec.

Holland, Thomas            Elizabeth Selby           12 Jan 1799
                             of Nancy
       Thomas Cropper, Benj. Potter and Edmund Bayly, sec.

Holland, William           Elizabeth Massey          16 Jan 1811
       William R. Drummond, sec.

Holland, William           Elizabeth Merrill          2 Jul 1816
       (wdr)                 of Joseph
       David Miles and Richard D. Bayly, sec.

Holland, William           Mary Broadwater of Jos.   18 Jan 1814
       Caleb Broadwater, sec.

Holly, Abel                Elizabeth Chandler         8 Aug 1840
       James J. Ailworth, sec.


Holmes, Thompson           Elizabeth A. Stockly      29 May 1805
       Richard D. Bayly, sec.

Holston, John              Catey Prewit              11 May 1784
       Thomas Snead, sec.

Holston, John              Nancy Bell                20 Dec 1817
                             of Thorowgood
       William Rayfield, sec.

Holstone, John (wdr)       Sally West of John        24 Mar 1818
       Mary West, widow John, sec.

Holt, Capt. Edward         Margaret A. Beach         14 Jul 1841
                           ward of James Ashley

Holt, James S.            Ann T. Mapp               19 Jun 1829
       George L. Mapp, sec.

Holt, James S.            Mary Ashly                27 Jul 1835
       (wdr)                of George
       Albert G. Ashly, sec.

Holt, John                Elizabeth Taylor          28 Mar 1808
                           (wid John)
       John Field, sec.
```

```
Holt, Samuel              Patty Wheatley           10 Dec 1827
     alias Hancock
     Dennis Kelly and son Sally Taylor, widow of Purnel, and
     William R. Custis, sec.

Hope, Charles             Rachel Bell               6 May 1786
     Caleb Broadwater, sec.

Hope, Elijah              Leah Small               12 Nov 1813
                          (wid Levi)
     George Abbott, sec.

Hope, George              Priscilla Watson         30 Dec 1822
     (wdr)                (wid Gilette)
Kendall Hope, sec.

Hope, George              Laura J.T. Wessells      26 Jul 1841
                          of Thomas
     James Wessells, sec.

Hope, George              Nance Taylor             21 Jun 1811
     Crippen Taylor, sec.

Hope, George              Laura J. Wessells        29 Jul 1841


Hope, George              Ann Ritta Fitchet        24 Nov 1818
     (wdr)                of Jonathan
     Samuel G. Taylor, sec.

Hope, James (wdr)         Elizabeth Johnson        22 Mar 1826
                          of Samuel
     Richard Gillespie, sec.

Hope, James              Betsy Foster             18 Apr 1811
     Elijah Beauchamp, sec.

Hope, James (wdr)         Margaret Young           18 Sep 1832
     Richard Gillespie, sec.

Hope, James L.           Eliza Budd                4 Jan 1841
     Major D. Colonna, sec.

Hope, John               Ann James                20 Feb 1837
     Samuel Hope, sec.

Hope, John (wdr)         Elizabeth S. Hope (wid)  14 Dec 1843

Hope, Kendall            Molly Bundick of Wm.     27 Dec 1813
     Kendall Hickman, sec.
```

```
Hope, Robert              Caroline Johnson        16 Jun 1847
                          of Samuel
     Zorababel Chandler,  sec.

Hope, Samuel C.           Elizabeth S. Wright       6 Dec 1837
                          ward of Henry P. Parks
     Southy Lewis, sec.

Hope, Thomas              Margaret Savage           4 Feb 1812
     Robert Broadwater,   sec.

Hope, William             Ann Wright                2 Apr 1839
                          of Thomas
     James H. Rew, sec.

Hopkins, Capt. Henry      Mary Matthews            25 Aug 1851

Hopkins, Ellison A.       Jane Hall Deeble         29 Sep 1828
     John Smith (CRad) and James B. Poulson, sec.

Hopkins, Henry            Margaret Dix             22 Apr 1841
                          of Nancy
     Thomas Lewis, sec.

Hopkins, Henry            Polly Tarr               17 Jan 1806
     David Watts, sec.

Hopkins, Isaac            Hetty Coard              16 May 1831

Hopkins, Joseph           Patty Crockett           18 Jun 1803
     John Tyler, sec.

Hopkins, Joseph           Elizabeth Dix            30 Mar 1840
                          of Molly
     Samuel Hickman, sec.

Hopkins, Nathaniel        Betsey Thornton           7 May 1803
     David Watts, sec.

Hopkins, Stephen          Jane Melson              15 Dec 1819
     of Stephen           of Nancy
     William Lee, sec.

Hopkins, Stephen          Ann Nelson               15 Nov 1842

Hopkins, Stephen (wdr)    Susan M. Bull            16 May 1838
     Isaiah N. Bagwell and William P. Joyner, sec.

Hornsby, Eli              Betsy Hornsby (wid)      21 Dec 1807

Hornsby, Eli              Anne Bird                24 Apr 1800
     Edmund Hornsby, sec.
```

Hornsby, Eli   Betsy Hornsby   22 Dec 1806
                            (wid of Edmond)
        Epraim Outten, sec.

Hornsby, James   Elizabeth Bradford   30 Dec 1851

Hornsby, James   Mary Copes   12 Oct 1807
        Bennet Mason of Caleb, sec.

Hornsby, William   Polly Hornsby   16 Sep 1801
        James Hornsby, sec.

Horsey, Dr. James E.   Sarah Ann Custis   15 Jun 1839
        James W. Custis and Edmund R. Allen, sec.

Houston, John M.   Eliza J. Stant   24 Dec 1839
        Walter Broadwater, sec.

Howard, Charles   Tinny Savage Bloxom   23 Feb 1813
        Nicholas P. Godwin, sec.

Howard, George   Tabitha Bloxom   5 Jun 1807
                            of Stephen
        George Marshall, sec.

Howard, John   Mary Northam   25 Mar 1811
        Archibald Trader, sec.

Howard, Selby   Nancy Walker   9 Feb 1804
        William Hutson, sec.
Howe, William (wdr)   Shady Merrill (wid)   29 Dec 1840
        John Roulson, sec.

Hudson, George Gore   Molly Shay   2 Sep 1789

Hundley, Christopher   Euphemia Savage   4 Jun 1832
        Joseph Crocket and William P. Moore Jr., sec.

Hunt, John J.   Elisha Parks   27 Jun 1834

Hunt, Thomas   Abigail Sturges   1 Dec 1775
        John Barnes, sec.

Hurley, Robert   Comfort Ann Taylor   29 Aug 1853
                            of Samuel T. Taylor

Hurst, James   Susan Mister   20 Jan 1842

Hurst, Thomas   Susannah Millenner   2 Oct 1809
        Daniel Drummond, sec.

Hurst, William   Molly Colony   3 Jan 1796

```
Hurst, William              Sally Guy                   31 Jan 1801
    William Lewis, sec.

Hurst, William              Margaret Williams            7 Jan 1837
    of Thomas               of Jane
    John S. Lilliston, sec.

Hurst, William              Margaret                    11 Jan 1837

Huslay, John W.             Mary Dunton                  4 Sep 1832
                            (wid of Benjamin)
    William Wyatt, sec.

Husley, John W.             Mary Dunton                 10 Sep 1832

Hutchinson, Babel           Sarah Fisher                31 Jan 1820
    of Babel                of George
    George S. Fisher, sec.

Hutchinson, Edmund W.       Caroline E. Bloxom           6 Jan 1854
                            of William

Hutchinson, Edward G.       Elizabeth Snead             14 Jan 1817
                            (wid George)
    Henry Walker, sec.

Hutchinson, George          Laura Stephens               5 Jan 1843

Hutchinson, John            Leah Jones                   6 Aug 1807
    James Thornton, sec.

Hutchinson, John W.         Harriet T. Rodgers          25 Nov 1823
                            orphan Levi
    James Walker and James Eichelberger, sec.

Hutchinson, John            Catherine Revil Dunton      27 May 1807
    William W. Burton, sec.

Hutchinson, John            Cristobel Rodgers           25 Nov 1823

Hutchinson, Richard         Molly Rodgers of Molly      22 Dec 1807
    William Pitts, sec.

Hutchinson, Robert          Maria Mason of Nancy        28 Dec 1820
    Arthur R. Powell, sec.

Hutchinson, Robert          Elizabeth Walker            31 Mar 1806
    John Walker, sec.

Hutchinson, William         Elizabeth Window             1 Jan 1810
                            (wid Abel)
    James Hornsby, sec.
```

```
Hutson, Elijah          Sinah Hoffman              14 Jan 1814
     Teackle Trader, sec.

Hutson, John            Elizabeth Marshall         13 Jan 1813
     John Marshall Sr., sec.

Hutson, Thomas          Nancy Simpson              26 Aug 1789

Hylop, James            Mary Downing of Francis    28 Mar 1825
     Major Savage, sec.

Hyslop, John W.         Mary R. Ames               29 Oct 1834
     Edward H. Ames, sec.

Hyslop, Levin           Susey Davis                11 Sep 1798
     Kendall Hyslop, sec.

Hyslop, Smith of Geo.   Sally Savage of John       29 Sep 1817
     George S. Fisher sec.

Hyslop, Willliam        Nancy Mears                24      1803
     Zorobabel Kellam, sec.
```

Ironmonger, John of Geo. Sally Edwards of Zoro   31 Dec 1807
     Zadoc Poulson, sec.

Ironmonger, Levin   Sarah Chandler   25 Dec 1804
     Edward Ironmonger, sec.

```
Jackson, John              Rebecca Laws of Jno.    20 Feb 1815
     William Matthews, sec.

Jacob, James B.            Sally Ewell of Wm. (SS)  5 May 1818
     John B. Jacob, sec.

Jacob, John                Nancy Trader             8 Jul 1798

Jacob, Philip              May J. Bloxom            3 Jan 1840

Jacob, Phillip             Mary Bloxom             31 Dec 1838
     Charles Tatham and John Massey, sec.

Jacob, Richard             Margaret Burton         25 May 1789

Jacob, William  E.         Charlotte A. Mears      23 Nov 1847
                           orphan of William
          John E. Smith, sec.

Jacobs, John B.            Nancy Bundick of Wm.    12 Dec 1821
     William B. Blackstone, sec., William Bundick, cons.

James, David               Leah Young              23 May 1807
     Robert Young and Richard R. Savage, sec.

James, Edward              Sarah Whealton of Wm.   18 Jun 1850
     N. H. Watson and Isaac K. Stevenson, sec.

James, Ezekiel H.          Elizabeth McMaster      18 Jan 1812
                           (wid William)
          Thomas James, sec.

James, George W.           Margaret A. Barnes       5 Dec 1852
                           of Elizabeth

James, James               Molly Hope              15 Jan 1801
     Selby Lilleston, sec.

James, Jesse K.            Virginia A. Lane        18 Oct 1850
                           (wid of Sewell J.)

James, Levin of Wm.        Eliza Bird of Eburn      1 Oct 1821
     William Bird, sec.

James, Levin               Eliza Bird               1 Oct 1821

James, Levin T.            Elizabeth K. Mears      21 Jan 1848
     William H. Wise and George K. Turner, sec.

James, Levin T.            Eliza R. Mears          26 Jan 1848
```

```
James, Thomas of Thos.     Susan E. Haley            20 Jun 1847

James, Thomas of Wm.       Molly Mason of Geo.       29 Jan 1816
     Levin James and Robert Kellam, sec.

James, Thomas              Anne Bagwell Watson       15 Dec 1808
     John W. Watson, sec.

Jenkins, Benjamin          Sally D. Drummond of Wm.   7 Dec 1847
     Henry Parker and Mears Smith, sec.

Jenkins, Custis            Sally Corbin              25 Jun 1788

Jenkins, George FN         Betty Rosary FN           17 Sep 1814
     George Harmon, sec.

Jenkins, George            Rebecca Broadwater        30 Jan 1832
     Savage Broadwater, sec.

Jenkins, James             Polly Corbin              15 Dec 1797

Jenkinson, Robert          Elizabeth Gascoynes       20 Jun 1786
     John Smith, sec.

Jennings, Robert C.        Mary Jones of John        25 May 1835
     Samuel Carey and John Jones, sec.

Jester, Charles            Delilah Sharpley of Wm.   23 Mar 1849
     John Thornton, sec.

Jester, Elijah             Hetty Birch               11 Apr 1839

Jester, Jacob              Elizabeth Edwards         14 May 1827
                           of Laban
     John Jester and Francis Lindsay, sec.

Jester, James of Jms.      May Jones                 25 Oct 1821

Jester, James              Molly Taylor              18 Jul 1812

Jester, James              Rebecca Jones             31 Dec 1803
     Parker Thornton, sec.

Jester, James of Jms.      Euphemia Russell          25 May 1839

Jester, James             Leah Gillespie              1 Aug 1835
     of John               of Esther Bloxom
     Argyl E. Hinman, sec.

Jester, James             Nancy Jones               28 May 1838
     (wdr)                 (wid of David)
     Timothy Hill and John Lewis, sec.
```

- 141 -

```
Jester, James (wdr)        Hetty Hall (wid)          11 Aug 1834
     Esan Boston and Levin Core, sec.

Jester, James of Jno.      Mary Jones of Jms.        27 Aug 1821
     Josiah Doughty, sec.

Jester, John               Anna Hall                 12 May 1833

Jester, John of Isaiah     Nancy Edwards of Laban    13 Jan 1823
     William Dolley and William Killmon, sec.

Jester, John               Nancy Bloxom of Molly     20 Jan 1834
     Samuel C. Johnson, sec.

Jester, John               Rachel Trader             28 May 1815
                           (wid Levi)
          Jesse Miles, sec.

Jester, John M.            Mary Turlington            1 Jun 1814
     Jacob Warner, sec.

Jester, John               Anna Hall of John          6 Apr 1833
     Henry Bagwell, sec.

Jester, Joseph             Susan Edwards of Laban    10 Jan 1824
     John Jester, sec.

Jester, Kendall (wdr)      Eliizabeth Lewis of Wm.    6 Jun 1833
     Isaac Lewis and William W. Dix, sec.

John FN                    Peggy FN                  22 Jun 1789

Johnson, Amos              Susanna Stockly           27 Apr 1808
     Jacob Edwards, sec.

Johnson, Caleb             Peggy Henderson            5 Apr 1802
     John Johnson, sec.

Johnson, Caleb             Euphamia Marshall         20 Jun 1814
                           of Solomon, dec'd.
          William Johnson, sec.

Johnson, George M.         Mary Ann Mears            25 Dec 1849
                           of Michael
          Richard B. East, sec.

Johnson, Harvey            Sally Wessells            25 Mar 1833
                           (wid of Harvey Johnson)
          John W. Bird, sec.

Johnson, Isaiah Sr.        Sally Ewell               23 Nov 1829
                           (wid William Ching)
```

John P. Drummond, sec.

Johnson, Isaiah	Tabitha J. East	28 Oct 1850

Johnson, Isaiah of Tho.   Abby Russell   18 Feb 1809
    Josiah Speight, sec.

Johnson, James T.   Mary Sterling   14 Jan 1857
   (wdr)   of Samuel

Johnson, James   Adah Garrison   25 Nov 1816
    of Edmund   of Archibald
    John Darby, sec.

Johnson, James   Laney Harmon   30 Mar 1801

Johnson, James   Mary Delastatius   28 Jan 1829
                    of Thomas C.
    Thomas C. Delastatius, sec.

Johnson, John S. (wdr)   Elizabeth Somers   24 Feb 1839
    Samuel C. Johnson and Zadock Nock, sec.

Johnson, John of Jno.   Charlotte Taylor of Jms.   7 Aug 1826
    Stringer Marshall, sec.

Johnson, John P.   Tabitha Ames   4 Oct 1803
    Jesse Ames, sec.

Johnson, John S.   Anna P. West of Jno.   23 Dec 1828
    John D. Parkes, sec.

Johnson, John R. Jr.   Elizabeth Mitchell   3 Jan 1837
                    of Stephen
    George S. Rew, sec.

Johnson, John S. of Sam. Nancy Bell of Wm.   26 Oct 1819
    Isaiah Johnson, sec., Nicey Bell, parent and guardian, cons.

Johnson, John   Polly Shrieves   17 Jan 1816
    Isaiah Johnson, sec.

Johnson, John S. (wdr)   Mary Ann Tatham (wid)   25 Jun 1855

Johnson, John   Polly Marshall   31 Jan 1801
    Isaac Holland, sec.

Johnson, John   Maria Bell   28 Feb 1833
    of William   of Anthony
    William Johnson and Anthony Bell, sec.

Johnson, John   Elizabeth Mitchell   4 Jan 1837

Johnson, John   Elizabeth Taylor   20 Sep 1799

Johnson, John   Polly Sharpley   27 Jul 1805
    Henry Thornton, sec.

Johnson, John T.   Margaret Fisher   20 Jul 1842

Johnson, Peter FN   Phillis Morris FN   30 Mar 1813
    Daniel Morris FN, sec.

Johnson, Purnel   Peggy Bull   27 Aug 1798
    George Finney, sec.

Johnson, Samuel   Rosey Corbin   4 Mar 1800
    Richard Kelly, sec.

Johnson, Samuel   Caroline Russell   25 Jan 1846

Johnson, Samuel   Charlotte Ball   10 Mar 1829
    of William   (wid Noah Ball)
    Wallop Read and Peter Copes, sec.

Johnson, Samuel (wdr)   Hetty Merrill   16 Jun 1841

Johnson, Samuel of Wm.   Hester Ann Copes of Peter 4 Jan 1826
    Peter Copes and William Johnson, sec.

Johnson, Thomas   Sally Latchum   4 May 1818
    of John   (wid Obed.)
    William Davis of Samuel, sec.

Johnson, Thomas   Nancy Adams   30 Jul 1832
    Obed Adams, sec.

Johnson, Willaim   Sally Beavans   22 Apr 1801
    James Collins, sec.

Johnson, William   Polly Mason   18 Mar 1823
    (wdr)   (wid Ayres)
    Walter Douglass and Henry Harvey, sec.

Johnson, William S.   Lucinda Henderson   23 Jun 1842

Johnson, William   Sally A. Rew   3 Jul 1838
    of Isaiah   of Dennis H.
    Dennis H. Rew, sec.

Johnson, William   Nancy Lingo   30 Mar 1812
    William Smith, sec.

```
Johnson, William          Peggy Gibb of William      22 Mar 1806
     John Young, sec.

Johnson, William (wdr)    Mary Allen                 30 Jan 1818
     of William           of Zadock
     John Matthews, sec.

Jolliff, Richard          Eckey Aimes                22 Sep 1800
     Robert Twiford, sec.

Jones, Daniel             Nancy Sharpley             18 Oct 1834
     (wdr)                (wid of Daniel)
     Major Budd, sec.

Jones, Daniel             Sally Merrill              28 Oct 1833
     (wdr)                (wid of William)
     Henry Fletcher, sec.

Jones, Daniel             Comfort Tunnell            27 Mar 1810
     William Thornton, sec.

Jones, Edward             Polly Whealton              6 Sep 1790

Jones, George             Sarah Waters                3 Oct 1809
     John Jones, sec.

Jones, George             Elizabeth Whealton         10 Oct 1805
     (ward of T. Hill)

Jones, Hiram              Harriet Bloxom             24 Mar 1829
                          orphan Woodman
     Samuel Bloxom and Michael R. Whealton, sec.

Jones, James of Jms.      Sally Read of Wm. P.       25 Feb 1822
     William Read and James Jester, sec.

Jones, James             Anne Cherricks              1 Aug 1853
                          of Daniel

Jones, James Jr.          Euphemia Taylor            27 Mar 1833
     Nathaniel Ssmart and Alfred O. Melvin, sec.

Jones, James             Sally Staton                4 Apr 1804
     Joseph Andrews, sec.

Jones, John               Ann Lewis                  15 Jul 1835
     of John
     John Jones and Peter Blades, sec.

Jones, John H.            Mary Scott                 16 Jun 18852
     (wdr)                (wid of Thomas W.)
```

Jones, John B.   Francis T. Custis   13 Apr 1840
    William H. B. Custis, sec.

Jones, Levi   Luda Lewis   7 Apr 1803
    Ralph Justice, sec.

Jones, Samuel C.   Elizabeth J. Brittingham 27 Nov 1848
    John Brittingham and James H. Fletcher, sec.

Jones, Smith   Mary Staton   2 Dec 1831
                            of Warrington
    Henry E. Phillip and John S. Dix, sec.

Jones, William (wdr)   Elizabeth Hones of Tho. 27 Oct 1823
    James Wishart and William Bird, sec.

Jones, William   Sarah Whealton   3 Dec 1805
    John Jones, sec.

Jones, William   Betsy Lawrence   14 Apr 1820
    (wdr)   (wid William)
    George D. Fisher, sec.

Jones, William   Sophia Parramore   24 Mar 1853
                           of John Parramore

Jones, William   Sarah Wheelton   10 Apr 1805

Jones, William   Maria J. Crockett   18 Dec 1844

Jones, William   Susa Fisher of Philip   4 Jan 1808
    George D. Fisher, sec.

Joyne, William   Margaret Mears   2 Dec 1774
    John Powell, sec.

Joynes, Edward D.   Ann Scott   25 Jul 1835

Joynes, Edward A.   Elizabeth S. Andrews   30 Mar 1818
    of Wm. dec'd.   of Robert, dec'd.
    Thomas W. Mears and Thomas Parker, sec.

Joynes, Edward D.   Ann Scott of Catharine   25 Feb 1835
    George C. Waters, sec.

Joynes, Elias   Margaret Smith   25 Jul 1814
    William Joynes, sec.

Joynes, Elias   Jane Smith   16 Mar 1808
    Stephen Warrington, sec.

Joynes, James of Jno.   Mahala Stringer of Jacob 5 Dec 1820

William Garrison, sec.

Joynes, John T.R.   Catherine K. Bayly   15 Nov 1830
    Thomas R. Joynes, sec.

Joynes, John   Attalantic Gectridge   6 Feb 1785
    William Gibb, sec.

Joynes, John R. of Wm.   Susan J. Colonna   29 Apr 1833
                          of Elizabeth
    John W. Colonna, sec.

Joynes, John   Anne Davis   27 Jun 1803
    Major S. Pitts, sec.

Joynes, Levin S.   Charlotte B. Satchell   10 Jul 1809
    Edmund W. Downing, sec.

Joynes, Thomas R. Jr.   Nancy Ames   31 Dec 1851

Joynes, Thomas R. Jr.   Nancy B. Ames   29 Dec 1851
                          (wid of Joseph)

Joynes, Thomas R.   Anne Bell Satchell   2 Apr 1812
    Alexander McCollom, sec.

Joynes, William   Levice Ann Snead   13 Sep 1813
    Bowdoin Snead, sec.

Joynes, William P.   Adeline R. Custis   6 Jan 1841

Joynes, William   Tabitha Snead of Tully   14 May 1813
    Joseph Ames, sec.

Joynes, William   Nancy Nock   28 Oct 1811
    John Nock, sec.

Joynes, William P.   Adeline R. Custis   28 Dec 1840
    Isaiah N. Bagwell, sec.

Joynes, Wm. of Reuben   Haddasa Rodgers   10 May 1807
    Walter Welsh, sec.

Jubilee, Asa FN   Sarah Sample FN   29 Dec 1834
    William S. Sturgis, sec.

Jubilee, Custis FN   Eliza Roan FN   10 Feb 1835
                          of Daniel FN
    William S. Sturgis and Levin Core, sec.

Jubilee, John FN   Nancy Bayly FN   29 Oct 1832
    James D. Benson, sec.

```
Jubilee, Otto              Nanny Teague              25 Mar 1811
     Shadrach Ames, sec.

Jubilee, Samuel FN         Mary Morris FN             8 Feb 1853
                           of Levin FN

Jubilee, Shepherd FN       Rachel Holt of Wm. FN     31 Jan 1820
     William Holt, sec.

Jubilee, William FN        Henny Holt FN             29 Mar 1847
     Charles T. Sturgis and George E. Coleburn, sec.

Jubilee, William FN        Sally Sample FN           28 Sep 1842

Justice, Isaiah            Tabitha Lewis of Geo.     24 Jan 1811
     George Lewis, sec.

Justice, Isaiah            Sally Lewis               17 Jan 1803
     Samuel Russell, sec.

Justice, James of Caty     Hetty Adams of Obed       20 Feb 1826
     Obed Adams and Edmund Baker, sec.

Justice, James            Sally Conquest of Jos.     27 Feb 1833
     David Abbott and Levin Core, sec.

Justice, James of Geo.    Milly Taylor                8 Jul 1812
     William Ailworth, sec.

Justice, John H.          Adeline Spence of John     26 Jun 1849
     Gillet Marshall, sec.

Justice, John             Catharine Barnes           20 May 1839
     James Barnes, sec.

Justice, John             Maria Annis                30 Dec 1837
     Custis Annis, sec.

Justice, John             Catherine Barner           23 May 1839

Justice, John             Malinda Wright             30 Aug 1854
                          of Catherine

Justice, Joseph C.        Mary R. Nock               21 Jun 1856
     ward of              (wid of Albert)
     Richard Conquest

Justice, Parker           Scarburgh Melson           12 Nov 1834
     Raymond Riley, sec.

Justice, Preeson          Molly Hutson               29 Oct 1832
     James S. Corburn and henry Taylor, sec.
```

```
Justice, Ralph              Bridget Clemmons            31 Jan 1787
     Nathaniel Beavens, sec.

Justice, Revell             Nancy Lewis of Levina        5 Jan 1835
     Spencer Lewis, sec.

Justice, Richard            Esther Lewis               22 Apr 1812
                            of Absalom
     Absalom Lewis Jr., sec.

Justice, Richard            Elizabeth Robinson         22 Oct 1789
     James Rooks, sec.

Justice, Samuel L.          Rose Ann Miles             27 Feb 1849
                            of Parker
     Henry B. Taylor and John T. Custis, sec.

Justice, Samuel A.          Molly Mears                10 Aug 1842

Justice, Samuel A.          Elizabeth Powell           21 Mar 1814
     Levin Crowson, sec.

Justice, Samuel            Priscilla West              1 Sep 1825
     of Richard           (wid George)
     Richard Justice of Robert and James Justice, sec.

Justice, Samuel A.          Rose Ann Bloxom            20 May 1834
                            of Dewey
     Samuel Wright, sec.

Justice, Teackle            Rose Taylor                10 Jul 1812
     Samuel Walston, sec.

Justice, Thomas             Molly Wright               11 Oct 1802
     Rodger Miles, sec.

Justice, Thomas             Mary H. Taylor              8 Aug 1848
                            of Richard
     Edward Nock and Edward D. Trader, sec.

Justice, William            Elizabeth B. Hall          30 Jun 1852
                            (wid of William)

Justice, William            Susan Taylor of Samuel     15 Jun 1840
     Samuel Taylor, sec.

Justice, William (wdr)    Tabitha Bloxom of Jacob      5 May 1830
     David Watts and Thomas B. Custis, sec.

Justice, William            Comfort Barnes             21 April 1807
     (Back Creek)
     Laban Moore, sec.
```

Justice, William James Ewell, sec.	Sally Taylor of Jms.	28 Jan 1833
Justice, William John Taylor, sec.	Eliza Killman of Chas.	11 Jan 1840
Justice, William (wdr)	Tabitha Bloxom	14 May 1830
Justice, Wm. of Robt. John Nock, sec.	Rebecca Gladding	30 Mar 1812

Keaton, Haywood   Margaret Belote   16 Dec 1848
    Arthur Mears and John J. Blackstone, sec.

Kellam, Abel   Esther Kellam   3 Feb 1812
    Steward Kellam, sec.

Kellam, Abraham   Anne Sinah Lecatte   before 1800
    Shadrack Lecatte, sec.

Kellam, Argel   Leah Kellam   27 Apr 1811
                         (wid Thomas)
    John Kellam, sec.

Kellam, Capt. Walter J. Margaret H. Kellam   25 Sep 1837

Kellam, Charles   Margaret Bird   5 Feb 1821
    of James   of Eburn
    William Bird, sec.

Kellam, Custis   Elizabeth Bird   14 Apr 1825
    (wdr)   orphan Jacob
    Richard Bull Jr., sec., Jno. G. Joynes, Gdn, cons.

Kellam, Custis   Elisabeth Smith   7 Sep 1805
    John Finney, sec.

Kellam, Custis W.   Leah Parkes   12 Oct 1830
                         (wid George)
    John Turlington, sec.

Kellam, Custis   Jane P. Ames   9 Oct 1840

Kellam, Dr. Frederick C.A.   Eliza E. Wise   8 Aug 1841

Kellam, Edmund   Betsy Rodgers   26 Aug 1816
    of John   of Laban
    George S. Fisher, sec.

Kellam, Edmund   Sally Watson   30 Jun 1826
    (wdr)   of William
    Stephen Peusey, sec.

Kellam, Edward W.   Rosa Ann Hyslop   1 Apr 1854
    of Argyl   of James

Kellam, Edward   Nancy Gillispie   12 Jan 1802

Kellam, Elijah S.   Margaret S. Bayly   11 Jun 1845

Kellam, Elijah S.   Henrietta Bird   27 Aug 1838
    of Nathaniel   (wid of Jacob)
    Edmund Garrison, sec.

Kellam, Esau   Elizabeth L. Joynes   21 Jul 1823
    Thomas Mehallonis, sec.

Kellam, Ezekiel   Euphamia Alexander   3 Feb 1812
    Thomas Alexander, sec.

Kellam, Francis   15 Jun 1847

Kellam, Frederick C. A. Eliza E. Wise   15 Feb 1841
                         (wid of John R.)
    Edward C. Russell, sec.

Kellam, George G.   Margaret Joynes   9 Feb 1842

Kellam, George   Adah Kellam   30 Dec 1805
    Esme Bayly, sec.

Kellam, George A.   Ann Hyslop of Smith   1 Apr 1850
    Abel J. Beach, sec.

Kellam, Hauson P.   Valeria Bayly   18 Aug 1837
    Jonathan W. Kellam, sec.

Kellam, Howsen   Betty Turlington   3 May 1787
    George Taylor, sec.

Kellam, Howson   Elizabeth Rodgers   1 Jun 1822
                         (wid Thomas (caulker))
    Howson Mapps, sec.
Kellam, Hutton   Susan Stringer   22 Jan 1827
                         of Jacob
    William N. Ames, sec.

Kellam, Hutchinson   Elizabeth Milby   14 Sep 1814
                         orphan John
    Henry S. Copes, sec.

Kellam, James L.   Sally P. Goffigon   23 Dec 1840

Kellam, James   Esther Elliott   4 Aug 1810
    Thomas Elliott, sec.

Kellam, James   Patience Belote   30 Dec 1839
                         (wid of George)
    Littleton Savage, sec.

Kellam, Jesse L.   Margaret Shields   12 Nov 1823
                         orphan Asa
    Anderson P. Bloxom, sec.

Kellam, John   Eliza Poolman   27 Sep 1803

John Wise, sec.

Kellam, John W.	Margaret W. Kellam of Frederick	14 Jun 1812
Frederick Kellam, sec.		
Kellam, John	Peggy Martin	8 Feb 1806
Smith Martin, sec.		
Kellam, John	Sally Savage of Jacob	1 Dec 1806
Savage of Nelson, sec.		
Kellam, John C. (wdr)	Jane M. K. Scarburgh	8 Nov 1837
Joseph S. Hill and William Burton, sec.		
Kellam, John R. (ward of Custis)	Mary F.	8 Jan 1844
Kellam, John Henry	Elizabeth Shield of Asa	5 Nov 1858
Kellam, John Jr.	Elizabeth Welch of William	11 Oct 1824
George H. Bell, sec.		
Kellam, Levin	Betsy Sturgis	10 May 1803
John A. Bundick and Purnell Twyford, sec.		
Kellam, Michael P.	Ann A. Kellam	12 Sep 1841
Kellam, Nash	Nancy Bloxom of Southy	21 Nov 1807
Southy Bloxom, sec.		
Kellam, Reuben	Nancy Parkinson	15 Mar 1808
William Mehollems, sec.		
Kellam, Revel	Jane Mears of Betsy	16 Jan 1850
Johnna N. A. Elliott and Charles B. Duffield, sec.		
Kellam, Revel	Leah Hornsby	11 Jan 1800
William Budd, sec.		
Kellam, Revel	Jane Mears	27 Jan 1850
Kellam, Revell	Mary Ann Kellam of Spencer	6 Jul 1807
Spencer Kellam, sec.		
Kellam, Robert	Polly Darby	14 Sep 1811
Severn Kellam, sec.		

Kellam, Shepherd	Rosey B. Stewart orphan Andrew	20 Mar 1815
John S. Walker, sec.		
Kellam, Smith of Sacker	Polly Trehearn of Jno.	6 Oct 1819
John Nelson, sec.		
Kellam, Smith	Molly Parker	18 Sep 1787
William Gibb, sec.		
Kellam, Spencer (wdr)	Peggy Smith of Wm.	30 May 1831
Jacob Phillips and Thomas R. Joynes, sec.		
Kellam, Spencer	Margaret Rodgers (wid John)	26 Nov 1827
William D. Chandler and John J. Wise, sec.		
Kellam, Stewart	Ann Maria H. Bradford	15 Jan 1810
Mitchell S. West, sec.		
Kellam, Stockley of Geo.	Comfort Stringer of Jacob	26 Jun 1820
John F. Mears, sec.		
Kellam, Stockley	Elizabeth Stringer	5 Feb 1843
Kellam, Thomas of Shad.	Jane Meers	19 Jun 1809
William Smyth, sec.		
Kellam, Thomas	Mary Lawson	15 Jan 1852
Kellam, Thomas H. Jr.	Susan P. Moore	21 Jan 1833
John Arlington, sec.		
Kellam, Thomas of Argyle	Mary Lawson of W. Lawson, Jr.	12 Jan 1852
Kellam, Thomas R.	Maria Groten	16 May 1844
Kellam, Thomas	Eliza Pusey	15 Aug 1832
Kellam, Thomas	Susanna Bradford of John, dec'd.	14 Sep 1822
William Smyth, sec.		
Kellam, Thomas	Polly Savage	26 Oct 1841
Kellam, Thomas T.	Margaret A. Bradford of Jacob	21 Dec 1831
Henry Walker, sec.		

Kellam, Walter J.   Margaret S. Kellam   25 Sep 1839
     Richard T. Ayress, sec.

Kellam, William L.   Betsy Chambers of Edward 27 Aug 1828
     John Jester and Jacob Jester, sec.

Kellam, William   Anna Underhill of Tho.   4 Feb 1839
     William and Thomas Kellam, sec.

Kellam, William B.   Harriet Poulson   22 Aug 1833

Kellam, William H.   Sarah Miles   9 Jan 1845

Kellam, William A.   Patsy A. Jolliff   29 Mar 1830
                         of Ecky Watson
       Samuel Coleburn, sec.

Kellam, William B.   Harriet Poulson   22 Aug 1835
                         of Zadock
       James Carmine, sec.

Kellam, William E.   Elizabeth S. Bloxom   4 Aug 1852
     of Charles   (wid of Ezekiel R.)

Kellam, William   Anna Underhill   1 Feb 1839

Kellam, William of Jms. Ann Belote of Jms.   23 Sep 1819
     James Belote of Hancock, sec.

Kellam, Zorababel   Bridget Addison   2 Oct 1798
     David Bowman, sec.

Kellen, Sherwood   Peggy Booth   4 Oct 1801
     John Burton, sec.

Kelley, Daniel John   Betsy S. Spence (wid)   3 Oct 1855
     (wdr)

Kelley, George W.   Elizabeth Ann Duncan   26 Dec 1849
                         of Meshack
       George N. Kelley and Noah Davis, sec.

Kelley, Richard   Bridget Brimer   10 Feb 1806
     John Madox, sec.

Kelley, Richardson   Sally Johnson   4 Mar 1800
     Samuel Johnson, sec.

Kelley, Samuel   Mary A. Pitts   31 May 1830
                         of John, dec'd.
       John Kelly, sec.

Kelly, Abel   Elizabeth White Badger   6 Oct 1824
                           of Ezekiel
      Edward Gunter, sec.

Kelly, Arthur   Margaret Badger (wid)   30 Nov 1835
      Geodiah Bell, sec.

Kelly, Arthur   Margaret Boggs   3 Dec 1835

Kelly, Charles   Adah Chandler   17 Jun 1808
                           (wid Solomon)
      Timothy Kelly, sec.

Kelly, Daniel   Nancy Wessells   4 Sep 1846

Kelly, Daniel, hatter   Nancy James of Sally   28 Oct 1828
      James Mears of Arthur, sec.

Kelly, Daniel (Hatter)   Nancy James   27 Oct 1830

Kelly, Daniel   Bridget Brimer (wid)   10 Feb 1806
      John Madux, sec.

Kelly, Dennis   Tabitha Smith   7 May 1821
      Kendal Silverthorne and Samuel Tunnell, sec.

Kelly, Edmund   Rosey Bradford of Chas. 28 Jan 1835
      Henry Davis and David Mears, sec.

Kelly, Elijah B.   Eveline Byrd   5 Jan 1854
      of James, dec'd.   of John W.

Kelly, Henry   Elizabeth Willett   24 Apr 1841
                           ward of Bagwell C. Mason
      William Damlin, sec.

Kelly, Isaiah   Elizabeth Kelly (wid)   26 Feb 1835

Kelly, Jacob   Rachel Byrd   3 Apr 1804
      Arthur Watson, sec.

Kelly, Jacob   Euphanica Harmon   13 Jan 1814
                           (wid Savage)
      Richard H. Taylor, sec.

Kelly, James   Euphanica Sterling   26 Oct 1829
      John Taylor of E. and Levin Core, sec.

Kelly, James (wdr)   Agnes Bloxom of George   14 Oct 1829
      William C. White, sec.

Kelly, James   Anne Berry   4 Mar 1806

John F. Fisher, sec.

Kelly, Jesse   Susanna Colony   27 Jun 1808
   George S. Fisher, sec.

Kelly, Jesse   Anna Woods   3 Dec 1807
   William Duncan, sec.

Kelly, John   Mary Gelchrist   8 Dec 1810
   Thomas H. Bradford, sec.

Kelly, John   Polly Mears (wid John) 11 May 1814
   Richard Kelly, sec.

Kelly, John   Nancy Bell   3 Jan 1849
   (wdr)   (wid of Jacob)
   William S. Sturgis, sec.

Kelly, Josiah   Elizabeth Kelly   25 Feb 1835
                  (wid of Abe)
   Geodiah Bell and James P. Taylor, sec.

Kelly, Major   Susanna Winborough   2 Jan 1813
   James James, sec.

Kelly, Obed (wdr)   Elizabeth Hansby of John 20 Nov 1834
   Littleton LeCato and John Hansby, sec.

Kelly, Obid   Margaret W. Bradford   28 Jun 1724

Kelly, Richard   Ann Foster   22 Nov 1810
   William R. Custis, sec.

Kelly, Richard R.   Elizabeth A.W.   1 Sep 1842

Kelly, Thomas   Peggy Bird   16 Oct 1805
   Major Bird, sec.

Kelly, Thomas   Sophia Bloxom of Stephen 16 Jun 1836
   Samuel C. Abbott, sec.

Kelly, Westket   Betsy Mears of Arthur   1 Jan 1817
   Richard Bull, sec.

Kelly, William of Dennis Rebecca Marshall   27 Aug 1827

Kelly, William of Wm. Susan Crowson of John   24 Oct 1831
   John Crowson, sec.

Kendall, John   Fanny Gutridge   24 Dec 1785
   Edward Arbuckle, sec.

Kennehorn, William (wdr) Delany Butler   14 Jan 1824

Kennett, William   Mary Daizey (wid Wm.)   7 Aug 1827
    Mordich Andrews and James W. Twiford, sec.

Kew, Edward H.   Margaret Ann Bayly   27 Apr 1820
    Richard D. Bayly and John H. Bayly, sec.

Killman, Edward   Tabitha Gray   2 Aug 1792

Killman, Ellis of John   Rachel E. White of Wm.   14 Mar 1853

Killman, John   Polly T. Justice   12 Feb 1850
    of C.   of Isaiah
    William Justice, sec.

Killman, Samuel   Nancy Riggs   22 Mar 1841
    Joseph Riggs, sec.

Killman, Samuel   Caty Dennis   14 Oct 1835
    William Killman, sec.

Killman, Samuel   Patsy Fitchett   23 Dec 1822
    Thorowgood Taylor and James W. Twiford, sec.

Killman, William   Jane Taylor   1 Aug 1849
                          of Teackle
    Charles Taylor and John E. Wise, sec.

Killmon, William of Ed.   Keiziah Fisher of Geo.   28 Aug 1826
    Babel Hutchinson and Edward Kilmon, sec.

Kilman, Charles   Abbe Kilman   29 Oct 1806
    William Kilman, sec.

Kilman, Edward Jr.   Jane Shores   28 Jul 1823
                          orphan Solomon
    Ezekiel Kilman sec.

Kilman, Edward   Margaret Dolby   14 May 1849

Kilman, James of Edward   Eliz. Charnock of Owen   30 Dec 1821
    Thomas Charnock sec.

Kilman, Thomas   Amey Justice   13 Mar 1802
    Edward Hillman, sec.

Kilman, Thomas   Sarah Sparrow   8 Jan 1808
    William Taylor, sec.   (Jobs Island)

Kilmon, Ezekiel   Polly Parks   19 Mar 1799

Kilmon, John   Nancy Parks of John   15 Oct 1816
      John Parks, sec.

Kilmon, Samuel Jr.   Nancy Riggs   23 Mar 1841

Kilmon, Samuel   Caty Dennis   15 Oct 1835

Kilmon, William (wdr)   Jane Taylor   4 Aug 1849

Kilpen, Warner   Tabitha Stocks   21 Jun 1814
                             (wid John)
William Hancock and Henry S. Copes, sec.

Kirtland, George   Elizabeth Charnock   6 Feb 1850

Knight, Dunreath M.   Elizabeth Marshall   12 Nov 1823
                             of Hessey
      Henry Marshall, sec.

Knox, John   Esther Fields   11 Jun 1816
      of Nicholas   (wid John)
      Thomas Hargis Jr., sec.

Knox, Nicholas   Barbara Marshall   28 Dec 1785
      John McLane, sec.

Knox, Nicholas   Esther Fiddeman   18 Jun 1799
      Thomas Alexander, sec.

Knox, Oliver W.   Elizabeth A. Parker   29 Dec 1847
                             of Edmund
      James D. McAllen, sec.

Lambden, John   Catherine Copes   18 Jan 1810
     James Eichelberger sec.

Land, Alexander Sr.   Sarah Maloney   13 Aug 1819
                             (wid Jno.
          Isaac Henderson, sec.

Landford, William   Susan Fletcher   22 Jan 1840
                             (wid of John)
          Marshall Gaskins and Levin T. Ross, sec.

Landing, Ezekiel   Sarah Russell   2 Oct 1826
     of Nicholas   of Tabitha
          Custis Annis, sec.

Landing, William   Nancy Justice   3 Feb 1842

Lang, Alexander   Roxanna Bloxom   10 Jun 1817
     of Alexander   of Stephen
          Stephen Bloxom, sec.

Lang, Alexander   Esther Bishop   10 Jun 1809
                             of Mons
          James Rawley, sec.

Lang, Nathaniel   Nancy Phillips   22 Jan 1814
                             of Matthew
          Thomas Fox, sec.

Lang, Nathaniel   Nancy Bull   25 Dec 1816
                             of Custis
          Custis Bull, sec.

Langdon, James   Ann Parkes   8 Jan 1831
     John Lewis, carpenter, sec.

Langford, Selby   Margaret Young   2 Aug 1841
                             of Robert
          Ephriem Wessells, sec.

Langsdale, John H.   Margaret Garrison   23 Feb 1837

Lankford, Abraham   Patience Marshall   30 Jul 1813
     John Marshall and William Marshall, sec.

Lankford, James L.   Hester A. Gladding   28 Jun 1847
                             of Sally
          Lankford and David Mears, sec.

Lankford, Selby   Amey Lewis   26 Feb 1805
          Absalem Lewis, sec.

                          - 160 -

Lawrence, Kendall   Molly Kellam   15 May 1817
     (wdr)   (wid Revell)
     William Lawrence, sec.

Lawrence, William   Euphania Mahorn   7 Oct 1803
     Kendall Lawrence, sec.

Lawrence, William   Elizabeth Kellam   28 Jun 1811
     Levi Rodgers, sec.

Laws, John Sr.   Polly Welbourn   4 Aug 1831
                          (wid Drummond)
     Levin Core, sec.

Laws, John Sr.   Elizabeth Abbott   2 Jul 1819
     (wdr)   (wid Tommy)
     Isaac Henderson, sec.

Laws, John   Ann Adair   23 Dec 1816   6
John   of Doctor Adair   Robert
Townsend, sec.

Laws, John W.   Catherine Bloxom   2 Nov 1852
     of L. C. Laws   of Dennis

Laws, Joshusa FN   Sylvia Allen FN   3 Jul 1834
                         of Daniel FN
     Thomas K. Watson and Fevin Core, sec.

Laws, Martin   Keziah Bull   29 Aug 1811
     Samuel Crippen, sec.

Laws, Rev. William   Mary Ann Wright   17 Jun 1840
                         (wid of James)
     Thomas P. Bagwell, sec.

Laws, William   Nancy Dillastatrus   26 Mar 1821
     (wdr)   (wid William)
     John Laws Jr. and Robert Townsend, sec.

Laws, William   Sarah Robins   8 Apr 1819
     of John   of Thomas
     Robert Townsend and Levin Core, sec.

Laws, Zorababel C. (wdr) Betsy Hope (wid)   16 Sep 1850

Laws, Zorobabel C.   Ann J. Coleburn   7 Aug 1827
     of John   of William
     Coleburn Nock and Levin Core, sec.

Laws, Zorobabel C.   Ann Riley   8 Jan 1830

(wdr)
Levin Core and Timothy James West, sec.

Lawson, Ephrain   Molly Watson   24 Aug 1798
    William Mister, sec.

Lawson, William   Mary Turner   26 Feb 1812
    Thomas Nelson, sec.

Lawson, William   Rebecca Gilchrist   15 Mar 1820
                   of Andrew
    John B. Wyatt, sec.

Lawson, William   Sarah Turlington   14 Feb 1831
    Robert R. Ringo, sec.

Layfield, George   Molly Melson   10 Sep 1811
                   (wid Daniel)
       Samuel Waples, sec.

Layfield, William   Nancy Ellis   27 Jun 1809
                   of John
    Thomas Milburn and John Ellis, sec.

Laylor, John P.   Harriet Jones   9 Aug 1836
                   (wid of Dr. Hiram)
    John A. Rowley and Leven Core, sec.

Laylor, Levin   Joice Justice   23 Mar 1816
                   of William
    James Justice, sec.

Laylor, William J.   Athelia W. Pool   11 Feb 1837
    of Levin   of Mary
    William H. and Thomas S. White, sec.

Leatherbury, Charles Elizabeth Kellam   2 Oct 1807
    John Snead, sec.

Leatherbury, Edmund   Elizabeth Savage   24 Jun 1817
                   of Jacob
    Caleb Belote, sec.

Leatherbury, Geo. P. Sarah Underhill   8 Sep 1819
                   sister Capt. Thomas Underhill
    Arthur R. Dunton, sec.

Leatherbury, Gilbert M. Nancy Dunton   15 Apr 1806
    William Seymour, sec.

Leatherbury, Gilbert M. Hennretta R. Johnson 17 Dec 1817
                   of Isaiah Sr.

James Russell, sec.

Leatherbury, John   Sarah Window   11 Feb 1809
   of Charles
John Leatherbury of Edmund, sec.

Leatherbury, John L.   Ann C. Oliver   24 Nov 1828
   Americas Scarburgh, sec.

Leatherbury, Thomas   Nancy Elliott   31 Mar 1806
   Charles Elliott, sec.

Lecato, Edwin   Mary H. Scarbrugh   15 Nov 1852

Lecato, Littleton Jr.   Nancy Fletcher   29 Sep 1834
                  of Margaret
   James B. Glen, sec.

Lecato, Littleton   Esther Bradford   24 Nov 1806
   Abel Bradford, sec.

Lecato, Luther A.   Mary Fosque   6 Jun 1836
                  of Sally
   John W. Elliott, sec.

Lecato, William R.   Jane E. Mapp   16 Jun 1836
                  of Robins H.
   Robins H. Mapp, sec.

Lecato, William H.   Cornelia Pool   4 Sep 1841

LeCato, Edwin W.   Mary Henry Scarborough   15 Nov 1852
                  of Samuel H. Scarborough

Lecatt, Augustine   Elizabeth Rodgers   14 Feb 1795
   William Gibb, sec.

Lecatte, Major   Nancy Churn   26 Mar 1808
                  of John
   John Churn, sec.

Lecatte, William   Elizabeth Elliott   10 Apr 1817
   of Augustine, dec'd.   (wid William)
   Phillip Fisher, sec.

Lecatto, Nathaniel   Elizabeth G. Walters   9 Jan 1829
   Littleton Lecato and Richard Walters, sec.

Lecoumpt, William   Mary Paul   16 May 1816
                  of Thomas
   Thomas Paul and Wilson Bishop, sec.

Lee, Andrew (wdr) James Walker, sec.	Betsy Tignal	3 Jan 1838
Lee, Andrew George Willis, sec.	Nancy Lumber	8 Jun 1812
Lee, Joseph	Wooney Ranger	26 Dec 1787
Lee, William (wdr) W. E. Wise and John Finney, sec.	Margaret West	8 May 1833
LeNoel, Flavins Edward A. Revells, sec.	Maria H. West	22 Feb 1814
Lenten, Jacob	Mary A. Dazy	10 Jun 1820
Levi (F.N.) Thomas Custis, sec.	Scarburgh Fortune	16 Apr 1803
Levinston, Whittington George S. Fisher, sec.	Nancy Beasley of Smith	7 Mar 1819
Lewis, Absalem (wdr) John R. Drummond, sec.	Elizabeth Lewis of Revel	27 Feb 1849
Lewis, Absalom William R. Custis, sec.	Rachel Ross	28 Nov 1805
Lewis, Absalom	Molly Killmon	28 Jan 1789
Lewis, Absolem John Thomas and William R. Custis, sec.	Ann Crockett of Eliza	27 Jan 1834
Lewis, Asa James Lewis, sec.	Susan Lewis of James	11 Aug 1840
Lewis, Charles George Lewis, sec.	Ann Prewitt of William	30 Apr 1810
Lewis, Custis Thomas M. Bayly, sec.	Eliza Drummond of William	22 Sep 1809
Lewis, Daniel Arthur Parks, sec.	Elizabeth Parks of Arthur	16 Jan 1833

```
Lewis, Ebed              Nancy Copes              20 Jan 1814
                         of Major
         Thomas Bloxom and Henry S. Copes, sec.

Lewis, Ebenezer          Nan Hill                 28 Nov 1851

Lewis, Edward            Francis Lang              6 Dec 1837
                         of Nancy
         Walter Lewis, sec.

Lewis, Edward            Eliza Hansby             28 May 1832
         M. B. Revell and John W. Colonna, sec.

Lewis, Edward            Frances Lang              9 Dec 1837

Lewis, Evan              Love Davis               27 Jul 1807
         William Sharply and Isaac Lewis, sec.

Lewis, Evans             Leah Read (wid)          20 Sug 132
         Edward Taylor and George Claywell, sec.

Lewis, Frederick C.      Maria Booth              22 Feb 1850
                         (wid of James)
         John Henderson, sec.

Lewis, George            Mary Taylor              16 Jan 1800
         John Lewis, sec.

Lewis, George            Elizabeth A. Hinman      21 Nov 1822
      (wdr)              (wid William)
         Samuel Walston, sec.

Lewis, Henderson         Nancy Elliott            25 Feb 1833
         Leven James and Rachel Elliott, sec.

Lewis, Henry             Charlotte Phillips       27 Aug 1857

Lewis, Isaac             Betsy Welburne           20 Feb 1810
         Zorobabel Chandler, sec.

Lewis, Isaac             Sophia Landing           25 Dec 1826
      of Thomas          of Michael
         Robert Taylor, sec.

Lewis Isaac              Ann Taylor               30 Mar 1825

Lewis, Isaac             Elizabeth Taylor          3 May 1819
      of John            of Thomas
         Samuel Mallet, sec.

Lewis, Isaac             Annamaria Holloway       31 Jul 1820
      (wdr)              of Aaron
```

Aaron Holloway and Peter Roberts, sec.

Lewis, Isaac Jr.   Vesta Lewis   21 Nov 1826
   (wdr)   of William
   David Watts Sr. and Americus Scarburgh, sec.

Lewis, Isaac   Polly Watson   19 Dec 1808
   Evan and Selby Lewis, sec.

Lewis, Major   Elizabeth Taylor   6 Dec 1848
   David Mason and Henry Mason, sec.

Lewis, James   Mary Lewis   18 Jan 1849
   of William K.   of Samuel
   James and Benjamin Thomas, sec.

Lewis, James   Ann Berry Hickman   10 Mar 1836
   Major Lewis, sec.

Lewis, James   Kessy Lewis   11 Jan 1820
   of William, dec'd. of William
   William Lewis, sec.

Lewis, John   Tabitha Drummond   10 Mar 1810
   of Thomas   of John
   Richard Drummond, sec.

Lewis, John   Ann Cheshire   15 Jan 1822
   of Hunting Creek of Shadrach
   Samuel Lewis, sec.

Lewis, John (wdr)   Nancy Bull   8 Jun 1822
   of Thomas   of William
      John Y. Bagwell, sec.

Lewis, John   Levinia Taylor   27 Nov 1797

Lewis, John   Sarah Clayvill   28 May 1838
   Timathy Hill, sec.

Lewis, John Jr.   Nancy Bull   12 Mar 1822

Lewis, John   Margaret G. West   28 Feb 1822
   of James   of John., dec'd.
   Mary West, sec.

Lewis, John T.   Sarah E. Justice   27 Nov 1850

Lewis, John   Polly Colona   7 Dec 1830
   of Daniel   of James
   Elizah Bloxom, sec.

```
Lewis, John of Eby.      Miss Clavell              5 Jun 1838

Lewis, John             Elizabeth Mister          1 May 1827
    of William              of William
John Bull Sr., sec.

Lewis, John T.          Sally Spence             17 Jan 1852
                            of John

Lewis, John             Elizabeth Whealton       21 Dec 1843

Lewis, John             Bridget Melson           28 Dec 1819
    of John                 of Levin
Henry S. Copes, sec.

Lewis, Levin D.         Mary Ann Melson          19 Dec 1849
                            of Smith
    Lewis D. Drummond, sec.

Lewis, Levin (of Tho.)  Susan Kellam             24 Feb 1820

Lewis, Levin            Elizabeth Prescot        13 Dec 1840

Lewis, Levin D.         Mary A. Mason            20 Dec 1849

Lewis, Levin            Susan Kellam             26 Feb 1820
    of Thomas               of Frederick
Richard Lewis, sec.

Lewis, Major            Elizabeth Powell          7 Apr 1830
                            of William
    Arthur Barnes, sec.

Lewis, Parker           Elizabeth Lewis          31 Mar 1851
                            of Isaac

Lewis, Revel J.         Elisha A. Marshall       29 Jan 1845

Lewis, Revell           Milly Marshall            5 Jan 1808
                            of Samuel
    Solomon Marshall and Washington Milbourn, sec.

Lewis, Revell           Polly Young              21 Dec 1822
                            (wid James)
    George White, sec.

Lewis, Richard          Adah Savage              28 Dec 1807
    William Badger, sec.

Lewis, Richard          Hester Hickman           19 Dec 1821
    of Thomas, dec'd.       (wid Revell)
    Thomas Lewis, sec.
```

```
Lewis, Richard           Catey Colonney          8 May 1838
     (wdr)               of Kendall
     Levin Petitt, sec.

Lewis, Robert            Tabitha Nock            30 Mar 1826
     (wdr)               of Benjamin
     John L. Lilliston, sec.

Lewis, Robert            Rachel Ross             30 Jul 1814
     William Rayfield, sec.

Lewis, Samuel            Margaret A. Kellam      27 Apr 1835
                         of Argyle
          Lewis S.  overts, sec.


Lewis, Samuel            Sally Thomas            26 Jul 1831
                         of Jno.
          Absolom Lewis, sec.

Lewis, Samuel            Polly Russell           27 Sep 1822
     of Spencer          of Milby
     Thomas Russell, sec.

Lewis, Samuel            Susan R. Lewis           1 Dec 1827
     of John             orphan William
     James Berry sec.

Lewis, Samuel            Rosey Watson            20 Apr 1826
     of Samuel           of James
     Edmund Lilliston, sec.

Lewis, Samuel            Susan Wessells          26 Jul 1823
     (wdr)               orphan Elijah, ward of Jno. Lilliston
     John Lillison, sec.

Lewis, Selby             Polly Burch             27 July 1807
     Isaac Lewis and William, Sharpley sec.

Lewis, Selby             Eliza R. Conner          3 Jun 1829
                         of George
     Isaac Lewis and William A. Matthews, sec.

Lewis, Selby (wdr)       Sally Burch             25 Jul 1853
                         (wid of John)

Lewis, Solomon           Seymour Hickman          3 Nov 1812
     Raymond Parks, sec.

Lewis, Spencer           Nancy Taylor            15 Feb 1836
                         of Major
     John Johnson, sec.
```

```
Lewis, Thomas              Margaret Monger           12 Jan 1832
     of Thomas
     Southy W. Bull, sec.

Lewis, Thomas D.           Demeriah White            11 May 1842

Lewis, Thomas              Margaret Ann Parks        27 Jan 1834
     of Spencer                 of John
     John Parks, sec.

Lewis, Thomas (wdr)        Sarah Ann Hart             9 Feb 1837
     of Spencer                 of John
     John Hart, sec.

Lewis, Thomas              Sally Russell             20 Jul 1835
                                of Robert
     William Shreaves, sec.

Lewis, Thomas              Euphemia Monger           21 Dec 1841

Lewis, Thomas  (wdr)       Nancy Damerlin            30 Aug 1823
     of Richard
     Zorobabel Chandler, sec.

Lewis, Thomas              Ann Kelly                  9 Feb 1815
     of Richard
     Zadock Lewis, sec.

Lewis, Thomas              Sarah Clark               29 Oct 1787
     William Gibb, sec.

Lewis, Thomas              Susanna Rayfield           7 Sep 1826
     of Spencer                 (wid William)
     Levin Core, sec.

Lewis, William             Elizabeth Snead           27 Dec 1827

Lewis, William             Mary Nottingham Kelly      1 Feb 1819
     of Richard                 of Nicholas, dec'd.
     Thomas Lewis, sec.

Lewis, William             Nancy East                25 Aug 1831
     (wdr)                      of Parker
     Abel Elliott, sec.

Lewis, William             Alicia Russell             8 Feb 1822
     of William                 of Robert
     Thos. Lewis of Spencer, sec.

Lewis, William             Eliza Snead               24 Dec 1827
     of William                 of William
     James W. Twiford, sec., William Snead cons.
```

Lewis, William   Ann Robins   16 Feb 1828
    of Laban   of Thomas
    Elijah W. Nock, sec.

Lewis, William   Nancy Parkes   23 Apr 1849
                        of Arthur, sec.

Lewis, William (wdr)   Nancy Parker   2 Sep 1852
                        (wid of Arthur)

Lewis, William   Sophia Bull   18 Oct 1800
    Laban Gunter, sec.

Lewis, William E.   Leah Lewis   29 Jun 1835
                        (wid of Evans Lewis)
        David Watts, sec.

Lewis, William H.   Elizabeth Bloxom   27 Dec 1836
    Eburn Bird, sec.

Lillaston, Jacob   Susanna West   28 Jul 1787
    Levin Copes, sec.

Lillaston, John   Bridget Lilliston   13 Jul 1809
    Tully Lilliston, sec.

Lilleston, Edmund   Sally Broadwater   1 Nov 1797

Lilliston, Asa   Nancy Hargis   13 May 1845

Lilliston, Bowman   Tabitha Crummond   7 Feb 1835
                        of Richard
        John W. Custis, sec.

Lilliston, Edmund   Rosa Chandler   19 Jul 1836
    Levin Core and Henry A. Wise, sec.

Lilliston, Elijah   Ann Welch   8 Oct 1821
                        of William, dec'd.
        John Leatherbury, sec.

Lilliston, Elijah   Ann Savage   5 Dec 1816
    of John   of Richard
    Michael Higgins, sec.

Lilliston, Henry P.   Mary A. Finney   2 Aug 1841
                        of Sarah S.
        George Hickman, sec.

Lilliston, Henry P.   Elizabeth Powell   30 Jun 1853
    (wdr)   of Seth

```
Lilliston, Isaac W.        Sally Ewell                 8 Oct 1821
    of Jacob                  of Solomon
    Dennis Clayton and Solomon Ewell (BS), sec.

Lilliston, Isaac W.        Nancy Budd                 24 Jan 1835
                              of John
        Thorogood Bell, sec.

Lilliston, James           Elizabeth Hickman          29 Dec 1840

Lilliston, John            Rosey Wise                  3 Jan 1828
    of Selby                  of Samuel
        Isaac Lilliston, sec.

Lilliston, John S.         Anne Hurst of Thos.        21 Apr 1829
        Smith Milliner, sec.

Lilliston, John            Patsy Andrews (wid)         9 Apr 1811
        Robert Lilliston, sec.

Lilliston, Samuel          Mary Handrick (wid)        23 Dec 1841

Lilliston, Selby           Margaret Joynes            10 Feb 1826
                              of William, dec'd.
        James W. Twiford and John Wise, sec.

Lilliston, Thomas          Charlotte R. Gibbons       28 Oct 1840
        James T. Gibbons and Richard B. Drummond, sec.

Lilliston, Thomas          Mahala Justice             25 Jul 1849
    (wdr)                     of William (Bayside)
        James H. Scott, sec.

Lilliston, Thomas          Juliet Ann Fitzgerald      15 Dec 1821
    of Edmund
        Nehemiah Stockley, sec.

Lilliston, Thomas          Mary Tunnell               25 Sep 1839
        Thomas R. and William T. Joynes, sec.

Lilliston, Thomas (wdr)    Mary McCollem              19 Oct 1850
                              (wid of James)

Lilliston, Tully (wdr)     Margaret G. Revell          7 Nov 1840
        John R. Watson, sec.

Lindsay, Francis           Margaret Edwards           14 May 1827
                              of Laban
        Jacob and John Jester, sec., Laban Edwards cons.

Lindsay, Thomas            Betsy Conaway              28 Dec 1807
                              (wid William)
```

Matthew Dowty, sec.

Lindsay, Thomas	Nancy Bull (wid Edmund)	7 Oct 1815
Phillip Fisher, sec.		
Lingo, David of Robinson, dec'd.	Margaret Taylor of William	27 Mar 1820
Joshua Taylor, sec.		
Lingo, John George Guy, sec.	Nancy Martin	3 Dec 1805
Lingo, Robert	Maria Downing	26 Sep 1827
Lingo, Robert R.	Margaret Lingo (wid David)	4 Jul 1825
William Smith, sec.		
Lingo, Robinson Kendal Richardson, sec.	Peggy White	18 Apr 1787
Lingo, Thomas Thomas Mears, sec.	Agnes Kellam	15 May 1797
Lingo, William George Guy, sec.	Thamar Martin	3 Dec 1805
Linsey, Matthias	Ann M. Slocomb of Levenah	4 Mar 1831
Walter Slocomb and John H. Powell, sec.		
Linton, Elijah	Fosset Sterling	7 Apr 1812
Nathaniel Linton and Stephen Linton, sec.		
Linton, George	Nancy Colonna of James	10 Mar 1852
Linton, George	Maria Spence of John	3 Apr 1849
George Linton, sec.		
Linton, Henry C.	Rachel Linton of William	28 May 1853
Linton, Major	Polly Bratcher of Tyler	9 Jul 1818
John Tyler, sec.		
Linton, Thomas Daniel Ardis, sec.	Susanna Annis	12 Sep 1807

```
Linton, William              Louisa Marshall           9 Dec 1851
                             of Zachariah

Linton, William              Triffy Marshall          23 Feb 1816
    of Nathan                of James
    Aaron Marshall, sec.

Littleton FN                 Betsy Godfree FN          5 Jun 1816
                             of Alice
        Richard D. Bayly, sec.

Littleton, George            Susannah Savage          18 Mar 1812
        John Sparrow, sec.

Littleton, Richard           Mary Shreives (wid)      11 Dec 1844

Littleton, Southy            Mary Taylor               5 Jan 1810

Littleton, Thomas            Sally White              24 Mar 1847
                             of Willliam A.
        James T. Hinman and Charles Wright, sec.

Livingston, Whittington  Nancy Beasley               29 May 1819


Lofland, Alfred              Casandra W. Scarburgh     2 Jul 1839
        Isaiah Bagewll, sec.

Logan, Oliver                Mary Ann S. Gillett      10 Feb 1823
                             of James
        Ezekiel H. James, sec., James Gillett cons.

Lomay, Samuel F.             Elizabeth Lewis           7 Mar 1850
                             of Samuel Lewis of John
        Robert A. Lomay, sec.

Long, Isaac                  Nancy Taylor             21 Apr 1836
                             of William Tylor of E.
        William Tylor, sec.

Long, Isaac                  Ann Gladden of John      13 Aug 1830
        John Gladden, sec.

Long, John FN                Laura Conner FN          31 Jul 1850
                             of George FN

Long, Thomas                 Mary E. Leppengcott       2 Mar 1831
                             orphan Samuel
        Whittington B. Pool and Vespanean Ellis, sec.

Longe, Coleburn              Nancy Thomas             27 Nov 1788
```

Longsdale, John H.   Margaret Garrison   20 Feb 1837
                               of Abel
        Levin Core and James Ailworth, sec.

Lucas, Elijah   Comfort Lewis of John   14 Dec 1827
        Samuel Lewis, sec.

Lucas, Elijah   Catherine Bird   31 Dec 1838
                               of Jacob
        James Northam and Southy Lucas, sec.

Lucas, Elijah   Betsy Taylor   27 Oct 1800
        Richard Taylor, sec.

Lucas, Luke   Susanna Hinmon   27 Aug 1821
                               of Moses, dec'd.
        Thomas Hinmon, sec.

Lucas, Major   Polly Sprungs   31 Jul 1805
        Zadock Bayly, sec.

Lucas, Samuel   Tabitha White   25 Jan 1858
        of Catherine Andrews   of Sofian White

Lucas, Solomon   Elizabeth Merrill   6 May 1820
        of Parker   of Kendall
        James Justice, sec.

Lucas, Southey T. (wdr)   Harriet A. Powell   6 Sep 1852
                               of William, Jr.

Lucas, Southy P.   Nancy White   4 Jul 1835
        Edmund Bell, sec.

Lucas, Southy   Naomi Taylor   *25 Feb 1799
        Teackle Taylor, sec.

Luker, John   Sarah Finney Read   6 Oct 1786
        Daniel Richardson, sec.

Lumber, Stephen   Nancy Whealton   5 Jan 1808
        William L. Lucas, sec.

Lumber, William S.   Elizabeth Willett   9 Feb 1820
        of William   of George
        Samuel Lumber and John C. Copes, sec.

Lunn, James   Elizabeth Snead   21 Jul 1842

Lunn, James   Sally Helms (wid)   10 Dec 1835

Lunton, Jacob   Nancy Shoars   18 Jan 1820

```
        of James              of Solomon
        Edward Charnick, sec.

Lurton, Jacob (wdr)      Suky Charnock            26 Feb 1838
                         of Oliver
        Edward Charnock, sec.

Lurton, Littleton        Patience Bishop          26 Sep 1785
        Babel Chandler, sec.

Lyon, Ethel              Louisa H. Gillett        14 May 1827
                         of James
        Richard D. Bayly and Littleton P. Henderson, sec.
```

```
MacMath, John            Sally Trader            18 Jun 1805
      Thomas Custis, sec.

Madrick, John            Tabitha Shipham of Ben.   3 Aug 1816
      Asa Mathews and Richard D. Bayly, sec.

Mago, Peter D.           Leah C. Upshur           3 Aug 1823

Major, Edmund FN         Sally Bagwell FN        22 Feb 1821
                         of George
      Levin Stockley FN and George Bagwell FN, sec.

Major, George FN         Rachel Phillips FN      25 Dec 1848
      Levin N. Phillips, sec.

Major, John FN           Louisa Thompson FN      13 Aug 1858

Major, Thomas FN         Susan Phillips           7 Dec 1852

Major, Thomas FN         Louisa Phillips FN       7 Dec 1852

Major, William           Betsy Darby             27 Oct 1802
      Joseph Moore, sec.

Mallett, Samuel          Polly Lewis of John     30 Sep 1816
      John Cherix and Nichokas Knox, sec.

Manuel, Moses FN         Rebecca Church FN        5 Jun 1807
                         of Jonathan
      Jonathan Church, sec.

Mapp, George S.          Margaret Shield         29 Jun 1840
      (wdr)              (wid of Samuel)
      Wilburn Walker, sec.

Mapp, George B.          Ann Jane Edmunds        11 Feb 1834
                         of James
      James F. Hall and James Edmunds, sec.

Mapp, George S.          Susan T. Scarburgh      10 Aug 1840
      James H. Dix, sec.

Mapp, George             Catherine C. Ames       13 May 1829

Mapp, George S. (wdr)    Catherine C. Ames       11 May 1829
                         of Zoro
      Abel Edwards, sec.

Mapp, George             Leah Harrison           10 Jan 1807
      Thomas Bradford, sec.

Mapp, George S.          Susan Scarburgh         12 Aug 1825
```

Mapp, George T.   Elizabeth P. Major   30 May 1825
    of Howson, dec'd.   of William, dec'd
    James Kellam Sr.

Mapp, James   Margaret J. Nottingham   12 Sep 1853
    of George S.   of David B., dec'd.

Mapp, John D.   Tabitha A. Ames   14 Sep 1832
    of George L.   of Richard
    George L. Mapp, sec.

Mapp, John   Susanna Potter   18 Dec 1809
                           of John, dec'd.
        Kendall Richison, sec.

Mapp, Robins   Achsah Bogg   23 Sep 1809
    Thomas Smith, sec.

Mapp, Samuel   Critty Nock   15 Mar 1809
    George Thomas, sec.

Mapp, William C.   Catherine R. Turlington   4 Feb 146

Mapp, William R.   Sally E. Henderson   2 May 1849

Mariner, George B.   Elizabeth Taylor   24 Mar 1848

Mariner, Levin (wdr)   Polly Winbrow (wid Jno.) 31 Aug 1831
    John Marshall and Oliver Logan, sec.

Mariner, Major   Sophia Ellis   31 May 1833
                           (wid of Josiah)
        John D. Welburn Jr. and Levin Core, sec.

Maritn, William Henry   Mary Ann Jacob   8 Nov 1852
    of Peter   of Arthur

Marriner, George   Euphamy Dunstan   1 Feb 1814
    William W. Hickman and John Custis, sec.

Marriner, Levin   Elizabeth Taylor   1 Feb 1811
    George Marriner, sec.

Marshall, Aaron of Jms.   Tinny Fisher of Wm.   20 Nov 1821
    Jesse Dickerson, sec.

Marshall, Benjamin   Betsey Bunting   29 Aug 1803
    Edward Arbuckle, sec.

Marshall, Caesar FN   Joyce Williams FN   5 Feb 1812
    Henry Douglass, sec.

Marshall, Caesar	Joyce Williams	5 Feb 1812
Marshall, David	Milcah Taylor	11 Apr 1846
Marshall, Geo. E. (wdr)	Rebecca Smith	12 Apr 1841
Marshall, George	Catherine Bull of William	3 Jan 1850

John W. Melson, sec.

Marshall, George	Sally Davis	17 Nov 1792
Marshall, George E. (wdr)	Rebecca Smith	12 Apr 1841

David L. Drummond, sec.

Marshall, Gilbert	Sarah Ann Hoffman of James	11 May 1830

Zachanial Marshall, sec.

Marshall, Henry	Nasha Chase	18 Jul 1795
Marshall, Isaac, mulatto	Elizabeth Lee, mulatto	6 Jan 1800
Marshall, Isaac	Nasha Chase of Robt.	1 Feb 1815

Sampson Marshall Jr., sec.

Marshall, Jacob	Margaret Warrington	7 Jan 1791
Marshall, James FN	Harriet Griffin of Sabra FN	27 Jan 1834

David Broadwater and John Savage of R., sec.

Marshall, James W.	Hetty Bayly of Betsy Bayly	9 Nov 1854
Marshall, James	Esther Nock	11 Sep 1805
Marshall, John	Adah Marshall	14 Jun 1802

William Cheshire, sec.

Marshall, John S. of Sally	Esther Adderson	11 Jun 1834

Southy Taylor and Michall Smith, sec.

Marshall, John	Eleanor Evans of Richard	2 Sep 1833

Tully R. wise, sec.

Marshall, John (of Tho.)	Rebecca Matthews	1 Nov 1827
Marshall, John	Eleanor Evans	btw 1825-1837

Marshall, John T. (wdr) Matilda Tindal (wid)   10 Jan 1849
    James D. McAllen and James W. Gibb, sec.

Marshall, John T. (wdr) Matilda Tindal (wid)   11 Nov 1849

Marshall, John W. (wdr) Nancy Taylor (wid Wm.)   5 May 1825
    David Watts and John R. Potter, sec.

Marshall, John L.   Rebecca Collins   4 Jan 1826
    of James   of Joshua
    Sebastian Cropper, sec.

Marshall, John B.   Sally Elliott   15 Nov 1811
    Shadrach Sterling, sec.

Marshall, John D.   Hester Ann Welborne   20 Dec 1830
    Peter Welborn and Elisha D. Davis, sec.

Marshall, John   Polly Cropper   10 Dec 1798
    Levin Townsend, sec.

Marshall, John of Geo.   Henrietta Watts of Wm.   1 Jul 1817
    David Watts and Richard D. Bayly, sec.

Marshall, John T.   Rebecca Copes   31 Mar 1821
                     (wid Revell)
    Caleb Johnson, sec.

Marshall, Levin   Esther Dennis   29 May 1788

Marshall, Levin T.   Ann Elizabeth Kelly   28 Dec 1852
                     of William

Marshall, Richard   Nancy Shay   28 Dec 1857
    ward of Henry B. Northam

Marshall, Robert J.   Elizabeth J. Wood   26 Mar 1850
                     of Ally
    Samuel T. Taylor and John E. Wise, sec.

Marshall, Robert   Levinah Marshall   16 Dec 1815
                     of Samuel
    Levin Harman, sec.

Marshall, Robert   Mohola Linton   28 Feb 1831
    Revell Lewis and George, Croswell sec.

Marshall, Sampson Jr.   Nancy Barnes   23 Jan 1809
                     of Tabitha
    John Snead, jailor, sec.

```
Marshall, Sampson          Molly Tunnell            16 May 1812
     of Sampson
  Robert Corbin, sec.

Marshall, Samuel FN        Caroline Church FN       13 Apr 1843

Marshall, Samuel           Margaret Henderson (wid) 26 Jan 1849

Marshall, Shadrach D.      Mohola Evans             30 May 1814
     Savage Corbin and William L. Lucas, sec.

Marshall, Soloman          Ann Marshall             16 Jun 1856
     (wdr)                 (wid of Thomas W.)

Marshall, Solomon          Judah Evans              20 Jun 1796

Marshall, Solomon          Polly Thomas              5 Jan 1803
     John Martin, sec.

Marshall, Solomon          Sally Gladding of Jno.   31 Dec 1821
     William Marshall, sec.

Marshall, Stephen          Elizabeth Burton         27 Dec 1831
                           (wid John)
          George Window, sec.

Marshall, Stephen          Tabitha Marshall         12 Oct 1787
     Robert Pitt, sec.

Marshall, Stephen          Patience Drummond        23 Dec 1837
     John P. Drummond, sec.

Marshall, Stringer A.      Narissa Taylor           16 Jan 1854
     of Stringer, dec'd.        of Southy

Marshall, Thomas W.        Leah C. Staton            4 Dec 1839

Marshall, Thomas W.        Leah C. Staton           29 Jan 1839
     Edward P. Pitts, sec.

Marshall, Thomas E.        Charlotte Johnson        16 Jan 1849
                           of Euphemia
          Thomas Walton, sec.

Marshall, Thomas A.        Ann Ashly                26 Jul 1841
                           of Thomas
     James A. Dowty and Spencer Drummond, sec.

Marshall, Thomas          Emmaline Marshall          9 Dec 1851
     of Robert            of Zachariah

Marshall, William          Betsy Bloxom              7 Dec 1820
```

```
    of Henry                of Stephen
    Noah Riggin, sec.

Marshall, William H. (wdr)    Henrietta Trader    25 Sep 1849
    Thomas Walters, sec.

Marshall, William          Peggy Stringer        15 Jun 1784
    William Gibb, sec.

Marshall, William T.       Caroline Gillett      25 Oct 1843

Marshall, William          Margaret Knox         26 Aug 1822
    of Solomon             orphan George
    Levin Townsend and Thomas Allen, sec.

Marshall, William D.       Sally Taylor          31 Aug 1835
    (wdr)                  (wid of Henry)
    Nathaniel W. Bird and Samuel S. Lucas, sec.

Marshall, William          Pamelia Knight        27 Jan 1848
    of Henry               of Elizabeth
    James C. Johnson and Thomas D. Trader, sec.

Marshall, William          Fanney Hutson         30 Jan 1817
    of Samuel              of Robert
    John Hutson, sec.

Marshall, William          Betty Bloxom           7 Dec 1820

Marshall, William          Hetty Parkes           6 Mar 1818
    of William             (wid John)
    Littleton Nock, sec.

Martin, Albert (FN)        Mahala Collins        17 Dec 1833

Martin, Andrew             Comfort Turlington     5 Feb 1787
    John Savage, sec.

Martin, Edmund             Betty Riggin          29 Nov 1803
    John Martin, sec.

Martin, Edward             Tressey Tatham        11 Jan 1822
                           (wid William)
    John Edwards, sec.

Martin, George             Esther Bayly          15 Aug 1816
    Abbott Trader, sec.

Martin, George             Elizabeth Russel       1 Jan 1849
    (wdr)                  of William
    Samuel Ewell and Robert Andrews, sec.
```

```
Martin, Henry              Susanna Derby            28 Sep 1787
     Edmund Scarburgh, sec.

Martin, James              Louisa Davis             26 Jan 1852
                           of Noah

Martin, James (FN)         Fanny Collins            27 Dec 1827

Martin, James (wdr)        Nancy Fletcher of Step.  24 Oct 1822
     Isaac Melson, sec.

Martin, James FN           Ann Major FN              9 Jan 1854
                           of Annis Major FN

Martin, James FN           Fanny Collins FN         26 Dec 1827
                           of Southy
          Southy Collins, sec.

Martin, James of Caleb     Catherine Kennehorn      22 Apr 1816
                           of John
          James Ames, sec.

Martin, James              Eliza Chase              10 Apr 1810
     Edward Martin, sec.


Martin, John J.            Esther Savage            21 Jan 1850
                           (wid of Colin)
          William G. Johnson and W.H. Parker, sec.

Martin, John S.            Anna Brown               30 Dec 1843

Martin, John               Betsy Sample             25 Jan 1830
          James Martin and James Kellam of A., sec.

Martin, John               Hetty Downing            28 Feb 1831
     James Hyslop, sec.

Martin, Peter              Rosey Warrington         23 May 1827
     of Smith                of James, dec'd.
     Joseph Turlington and James Walker, sec.

Martin,  Peter            Caty Savage                1 Aug 1818
     of Smith
     John S. Walker and James Walker, sec.

Martin, Peter (of Smith) Rosey Warrington           27 May 1823

Martin, Peter              Elizabeth A. Bradford    20 Nov 1845

Martin, Samuel FN          Rachel Collins FN        29 Dec 1817
                           of Southy
```

Edmund Nutts, sec.

| Martin, Smith K. | Maryann Badger | 2 Dec 1840 |

| Martin, Smith | Mary Ann Badger of Nathaniel | 30 Nov 1840 |

George Nock and Nathaniel Badger, sec.

| Martin, Smith | Sophia Beach of Kendall | 20 Feb 1816 |

Edmund Nock, sec.

| Martin, Smith Sr. (wdr) | Sarah Harman (wid Kendall) | 2 Jan 1823 |

William D. Groten and Richard D. Bayly, sec.

| Martin, Smith K. | Louisa A. Badger | 18 Apr |

| Martin, Thomas | Tabby Mears | 31 Jan 1804 |

William Mears, sec.

| Martin, Thomas | Malinda Cropper | 26 Apr 1842 |

| Martin, Thomas | Sarah Abdell | 20 Aug 1827 |

| Martin, Thomas | Sally Poulson | 7 Mar 1808 |

Mitchell S. West, sec.

| Martin, Thomas of Henry | Sarah Abdellof Revell | 20 Aug 1827 |

James Kellam of Robt., sec.

| Martin, William of Caleb | Margaret Harmon | 19 Mar 1821 |

James Martin, sec.

| Martin, William S. | Mary A. Jacob | a. 1800 |

| Martin, William S. of Smith | Rosey Savage of Jacob of Littleton | 4 Sep 1817 |

Jacob Savage, sec.

| Martin, William of Caty | Catherine Bird of Jno. | 31 Dec 1827 |

Solomon Gladding and Solomon Small, sec.

| Martin, William (wdr) | Arady Marow | 10 Sep 1825 |

William C. Watson, sec.

| Masey, John | Patty Walters | 29 Jan 1833 |

Oliver Logan and Thomas R. Joynes, sec.

| Mason (Mayson),Bennett | Rachel Duncan | 11 Mar 1799 |

Solomon Johnson, sec.

Mason, Ace	Tabitha Bloxom	18 Nov 1841
Mason, Babel	Nancy Bull	23 Jan 1790
Mason, Bagwell C. Edmund Mason, sec.	Margaret East of Severn	10 Oct 1831
Mason, Bagwell C. (wdr)	Ann Rayfield (wid of Levi)	24 Nov 1851
Mason, Bennett of Caleb William Doughty sec.	Aroda Heath	28 Nov
Mason, Bennett Edmund Mason, sec.	Tinne Mason of Severn	17 Dec 1814
Mason, Charles	Mary Grinalds	8 Nov 1837
Mason, Edmund Zorobabel Chandler, sec.	Betsy James of Patience	4 Nov 1815
Mason, Edmund B. Edmund J. Poulson and James H. Dix, sec.	Margaret Tignall	26 Dec 1833
Mason, Edward B.	Margaret Tyndal	26 Dec 1839
Mason, Ezekiel William Watson, sec.	Tabitha Watson of Wm.	3 Aug 1814
Mason, George W. John Belote, sec.	Ann Bundick of John B.	9 Sep 1839
Mason, George William Mister, sec.	Scarburgh Turner	1 Oct 1803
Mason, George	Sarah Phillips	2 Dec 1848
Mason, Henry James Russell, sec.	Betsy Bonwell (wid John)	4 May 1829
Mason, Henry Edward Martin, sec.	Polly Heath	18 Jan 1802
Mason, Jacob James Parker of Robert of Phillip, sec.	Damy Taylor	8 Feb 1810
Mason, James of Major	Sarah A. Bird of John A.	16 Feb 1848

Henry Mason, sec.

Mason, James	Betty Northam	30 Jun 1789

Mason, John (wdr)   Charlotte Upshur   27 Nov 1831
    John Bull Sr. and Southy W. Bull, sec.

Mason, John   Margaret Only   11 Nov 1802
    Major Rodgers, sec.

Mason, Major Jr.   Nancy Grinnalds   25 Dec 1826
                     orphan South
    James Berry and William Taylor, sec.

Mason, Major   Berndette Justice   3 Jan 1856
    (wdr)   of Samuel

Mason, Middleton   Margaret R. Ewell   17 Mar 1842

Mason, Peter H.C.   Sarah Logan   11 Nov 1856
    (wdr)   of Oliver, dec'd.

Mason, Richard   Elizabeth Justice   26 Nov 1827
    of Major   of Isaiah
    Littleton P. Henderson and Isaiah Justice, sec.

Mason, Sacker   Elizabeth Ironmonger   5 Dec 1808
                   alias Monger, (wid Zadoch)
        Major Mason, sec.

Mason, Samuel   Eliza Smith   10 Feb 1842

Mason, Samuel   Adeline Metcalf   8 Jan 1845

Mason, Samuel   Adeline W. Wessells   8 Jan 1845

Mason, Stephen   Ann Parker   20 Mar 1844

Mason, Stephen of Wm.   Harriet Guy of Jona.   22 Feb 1830
    Jacob Jester and Thomas W. Finny, sec.

Mason, Teackle   Sally Savage   27 Jul 1807
    Richard R. Savage, sec.

Mason, Teackle   Hetty James   17 Mar 1812
    Dennis Bloxom and Coventon Mason, sec.

Mason, Thomas   Ann Phillips   1 Aug 1838
                   of William
    Bagwell C. Mason, sec.

Mason, Thomas of Caleb   Ann Snead of Bowdoin   12 Dec 1816
    Bowdoin Snead, sec.

Mason, William   Tabitha Justice   24 Jan 1833
    Josiah Justice, sec.

Mason, William   Esther Howarth   25 Dec 1806
    John Howarth and Edward Mason, sec.

Mason, William of John   Elizabeth Boggs of Art.   5 Nov 1829
    William S. Harrison sec.

Mason, William J.   Hester Belote   25 Oct 1843

Mason, Zadock   Leah Grinnalds   8 Oct 1835
    Major Mason Jr., sec.

Mason, Zadock   Nancy Grinalds   9 Oct 1835

Mason, Zorobabel   Polly Grinnalds   27 Dec 1830
                           orphan Southy
    Major Mason Jr., sec.

Mason, Zorobabel (wdr)   Sarah Kelly (wid)   5 Feb 1817
    William Kendall, sec.

Massey, Adkins   Mary Mathews   9 Mar 1790

Massey, Caleb   Salley Thornton   28 Apr 1800

Massey, James   Nancy Jones   31 Aug 1807
    William Downing, sec.

Massey, John   Mary S. Tunnell   15 Jun 1812
                           (wid John)
        John Cole, sec.

Massey, Luther   Sally Young   19 Sep 1827
    of Caleb

Mathews, Anthony   Bridget Elliott (wid)   2 Feb 1814
    Abel Window, sec.

Mathews, Asa   Sally Thornton   30 Dec 1816
    John Thornton, sec.

Mathews, Edmund   Jane Taylor   12 Nov 1839
                           of William
    John Taylor of E., sec.

Mathews, Evans   Elizabeth Merrill   15 Feb 1790

```
Mathews, Frederick        Eliza Johnson              30 Dec 1840
     Soloman Marshall, sec.

Mathews, George           Azenith Benston            30 Nov 1807
     Nathaniel Benston, sec.

Mathews, George           Hessy Sterling             27 Feb 1810
     Abel Coleburn, sec.

Mathews, George           Mrs. Peggy Milburn         24 Apr 1797

Mathews, James            Anne Silverthorn            9 Feb 1787
     Elijah Mathews, sec.

Mathews, Lewis            Maria Han                   6 Jan 1846

Mathews, Lewis W.         Maria Hannah Wyatt         18 Nov 1846

Mathews, Nathaniel        Leah Medad                  7 Feb 1806
     Peter Medad, sec.

Mathews, Samuel           Eliza Bloxom               17 Dec 1839
     of William
     Zadock Nock and Thomas Kelly, sec.

Mathews, Thomas           Sarah Robins               30 Oct 1810
     of Staton
     Ralph Corbin, sec.

Mathews, William J. (wdr)    Maria H. Boggs          29 Jun 1840
     Robert W.H. Wilburn, sec.

Mathews, William of Wm.   Rebecca Sterling           26 Mar 1810
     Elias Broadwater, sec.

Mathews, William         Sarah Thorn                 1 Jan 1812
     James Jones, sec.

Matthews, Adkins          Hessy Taylor               23 Feb 1819
     of Elias              of John
     Asa Matthews, sec.

Matthews, Adkins          Polly Taylor               16 Jul 1829
     (wdr)                 (wid Shadrach)
     Asa Matthews, sec.

Matthews, Adkins          Hetty Staton               31 Dec 1827
     of Elias              of Warrington
     Joseph Showard, sec.

Matthews, Alfred E.       Elizabeth Hinman           26 Feb 1856
                          of Perry
```

Matthews, Edward	Jane Duncan	14 Oct
Matthews, Edward	Janet Drummond	14 Nov 1839
Matthews, George of Wm. Oliver Logan, sec.	Patty B. Beavans of Wm.	28 Dec 1820
Matthews, Geroge W. of George John T. Joynes and William Byrd, sec.	Mary E. Matthews of William S.	10 Jan 1848
Matthews, Jacob George P. Ewell, sec.	Seymour Ewell of Jms.	24 Dec 1829
Matthews, James E. William B. and John P. Twyford, sec.	Margaret Wallop of John D.	19 Apr 1848
Matthews, James E. (wdr)	Martha S. Fedderman (wid)	15 Nov 1855
Matthews, John Samuel L. Brimer, sec.	Eliza Brimer	11 Mar 1839
Matthews, John, Jr.	Sally Kellam	22 Mar 1799
Matthews, John K. of John	Sally Whealton (wid)	7 Oct 1824
Matthews, John Michael Dickinson, sec.	Eliza Taylor	31 Jan 1804
Matthews, John W. of John Thomas Crippen Delastatious and Thomas R. Matthews, sec.	Elizabeth Tatham of John	1 Nov 1826
Matthews, John	Margaret Hopkins	18 Aug 1851
Matthews, John William	Ann R.S. Matthews of William S., dec'd.	17 Feb 1852
Matthews, Levin George Matthews, sec.	Elizabeth Thornton	22 Feb 1803
Matthews, Meshach of George	Elizabeth Matthews	6 Jan 1823
Matthews, Samuel Thomas C. Delastatious and Samuel Walston, sec.	Mary Showard (wid George)	20 Dec 1830
Matthews, Samuel	Euphamy Broadwater	1 Sep 1841

```
Matthews, Thomas R.        Elizabeth Whealton (wid)   5 Dec 1854

Matthews, Thomas          Elizabeth Merrill          6 Dec 1819
    of Evans              (wid John)
    Caleb Broadwater and James Wright, sec.

Matthews, Washburn        Euphamey Taylor           27 Jun 1803
    George Staton, sec.

Matthews, Washington      Nancy Matthews            29 Dec 1836
                          (wid of Meshack)
        Thomas Bayly, sec.

Matthews, William W.      Martha E. Taylor          12 Dec 1848
                          of Henry N. Taylor
    W.H. Marshall, sec.

Matthews, William         Maria Berry                1 Jul 1840

Matthews, William         Mary Richardson            2 Mar 1848
                          of James
        Parker N. Parks, sec.

Matthews, William S.      Margaret P. Dunton (wid)   5 Oct 1849

Matthews, Willliam        Peggy Taylor              20 Dec 1798
    John Taylor, sec.

Maybe, Thomas             Lucinda Bradford           3 Aug 1823

Mayson, Ezekiel           Sally Matthews            25 Jan 1805
    Charles Smith, sec.

Mazell, Thomas            Lucretia Bradford         31 Jul 1823
    Nehemiah Stockley and William Parramore Jr., sec.

McClain, William         Elizabeth Cobb            12 Feb 1842

McCollon, James          May Dix                   19 Jul 1837

McCready, George         Nancy Bunting of Geo.     21 Nov 1807
    George Bunting sec.

McCready, James          Elizabeth Marshall        28 Jun 1786
    John McLane, sec.

McCready, James          Sally Marshall            22 Feb 1830
                         orphan John, ward of Jms. McCready
        Thomas Russell of Geo., sec.

McCready, Stephen        Eliza Matthews            10 Dec 1811
    Thomas Mathews, sec.
```

McCready, William Jr.   Cretty Hinman   31 Oct 1836
                       of Hetty
    James R. Duncan, sec.

McCready, William   Lucy Berry (wid Jms.)   3 Nov 1828
    Custis W. Bird, sec.

McCredy, William   Sarah Bunting   13 Jul 1804
    John Slocomb, sec.

McGuire, John   Sarah Finney   6 Oct 1803
    Edmund Bayly, sec.

Mchollow, William   Polly Kellam   15 Apr 1813

McKeel, Budd Sr.   Sally Bull   19 May 1842

McKell, Arthur D.   Sally R. Elliott   19 Oct 1842

McLean, Arthur   Mary Mason   16 Oct 1811
    Zorobabel Kellam, sec.

McLean, Robert   Elizabeth Watefield 30 Nov 1818
                       of Augustine
    Stephen Pewsey, sec.

McMaster, James   Charlotte Henderson Jr 29 Dec1809
    Samuel Henderson, sec.

McMaster, William   Elizabeth Henderson   7 Dec 1805
    Levin Hicks Dollinor, sec.

McMath, John T.   Kaziah A. Kelley   10 Aug 1853
    (wdr)   of Weston

McMath, Littleton R.   Margaret Kelly   9 Mar 1840
                       of Wescott
    Wescott Kelly, sec.

McMath, Samuel T.   Ann Elizabeth J. Kelley 21 Jan 1854
    of John   of William

McMath, Zadock   Polly Copes   28 Feb 1792

Mears, Abel B.   Barsheba Taylor   2 Apr 1836

Mears, Abel B.   Barsheba Taylor   31 Mar 1836
    Solomon Phillips, sec.

Mears, Abel Sr.   Elizabeth Spiers of Jno. 15 Mar 1817
    Joseph Beach, sec.

```
Mears, Abel                Peggy B. Edmunds          21 Nov 1825
    of Abel Sr.            of James
    James Edmunds, sec.

Mears, Abel (wdr)          Elizabeth Wallace         19 Aug 1828
    William Beach, sec.

Mears, Able                Elizabeth Lingo           29 Dec 1846
    of John

Mears, Alexander           Margaret Ann Taylor       23 Jan 1837
    John W. Johnson, sec.

Mears, Armstead            Nancy Kellam              25 Mar 1799
    William Joynes, sec.

Mears, Arthur              Peggy Mears               25 Oct 1802
    William Poulson, sec.


Mears, Arthur              Mary Ann Williams          2 Aug 1847

Mears, Arthur              Sally Cropper Cole         5 Nov 1785
    Major Bayley, sec.

Mears, Arthur              Ann Gardner of Wm.         3 Nov 1831
    William Gardner, sec.

Mears, Arthur              Ann G. Ames               3 Nov 1831

Mears, Arthur              Margaret Williams         21 Mar 1848
    (wdr)                 of Seth
    Seth Williams, sec.

Mears, Bagwell B.          Elizabeth Mister          15 Jul 1839

Mears, Bagwell B.          Elizabeth A. Custis       29 Jun 1840
                          of Isaac

Mears, Bartholomew         Rebecca Bird              31 Aug 1795

Mears, Bartholomew         Elizabeth Copes           29 May 1805
    Richard Sparrow, sec.

Mears, Caleb               Patience Pratt            20 Feb 1805
    Robert Twyford, sec.

Mears, Coventon            Nancy Roberts             19 Jul 1784
    Arthur Roberts, sec.

Mears, David               Juliet Ann Ames            4 Jan 1830
    Abel R. Harmon, sec.
```

```
Mears, David              Nancy Bowden of Edward    26 Mar 1816
     Eleanah Andrews, sec.

Mears, David (wdr)        Mary Ann Hinman            4 Jan 1844

Mears, Edward             Mary Elliott               7 Dec 1836

Mears, Edward             Mary E. Scott              8 Dec 1836
                            of Catharine
          Obed P. Twiford and Charles Tignal, sec.

Mears, Edward             Susan Gunter              23 Nov 1842

Mears, Edward             Fanny Folio               11 Jan 1835
                            of Joyce
     Major R. Dowty, sec.

Mears, George             Nancey Shay               11 Nov 1816
     of Shadrach            of Teackle
     Jesse Duncan, sec.

Mears, George             Patsy Turlington          29 Dec 1824

Mears, George of Milly    Ann Hargis of Levin       25 Jul 1815
     Thomas Harrison and John, Roberts sec.

Mears, Gilbert            Elizabeth Harris          26 Dec 1853
     of James              of George B.

Mears, Henry             Patience Fisher            19 Jun 1842

Mears, Henry             Mariah Barnes              15 Dec 1842

Mears, Hillary           Uphemy Bell                23 Sep 1787
     Arthur Mears, sec.

Mears, James             Mary Phillips              12 May 1852

Mears, James of Elisha   Nancy Hyslop of Levin       1 Sep 1821
     John Davis, sec.

Mears, James             Mary Phillips              26 Apr 1852
     (wdr)                of Labin

Mears, James             Rosey Turlington           25 Feb 1817
     William Mears, sec.

Mears, James of Jms.     Mary Belote                27 May 1827
                           of James H., dec'd.
     Charles Belote, sec.

Mears, James             Sally Wallace              28 Mar 1814
```

James Mears of James and George Beach, sec.

Mears, James   Mary Harrison   25 Jun 1838
    ward of William W. Oliver   (wid of Evans)
    William W. Oliver, sec.

Mears, James R.   Catharine T. Wyatt   14 Sep 1839
    James R. Garrison, sec.

Mears, James   Hessy N. Harmon of Jno. 10 Oct 1806
    John Harmon sec., cons.

Mears, Jesse   Betsy L. Wyatt   8 Aug 1814
    Hillery Mears, sec.

Mears, John   Scarburgh Smith   2 Mar 1808
                        of Valentine
    William Ailworth, sec.

Mears, John   Elizabeth Stephens   24 Dec 1839
    of Richard   of Charles
    Samuel T. Rayfield, sec.

Mears, John S.   Sarah D. Mapp   6 Mar 1826
                        orphan Howsen
    Abel Garrison, sec.

Mears, John   Sally Gunter   30 Oct 1833

Mears, John W.   Margaret S. Kellam   23 Mar 1835
                        of Nathaniel
    James Mears, sec.

Mears, John B.   Jane Ames   31 Dec 1832
    William Garrison, sec.

Mears, John   Sally Gray   31 Jul 1847
    of Shadrock   of John
    David Mears and W.B. Finney, sec.

Mears, John W.   Margaret Kellam   25 Mar 1835

Mears, John W. A.   Hester Pusey   10 Dec 1839

Mears, John   Elizabeth Stephens   25 Dec 1839

Mears, John B.   Jane Ames   31 Dec 1837

Mears, John W. A.   Hester Puzey   10 Dec 1839
    John T. Johnson and Frederick Kellam, sec.

Mears, John of Richard John Mears of John, sec.	Elizabeth Garrison (wid John)	11 Mar 1813
Mears, John B. John Mears, sec.	Nancy Mears of Jno.	24 Dec 1823
Mears, John F. Thomas C. Mears, sec.	Elizabeth Kellam of Geo.	10 May 1814
Mears, John of Jno. William Mears, sec.	Katherine Tignal	15 Aug 1810
Mears, John T.	Virginia Mears of Thomas	4 Dec 1850
Mears, John Sr. (wdr) Smith Ashby, sec.	Elizabeth Wyatt (wid Thomas)	18 Mar 1826
Mears, John (K) Anthony Bell, sec.	Esther Linton of Laban	3 May 1830
Mears, John George Taylor, sec.	Nancy Phillips	10 Feb 1802
Mears, John Richard P. Read, sec.	Sally Gunter ward of Rilchard P. Read	28 Oct 1833
Mears, John of Jno.(King) Littleton Lecato, sec.	Eleanor Lurton of Laban	20 Aug 1828
Mears, John of Shadrock	Sally Guy	4 Jun 1847
Mears, John of Meshack Henry B. and Elijah Northam, sec.	Nancy Northam of W.	19 Nov 1839
Mears, Jonathan Custis Willis, sec.	Leah Hyslop	17 Oct 1798
Mears, Julius C. of George	Susan Jane Young of Henry, dec'd.	3 Jan 1853
Mears, Levin of Arthur Charles Belote, sec.	Tabitha Belote orphan James of H.	28 May 1827
Mears, Lorenzo	Sophia Kellam	11 Nov 1835

```
Mears, Lorenzo T.          Sarah Belote            31 Oct 1855
    of Jesse                  of George

Mears, Luther              Sally Ames               7 May 1812
    John Snead, sec.

Mears, Luther              Mary S. Mears           22 May 1852

Mears, Meshack             Margaret Baker          27 Aug 1810
    William Baker, sec.

Mears, Meshack             Elizabeth Hickman       16 Jan 1845
                             ward of Wm. Hope

Mears, Michael             Ann Mears                4 Nov 1826
    of Kendall                of Richard, dec'd.
    James Edmund, sec.

Mears, Michael (wdr)       Nancy Elliott           25 Jun 1849
    George S. Rogers, sec.

Mears, Patrick             Rosey B. Mears          28 Dec 1835
    Lorenzo D. Mears and Levin Core, sec.

Mears, Patrick B.          Mary Emeline Ames       28 Sep 1840
    (wdr)
    Richard P. Rew and Edward H. Ames, sec.

Mears, Patrick             Rosey B. Mears          25 Mar 1835

Mears, Richard             Elizabeth Lecato        11 Mar 1826
    of Richard                (wid William)
    William Beach, sec.

Mears, Richard             Polly Mears             31 Jul 1809
    James Mears, sec.


Mears, Richard of Wm.      Margaret Morrison       30 Jul 1810
    Shadrach Ames and Alexander Morrison, sec.

Mears, Robert of Shad.     Ann Stant of James      28 Dec 1824
    Samuel Stant and Samuel Walston, sec.

Mears, Robert              Elizabeth Wyatt         24 Nov 1837
                             of James
    James Wyatt, sec.

Mears, Robert (wdr)        Margaret Boone           6 Jan 1854
```

```
Mears, Robert            Casey Gillett            15 Jan 1838
     Robert and Patrick Mears, sec.

Mears, Robert            Sarah Melson              9 Jun 140
     Thomas Harrison, sec.

Mears, Robert (wdr)      Nancy Underhill          26 May 1819
     of John               (wid James)
     Elijah Floyd, sec.

Mears, Robert            Cassey Gillett           17 Jun 1838

Mears, Robert            Sarah Melson              4 Jun 1840

Mears, Robert            Elizabeth Wyatt          25 Jul 1837

Mears, Severn            Nancy Watefield           1 Sep 1798
     Isaac Melson, sec.

Mears, Solomon FN        Bridget Dury FN          25 Feb 1839
     Benjamin Stringer and Elongo Mears, sec.

Mears, Thomas W.         Anna P. Smith of Chas.   28 May 1823
     Charles Smith, sec.

Mears, Thomas C.         Hessy Hancock of Elijah   3 Jan 1815
     Levi Ames, sec.

Mears, Thomas Walton     Catherine Smith of Geo.  19 Sep 1808
     John Ames, sec.

Mears, Thomas            Mary Fox                 17 Feb 1853
     of John (wdr)         of James

Mears, Thomas            Catherine Justice         8 Jun 1822
     orphan Jonathan       of Ralph, dec'd.
     William Parramore Jr., sec.

Mears, Thorogood         Caroline Richardson      26 Nov 1844

Mears, Thoroughgood      Mahala Melson            10 Jul 1833
                          (wid of George)
     Edward Mears, sec.

Mears, William (wdr)     Tinney Bishop            10 Jun 1829
     of Sarah              (wid Jacob)
     Thomas Johnson, sec.

Mears, William (wdr)     Elizabeth Ashby          27 Jul 1818
     of William            of Samuel, dec'd.
     James Ames, sec.
```

```
Mears, William            Sally Johnson            30 Aug 1821

Mears, William            Bridget Bull             2 Jan 1808
     Francis Downing, sec.

Mears, William            Elizabeth Shurlock       24 Dec 1824

Mears, William B.         Mary Phillips            28 Aug 1815
     John Mears, sec.

Mears, William T.         Harriet Mason            28 Jan 1852

Mears, William            Margaret Gibson          23 Mar 1814
     of Ritter
     Isaac Nelson, sec.

Mears, William            Elizabeth Johnson        29 Aug 1821
     orphan Sally Johnson      of Thomas
     Thomas Johnson and Southy Northam, sec.

Mears, William            Elizabeth Ashby          15 May 1806
     of Elisha
     David Ashby, sec.

Mears, William            Elizabeth Sherlock       21 Dec 1824
     of Molly                 of Charlotte
     John B. Walker, sec.

Mears, William            Margaret Hatton          22 Jun 1827
     of Arthur                of Margaret
     George Nelson Jr. and Marg. Hatton and Mary N. Bundick, sec.

Medad, Jacob of Levin     Peggy Jenkins of Frank   30 Dec 1819
     Robert Spark and Richard D. Bayly, sec.

Medad, James FN           Sukey Drummond FN of Athy 2 Apr 1825
     Samuel Walston, sec.

Medad, Levin FN           Betsy Gardner FN         26 Aug 1817
     of Betty                 of Tinsey
     Stephen Medad, sec.

Medad, Robert S. FN       Sally Beavans FN         10 Mar 1820
     William Custis, sec.

Meers, William            Elizabeth Arlington      6 Jan 1806
     John Ames, sec.

Mehollem, William         Nancy Sterling           16 Dec 1803
     John Gunter, sec.

Mehollons, William        Polly Kellam             15 Sep 1813
```

Revell Abdale, sec.

Mehollons, William William Davis, sec.	Susanna Luker	20 Dec 1811
Melbourn, Elijah Samuel Downing, sec.	Euphamy Wilkerson	26 Jan 1807
Meloney, John N.	Sally Fox	12 Mar 1807
Melson, Caleb	Tabitha West	2 May 1789
Melson, Capt. James (wdr)	Mary H. Taylor	21 Jun 1837
Melson, Daniel Thomas Evans, sec.	Sophia Drummond (wid. of David)	6 Aug 1796
Melson, Daniel Henry Fitzgerald, sec.	Amey Drummond	24 Dec 1785
Melson, Daniel	Tabitha Ayres	2 Jul 1794
Melson, Daniel Sr.	Molly Pruitt (wid of John)	29 Jan 1805
Melson, Daniel	Betsy Wise	9 Feb 1801
Melson, David	Nancy Fitzgerald	25 Jul 1791
Melson, David	Susan Turner of John	21 Dec 1855
Melson, Edmund Robert Melson, sec.	Hetty Bonwell	26 Dec 1809
Melson, Elijah John Lewis of Daniel, sec.	Elizabeth Gray of Tho.	5 Apr 1832
Melson, George	Nancy Smith	12 Sep 1830
Melson, George William Willett, sec.	Sarah Taylor	23 May 1805
Melson, George Arggle Kellam, sec.	Mahala Kellam of Tho.	1 Nov 1830
Melson, George of Isaac Benjamin Floyd, sec.	Susan Mehollons of Jno.	17 Apr 1827
Melson, George	Tabitha Kelly	13 Mar 1794

```
Melson, Henry              Emma James                20 Jan 1852
    of P.                      of Molly

Melson, Henry              Emiline Justice            5 Jun 1849
                               of William, dec'd.
       Major Scott and Lewis L. Snead, sec.

Melson, Isaac of Geo.      Susanna Mears of Zoro     24 Feb 1818
       William Mears of Jno, sec.

Melson, James              Betsy Dickerson           27 Nov 1797

Melson, James              Susanna Poulson            4 Oct 1820
    of Robinson                of Molly
    Robinson Melson, sec.

Melson, James Thomas       Tabitha Hinman            10 Feb 1851

Melson, James Sr.          Scarburgh Snead           28 Dec 1829
       William Coard, sec.

Melson, James              Polly Dix                 28 Dec 1797

Melson, James H.           Eliza Milliner of Smith    3 Feb 1832
       John S. Lilliston, sec.

Melson, James Thomas       Sophia Scott               3 Jan 1844

Melson, Jeremiah           Elizabeth Hinman           7 Aug 1798
       Bennet Mason, sec.

Melson, Jeremiah           Tabitha Gladding of Geo.  25 Aug 1817
       John Mears, sec.

Melson, John D.            Margaret Kelly            21 Mar 1848
                               of Thomas
       George T. Mears and Joseph Federman, sec.

Melson, John W.            Maria Marshall            15 Dec 1835
       William S. Melson and Aaron Marshall, sec.

Melson, Jonathan          Seymour Melson            11 Jun 1803
       Smith Melson, sec.

Melson, Joseph             Nancy Colony               6 Jan 1809
       Benjamin Parks, sec.

Melson, Lorenzo Smith     Mary Bell of Edward       23 Dec 1826
       Edward Bell, sec.

Melson, Middleton          Rodey Mears               25 Mar 1797
       Elijah Fitzgerald, sec.
```

```
Melson, Noah              Patty Lumber              20 Mar 1807
     John Lambden, sec.

Melson, Robert            Margaret Hickman          25 Dec 1809
                          of Edward
     John K. Warrington, sec.

Melson, Robinson          Susanna Bunting           30 Jul 1810

Melson, Smith of Jona.    Anna Willett of Wm.        1 Feb 1816
     William Willett, sec.

Melson, Thomas            Suky Bunting              29 Jun 1841
                          of Solomon
     James H. East, sec.

Melson, William           Sally Gray                10 Feb 1789

Melson, William Henry     Bridget Bull              23 Dec 1834
                          of Southy

Melson, William S.        Sally Bloxom              25 Jan 1835
                          of Levin
     Levin Bloxom, sec.

Melson, William Henry     Bridget Bull              24 Dec 1834

Melvin, Aora              Caty Bayly of Tho.        16 Oct 1813
     William Seymour, sec.

Melvin, Obadiah           Molly Dreddon              4 Aug 1789

Melvin, Rev. Avra         Caty Baily                17 Oct 1813

Merril, John of Jos.      Sarah Bowles of Jno.      20 Dec 1819
     John Mathews of Evans, sec.

Merrill, Asa J.           Ann A. Mason              15 Nov 1832
                          of Agnes
     Peter Hargis, sec.

Merrill, Elisha           Sally Watson              15 May 1827
     of George            orphan John
     Wm. Walters Jr., John Coleburn of Abel and Moses W.    Hinman,
sec.

Merrill, James            Esther Mariner            19 Nov 1856

Merrill, John of Tho.     Damey Melson of Geo.      21 Dec 1825
     George Melson and Michael Robins, sec.

Merrill, John             Elizabeth Coleburn         3 Dec 1816
```

Asa Mathews, sec.

Merrill, Joseph David Miles and Isaac Henderson, sec.	Metsy Lambden of Tho.	5 Mar 1819
Merrill, Joseph John Merrill, sec.	Hester B. Loyd (wid of James)	17 Apr 1838
Merrill, Maximilian Charles Stockley, sec.	Mary Chapman	30 Jul 1800
Merrill, Maximillian John Nock, sec.	Hessey Richardson	28 Mar 1803
Merrill, Thomas H. (wdr)	Elizabeth A. Burton of John	28 Dec 1857
Merrill, Thomas Thomas Bunting, sec.	Tabitha Bunting	11 Dec 1798
Merrill, William	Rosy Parker	-- Aug 1790
Metcalf, Charles Thomas Copes, sec.	Sarah Hooke	15 Jun 1775
Metcalf, Jesse	Tabitha Cropper	20 Oct 1842
Metcalf, Jesse John K. Warrington, sec.	Sarah Warrington (wid John)	26 May 1817
Metcalf, John Ezekiel R. Bloxom, sec.	Mary A. White of Henry C.	3 July 1848
Metcalf, John William Haley, sec.	Susanna Custis	23 Dec 1807
Metcalf, Mark John Metcalf, sec.	Sarah Mathews	1 Nov 1783
Metcalf, Thomas M.	Sally G. Ward	13 Aug 1832
Metcalf, William George Fosque, sec.	Hessy Stokes	22 May 1821
Michael, William W. James Taylor, sec.	Amy Bunting	24 Dec 1810
Michael, William W. Thomas Wilkins, sec.	Charlotte S. Carpenter	26 Dec 1818

Middleton, George   Eveline Young   13 Dec 1848
     of Revel   of Catherine
George Middleton, sec.

Middleton, George   Elizabeth Russel   4 Jan 1805
     William Middleton, sec.

Middleton, John   Julia Ann Shreaves   29 Apr 1850
     (wdr)
     William S. Shreaves, sec.

Middleton, Major   Charity Wise   27 Jan 1795

Middleton, Revell   Elizabeth Taylor   29 Oct 1821
     of Major, dec'd.   of Charles
     Raymond Riley, sec.

Middleton, Thomas   Rosah White   7 Oct 1804
     Thomas West, sec.

Middleton, William   Susanna Topping   29 Apr 1816
     of William   of William, dec'd.
     Smith R. Carmine, sec.

Middleton, William   Sally S. Topping   22 Oct 1816

Middleton, William   Elizabeth Drummond   11 Jan 1822
                           of Step.dec'd., ward of Chas. Willite
     Charles Willite, sec.

Middleton, Wm. Sr.   Sally S. Topping   22 Oct 1816
                           (wid William)
     William Middleton Jr., sec.

Milburn, James   Anna Milburn   26 May 1806
     Elijah Milburn, sec.

Milburn, Thomas   Elizabeth Ellis   5 May 1807
     John Milbourn, sec.

Milby, John   Nancy Finney   27 Dec 1802
     Richard Rogers, sec.

Milby, John   Amey Groten   5 Jul 1784
     Zorobable Groten, sec.

Milby, William R.   Ann S. Roberts of Wm.   25 Apr 1828
     Thomas Kellam (SS), sec.

Miles, David   Caty Beacham   23 May 1833

                        (wid of Asa)
        Thomas Matthews and John Gladding, sec.

Miles, George   Nancy Poulson   15 Mar 1810
     William Major, sec.

Miles, George   Archania Spence   20 Dec 1852
                         of John

Miles, George   Comfort Taylor   9 Jan 1790

Miles, George (of Wm.)   Nancy Smith   21 Jul 1830

Miles, George   Nancy Smith of Elisha   21 Jul 1830
     William J. Matthews, sec.

Miles, Henry of Henry   Anna Harmon of Savage   25 Jun 1821
     Thorowgood Taylor, sec.

Miles, Henry   Elizabeth S. Mitchell   17 Nov 1852
     (wdr)   (wid)

Miles, James (wdr)   Margaret Bradwater   26 Mar 1838
     Elijah Miles and Revel Taylor, sec.

Miles, James S.   Mary A. Bird   24 Nov 1851
                         of Custis

Miles, James   Mary Crockett   25 Dec 1851
     of Parker   of George

Miles, James   Elizabeth Barnes   26 Dec 1831
     Elijah Miles and Elijah Hinman, sec.

Miles, Parker (wdr)   Ann Tyler   31 Mar 1835
     Gilbert Marshall and Jabez Tyler, sec.

Miles, Parker of Jno.   Rosanna Marshall of Sam. 3 Jan 1820
     Aaron Marshall, sec.

Miles, Rodger   Rachel Justice   23 Dec 1797

Miles, William of Geo.   Sally Bloxom of Custis   19 Apr 1820
     William R. Bunting, sec.

Miller, Francis D.   Louisa Lyon   27 Nov 1835
     (wdr)   (wid of Ethel)
     William Berry and William W. Dix, sec.

Miller, Rev. Benjamin   Ann D. Bayly   11 Nov 1840
     Thomas H. Bayly and Thomas R. Joynes, sec.

```
Miller, William E.          Mary Smith                28 May 1853
                            of Ezekiel

Milligan, John              Sally Tunnell             10 Mar 1800
      William Tunnell, sec.

Milliner, James             Ann Smith                 23 Dec 1822
      William S. Gunter, sec.

Milliner, John              Elizabeth James           12 Jan 1846

Milliner, Thomas            Harriet Bull              28 Nov 1834
                            of Custis
            Custis Bull, sec.

Mills, John                 Susanna Logan             13 Mar 1809
      James W. Melvin, sec.

Mills, Levin                Barbara Melvin            28 Nov 1806
      Gilbert Mills, sec.

Minson, Samuel              Sarah Joynes              24 Dec 1805
      Carvy Dunton, sec.

Mister, Azariah             Martha Duet               19 Aug 1807
      Custis Darby, sec.

Mister, Capt. Thomas        Margaret Ann Watson        2 Aug 1840

Mister, Edward C.           Sarah G. Mears            11 Sep 1850

Mister, Henry of Isaac   Susanna Mister of Wm.         2 Jan 1827
      William Martin, sec.

Mister, James               Rachel Mason              21 Oct 1803
      Robert Saulsbury, sec.

Mister, James F.            Catherine Salisbury        5 Feb 1812
      McKell Bonwell, sec.

Mister, John of Wm.         Lovea Mason               28 May 1827
                            of Middleton
            Coleburn Salisbury and Middleton Mason, sec.

Mister, John M.             Maria Pitts                9 Mar 1835
      Richard P. Read, sec.

Mister, Severn              Keziah Evans               2 Jul 1805
      Benjamin Evans, sec.

Mister, Solomon             Sally Snead                4 May 1836
```

Henry Walker, sec.

Mister, Thomas   Mary Johnson   19 Oct 1835
        William B. Kellam,   of Hamilton
                              sec.

Mister, Thomas   Margaret Ann Watson   30 Dec 1839
                              of William C.
        William Mister and William C. Watson, sec.

Mister, William Jr.   Ann D. Kellam   28 Feb 1825
        William P. Moore, sec.

Mister, William   Elizabeth Ward   20 Jul 1812
        James Mister, sec.

Mister, William   Sally Bull   29 Dec 1853
        of John   of William H., dec'd.

Mitchel, Alfred   Elizabeth Bonnawell   28 Oct 1846

Mitchell, Stephen   Mary Annis of Levi   1 Feb 1820
        James Grey, sec.

Mongue, Levin   Nancy Turlington   10 Aug 1804
        Geprge Harman, sec.

Montgomery, John   Patience Drummond   16 Jun 1775
        John Powell, sec.

Moore, Bratcher   Molly Hickman   9 Aug 1790

Moore, Ezekiel   Elizabeth S. Leatherbury   6 Dec 1849
                             of Thomas
        Perry A. Leatherbury, sec.

Moore, George   Ann Hickman   18 Dec 1832
        of Levi
        Levi Moore, sec.

Moore, Isaac   Lucy A. Boggs   5 Dec 1837
        Solomon Phillips, sec.

Moore, John   Elizabeth Belote   18 Apr 1808
        Stephen Moore, sec.

Moore, John J.   Sally Ann Purnell   17 Dec 1828
        James B. Robins and Zadoch Selby, sec.

Moore, John   Elizabeth Kilman   20 Dec 1797

```
Moore, Laban              Mary Lankford              3 Jul 1792

Moore, Laban              Mary Wessels              14 Jul 1807
   William Justice, sec.

Moore, Levi               Mary Belote               31 Dec 1818
   of Stephen                of Hancock
   William Jones, sec.

Moore, Levi               Mary Howarth              12 Aug 1816
   (wdr)                     of Rebecca
   Elijah Bonwell, sec.

Moore, Levi               Elizabeth Smith           24 Dec 1805
   Stephen Moore, sec.

Moore, Levi               Petunia Simpkins          13 Mar 1804
   Charles Stevens, sec.

Moore, Levin              Susanna Hickman of Edw.   19 Mar 1827
   John S. Ames, sec.

Moore, Stephen            Margaret E. Taylor         1 Sep 1841
                             of James
   George U. Parker, sec.

Moore, Stephen            Jemimah Lawson of Jno.    10 Aug 1815
   Thomas Nelson, sec.

Moore, Thomas             Susan Roberts             28 Nov 1825
                             of Tabitha
      Raymond Riley, sec.

Moore, William            Jane S. Boggs             20 Mar 1835
                             of Arthur
      William and Isaac Moore, sec.

Morgan, Ayres             Fanny Bloxom              12 Jan 1799

Morgan, James             Martha Ann Sasbery         4 Apr 1848

Morris, Daniel            Nancy Drummond             9 Nov 1815
                             of Atha/Otho?
      Atha Drummond, sec.

Morris, Gilbert           Elizabeth Richardson      26 --- 1805

Morris, Gilbert (wdr)     Polly Marriner of Geo.    22 May 1817
   William W. Hickman, sec.

Morris, James             Elizabeth Watson          27 Jul 1804
   Custis Kellam, sec.
```

Morris, John   Harriet Bayly   31 Dec 1857
                            of Custis

Morrison, John   Comfort Potter   4 Dec 1805
    James Ironmonger, sec.

Morrison, Alexander   Rachel Mears   30 May 1808
    George S. Savage, sec.

Moses FN   Leah Davis   FN   20 Mar 1808

Muliner, John R.   Caroline Hutson   13 Dec 1843

Mullins, James   Ann Smith   24 Dec 1822

Mullins, Smithy   Ann T. Taylor   18 Dec 1834

Mullins, Thomas   Harriet Bull   29 Nov 1834

Mullowny, John   Sarah Fox   30 Jan 1807
    Richard D. Bayly, sec.

Mum, John   Polly Matthews   17 May 1803
    John Young, sec.

Mumford, Riley   Caty Smallwood   26 Sep 1803
    John Jester, sec.

Munford, Jesse   Nancy Collins   4 Sep 1816
                            (wid John)
    James Brittingham, sec.

Murray, William   Nancy Williams   20 Sep 1803
    John Melvin, sec.

```
Nedab, John                 Henny Bundick            24 Feb 1830
                            orphan John Bundick, alias James FN
        Levin Core, sec.

Nedab, Levin                Comfort Nedab             2 Apr 1790

Nedab, Stephen FN           Patience FN              22 Apr 1807

Nedab, William              Sally Harmon              4 Dec 1848

Nedab, William FN           Sally Harmon             20 Dec 1848
                            of George FN
          John N. Poal and John E. Gibbons, sec.

Neely, John                 Amelia W. Bayly           5 Mar 1827
        John B. Revell, sec.

Nelson, Edward              Sally Nelson of Jno.     20 Jun 1829
        John S. Gibbs, sec.

Nelson, George Jr.          Hessy Hatton             23 Aug 1825
        of George               of Benjamin
        Sacker Scott, sec.

Nelson, George             Delaney Vessels          25 Mar 1797

Nelson, George             Betsy Melson              8 Nov 1798
        Asa Shield, sec.

Nelson, George H.          Elizabeth Whealton       15 Feb 1853
        of John                 (wid of John)

Nelson, James              Nancy Bull               16 May 1835
                            of John and Harriet
          William R. Custis, sec

Nelson, James              Delilah Prescoat          9 Oct 1801

Nelson, James              Nancy Bull               17 May 1832

Nelson, John (wdr)         Anne Hickman             14 Apr 1854
        of George               (wid of Robert)

Nelson, John Jr.           Barbara Savage of Jacob  14 Jan 1829
          John Nelson Sr. and Joseph Turlington, sec.

Nelson, John (wdr)         Rosey Ann Broadwater      9 Dec 1852

Nelson, John               Leah Trehearn             5 Jun 1803
        Richard Drummond, sec.

Nelson, Spencer            Elkanah Beach            30 Jul 1832
```

of George S.
John Nelson and George S. Nelson, sec.

Nelson, Thomas of King   Nancy Cox of Leah   5 Jul 1815
    Thomas Nelson Sr. and Elijah Sterling, sec.

Nelson, Thomas   Sally A. Lucass   1 Feb 1854
    of John

Nelson, William   Ann Mason   31 Dec 1805
    Jacob Edwards, sec.

Nelson, William   Hessey Pruitt   27 Jan 1804
    George Nelson, sec.

Nickolson, Levin   Harriet Stuart   7 Dec 1839

Niffen, Henry   Eliza Payne   5 Apr 1815
                  (wid Levin)
    Thomas Chandler, sec.

Night, Jacob FN   Martha Walker FN   11 Mar 1815

Nocholson, John   Elizabeth Whittington 1 Feb 1775
                  of Southy
    Sebastian Cropper, sec.

Nock, Benjamin   Tabitha A.P. Willia 21 May 1839
                  of Zorababel

Nock, Charles   Sarah Barnes   18 Dec 1807
                  of Archibald
    John Cole, sec.

Nock, Edmund   Catherine Nock   31 Oct 1806
    Solomon Nock, sec.

Nock, Elijah   Lydia Hope   22 Nov 1798
                  of Rachel Broadwater
    John Nock sec.

Nock, Elizah   Margaret Charnock 29 Dec 1825

Nock, George W.   Julia F. Duncan   2 Jan 1854
    of Sally   of Meshack

Nock, George   Margaret Guy   8 Dec 1784
    Robert Nock, sec.

Nock, Gillet   Mary A. Marshall 24 Dec 1841

Nock, James   Esther Garrison   6 Dec 1824

(wdr)   (wid William)
John W. Nock of Jas., sec.

Nock, John   Polly Mears   21 Dec 1809
                          (wid John)
     Elijah Baker, sec.

Nock, John   Elizabeth Nock   20 May 1813
                          (wid Zadock)
     Zorobabal West, sec.

Nock, John of James   Elizabeth Mapp of Housen 27 Oct 1823
     James Nock and Littleton A. Lecato, sec.

Nock, John   Peggy Broadwater   18 Dec 1797

Nock, John   Sarah Duncan   28 Jul 1834
     Edward Nock and J.J. Ailworth, sec.

Nock, Levin W.   Polly W. Edmunds of Jms. 27 Oct 1821
     James Edmunds, sec.

Nock, Levin W.   Sarah C. Floyd   16 Oct 1849
                          of Matthew, dec'd.
     Robert T. Harmon, sec.

Nock, Lewis J.   Susan Phillips   7 Mar 1849

Nock, Lewis   Tabitha Johnson   11 Mar 1829
                          of Isaiah
     George Ellis and Zadock Selby, sec.

Nock, Lewis J.   Susan Phillips   7 Nov 1849
                          of William
     John W.H. Parker, sec.

Nock, Lewis of Zadock   Jane Fitchett of Jona.   16 Feb 1819
     Samuel Mapp, sec., Wm. Nock, guardian, cons.

Nock, Littleton   Susan P. Dix   27 Jun 1838
     Colmon C. Hinman and Thomas Lilliston, sec.

Nock, Littleton   Mary Johnson   29 Dec 1808
                          (wid John)
     George Thomas, sec.

Nock, Robert   Elizabeth Heath   17 Feb 1787
     Thomas Nock, sec.

Nock, Samuel   Elizabeth Savage   13 Jan 1820

- 210 -

```
        of John              of John, dec'd.
        Elias D. Joynes, sec.

Nock, Samuel of John    Sally Bunting of Jana    28 Feb 1820
        Noah Jones, sec.

Nock, Thomas            Susan Kellam            12 Jan 1833
                        (wid of Thomas S.)
        Hugh Smith, sec.

Nock, William           Bridget Bundick         30 Nov 1784
        William Gibb, sec.

Nock, William           Meliah Watson           30 Mar 1814
        Richard D. Bayly, sec.

Nock, William           Sinah Bloxom            16 Feb 1818
        of Elijah           of Levin, dec'd.
        Staton Taylor, sec.

Nock, Zadock            Evaline W. Riley         3 Dec 1840
        Jesse Dickerson and Augustus J.F. Johnson, sec.

Nock, Zadock            Elizabeth Warner         c. 1786
        John Moore, sec.                        (not dated)

Northam, Custis         Nancy Boggs of Arthur   29 Jul 1816
        Elijah Boggs, sec.

Northam, Custis         Mary Boggs               1 Aug 1816

Northam, Custis         Eliza Northam           16 Nov 1803
        John Northam, sec.

Northam, David B.       Julia A. Bull (wid)      1 Apr 1846

Northam, Edward J.      Elizabeth Ann Justice   19 Aug 1834
        Henry Miles and John Watson, sec.

Northam, Edward         Polly Coke of Richard   27 May 1829
        Shadrach Taylor and Samuel Walston, sec.

Northam, Elijah         Margaret Young           1 Jun 1853
        (wdr)               (wid of David)

Northam, Elizah         Comfort Trader          19 Mar 1827
        son Wm. of E.       of Sacker
        Dan. Shay, Whittington Trader, sec.

Northam, Geo. of Major  Ann Bird of Major       25 Nov 1816
        Major Bird, sec.
```

Northam, Gillett   Elizabeth Bird   5 Feb 1840
                          of Bennett, Sr.
     Bennell M. Bird, sec.

Northam, Gillett   Elizabeth Cole   13 Mar 1834
     Meshack and James K. Duncan, sec.

Northam, Henry B.   Milky Northam   30 Apr 1832
                          orphan of Custis
     Elijah Northam, sec.

Northam, Henry   Sally Duncan   4 Apr 1818
     of Major   (wid Edmund)
     George Northam and John Cole Jr., sec.

Northam, Henry B. (wdr)   Elizabeth Young (wid) 28 Aug 1847
     M.C. Northam, sec.

Northam, Henry B. Jr.   Hester Prescott   26 Apr 1858
                          of Hester

Northam, James M.   Sarah A. Landing   26 Jul 1858
     of Henry B.   of James

Northam, James of Jacob   Elizabeth Wright of Geo. 1 Nov 1819
     Revell Parker, sec.

Northam, James   Rosey A.G. Dix   7 Mar 18388
     (wdr)   of Levi
     Levi Dix, sec.

Northam, John   Adeline Trader   2 June 1854
     of William   of Ishmeal

Northam, John   Elizabeth Northam   31 Aug 1829
     of Custis   of William of E.
     Wm. Northam and Henry B. Northam, sec.

Northam, Southy   Neomy Bird   29 Jan 1805

Northam, William   Betsy Northam   10 Aug 1803
     John Northam, sec.

Northam, William   Drucilla Bayly   6 Jan 1858
     of Elijah   of Elizabeth Harris

Northam, William C   Margaret Bird   30 Nov 1847
                          of Johannas
     Henry B. Northam and E.P. Pitts, sec.

Northam, William of Wm.   Susanna Christopher   8 Dec 1819

                              of George
        George Christopher, sec.

Nottingham, David B.   Leah G. Floyd   30 Aug 1813
     William F. Savage, sec.

Nottingham, Thomas   Mary A. Scott   27 Jul 1835

Ogue, William   Susey James   10 Jan 1801
        Robert James, sec.

Oliver, James M.   Ann R. Custis   12 Apr 1843

Oliver, William N.(wdr) Catherine Susan Martin   28 Dec 1848
        Thomas N. Smith, sec.

Oliver, William W.   Juliet Savage   26 Feb 1834
        William P. Moore, sec.

Onions, Henry   Nancy Wilkinson   17 May 1803
        John Onions, sec.

Onions, Hezekiah   Betsy Stockly   31 Jan 1792

Onions, John   Linany Littleton   10 Feb 1804
        Elijah Wright, sec.

Onions, John   Tabitha Young   20 Jun 1790

Onions, Wesley   Eliza Thomas of Polly   12 Jul 1852

Onions, William Selby   Sally Bundick   6 Dec 1792

Onions, William   Polly Vessels   10 Dec 1811
        Isaac Vessells, sec.

Onley, Samuel   Elizabeth Marshall   7 Feb 1831
                         of John
           James McCready, sec.

Onley, William of John   Tiffany Hickman of Tho.   6 Nov 1854

Only, John   Nancy Groten   26 Jan 1786
        Thomas Bonewell, sec.

Only, John   Critty Wilson   11 Oct 1843

Only, John of Edmund   Polly Clarke of Nancy   31 Jan 1817
        Daniel Baker, sec.

Only, John   Pamelia Melson   27 Aug 1832
        William Nelson and Revel Gaskins, sec.

Only, Major of Edmund   Ann Justice of Tho.   19 Dec 1820
        Samuel Justice, sec.

Only, Richard   Margaret Delastatius   30 Dec 1808
                         of Selby
           Thomas Allen, sec.

Only, Thomas	Sally Davis	4 Apr 1841
Only, William of Edmund John Savage Sr., sec.	Ann Maria Bundick	12 Dec 1826
Only, William William Drummond, sec.	Mary Delastatius	31 Jan 1814
Outten, Abraham Peter Mack, sec.	Mary Wise	2 Feb 1785
Outten, Ephraim John O. Twyford, sec.	Susanna Leatherbury	8 Dec 1803
Outten, Isaac Eli Hornsby, sec.	Margaret H. Colony	21 Dec 1802
Outten, Jacob Ephraim Outten, sec.	Mary Hancock	23 Jun 1806
Outten, Jacob James Justice Abbott, sec.	Keziah Conquest	5 Aug 1804
Outten, Purnal Joshua Taylor, sec.	Elizabeth Taylor	16 Jul 1785
Outten, Purnell T. Thomas Sturgis, sec.	Ann Sturgis of Tho.	8 Jan 1821
Outten, Shadrack W. Smith Hyslop, sec.	Margaret Moore of Jno.	25 Feb 1817
Outten, William (FN)	Tinny Medad	30 Dec 1841
Outten, William Alexander McCollom, sec.	Tabitha Burton	19 Jul 1809
Owen, Henry Arthur Addison, sec.	Nancy Thornton	31 Mar 1806
Owen, John John Thornton, sec.	Peggy Warner	17 May 1803
Owen, John	Anne Taylor	20 Dec 1797
Owen, Samuel James B. Jacob, sec.	Margaret C. Welburn of John	28 Feb 1825
Owen, Taylor	Scarburch Taylor	2 Oct 1789

Owen, Taylor   Elia Young of Wm.   13 Nov 1813
   Richard Young, sec.

Owens, Taylor   Caty Guardinir   9 Feb 1808
   Thomas Hancock, sec.

Padget, Nathaniel	Peggy Connah	30 Jul 1788
Padget, William Levi Brittingham, sec.	Polly Brittingham of Levi	10 Aug 1812
Pairs, William Dennard Paul, sec.	Euphamy Paul of Zorobabel	4 Sep 1829
Palmatary, George H.	Irene Bagwell	2 Sep 1858
Palmer, Capt. James	Elizabeth B. Cropper of William	29 Apr 1846
Parker, Anderson Southy Bloxom, sec.	Nancy Kellam	27 Dec 1802
Parker, Arthur H.	Nancy Taylor	20 Nov 1847
Parker, Capt. Robert	Betsy Thornton	8 Dec 1845
Parker, George William A. Parker, sec.	Sarah Ann D. Taylor of Thomas T.	18 Sep 1826
Parker, George of Samuel Joseph Turlington, sec.	Peggy Jones Fosque of John	3 Jun 1816
Parker, George	Sally Rodgers	21 Nov 1820
Parker, George S. (wdr)	Rachel	11 Oct 1837
Parker, George W. minor son Henry John M. Watson and John W. Hutchinson, sec.	Jane M. Rodgers	27 Nov 1826
Parker, George	Margaret East	8 Jan 1851
Parker, George FN	Mary Major	13 may 1852
Parker, George E. of Michael Joseph C. Parker and Levin Core, sec.	Nancy Taylor of James	18 Jan 1825
Parker, Henry P. John A. Scarburgh and John B. Ailworth, sec.	Elizabeth Riley of Raymond	4 Mar 1830
Parker, Henry	Emiline Corbin of Sarah Ann	8 Jun 1847

John Kilmon, sec.

Parker, James   Hanney Savage   29 Aug 1836
    of Robert   (wid of Jesse)
    Robert and Pete East, sec.

Parker, James   Nancy East   21 Dec 1801
    Parker East, sec.

Parker, James   Henny Savage   27 Jun 1838

Parker, James   Ann Paul   29 Aug 1836
    of Robert
    Willaim Payne, sec.

Parker, James   Susan Mason   4 Jan 1843

Parker, John   Agnes Mason   31 Dec 1832
    of Sacker
    Custis Annis, sec.

Parker, John FN   Margaret Major FN   25 Jun 1855

Parker, John FN   Ada Wittus FN   28 Dec 1835
    Mitchell Chandler and John C. Wise, sec.

Parker, John W.   Ellen M. Hopkins   10 Feb 1847

Parker, John N.H.   Sarah A.S. Topping   27 Dec 1847
                         of Nathaniel
    Edward P. Pitts, sec.

Parker, John   Margaret Boggs   17 Nov 1819
    of Richard   of Arthur
    William D. Chandler, sec.

Parker, John (FN)   Ada Outten   29 Jan 1826

Parker, John   Leah Savage   28 Dec 1819
    of Robert   of Jacob
    Edmund Leatherbury, sec. and Jacob Savage consent

Parker, John   Margaret Boggs   17 Mar 1829

Parker, John, Jr.   Mary Twiford   1790

Parker, John   Nany Dix   22 Dec 1801
    of John
    John Burton sec.

Parker, John   Nancy Ann Middleton   29 Jun 1847
    of Benjamin   of Russell

Samuel Wessells and Raymond Parks, sec.

Parker, John	Molly Grinalds	14 Dec 1790
Parker, John	Sarah Simpson of Southy	31 Jul 1775

     John Riley sec.

Parker, John FN	Mary Jane West FN	29 Dec 1856
Parker, Josiah	Hetty Mears of Robert	6 Aug 1812

     Jesse Dickerson, sec.

Parker, Levin	Alice A. East of John	12 Jul 1853
Parker, Major FN	Sabra Stran FN of Rike FN	21 Nov 1849

     Sylvester R. Chandler, sec.

Parker, Major (FN)	Sabra Stevens	24 Nov 1849
Parker, Revell	Elizabeth Hornsby of Major, dec'.d	17 Dec 1822

     Bagwell Topping, sec.

Parker, Samuel of Samuel	Margaret Watson of John, dec'd.	11 Jan 1819

     George S. Fisher, sec.

Parker, Samuel	Mary Stephens of Charles	25 Dec 1839

     Nathaniel Fosque, sec.

Parker, Samuel	Anne Celly (Kelly?)	c. 1787 (not dated)

     Jacob Savage, sec.

Parker, Samuel of Samuel	Sally Phillips of Thomas	29 Dec 1828

     John G. Joynes, sec.

Parker, Southy	Hessey Grinnalds	3 Aug 1803

     Robert Lilliston, sec.

Parker, Thomas Jacob	Anne M. Galt of Dr. Samuel, dec'd.	19 Dec 1817

     William P. Moore, sec.

Parker, Thomas of James	Mary Smith orphan William W.	28 Dec 1829

     Edward Phillips, sec.

```
Parker, Tully W. (wdr)      Susan A. Neely           16 Jul 1851
                            ward of Edward B. Neely

Parker, William L.          Margaret L. James          7 Feb 1852
   of Levin                 of Mary James (wid of Thomas)

Parker, William H.          Margaret Fletcher         16 Apr 1823
                            (wid William)

Parker, William O.          Sudey Wise                11 Mar 1816
                            of Tully
      William P. Custis, sec.

Parkes, Benjamin            Polly West of Esther      21 Feb 1832
      John Shrieves, sec.

Parkes, Charles             Margaret D. Russell       25 Dec 1848
                            of George
      William Hillman, sec.

Parkes, Edward of John      Nancy Mason of Richard    27 Dec 1852

Parkes, George              Mary Russell of Eliz. B.  16 Nov 1852

Parkes, John (wdr)          Elizabeth Bradford (wid)  26 Jul 1850

Parkes, William T.          Mary A. Stephens          26 Jul 1848
      William D. Parks, sec.

Parkinson, Richard          Nancy Watson               5 Jan 1809
      Obediah Thorman, sec.

Parks, Benjamin             Damy Bundick              19 Dec 1818
   of Benjamin              of Richard
      Southy Grinnalds of Wm, sec.

Parks, Benjamin             Betsy Savage              16 Sep 1797

Parks, Charles             Margaret H. Resssell       27 Dec 1848

Parks, Edmund (wdr)         Yearly Russell (wid)      16 Oct 1821
      Southy Grinnalds, sec.

Parks, Edmund               Peggy Bird                24 Dec 1798

Parks, Elijah               Sally Stephens            21 Feb 1804
      Dennis Simpson, sec.

Parks, Gabriel              Elizabeth Pruitt          15 Jan 1845

Parks, George               Leah Turlington           19 Oct 1825
```

```
Parks, George S.            Leah Turlington            15 Oct 1825
     of Benjamin            of John
John Turlington, sec.

Parks, George S.            Rachel Bunting              9 Oct 1837
     (wdr)                  (wid of William)
Elijah Sabage, sec.

Parks, John Jr.            Caty Cutler                  7 Dec 1833

Parks, John               Agnes Mason                 31 Dec 1837

Parks, John D.            Sarah Rew                   23 Apr 1823
                          of Charles, dec'd.
     Charles Willett, sec.

Parks, John (wdr)         Polly Phillips          Sep 1835-1837

Parks, John               Tabitha Young               19 Jul 1809
     Solomon Ewell, sec.

Parks, John H.            Betsy Shreves               31 Jul 1832
                          (wid of John)
     Daniel Lewis, sec.

Parks, John H.            Betsy  Shreives              2 Sep 1838

Parks, John Jr.           Caty Cutler                 29 Apr 1833
                          of John
     John Parks, Sr., sec.

Parks, John (wdr)         Polly Phillips              29 Oct 1832
     of Smiths Island
Reuben Parks and William Drummond, sec.

Parks, Mark               Elizabeth Thornton          27 Dec 1834
     of John              of Laura
James Wessells, sec.

Parks, Raymond            Nancy Outten                 1 Nov 1809
     Samuel Johnson, Richard Dix and John West, sec.

Parks, Raymond Jr.        Nancy Wessells              19 Feb 1833
                          (wid of Willliam)
     Raymond Riley, sec.

Parks, Reuben             Pricilla Croswell           18 Sep 1805
     Peter Parker, sec.

Parks, Robert             Rosey Tignal                 5 Jul 1817

Parks, Robert             Nancy Holsten               22 Mar 1806
```

Parks, Robert Smith Melam, sec.	Nancy Holston	22 Mar 1808
Parks, Solomon Richard Young, sec.	Margaret Killman	7 Feb 1837
Parks, Solomon	Peggy Kilmon	7 Feb 1837
Parks, William J. (wdr)	Sarah E. Willet of Polly	5 Feb 1851
Parks, William	Amamda Wessells of John, dec'd.	17 Dec 1856
Parramore, John of Jms.	Jemimah Spence	5 Jul 1825
Parramore, John C. James N. Bayly, sec.	Harriet B.D. Parramore	29 May 1820
Parramore, John William Parramore, sec.	Sarah Holland (wid)	16 May 1808
Parramore, Thomas Peter Hack, sec.	Anne Hack	25 Jul 1786
Parramore, William	Margaret Teackle	27 Jun 1796
Parramore, Wm. Jr. Richard D. Bayly, sec.	Elizabeth C. Custis	25 Nov 1825
Parramore, Wm. Sr. John Henderson, sec.	Sarah Grinnalds	12 Nov 1802
Parridice, John James West, sec.	Betsy Littleton	3 Jul 1800
Parson, Elexander	Sarah Smith	28 Jan 1852
Patchet, William	Polly Brittingham	10 Jul 1812
Patterson, Anderson Arthur Hickman, sec.	Elizabeth Mills	29 Dec 18-- (damaged)

Patterson, James
    Charles Tatham and James W. Twyford, sec.
	Elizabeth Holland
	    of William
		17 Aug 1836

Paul, Dennard
    of Zorobabel
    Elisha Crockett, sec.
	Henny Crockett
	    of Jesse
		20 Sep 1826

Paul, Jacob	Sophia Linton	22 Sep 1797

```
Payne, Levin                Elizabeth Lumber          27 Sep 1810
    William White, sec.

Payne, Levin                Eliza Hickman              2 Feb 1803
    Selby Benson, sec.

Peacock, Cornelius          Elizabeth Lewis            7 Sep 1830
                            of Stephen
    Stephen Lewis and John T. Marshall, sec.

Peacock, Southy             Nancy Conner               7 Oct 1802
    Nehemiah Broughton, sec.

Peake, Robert (wdr)         Rosey Tignal of Phillip    3 Jul 1817
    John Taylor, sec.

Pearce, Gideon              Eliza Baynes               2 Nov 1814
    John T. Baynes and John H. Bayly, sec.

Pearson, William           Kessey Watson             25 Dec 1817

Pearson, William           Kessy Watson              24 Dec 1817
    of Thomas              of William
    Charles Smith, sec.

Peck, Samuel               Polly Abbott              24 Nov 1791

Perkins, James FN          Margaret Allen FN         28 Mar 1853

Perkins, Peter FN          Maria Roan FN             25 Dec 1838
    Thomas Harrison, sec.

Perkins, Stephen           Adah Andrews              17 Nov 1802
    Geodiah Bell, sec.

Peter FN                   Leah Frank FN             23 Dec 1807
    Littleton Armitrader, sec.

Peter FN                   Sally Medad FN            15 Apr 1826
                           of Peter
    Elisha H. Davis and Bloxom Thomas Lilliston, sec.

Peterson, Jeremiah F.      Elizabeth Powell           7 Aug 1833
    William Ewell and John C. Stevenson, sec.

Petitt, John               Triphamy Mason            13 Mar 1804
    Levi Ames, sec.

Pettet, Levin              Louisa Wright             20 Jun 1838
                           of Edward
    Thomas Hope, sec.
```

Pettit, Levin	Susanna Wright	26 Jun 1838
Pettit, Thomas Isaac Hickman, sec.	Kessy Melson orphan Noah	17 Sep 1828
Pettitt, George	Grace Litchfield	10 Jan 1801
Pettitt, James of Revell John Bull Sr., sec.	Margaret Beauchamp orphan Elizah, ward of John Bull	28 Dec 1829
Pettitt, James	Anna Maria Matthews of George	17 Nov 1856
Pettitt, John of Revel Levin Bloxom and William Baker, sec.	Elizabeth Baker of Wm.	30 May 1825
Pettitt, Levin (wdr)	Jane West of Robert and Peggy	13 Dec 1853
Pettitt, Levin (wdr)	Sarah Ann Fisher of Wm.	5 Oct 1858
Pettitt, Revel Southy Litchfield, sec.	Elizabeth Baker	3 Jul 1800
Pettitt, Thomas George Pettitt, sec.	Nancy Groten	24 Aug 1804
Pettitt, William M. William P. Moore, sec.	Louise W. Coward orphan Samuel, ward of Wm. P. Moore	28 Feb 1825
Pettitt, William	Molly Lang	nd 1815
Pettitt, William James Custis, sec.	Mary Hope (wid of Kendal)	7 Jan 1836
Pewsey, Stephen Elizah Hancock, sec.	Betsy Hancock of Elizah	12 Nov 1810
Pewsey, Thomas Thomas Lilliston, sec.	Sally Fitzgerald of Chas. dec'd., ward of Tho. Lilliston	3 Aug 1825
Pewsey, Thomas William of John, dec'd. W. Twiford, sec.	Ann Y. Hichman	9 Sep 1820 James
Phillips, Abel	Sally Dolby	27 Jan 1806

William Churn, sec.

Phillips, Abel   Margaret Edwards   18 Mar 1820
    of Thomas   of Babel
John Turlington, sec.

Phillips, Benjamin   Caty Elliott   31 Jul 1837
    of Jonathan   (wid of Thomas)
George East, sec.

Phillips, Charles   Leah Savage   3 Jan 1806
Francis Boogs Jr., sec.

Phillips, David   Patsy Stockley   19 Jun 1827
    of Thomas   of Margaret
Samuel Turlington, sec.

Phillips, Edward   Nancy Smith   14 Jan 1799
Matthew Phillips, sec.

Phillips, Eli   Mary Chandler   7 Apr 1839
William Gardner, sec.

Phillips, George B.   Margaret Hickman   25 Aug 1825
                            of Thomas
    Levin Phillips, sec.

Phillips, George   Betty Powell   31 May 1799
George Taylor, sec.

Phillips, Jacob (wdr)   Sarah C. Slocomb   14 May 1827
John R. Parker, sec.

Phillips, Jacob   Ann Wise of George   21 Jun 1814
William Finney, sec.

Phillips, Jesse   Mahala Bell   28 Jul 1823
James Glen, sec.

Phillips, John   Julia Satchell   13 Sep 1839
William Hinman, sec.

Phillips, John   Juliet Staton   15 May 1839

Phillips, John   Nancy Edmunds   19 Aug 1786
Thomas Willet, sec.

Phillips, John L.   Kessy Bell of Anna   23 Dec 1820
Edward Bell, sec.

Phillips, John   Rose Stephens   27 Nov 1844

- 225 -

```
Phillips, John          Rachel Fisher          27 Mar 1827
   of Thomas            (wid George)
Samuel M. Turlington, sec.

Phillips, Laban         Hessy Phillips of Thos. 14 Feb 1820
   John Turlington, sec.

Phillips, Laban         Betsy Melson           27 Sep 1808
   William S. Watson, sec.

Phillips, Levin         Sarah Phillips         30 Mar 1835
   Thomas Leatherbury, sec.

Phillips, Levin         Charlotte Vernelson     5 Feb 1828    6
Matthias     of Sally                                      John
Hickman, sec.


Phillips, Levin         Susan Ashly            14 Nov 1838
                        of Willliam
     William Ashly, sec.

Phillips, Levin         Elizabeth B.Phillips   15 Feb 1821    6
Thomas        of John
John Phillips of John, sec.

Phillips, Matthias      Nancy Nelson           28 Feb 1799
   John Satchell, sec.

Phillips, Sacker        Susan Savage           20 Jan 1840
                        of Bagwell
     George W. Mason, sec.

Phillips, Samuel (wdr)  Nancy Smith (wid)      13 Nov 1844

Phillips, Samuel        Mary Barnes            30 Jul 1849
                        of Parkes
     George S. Rea, sec.

Phillips, Smith         Elizabeth East         10 Dec 1834
                        (wid of Richard)
     Laben Phillips, sec.

Phillips, Solomon       Ann S. Phillips         7 Apr 1832
                        of Edward
     Edward Phillips, sec.

Phillips, Thomas        Betsy Lewis            17 Oct 1814
   John Hickman, sec.

Phillips, Thomas        Elizabeth Baker        12 Apr 1848
```

```
                            of Edmund
          P.T. Savage and T.H. Wessells, sec.

Phillips, Thomas        Nancy Vernelson          -- Feb 1795
     James Hanneford, sec.                       (badly damaged)

Phillips, Wesley S.     Sarah Harrison           9 Apr 1851

Phillips, William       Rachel Floyd            21 Feb 1844

Phillips, William       Molly Savage            23 Dec 1806
     Zorobabel Savage, sec.

Phillips, William       Mrs. Betsy Picket       29 Sep 1800
     George Taylor, sec.

Phillips, Wm. Fenry     Sally Turlington        20 Jun 1829
                        of Joseph
     Edmund Leatherbury, sec.

Pigott, Jecvhoma        Molly Lawrence          14 Sep 1787
     William Gibb, sec.

Pilchard, John          Elizabeth Taylor        20 Nov 1800
     Southy Lucas, sec.

Piper, Charles S.       Polly Marshall          11 Nov 1811
     John Marshall of Wm., sec.

Pitt, William           Elizabeth Hutchinson     1 Jan 1816
                        of Babel
     Eli Charnock, sec.

Pitts, Major S.         Margaret Custis         10 Dec 1803
     John Wise, sec.

Pitts, Major            Margaret Charnock        2 Jan 1843

Pitts, Robert           Susannah Conner         21 Dec 1813
     William Savage, sec.

Pitts, Robert           Ann Waterfield          30 Nov 1812
     James White, sec.

Pitts, Thomas C.        Elizabeth S. Gunter      3 Mar 1853
     of Robert            ward of George Savage

Pitts, William          Molly Long               1 Jul 1815
     Babel Hutchinson, sec.

Pitts, William C.       Ann M. Savage           30 Dec 1839
     James K. Savage, sec.
```

Pitts, William   Elizabeth Gunter   30 Dec 1808
    John Gunter, sec.

Pitts, Thomas H.   Ann Turner   2 Apr 1851

Planter, John FN   Haney Teackle FN   10 May 1831
    Benjamin Bradley, sec.

Poe, George   Rosey Elliott   7 Aug 1847
    (wdr)   of James
    James Parks of Samuel and Barnard B. Badger, sec.

Pool, Charles   Betsy Drummond   9 Oct 1804

Pool, James FN   Mary Ann Douglas FN   30 Dec 1850
                          of William FN

Poolman, Cato   Nancy Stephens   17 Dec 1811
    John Budd, sec.

Porter, Elijah   Sally Merrill   19 Jan 1835
                          (wid of Elisha)
        Thomas Bayly, sec.

Porter, John   Henrietta Mathews   24 Jan 1818
    of James   of James
    Caleb Duncan, sec.

Potter, John R.   Anna M. Moore of Wm.   14 Dec 1825
    George Parker, sec.

Potter, Laban   Sophia Spiers   18 Aug 1786
    Benj. Hayley, sec.

Potts, T. George   Nancy Hill   10 Oct 1854

Poulson, Edmund   Susan C. Hopkins   10 Jun 1824
    of James   of Maximilian
    Thomas H. Guy, sec.

Poulson, Eraster   Catherine Bagwell   25 Sep 1815
    William W. Burton, sec.

Poulson, Erasters   Tabitha Custis   8 Oct 1806
                          sister Thomas Wise
        Thomas H. Guy, sec.

Poulson, James B.   Sally Revell   7 Jun 1843

Poulson, John   Elizabeth Poulson   31 Dec 1832
    Custis Northam, sec.

```
Poulson, John              Polly Dix                    1 Dec 1785
    William Gibb, sec.

Poulson, John H. (wdr)     Margaret Mason              10 Jan 1854
                           of Jacob, dec'd.

Poulson, Robert            Catherine Custis            22 Jul 1833
    Thomas B. Custis, sec.

Poulson, Thomas            Rosey Windew                 2 Dec 1835

Poulson, Thomas            Rosey Window                 3 Dec 1835
    John M. Hack and Alexander W. Mears, sec.

Poulson, Wiliam            Betsy Savage of John        31 Oct 1816
    Stephen Pusey, sec.

Poulson, Zadock            Molly Edwards               10 Aug 1805
    Zorobabel Edwards, sec.

Powell, George L.          Sally E. Wise                5 Jul 1851

Powell, Geroge P.          Margaret A. Johnson         15 Jan 1851

Powell, Hugh L.            Catherine Wise              22 Jan 1849

Powell, Isaac              Polly Gootee                20 Jun 1792

Powell, James              Polly Roberts               29 Oct 1817
    of Levin               of John
    John Roberts, sec., Levin Powell consent

Powell, Jesse              Peggy Savage                16 Jul 1811
                           of Littleton
    Littleton Savage, sec.

Powell, Jesse              Betsy Cobb                  30   Dec    1831
                           of Shadrock
    James Hyslop, sec.

Powell, John               Elizabeth Buntin            23 Aug 1812
    Samuel Justice, sec.

Powell, John               Susan Mister                30 Mar 1835
    James Savage, sec.

Powell, John T.            Arinthia S. Ewell           19 Dec 1849
                           of George P. Ewell
    George P. Ewell, sec.

Powell, Joseph             Nancy Townsend               9 Jul 1810
                           of Teackle
```

Edmund Bell, sec.

Powell, Joseph Elias Taylor, sec.	Rachel Mathews	26 Sep 1808
Powell, Laban	Mary Rew	23 Aug 1792
Powell, Nathan Littleton Trader, sec.	Catherine Watson	30 Dec 1800
Powell, Nathaniel (wdr) Smith Melson, sec.	Sally Turnell of Major	17 Nov 1821
Powell, Nathaniel	Mary L. Winder	15 Dec 1847
Powell, Nathaniel John West, sec.	Leah Lewis	17 Dec 1804
Powell, Nicholas	Elizabeth West	22 May 1792
Powell, Seth of Laban Major Rayfield, sec.	Mary Rayfield of Major	28 Dec 1818
Powell, William R.	Indiana Margaret West	10 Nov 1849
Powell, William Levin Bloxom, sec.	Rachel Bloxom	1 May 1809
Powell, William William Lewis, sec.	Caty Lewis	16 Apr 1806
Powers, James Edward Ironmonger and Southy Copes, sec.	Esther Copes	12 Nov 1807
Prescott, George Coventon Mason, sec.	Tenny Young	29 Jan 1813
Prescott, Thomas Thomas Hope and George Prescott, sec.	Bridget Barnes (wid William)	11 Dec 1822
Prewet, Elijah George Prewit, sec.	Arcadia Dies	14 May 1804
Prewet, Ruben Severn Evans, sec.	Sally Evans	2 Jun 1841
Prewitt, George (wdr) Gabriel Parkes and John M. Fosque, sec.	Sally Evans of George	5 Jul 1848

```
Prewitt, William          Rachel Shield              30 Nov 1818      6
Molly                of Reuben
John Shield, sec.

Prewitt, William          Rachel Dority              21 Feb 1827
     Planner Crocket and Thomas Crockett, sec.

Price, James H.           Matilda Lewis of James     22 Jun 1853

Price, Phillip,           Louisa E. Lewis            11 Aug 1852
                          of James, Jr.

Pruit, Benjamin           Ritter Melson              16 Nov 1796
  Prewit, John            Molly Parker                8 Nov 1798

Pruitt, George            Sally Evans                13 Jul 1848

Pruitt, George            Sarah Bloxom               24 Dec 1854

Pruitt, Raymond           Margaret Ann Killman       16 Feb 1852
     of William           of William E.

Pruitt, Willizm           Rachel Dority      Jun 1823-Sep 1837
```

Raleigh, William of Wm.   Polly Bull of Custis   12 Jan 1820
    Custis Bull, sec.

Rayfield, Asa FN   Jane Scarburgh FN   26 Mar 1855

Rayfield, Asa FN   Sally Broadwater FN   3 Feb 1858

Rayfield, Custis   Betsy Sterling   4 May 1803
    Edward Martin, sec.

Rayfield, Edward   Margaret Ashby of Ann   28 Jul 1831
    John S. Wilson, sec.

Rayfield, George   Mary Mears (wdi)   29 Dec 1856

Rayfield, John W.   Margaret Powell   10 Jan 1844

Rayfield, John of Levi   Nancy Kellam of Jms.   25 Dec 1826
    Thomas Lewis of Thos., sec.

Rayfield, Levi R.   Ann S. Arlington of Tho.   7 Jan 1829
    Henry P. Mister, sec.

Rayfield, Levi Sr.   Nancy Lewis   28 Sep 1829
                           (wid Thomas)
        William D. Chandler, sec.

Rayfield, Major   Sarah Saunders   26 Jan 1848
    (wdr)   (wid of Jacob)
    Samuel Saunders, sec.

Rayfield, Major, Jr.   Elizabeth Fitchett   23 Feb 1852
    of Major, Sr.   of Rose

Rayfield, Major Jr.   Sally Hinman of Geo.   31 Dec 1827
    Major Rayfield Sr., sec.

Rayfield, Peter D.   Mary Hall of Tho.   28 Jan 1831
    Southy W. Bull and Samuel, Bloxom sec.

Rayfield, Samuel   Nancy Stephens   31 Dec 1827
    of Levi   of Charles
    Elijah Lilliston, sec.

Rayfield, Solomon FN   Tamar T. Chandler FN   26 Dec 1855

Read, ---   Peggy Lillaston   17 Jan 1807
    Tully Lillaston, sec.

Read, George   Esther Arbuckle   14 Oct 1805
    Joseph Doughty, sec.

- 232 -

```
Read, Hign                Edith Taylor              28 Jan 1811
    William Hancock, sec.

Read, John                Sarah Lewis of Tho.       27 Dec 1808
    Custis Bull, sec.

Read, Michael             Anna Russell             *31 Dec 1799
    William Read, sec.

Read, Michael of Wm.      Sally Sharpley of Jos.    16 Aug 1816
    William Sharpley, sec.

Read, Revel               Susan Bird                 4 Jun 1838

Read, Revell              Esther Taylor             27 Feb 1806

Read, Richard P.          Margarret A.P. Rodgers    30 Apr 1827
    of Sarah              of Richard, dec'd.
    Asa J. Badger and John R.Parker, sec.

Read, Richard            Jenny Bradford             10 Mar 1786
    Edmund Read, sec.

Read, Richard P.          Mary E. Durmmond          26 Aug 1833
                          ward of John K. Chandler
    John K. Chandler, sec.

Read, Samuel A.           Elizabeth Ward            22 Dec 1846

Read, Severn              Anne Bagge, Jr.           15 Oct 1785
    Henry Townsend, sec.

Read, Solomon             Sarah Wyatt (wid)         11 Feb 1775
    James Broughton, sec.

Read, William             Mary Ann Snead             6 May 1833
    of William P.
    David Watts and Levin Core, sec.

Read, William             Euphemia Jajor            18 Dec 1834

Read, Wm. of Michael      Leah Whealton             15 Jun 1824

Reid, William             Tabitha Mister            21 Jan 1784
    Edmund Reid, sec.

Revel, George C.          Eliza Fisque              17 Sep 1811
    Levin S. Joynes, sec.

Revell, George Corbin     Elizabeth Fosque          10 Apr 1811

Revell, John K.           Eliza S. Robins           26 Jun 1805
```

George Burton, sec.

Revell, John	Elizabeth Poulson	28 Feb 1787
William Gibb, sec.		
Revell, John B.	Rosy D. Seymour	18 Sep 1816
Revell, Nathaniel F.	Elizabeth Colbourn	25 Mar 1839
Revell, William	Sarah Fosque	14 Dec 1813
Levin S. Joynes, sec.		
Rew, Charles Jr.	Sarah Finny	8 Jul 1816
	(wid William)	
George Snead, sec.		
Rew, Charles	Comfort Hickman	23 Oct 1790
of Absalom		
Rew, Charles Jr.	Hetty Baker	31 May 1818
	of Solomon	
Charles Rew Sr., sec.		
Rew, Dennis	Sarah Ayres	1 Dec 1809
Levin R. Ayres, sec.		
Rew, George S.	Margaret S. Ayres	4 Mar 1851
	of Francis R.	
Rew, James	Elizabeth Adams of Wm.	6 Jan 1836
William Adams, sec.		
Rew, John (wdr)	Polly Davis (wid of Wm.)	7 Apr 1836
Rew, John D.	Elizabeth A. Snead	7 Jan 1840
	of Tully	
Americus Scarburgh, sec.		
Rew, John	Elizabeth Cheshire	26 Mar 1810
Arthur Watson, sec.		
Rew, Reuben	Leah Riggs	6 Jan 1792
of Reuben		
Rew, Reuben	Rachel Andrews	4 Feb 1811
John A. Bundick, sec.		
Rew, Richard S.	Ann Nock of Edmund	3 Jan 1837
John Mapp, sec.		
Rew, Smuel S.	Henrietta Bloxom	30 Dec 1833
James R. Duncan, sec.		

Rew, Southy   Nanny Taylor   28 Jun 1786
     Smith Melson, sec.

Rew, William   Juliet Mason   2 Jan 1834

Rew, William   Emeline Trader   1847-50
                       of Teackle

Rew, William S.   Juliet Mason of Geo.   1 Jan 1834
     Middleton Mason, sec.

Rich, Benjamin S.   Rachel S. Shield   20 Mar 1855
     of Milford   of James, dec'd.

Richardson, Isaiah   Polly Bradford   15 Dec 1832
     Argyle Kellam, sec.

Richardson, James   Elizabeth Potter   21 Dec 1825
     of Severn   of Laban
     Arthur Bradford sec.

Richardson, James   Mary Charnoc   28 Feb 1820
     of Daniel   of Robert
     Wiliam S. Drummond, sec.

Richardson, John   Margaret Hickman   15 Jan 1853
     of James

Richardson, John   Polly Chance   Nov 1824

Richardson, John of Jno. Molly Churn of Wm.   11 Nov 1824
     Jacob Bradford, sec.

Richardson, John   Margaret Hickman   16 Jan 1853

Richardson, Jonathan W. Susy Benston   16 Dec 1822
     John W. Sturgis, sec.

Richardson, Kendall   Joyce Lewis of Jms.   25 Dec 1809
     James Lewis, sec.

Richardson, Nathan   Matilda Bracher   6 Sep 1856
                       of Hambleton

Richardson, Severn   Mary Edwards   26 Jun 1837
                       ward of said Severn
     Arthur Bell, sec.

Richardson, Severn   Eliza Kelly   13 Dec 1843

Richardson, Thos. S.   Margaret Walters   6 Jan 1827

- 235 -

of Richard
John Floyd, sec., Richard Walters, cons.

Richardson, William   Rosey La   11 Mar 1851

Richison, Alexander   Fanny Townsend   15 May 1811
    Elijah Beauchamp, sec.

Richison, Major   Alicia Hyslop   26 Nov 1824
    John Hyslop, sec.

Richison, Zorobabel   Isea Watson   17 Oct 1810
    William Edwards, sec.

Riggen, John   Polly Garrett   30 Mar 1890

Riggen, Levin   Hannah Sterling   11 Jun 1806
    Josiah Sterling, sec.

Riggin, Noah   Elizabeth Gillespie   23 May 1821
                        of John
    John Powell, sec.

Riggs, George Day   Sarah Lewis   *30 Oct 1798
    License for Rev Thomas Evans to officiate granted by
    Littleton Savage, clerk of court.

Riggs, John B.   Elizabeth Leatherbury   27 Sep 1820
                        (wid)
    James Russell, sec.

Riggs, Joseph   Elizabeth Wessells   26 Dec 1838
                        of James
    Thomas Wessells, sec.

Riley, George   Fanny West   2 Feb 1802
    William Riley, sec.

Riley, Henry F.   Margaret R. Bagwell   1 Dec 1828
    of William   ward William Bagwell
    William Riley and William Bagwell, sec.

Riley, Henry F. (wdr)   Martha W. Wise   5 May 1834
    Levin Core, sec.

Riley, John   Crity McCready   11 Jul 1843

Riley, Raymond   Sally R. West   19 Feb 1812
    James Eichelberger, sec.

Riley, Raymond R., Jr.   Margaret A. Snead   30 Dec 1850

Riley, Thomas R.   Elizabeth Blackstone   7 Jun 1816
                          of John
     Richard D. Bayly, sec.

Riley, William   Nancy Riley   24 Feb 1806
     Thomas Riley, sec.

Riley, William M.   Elizabeth Snead   1 Mar 1828
     of George   of Thomas
     Americus Scarburgh, sec.

Riley, William   Mary Hickman   9 Jan 1815
     Thomas W. Finney, sec.

Roach, Rev. John A.   Elizabeth Bayly   7 Feb 1837
     John Hart, sec.

Roan, Daniel   Ader Morris   8 Jan 1806
     Levin Godfree, sec.

Roan, Stephen   Esther Becket   28 Aug 1805
     Jacob Morris, sec.

Roberts, Charles   Tabitha Churn   15 Sep 1787
     William Gibb, sec.

Roberts, Edmund   Esther Scarburgh   7 Jan 1811
     Zorobabel Henderson, sec.

Roberts, Edwin S.   Elizabeth S. Smith   6 Sep 1830
     George S. Savage, sec.

Roberts, Edwin S.   Elizabeth Smith   7 Sep 1830

Roberts, Francis   Betsy Bradford   24 Feb 1808
     Arthur Roberts, sec.

Roberts, Francis   Betsy Wharton   13 Mar 1802
     John Roberts, sec.

Roberts, John   Nancy Read   27 Oct 1806
                          (wid of Severn)
     Jonathan Mears, sec.

Roberts, John (wdr)   Adah Mears of Jno.   16 Mar 1818
     John S. Beach, sec.

Roberts, John   Ann Jacob Sturgis   25 May 1829
                          of John W.
     John W. Sturgis, sec.

Roberts, Joshua D.   Jane W. Watts   23 Apr 1833

(wid of William)

Roberts, Lewis FN   Margaret Justice FN   22 Feb 1836
    Southy Bull, sec.

Roberts, Louis   Margaret Justice   27 Feb 1834

Roberts, Louis   Sarah Ann Major   27 Jun 1825
    of William L.   of Wm., dec'd.
    James Kellam Sr.and Thomas Kellam, sec.

Roberts, Peter   Traney Holloway   5 Feb 1813
                           of Aaron
        Aaron Holloway, sec.

Roberts, Samuel of Chas. Catey Ewell of Geo.   20 May 1818
    Thorogood Taylor, sec.

Roberts, Thomas L. B.   Elizabeth Matthews   19 Oct 1843

Roberts, William J.   Ann E. Willis   28 Oct 1851

Roberts, William T.   Elizabeth Smith   10 Jan 1803
    Edmund Bayly, sec.

Robertson, William   Mary Waples   29 Oct 1844

Robins, Abraham   Elizabeth Robins   17 Jun 1844

Robins, Arthur   Susanna Smith   2 Feb 1807
    Nathaniel Badger, sec.

Robins, Isaac   Elizabeth F. Smith   22 Sep 1808
    Arthur Robins, sec.

Robins, John   Susanna Teackle   31 Mar 1786
    John Boisnard, sec.

Robins, John   Drucilla Conner of Fred   30 Dec 1833
    Geroge Mathews and Levin White, sec.

Robins, Joseph   Ann Eliza James   9 Nov 1830

Robins, Michael   Elizabeth Stockley   10 Jun 1807
                           of Kendall
        George Marshall, sec.

Robins, Parker FN   Ibby Griffin   21 Sep 1833
                           of Laban FN
        David Mears and James Marshall, sec.

Robins, Thomas W.   Margaret A. Wyatt   15 Jan 1835
                          of William
        William Wyatt, sec.

Robinson, John R.   Rachel M. Huslay   22 Dec 1812
        Shadrach Ames, sec.

Robinson, Thomas Jr.   Mrs. Nancy Turpin   8 May 1805
        Robert Twiford, sec.

Robinson, William   Mary C. Waples   29 Oct 1844

Rodgers, Finly   Amey Twiford   26 Jul 1786
        John Warrington, sec.

Rodgers, George S.   Margaret J.W. Moore   28 Sep 1829
                          of William P.
        Edward A. Revell and John G. Joynes, sec.

Rodgers, John   Rosanne Moore   27 Apr 1785
        Thomas Parker, sec.

Rodgers, John K.   Eliza Boggs   2 Jan 1845

Rodgers, John   Polly Schoolfield   7 Apr 1803
        John A. Bundick, sec.

Rodgers, John   Margaret Bradford   21 Dec 1829
        of Laban   of Sally
        John Carmine, sec.

Rodgers, John of Laban   Sally East of Parker   26 Dec 1825
        John Kellam of John, sec.

Rodgers, Levin   Ellen Mason   9 Mar 1840
                          of Middleton
        Edward B. Ayres, sec.

Rodgers, Levin   Elizabeth Reid   1 Apr 1783
        Thomas Coleburn, sec.

Rodgers, Reuben   Patty Mason   29 Dec 1806
        Daniel Twiford, sec.

Rodgers, Richard   Polly Marshall   12 Dec 1798
        John Marshall, sec.

Rodgers, Richard   Betsy Collins   29 Aug 1801
                          of James
        Peter Delastatius, sec.

Rodgers, Robert   Tabitha Bundick   31 Oct 1775

of Justic

John Smith, sec.

Rodgers, Thomas   Nancy Cutler   30 May 1785
    Smith Cutler, sec.

Rodgers, William   Susanna Smith   11 Jan 1811
    Edmund Phillips, sec.

Rodgers, William   Elizabeth Kellam   23 Feb 1813
                         (wid Custis)
        Edward Phillips, sec.

Rodgers, William W.   Rachel Boggs   7 Mar 1820
    (wdr)   of John
    James Boggs, sec.

Rodgers, William S.   Elizabeth F. Finney   11 Mar 1850
                         of Thomas W.
    John W. Chandler, sec.

Rogers, Major   Elizabeth Mason   11 Nov 1802
    John Mason, sec.

Roles, John   Susanna West   24 Mar 1785
    William Gibb, sec.

Roley, William   Polly Young   29 Feb 1808
                         (wid John)
        Obed Adams, sec.

Roley, William   Hepsey Silverthorne   25 Jul 1798
    Robert Twiford, sec.

Rooks, James   Peggy Hinman   22 Jul 1799

Rooks, Thomas   Mary Watson   17 Jul 1805
    Caleb Watson, sec.

Ross, Ezekiel   Esther Harmon   25 Oct 1789

Ross, Ezekiel   Sukey Chase   28 Oct 1811
    William Culworth, sec.

Ross, James of Eliz.   Patsy Bishop of Jacob   29 Nov 1821
    Littleton Bloxom and Jacob, Bishop sec.

Ross, James   Elizabeth Savage   23 Jan 1812
                         of Kendall
    John S. Cropper, sec.

Ross, James K.   Virginia D. Belote   10 Sep 1851

Ross, Kendall   Leah Woolridge   24 Jul 1815
                                  (wid Thomas)
     William Waters, sec.

Ross, Kendall   Rachel Thornton   15 Jul 1815
     John H. Watts and John, Follio sec.

Ross, Lewis T.   Nancy Kelly of James   20 Jan 1834
     Samuel C. Johnson, sec.

Ross, Samuel   Margaret S. Revell   5 Dec 1810
     Samuel Downing, sec.

Ross, William   Sally Taylor   25 Jul 1800
     John Thornton, sec.

Ross, William   Emiline Trader   20 Dec 1849
                                  of Teackle
     William S. Burton, sec.

Ross, William   Elizabeth White   6 Sep 1816
     William Henderson and John W. Crippen, sec.

Ross, William   Molly Hornsby   6 Feb 1806
     Thomas Edminds, sec.

Roward, Dustan   Elizabeth Stringer   31 Mar 1828
                                  (wid Smith)
     John W. Kellam, sec.

Rowell, William   Susanna Holston   22 Apr 1803
     Levin Crowson, sec.

Rowley, Henry   Peggy Massey   28 Jun 1819
     John F. James, sec.

Rowley, Henry (wdr)   Sarah T. Marshall   7 Jul 1837
     Thomas Melvin, sec.

Rowley, James   Amy Nock   2 Oct 1812
     William Rowley, sec.

Rowley, John A.   Mary P. Savage   11 Jul 1835
                                (wid of George)
     Luther Mapp and Drummond Massey, sec.

Rowley, John W.   Elizabeth B. Wilkins   2 Feb 1843

Rowley, Raymond   Margaret Willis   8 Dec 1810
     George Flehart, sec.

Rowley, Samuel   Elizabeth Stevenson   26 Nov 1832
                              (wid of Hugh)
        John D. Welburn and Henry A. Wise, sec.

Rowly, Edmond FN   Leah Church FN   24 Dec 1810
        James Upshur, sec.

Russel, James   Elizabeth Gray of Tho.   21 Dec 1809
        Elkanah Andrews, sec.

Russell, Abel   Leag Chambers   24 Mar 1785
        Gilbert Pielee, sec.

Russell, Andrew   Esther Bell   23 Apr 1800
        Richard Sparrow, sec.

Russell, Andrew (wdr)   Rachel Colona of Ken.   23 Mar 1824
        Joseph Godwin and Littleton Hickman, sec.

Russell, Colmore   Catherine Wessells   25 Nov 1833
        of James   of Ephram
        David Mears and James S. Corbin, sec.

Russell, Elijah (wdr)   Nancy Hall (wid)   26 Apr 1841
        Timathy Hall, sec.

Russell, George   Lucretia Russell   3 Jan 1814
                                  of Benjamin
        Elijah Russell, sec.

Russell, George   Sarah Kilman   15 Dec 1806
        George W. Burton, sec.

Russell, George of Geo. Peggy Wessells of Jno.   12 Jan 1820
        George H. Ewell, sec., John Wessells, cons.

Russell, George   Yeardly East of Severn   29 Oct 1811
        Severn East, sec.

Russell, Henry J.K.   Mary Ellen Poulson   8 Dec 1849
                              of James B.
        Josiah Bagwell and Joshua Wyatt, sec.

Russell, Ignatius (wdr) Betsy R. Groten   27 Jan 1817
        John C. Copes, sec.

Russell, Ignatus   Peggy Middleton   15 Mar 1815
        of Tabitha   of William
        William Middleton, sec.

Russell, Isaac   Mary Satchell   6 May 1850
                              of Zapporah

Ephriem Wessells of B., sec.

Russell, James   Mary Berry   14 Dec 1847
  Thomas N. Twyford, sec.

Russell, James of Tho. Keziah Bell of Southy 17 Dec 1817
  Gilbert M. Leatherbury, sec.

Russell, James   Susan Russell   30 Dec 1841

Russell, James   Rachel White   22 Dec 1813
  William D. Outten, sec.

Russell, John C.   Rose Ann Savage   18 Oct 1827

Russell, John W.   Polly Justice   21 Dec 1824
  of Mary   of William, dec'd., ward of Wm. Riley
  William Riley sec., cons.

Russell, Joshua   Jane Thornton   c. 1790
                 (not dated)

Russell, Levin   Ann Ironmonger   28 Aug 1827
  of Milby   of John, dec'd.
  John J. Wise, sec.

Russell, Robert   Comfort Parks   5 Mar 1790

Russell, Robert Jr.   Elizabeth Lewis   26 Oct 1822
          of Thomas, dec'd.
  Samuel Lewis, sec.

Russell, Robert   Sarah Crippen   8 May 1818
  (wdr)   of Thomas, dec'd.
  William C. White and Henry S. Copes, sec.

Russell, Samuel L. (wdr) Mary B. Laws   19 Feb 1845

Russell, Samuel S.   Caroline F.C. Wise 23 May 1837
          orphan of W.E. Wise
  John Savage and Edmund R. Allen, sec.

Russell, Solomon   Jemimah Flewhart 6 Aug 1805
  Charles Booth, sec.

Russell, Solomon   Susan Tunnell   8 Feb 1833
          (wid of Elijah)
  William W. Churn, sec.

Russell, Sylvanus W. Polly Hinman of Mary 5 Feb 1856

Russell, Tho. of Milby Sarah Adams of Obed 11 Jan 1825

Obed Adams and Richard D. Bayly, sec.

Russell, Tho. of Joshua   Eliz. Henderson of Jno.   23 Feb 1819
    John Henderson and William Welburn, sec.

Russell, Thomas   Elisha Gootee   19 Aug 1840
                         (wid of James)
    Thomas Russell of George and Edward Gunter, sec.

Russell, Thomas   Mary Dix of Molly   26 Jul 1848
    Sam Hickman, sec.

Russell, Thomas of Robt. Elender Evans of Josiah 26 May 1818
    Robert Russell, sec.

Russell, William   Susan Drury   24 Jan 1849
    (wdr)   (wid of Drury)
    Gilbert Marshall and Richard S. Taylor, sec.

Russell, William   Fannie Dix   31 Dec 1855

Russell, William (wdr)   Polly Russell (wid)   5 Jab 1842

Russell, Wm. of Benj.   Tabitha Ewell of Jms.   27 Aug 1827
    Thomas Russell, sec.

Rutter, John   Mary W. Teackle   27 Jan 1824

```
Sakes, William              Esther Kellam           29 Dec 1808

Salisberry, Thomas          Sally Topping           26 Nov 1791

Salisbury, Capt. John       Mary S. Crosby          15 Jul 1846

Salisbury, Elisha           Amanda Somers of Milly  19 Oct 1816
    Reuben Somers,, sec.

Saltonstale, Richard        Margaret Ann Savage     24 Oct 1822
    George Parker sec.

Sample, Dingler FN          Cathy Matthews FN       17 Jan 1812
    William Waterfield, sec.

Sample, Emerson FN          Molly Holt FN           27 Jan 1810
    William Holt, sec.

Sample, Emerson FN          Betsy Jamor FN          29 Oct 1838
    Benjamin Sturgis and George S. Rogers, sec.

Sample, Emerson FN          Betsy Major             14 Nov 1838

Sample, Isaac FN            Margaret Roan FN        31 Dec 1832
                            of David FN
        Patrick B. Colonna, sec.

Sample, Isaac FN            Margaret Bean            2 Dec 1833

Sample, Littleton FN        Mallie Collins          4 Nov 1836
    of Eady                 of Annie FN
    Elesha W. Mears and William Parramore Jr., sec.

Sample, Littleton          Margaret Collins        10 Aug 1829
                            of Southy FN
        Southy Collins,  sec.

Sample, Shepard FN          Tinny Gardner FN        21 Jul 1835
    James Benson, sec.

Sample, Shepherd, black  Rachel Anthony, black    26 Jan 1829
    Isaac Ames FN, sec.

Sample, William             Margaret Cast           23 Jun 1835
    Wilburn H. Core, sec.

Sanders, Samuel             Keziah Hinmon           29 May 1792

Sanford, James              Sarah Roberts           6 July 1774
    Severn Guthrey, sec.

Sartorius, William G.       Georgianna S. Barnes    13 Nov 1851
```

of George P. Jr., dec'd

Satchell, Christopher William Gibb, sec.	Anne Bell	28 Feb 1786
Satchell, George of Geo. George Satchell Sr., sec.	Nancy Melson of Wm.	29 May 1819
Satchell, George T.	Margaret Bundick	24 Feb 1847
Satchell, Jacobus	Jane Rodgers of John	4 Aug 1851
Satchell, John James Snead, sec.	Leah Drummond	18 Nov 1801
Satchell, Southy of William Samuel Nock, sec.	Rachel Hutchinson of Babel	6 Jul 1816
Satchell, William of George George Satchell and John G. Joynes, sec.	Betsy Bundick of Tabitha	18 May 1815
Satchell, William H. Samuel Rayfield, sec.	Tabitha Wise	6 Jun 1834
Saunders, Jacob Eli Bloxom, sec.	Sally Fitchett of Wm.	30 May 1823
Saunders, Thomas	Elizabeth Brimer	22 Dec 1789
Savage, Arthur R. Obedience White, sec.	Sarah Mears	23 Apr 1810
Savage, Bagwell of Jacob Waitman Willett, sec.	Elizabeth East of Severn	15 Aug 1816
Savage, Bagwell Walter R. Finney, sec.	Mary Rodgers of Ayres, dec'd.	24 Jun 1826
Savage, Bagwell Waitman Willett, sec.	Leanna East	4 Jan 1814
Savage, Cabel B. William M. Savage, sec.	Ellen Bradford of Margaret	27 Mar 1847
Savage, Caleb B.	Mary Ellen Bradford	31 Mar 1847
Savage, Charles	Lovey Smith	1 Jan 1807

William Custis of Wm, sec.

Savage, Edmund   Betsy Haley   21 Dec 1815
     Levin Savage, sec.

Savage, Edward G.   Elizabeth G. Bell   30 May 1849

Savage, Edward J.   Mary E. Belote   18 Oct 1847
   of George   ward of John Arlington
   John Fox and D. Broadwater, sec.

Savage Edward FN   Tabitha Morris FN   27 Dec 1852
                     (wid of Levin)

Savage, Edward P.   Charlotte S. Fosque   17 Nov 1834
                     of Sally
   Richard Walter Jr., sec.

Savage, Edward G.   Elizabeth G. Bell   29 May 1850
                     of Charlotte
   John N. Elliott, sec.

Savage, Geoge S.   Rachel Kelly   22 Aug 1837
   of Jacob
   Levin James, sec.

Savage, George S.   Margaret S. Henderson 6 Sep 1830
                     of Zorobabel
   Edwin S. Roberts, sec.

Savage, George G.   Susan C. Willis   28 Nov 1853
                     of Custis

Savage, George J.   Mary P.Holland   3 Dec 1818
   Calvin H. Read, sec.

Savage, George   Harriet Bull   26 Aug 1822
   of John   (wid John)
   James Heath, sec.

Savage, Henry FN   Elizabeth Conner FN   3 Mar 1841
                     of George FN
   John P. Taylor and Sebastian C. Marshall, sec.

Savage, Jacob   Mary Kellam   6 Jun 1786
   Zorabable Chandler, sec.

Savage, James   Mary P. Outten   11 May 1815
                     of Purnel?
   Shadrach W. Outten, sec.

Savage, James K.   Ann Harman of Jno.   12 Jan 1829

Smith Hyslop and John, Harman sec.

Savage, Jesse   Henny White   31 May 1834
     Levin White, sec.

Savage, Jesse   Sarah Fosque of Jno.   19 Dec 1816
     George S. Parker, sec.

Savage, Jesse   Henny White   31 May 1834

Savage, John of Rich.   Elizabeth Justice   23 Oct 1811
     Alexander McCollom, sec.

Savage, John C.   Sophia Kelly of Stephen   7 Oct 1828
     Samuel Kelly, sec.

Savage, John   Molly Savage   28 Jul 1802
     Jacob Edwards, sec.

Savage, John   Ann C. Arbuckle   19 Sep 1838
    (wdr of R.)   (wid of George)

Savage, Joseph   Peggy Sturgis   9 Dec 1799
     Arthur Savage, sec.

Savage, Levin   Ann Salesbury   24 Dec 1814
     of Kendall   of Thomas
   McKeel Bonwell, sec.

Savage, Levin FN   Jenny Copes of Dan. FN   29 Dec 1814
     Thomas Savage, sec.

Savage, Levin   Nancy Warrington   5 Jan 1811
     Charles Savage, sec.

Savage, Littleton (wdr)   Nancy Kellam   18 Mar 1817
     Thomas Stirges, sec.

Savage, Littleton   Caty Jones   2 Dec 1833
     Edward L. Bradford, sec.

Savage, Littleton   Nancy Kellam   20 Mar 1817

Savage, Major   Susanna Edmunds   27 Sep 1819
     of Robinson   of James
   James Edmunds, sec.

Savage, Major   Maria Turlington   31 Dec 1827
     of William   of Joseph
   Edmund Leatherbury and Joseph Turlington, sec.

Savage, Michael   Finetta W. Ames   2 Oct 1820

of Jesse Sr.
Thomas H. Ames, sec., Jesse Ames cons.

Savage, Nathaniel   Lacy Stringer   21 Oct 1811
    Francis Savage of Peter, sec.

Savage, Richard of Jno. Elizabeth H. Beavans   18 Mar 1829
    William Laws and Levin Core, sec.

Savage, Richard R.   Elizabeth Broadwater   7 Jul 1806
                         (wid)
        Smith Cutler, sec.

Savage, Richard T.   Livey Baker   11 Sep 1850

Savage, Robert   Nancy Kellam   29 Dec 1801
    James Ailworth, sec.

Savage, Robert   Mary Riley   14 Dec 1818
    of George   (wid William)
    Thomas Wright, sec.

Savage, Robinson   Betsy Mears   28 Aug 1792

Savage, Robinson   Molly Roberts   27 Jul 1804
    Francis Roberts, sec.

Savage, Samuel G.   Elizabeth Mears   11 Oct 1837

Savage, Sylvester H.   Sarah Ann Warner   6 Mar 1834
    William W. Dix and Hezekiah P. James, sec.

Savage, Thomas T.   Mariah J. Parker   28 Sep 1852
                         of George, dec'd.

Savage, Tobey FN   Ailsey Onley FN   30 May 1853
                         of Mariah Nedab

Savage, William   Lucy Phillips   11 Nov 1802
    John Phillips, sec.

Savage, William   Mary Henderson   10 Sep 1836
    of John of Hog Neck   of John
    James P. Selby, sec.

Savage, William   Rosey Trader   18 Sep 1813
    Robert Pitts, sec.

Savage, William B.(wdr) Rebecca Trader of Henry 27 Feb 1857

Savage, William F.   Suckey Addison   30 Oct 1807

- 249 -

Frances Savage, sec.

Savage, William FN	Ann Custis	25 Jan 1843
Savage, William	Rosey Chandler	19 Apr 1813
Savage, Zerobabel	Molly James	1 Sep 1804
Savage, Zorobabel John Gillespie, sec.	Sally Gillespie	6 Nov 1810

Scarborough, Abraham J.   Margaret Kellam   5 Nov 1821
                       of Hutchinson
    Littleton P. Henderson, sec., Hutchinson Kellam cons.

Scarborough, Bennett W.   Margaret A.F. Heath 15 Aug 1820
   of Edmund   of Fletcher
   Jesse Powell, sec., Edmund Scarborough cons.

Scarborough, Chas. P.   Hetty Talbert   8 Aug 1821
                    (wid Samuel)
   Abram Scarborough, sec.

Scarborough, Samuel W.   Elizabeth H. Bayly 29 Feb 1832
                    orphan Isma
   Levin Core, sec.

Scarburgh, Alfred FN   Juliet Ann Beckett FN 3 Aug 1836
   Americus Scarburgh, sec.

Scarburgh, Americus   Mary Turlington of Asa 22 Sep 1830
   William W. Riley, sec.

Scarburgh, Americus   Sally Q. Tunnell   22 Feb 1819
   of Americus   of John
   James Q. Selby and Richard D. Bayly, sec.

Scarburgh, Bennet W.	Margaret W. Wyatt	24 May 1843
Scarburgh, Bennet C.	Eliza Martin	9 Jan 1844
Scarburgh, Daniel FN	Mary Jubilee FN	26 Dec 1853

Scarburgh, George P.   Mary S. Joynes   9 Oct 1833
   Thomas Joynes, sec.

Scarburgh, Henry   Elizabeth Rodgers 22 Dec 1806
   Edward Bayly, sec.

Scarburgh, John   Sabrah P. Townsend 24 Sep 1807
   Luther H. Read, sec.

Scarburgh, John A.   Caroline C. Boggs   7 Nov 1836
                               of Elijah
        Elijah Boggs, sec.

Scarburgh, Samuel H.   Mary S. Mears   29 Jul 1833
   (wdr)
   John Arlington, sec.

Scarburgh, Samuel H.   Elizabeth H. Bayly   1 Mar 1832

Scarburgh, William M.   Ann P. Teackle   26 Sep 1808
   Edmund Read, sec.

Scherer, George   Frances Ann Hack   21 Dec 1812
   John K. Evans, sec.

Scott, Edward L.   Lovey Warrington   27 May 1833
                               ward of George Bull of B.
        George Bull, sec.

Scott, Geo. of Severn   Bridget Matthews   7 Jun 1819

Scott, George (wdr)   Susan Moore of Stephen   5 Jul 1827
   John W. Smith, sec.

Scott, George   Polly Bull   29 Oct 1810
                               (wid Benjamin)
        John Bull Sr., sec.

Scott, George   Bridget Matthews   7 Jun 1819
   of Severn   (wid Anthony)
   Severn Scott, sec.

Scott, George   Betsey Ewell   5 Jan 1801
   Mark Ewell, sec.

Scott, George of Severn Sally Waterfield   2 Dec 1836
   John Elliott, sec.

Scott, George   Polly Bull (wid)   29 Oct 1810

Scott, George R.   Elizabeth Metcalf   3 Feb 1842

Scott, George W.   Elizabeth Bonnawell   21 Feb 1844
                               (wid)

Scott, George   Sally Warrington   2 Dec 1836

Scott, James   Hetty Snead of Geo.   28 Apr 1835
   alias Smith orphan of Ruth Smith, dec'd.
   Henry A. Wise and Samuel Melvin, sec.

```
Scott, James               Elizabeth Bishop        14 Feb 1854
                           of Henry, dec'd.

Scott, John W.             Leah Bradford             3 May 1816
    of Walter              of Amy Chambers
William T. Rodgers, sec.

Scott, John                Rachel Hopman             7 Nov 1836

Scott, John                Eliza Justice            28 Nov 1836
    of Major
William and Raymond Riley, sec.

Scott, John of Walter      Tabitha Lewis of Spenc.  22 May 1817
    Spencer Lewis, sec.

Scott, John R.             Maria  Bird              11 Oct 1850
                           (wid of Ebern)

Scott, Littleton           Susan Chandler           29 Mar 1830
    of Walter              of James
Levin James, sec.

Scott, Major               Rosey Sharrod            22 Mar 1813
    John Hogshead, sec.

Scott, Sacker              Ann Bloxom               27 Mar 1827
                           orphan George, ward of John
       B. Downing, sec.

Scott, Sacker              Elizabeth Dunton          7 Mar 1820
    of Robinson            of George
William Custis, sec.

Scott, Severn              Bridget Smith            20 Sep 1809
    William Lee, sec.

Scott, Severn (wdr)        Ann Smith of Richard     23 Feb 1818
    William Chandler, sec.

Scott, Thomas              Catherine Carmine        26 May 1817
    of Thomas              (wid George)
Levin T. Joynes, sec.

Scott, Thomas              Peggy Fosque             27 Jun 1849
    John D. Heath, sec.

Scott, Tully               Tabitha Martin           29 Dec 1841

Scott, Walter              Matilda Lang             25 Dec 1838

Scott, William             Polly Lewis of Spencer    3 Aug 1815
```

Samuel Lewis, sec.

Scott, William P.	Margaret Badger	29 Feb 1840
William M. Riley and Nathaniel Revel, sec.		
Scott, William P.	Margaret Badger	4 Mar 1840
Scott, William C.	Elizabeth M Scott	14 Mar 1841
Selby, Albert	Margaret H. Joynes	25 Mar 1840
Selby, George	Polly Custis	18 Sep 1800
Arthur White, sec.		
Selby, Henry Q.	Betsy Bunting of Isma	6 Jan 1813
Isma Bunting and William Bunting, sec.		
Selby, James Q.	Lavinia W. Scarburgh	14 Jul 1818
of James	of Ameicus	
Robert Waters, sec.		
Selby, John of Jms.	Mary Massey	10 Feb 1807
Zadock Selby, sec.		
Selby, Thomas	Ann S. Milby	28 Sep 1840
	(wid of William)	
Thomas Bayly, sec.		
Selby, William W.	Mary P. Barnes	3 Jan 1851
Selby, William Jr.	Mary Ann Harmon of Major	1 Jan 1838
George Harmon and John Fidderman, sec.		
Selby, William	Sarah Henderson	19 Apr 1806
John Henderson, sec.		
Seymour, Abraham	Melvina Scarburgh	10 Sep 1835
	of Dinah FN	
Raymond Riley and Americus Scarburgh, sec.		
Seymour, Daniel FN	Jane Sample	31 Dec 1851
Seymour, Dr. Hugh G.	Elizabeth J. Custis	2 Dec 1841
	(wid)	
Seymour, Smith FN	Mary Johnson FN of Jingo	24 May 1823
Jingo Johnson FN, sec.		
Shalmanser, Davis	Elizabeth R. Riley	4 May 1842
Sharpley, Henry	Elizabeth Mumford	28 Apr 1807

John Wallop, sec.

Sharpley, John   Elizabeth Hancock   4 Oct 1819
    of John   (wid Mitchell)
    Thomas Sharpley, sec.

Sharpley, John w.   Elizabeth Daisey of Jms. 2 Apr 1850
    John Thornton, sec.

Sharpley, Parker   Mary Read   29 Aug 1825
    of Joseph   of Michael
    Wm.P. Drummond, Jno. Downing, sec.

Sharpley, Tho. of Jno.   Nancy Johnson of Wm.   7 Jul 1818
    Willliam Johnson Sr. and Isaac Henderson, sec.

Sharpley, William   Nancy Celpen   27 Jul 1807
    Isaac Lewis, sec.

Sharpley, William   Margaret Tarr   15 Mar 1841

Sharpley, Wm. of Jos.   Betsy Lewis   26 Apr 1813
    Joseph Sharpley and John Jester, sec.

Sharply, Henry   Pheebe Thornton   9 Aug 1810
    Daniel Jones, sec.

Sharply, John   Sally Cary   23 Mar 1801
    Levin Taylor, sec.

Sharply, John   Peggy Taylor   26 Apr 1813
    William Hancock and Michael Read, sec.

Sharply, William   Esther Whealton   15 Jan 1799
    Beverly Copes, sec.

Sharrod, George   Agnes Powell   4 Oct 1803
    John Satchell, sec.

Sharrod, George   Francis Taylor   22 Apr 1811
                          (wid Elias)
    John Taylor, sec.

Sharrod, Levin   Eliza Outten   20 Oct 1803
    James White, sec.

Sharrod, Revill   Betsy Wise   27 Jun 1811
    John Hogshire, sec.

Sharrod, Thomas   Betsy Boniwell   18 Feb 1815
    John Hogshear and Henry S. Copes, sec.

Sharrod, William   Nancy Lee   28 Mar 1814
      Andrew Lee, sec.

Sharwood, William   Mrs. Peggy Allen   14 Apr 1802
      Edmund Bayly, sec.

Shay, Daniel   Jernina Trader   7 Jan 1807
                          of Sacker
      Staton Trader, sec.

Shay, Eli   Agnes Trader   12 Nov 1788

Shay, Jenry of Eli   Catherine Crowson of Wm. 16 Jan 1828
      Whittington P. Pool, sec.

Shay, Martin   Elizabeth Crowson   7 Feb 1831
      Richard Gillispie, sec.

Shay, Teackle   Elizabeth Bunting   27 Dec 1847
      William C. Northam, sec.

Sheppard, Irving   Margaret Ann Hargis   17 Jan 1853
      of Elijah   of James

Sheppard, James   Sally Mears   15 May 1815
                          of Littleton
      William Heath, sec.

Sherrod, George   Molly K. Godwin   4 Mar 1805

Sherrod, Thomas   Elizabeth Mister   6 Apr 1805
      John Sherrod, sec.

Shey, John of Eli   Elizabeth Mariner   6 Jan 1823
      Andrew Lee, sec.

Shias, Teackle   Patsy Luker   28 Mar 1820
                          (wid John)
      Samuel Coward and Richard D. Bayly, sec.

Shield, Aser   Elizabeth Snead   29 Jun 1835
                          of Elizabeth
Anderson P. Bloxom and James Shield, sec.

Shield, James   Elizabeth Shield   21 Sep 1826
                          of Aser, ward of A.P. Bloxom
      Anderson Bloxom, sec.

Shield, James   Ann Kellam   28 Nov 1808
      Thomas Bagwell, sec.

Shield, James (wdr)   Elizabeth Shedd   27 Sep 1826

```
Shield, John              Mary Barnes              17 Oct 1801
    Spencer Barnes, sec.

Shield, Thomas            Mahala Gunter            22 Jun 1841

Shields, John W. of Jms. Elizabeth M.B. Outten    3 Nov 1834
    James I. Ailworth, sec.

Shores, Whittington       Mary Laws                3 Aug 1833
    Sewell Dix and Ezekiel Killman, sec.

Shores, Whittington       Nan Laws                 1 Aug 1833

Shores, Whittington       Elizabeth Kilmon         4 Dec 1833

Shores, Zorobabel         Elizabeth Killman       16 Mar 1825
    of Solomon            of Ezekiel
    Ezekiel Killman, sec.

Shores, Zorobabel         Margaret Kellam          1 Jun 1842

Shores, Zorubabel         Sally Moore             19 Mar 1825

Showard, George           Polly Taylor            20 Dec 1816
    (wdr)                 of John Sr.
    William Walters and John T. Dickerson, sec.

Showard, Henry            Mary Snead of Isaac     30 Dec 1834
    Raymond Riley, sec.

Showard, Hillary          Elizabeth Wilson of Jno. 19 Mar 1831
    John Wilson and Southy W. Bull, sec.

Showard, Hilly            Nancy Collins           26 Oct 1818
    (wdr)                 (wid John)
    Lemuel Henderson and Revell Taylor, sec.

Showard, John (wdr)       Frances Watson (wid)     7 Jul 1847

Showard, John             Elizabeth Rew           25 Oct 1839

Showard, Joseph of Geo.   Ann Staton of Geo.      31 Dec 1827
    Adkins Matthews, sec.

Showard, Southy           Susan A. West           26 Dec 1849
                          of George, Sr.
    Henry Melson and William H. Melson, sec.

Showard, William          Sally Gladding of Jesse 15 Nov 1839
    William Thornton and Edward Mears, sec.

Shreaves, Abraham         Levinia Scott           31 Dec 1838
```

Shreaves, James	Mary Starling	25 Jun 1840
Shreaves, John	Elizabeth Johnson	11 Sep 1839
Shreaves, Levin	Daney Bishop	9 Oct 1823
Shreaves, Thomas	Ann Russell	27 May 1844
Shreaves, William (wdr) of William John Barnes, sec.	Caroline Barnes of John	31 Dec 1849
Shreaves, William	Jane Barnes	5 Jan 1839
Shreaves, William	Polly Lewis	10 Apr 1817
Shreaves, Wm. of E.	Lusianna Guy	22 Feb 1826
Shreves, Abraham George Turner, sec.	Lovinia Scott ward of George Turner	31 Dec 1838
Shreves, David Parker Thomas, sec.	Sarah Ann Powell	31 Dec 1838
Shreves, James of Elizabeth Parkes Asa Lewis, sec.	Mary Starling	22 Jun 1840
Shreves, John Isaiah Johnson, sec.	Elizabeth Johnson of Isaiah	10 Sep 1839
Shreves, Parker Samuel A. Justice, sec.	Amy T. Justice of Sam.	31 Dec 1832
Shreves, Thomas Major Annis, sec.	Ann Russell of Thomas	26 May 1841
Shreves, William David White, sec.	Susan West of John	12 Aug 1841
Shreves, William S. David Mason, sec.	Tabitha Snead	24 Dec 1839
Shreves, William Arthur Barnes, sec.	Jane Barnes of Arthur	3 Jun 1839
Shrieves, John Absolom Lewis Jr., sec.	Betsy Lewis	7 Mar 1811

Shrieves, John   Nancy Davis   10 Dec 1830
                          (wid James)
     Benjamin Parker, sec.

Shrieves, Levin   Molly Hart   10 Dec 1811
     Parker Parradice, sec.

Shrieves, Levin   Daimey? Bishop   8 Oct 1823
     (wdr)   of Southy
     Alexander Lang Jr., sec.

Shrieves, Teackle   Molly Middleton   3 Sep 1798
     George Middleton, sec.

Shrieves, Thomas   Comfort Mears   25 Jan 1811
     Isaiah Baker, sec.

Shrieves, William   Susanna Guy   21 Feb 1826
     of Elias   of William
     William Guy, sec.

Shrieves, William   Polly Lewis   16 Apr 1817
     of William   of Absolom
     Raymond Rolly, sec.

Shuter, Edward   Tabitha Snead   31 Mar 1834
                          ward of William R. Coard
     William R. Coard, sec.

Silverthorn, Burton   Susanna Dunton   12 Dec 1800
     William Wyatt, sec.

Silverthorn, Henry T.   Jane Charnock of Robt.   23 Apr 1851

Silverthorn, John   Sarah Ann Cluff   16 Sep 1833
     Charles Tatham and Levin Core, sec.

Silverthorn, Kendal   Elizabeth Mathews   20 Jan 1836
     Edward Croswell, sec.

Silverthorn, Samuel   Mary Ann Taylor of Chas. 13 Jan 1841
     Charles Taylor, sec.

Silverthorn, William   Levinia Corbin   21 Oct 1796

Silverthorne, Crippen   Betsy Mears   8 Jan 1811
     George Russell Jr., sec.

Silverthorne, Kendall   Susan Jenkins   15 Jan 1823
     (wdr)   of Robert
     William P. Custis, sec.

```
Silverthorne, Kendall      Nancy Sandford              7 Mar 1809
     Isaiah Johnson, sec.

Silverthorne, Southy       Nancy Taylor               21 Dec 1809
     Elkanah Andrews, sec.

Silverthorne, Southy       Nancy Taylor                4 Jun 1806

Silverthorne, Wm.          Tabitha Ewell               8 Mar 1814
     Thorogood Taylor, sec.

Silverthorne, Wm. M.       Rebecca Moore of Jno.      30 Apr 1814
     John Moore, sec.

Simpson, Dennis            Betsy Parks                 3 Jan 1800
     Elijah Parks, sec.

Simpson, Elijah            Betsy Beasly               30 Jan 1802
     Zorobabel Budd, sec.

Simpson, George            Leah Melson                28 May 1801
     William Kelley, sec.

Simpson, Hancock           Anne Barnes                27 Jan 1786
     Richard Drummond, sec.

Simpson, John              Nancy West                 24 Feb 1784
     Charles West, sec.

Simpson, Reuben            Dorothy Rodgers            22 Jun 1814
     Charles Lewis, sec.

Simpson, Revil             Rebecca Cheshire           29 Dec 1803
     William Cheshire, sec.

Simpson, Southy            Hannah Rodgers              2 Jun 1786
     William Gibb, sec.

Simpson, William           Letitia Ayres              20 Nov 1833
     James R. Duncan, sec.

Singleton, Richard         Esther Shreaves            26 Mar 1790

Singleton, Samuel          Henrietta Dix              31 Jan 1825
                           of Isaac, dec'd.
          George West, sec.

Slocomb, John of Jno.      Mary Bowles of Jno.        26 Feb 1827
     John Matthews, sec.

Slocomb, Walter            Rebecca Bowles of Jno.     31 Aug 1826
     John Fidderman, sec.
```

Slocomb, William	Anne Banister	31 Oct 1797
Slocumb, William Sr. Richard Grinalds, sec.	Lavinia Silverthorne	28 May 1804
Slover, John Selby Foster, sec.	Peggy Twiford	26 Dec 1805
Small, Handy James and William Chesser, sec.	Maria Chessser of Wm.	16 Dec 1835
Small, Levi Teackle Trader, sec.	Leah Price	29 Jul 1811
Small, Robert	Hepsey Johnson	27 Aug 1804
Small, Steward Isaac Dix, sec.	Polly Kickman	20 Jan 1829
Small, Stewart (wdr) Samuel Hickman, sec.	Louisa Venelson of Wm.	16 Dec 1835
Smart, Henry Andrew Hoffman, sec.	Sally Hoffman	26 Nov 1806
Smart, Henry (wdr) William Ailworth and Richard D. Bayly, sec.	Betsy Lucas (wid Elijah)	17 Feb 1816
Smart, Nathaniel William Bunting, sec.	Nancy Bunting	18 Nov 1784
Smith FN William Seymour, sec.	Sarah FN	26 Mar 1816
Smith, Charles Thomas W. Mears, sec.	Sally Mears of Armtend?	1 Apr 1815
Smith, Custis	Rosanne Bunting	21 Jan 1856
Smith, Edward C.	Mahala Berry	24 Mar 1842
Smith, Elisha Levin Mathews, sec.	Nancy Wheatly	29 Jun 1804
Smith, Elizah Francis Boggs, sec.	Rachel Savage	24 Nov 1806
Smith, Ezekiel	Tabitha Parker of Nichols/Michael?	7 Nov 1808

Edmund Phillips, sec.

Smith, Ezekiel Y.   Mary Ann Harrison   29 May 1848
                           of James H.
     W.T.   Drummond and Thomas P. Hack, sec.

Smith, Ezekiel Y.   Margaret Jester   27 Sep 1852

Smith, Francis H.   Susan B. Teackle   4 Sep 1820
                           of John, dec'd.
     John B. Walker, sec.

Smith, George W.   Elizabeth S. Darby   5 Apr 1851

Smith, George W.   Eliza C. Wilkins   8 Sep 1828
                           orphan John
        William R. Milby, sec.

Smith, George   Ruth Parker   24 Dec 1798
        Edward Phillips, sec.

Smith, George W.   Eliza C. Wilkins   10 Sep 1828

Smith, George F.   Emily E. Scarburgh   18 Jul 1840

Smith, Henry   Mary Jane Benson of Ann   5 Jun 1852

Smith, Hugh G.   Margaret E.S. Rodgers   8 Feb 1832
                           orphan Richard
        George S. Savage, sec.

Smith, Isaac   Margaret Dowty   15 Jun 1802
        David Bowman, sec.

Smith, Isaac   Ann S. Teackle   4 Apr 1814
        John B. Upshur, sec.

Smith, Isaac   Alice Sterling   10 Dec 1803
        George Smith, sec.

Smith, Isaac   Emiline Turner   21 Feb 1843

Smith, James P.   Margaret Turner   31 Mar 1834
                           of Nathaniel B.
        George S. Christian, sec.

Smith, James   Sally Frances McCready   27 May 1850
                           of James
        John T. Fletcher, sec.

Smith, James   Mary Jackson   22 Jan 1787

Ezekiel Delastatius, sec.

Smith, James   Sophia Wilson   23 Feb 1818
    of Charles   of Jemima Russell
    William S. Watson, sec.

Smith, James D.   Margaret B. Turner   5 Apr 1834

Smith, James G.   Elizabeth S. Burton   14 May 1843

Smith, John   Elizabeth Lewis   8 May 1849
    George Elliott, sec.

Smith, John E.   Margaret C. Ward

Smith, John W.   Mary Ann Tyler   27 Jul 1839
                            orphan of Severn
        James B. Poulson, sec.

Smith, John   Elizabeth Lewis   9 May 1849

Smith, John W.   Melinda W. Bennett   13 Jun 1838
                            of Coventon
        William P. Joynes, sec.

Smith, John   Elizabeth Duble   26 Nov 1812
                            (wid William)
        Charles Smith, sec.

Smith, John   Elizabeth Milburn   30 Oct 1810
    Elias Joynes, sec.

Smith, John of Geo.   Mahola Powell   19 Oct 1807
    Thomas W. Rogers, sec.

Smith, John B.   Elizabeth Kellam   16 Aug 1838
                            (wid of Evans)
        James J. Ailworth, sec.

Smith, John of Geo.   Sally Garrison of Jms.   6 Nov 1820
    Abel Garrison and Francis Savage, sec., George Smith cons.

Smith, John W.   Sally Warrington   26 Jun 1816
                            (wid John W.)
        James Eichelberger, sec.

Smith, John W.   Melinda Bennett   1 Jun 1838

Smith, Levin   Margaret Savage   15 Aug 1817
    of Levin   of John, dec'd.

Elias D. Joynes, sec.

Smith, Levin   Henrietta Parker   3 Apr 1851
                            (wid of James)

Smith, Littleton   Rosey Bunting of Rosey   1 Apr 1834
   William Langford, sec.

Smith, Mears   Elizabeth Parker   24 Jun 1824

Smith, Mears   Ann M. Potter   16 Feb 1843

Smith, Michael   Maria Marshall   9 Dec 1833
   Southy Taylor and John S. Marshall, sec.

Smith, Nathaniel   Mary Ann Elliott   28 Sep 1857
                            ward of Nathaniel Smith

Smith, Nathaniel   Ann J. Garrison   14 Oct 1824
   of George   orphan James
   John Smith, sec., Sarah Garrison, mother, cons.

Smith, Noah   Nancy Gaskin of Wm.   12 Dec 1822
   David Miles and Thomas Matthews, sec.

Smith, Ralph of Ralph   Nancy Kelly   27 Dec 1826
                            of William, dec'd.
      Shadrack Taylor, sec.

Smith, Ralph   Scarburgh Whealton   29 Jun 1787
   Valentine Smith, sec.

Smith, Solomon   Betsey Outten   12 Sep 1786
   Robert Twiford, sec.

Smith, Thomas W.   Susan J. Harrison   8 May 1848
   Henry S. Davis, sec.

Smith, Thomas   Sally Gladding   15 Jun 1854
                            of George W.

Smith, Thomas B.   Susan Kellam   21 Mar 1823
                            sister of John Kellam of White Marsh
      Robert McLain, sec.

Smith, Thomas   Atta Kelly   9 Jan 1812
   William Ailworth, sec.

Smith, Valentine   Elizabeth Stant of Jms.   29 Dec 1834
   Henry White and Ralph Smith, sec.

Smith, Walter   Margaret Bonnewell   29 Apr 1833
    William C. Watson, sec.

Smith, William E.   Sarah E. Corbin   15 Feb 1853
                             of William H.

Smith, William   Emily West (wid of Wm.)   27 Dec 1852

Smith, William P.   Susan H. Joynes   4 Sep 1848
    Isaac Smith and William H. Walker, sec.

Smith, William S.   Margaret A. White of Wm. 26 Dec 1857

Smith, William   Adah Mears   14 May 1804
    William J. Roberts, sec.

Smith, William Wise   Margaret Drummond   24 Dec 1807
    Robert Drummond, sec.

Smith, William   Nancy Downing   15 Sep 1802
    David Watts, sec.

Smith, William B.   Maria Rew   9 Sep 1834
    Zorababel Miles, sec.

Smith, William P.   Susan H. Joynes   6 Sep 1848

Smith, Zophas   Mary Russell of Thos.   16 Dec 1848
    Thomas Russell, sec.

Smulling, ---m   Nancy Delastatius   25 Mar 1799
    William Brewigton, sec.

Smulling, William   Peggy Boniwell   24 Apr 1815
    William Wilburn and Drummond Wilburn, sec.

Snead, Bowdoin   Polly Kellam   29 Apr 1790

Snead, Bowdoin (wdr)   Mary Powell of Wm.   25 Jan 1841
    William Powell and Levin Gray, sec.

Snead, Charles F.   Matilda Wilson of Jms.   28 Dec 1829
    James Watson, sec.

Snead, Charles S.   Elizabeth Bonwell   10 Nov 1824
    of James   of Sarah
    Littleton Henderson, Levin Core and Elisha H. Davis, sec.

Snead, Charles S.   Rachel B. Elliott   1 Nov 1827

Snead, Edmund FN   Leah Poulson   2 Aug 1839
    Ezekiel R. Bloxom, sec.

```
Snead, Edward R.          Mary D. Wallop          22 Nov 1854
     of Edward S., dec'd.      of David, dec'd.

Snead, George            Nancy Bull              18 May 1804
     John Bull, sec.

Snead, George F.         Henrietta W. Snead       7 Jul 1829
                            of Thomas
     Americus Scarburgh, sec.

Snead, George            Betsy Davis              9 Jan 1810
     Levin Hyslop, sec.

Snead, George            Sarah Bayly             14 Mar 1790

Snead, George            Elizabeth Ironmonger    27 Jun 1805
     Daniel Ardis, sec.

Snead, George            Catherine Watson        26 Jan 1801
     Charles Snead, sec.

Snead, George L.         Harriet W. Snead        10 Jul 1829

Snead, Isaac (wdr)       Ann Boniwell            25 Jun 1831
     Borden Snead and James W. Twiford, sec.

Snead, Isaac             Nancy Sharwood           3 Dec 1801
     John Hogshire, sec.

Snead, James             Mrs. Sally Window       28 Oct 1801
     John Satchell, sec.

Snead, James             Susanna Satchell         7 Aug 1798
     John Satchell, sec.

Snead, John H.           Betsy Drummond of  Robt. 29 May 1801

Snead, John              Milly Chandler          26 Dec 1798
     Bowdoin Snead, sec.


Snead, John L.           Tabitha Bundick         19 Dec 1838
                            of Richard
     George P. Barnes Jr., sec.

Snead, John H.           Selby Floyd              4 Apr 1804
     Bowdoin Snead, sec.

Snead, John (wdr)        Christina Bowden (wid)  28 Nov 1851

Snead, John H. (wdr)     Mary White              18 Jun 1851
```

Snead, John of Robert   Leah Kellam of Edward   25 Mar 1822
     John Follio, Jos. Brimer and Samuel A. Justice, sec.

Snead, John H.   Peggy Hickman   28 Mar 1809
                         (wid Spencer)
          Joseph Ames, sec.

Snead Lewis L.   Hester Sturgis   18 Dec 1837
                         (wid of Thomas)
          Thomas Rogers, sec.

Snead, Louis S.   Hester H.   Oct 1831

Snead, Peter   Comfort Snead   13 Sep 1837
     Levin S. Joynes and Solomon Warren, sec.

Snead, Robert   Esther Scott   5 Aug 1783
     Bayly Hinman, sec.

Snead, Samuel   Lovey Starling   15 Feb 1833
                         ward of Major Savage
          Major Savage and Thomas W. Mears, sec.

Snead, Samuel   Lovy Starling   28 Feb 1833

Snead, Thomas   Elizabeth West   23 May 1785
     William Gibb, sec.

Snead, Thomas of Wm.   Katherine Booth   28 Jan 1807
     Edward Gunter, sec.

Snead, Tully   Molly Twyford   10 Aug 1840
     (wdr)   (wid of Revel)
          John D. Rew, sec.

Snead, Tully   Betsy Snead   22 Dec 1813
                         ward Levin C. Stewart
          Levin C. Stewart, sec.

Snead, Tully   Molly Twyford   13 Aug 1840

Snead, Willam   Elizabeth Coleburn (wid) 17 Dec 1806
     Francis Downing, sec.

Snead, William   Elizabeth Metcalf   31 Jan 1807
     Levin Payne, sec.

Snead, William B.   Emmie A. Gardner   1 Oct 1823

Solomon FN   Tamer FN   28 Dec 1798

Somers, John   Nancy Prescot   10 Aug 1813

Joshua Thomas, sec.

Somers, John   Elizabeth Wessells   7 Mar 1821
    of Horsey   of Arthur, dec'd.
    Thomas Wessells and Delight James, sec.

Somers, John   Nancy West of Alexander 31 May 1819

Somers, Richard   Elizabeth Lewis   4 Jul 1836
    (wdr)   (wid of George)
    John D. Parks and James J. Ailworth, sec.

Somers, William   Serina C. Bird   21 Jan 1852
    of John   of Eborn

Sommers, John Jr.   Vianna Bird of Eborn   5 Feb 1851

Sommers, Richard   Mary Young of David   25 Mar 1850
    David Young, sec.

Sparks, Robert   Sally Beavans   30 Mar 1820

Sparrow, David (wdr)   Molly Bundick (wid)   2 Feb 1857

Sparrow, George W.   Margaret Cherricks   17 Nov 1854
                          of Edward

Sparrow, Jacob   Molly Hall   24 Feb 1806
    Jonathan Mears, sec.

Sparrow, Jacob Jr.   Deliley Evans   3 Feb 1823
                          of Richard Sr.
      Henry Smith and John Phillips, sec.

Sparrow, Jacob Jr.   Delily Evans of Rich.   3 Feb 1823

Sparrow, John   Hessy Dix   11 Jul 1812
    Teackle Justice, sec.

Sparrow, Josiah   Rutha Evans   2 May 1827
    Major Evans and Charles Kilmon Jr., sec.

Sparrow, Laben   Nancy Howarth   7 May 1823
    James Hoffman, sec.

Sparrow, Richard   Sarah Riggs   3 Mar 1817
    (wdr)   (wid George D.)
    George White, sec.

Sparrow, Richard   Tabitha Wright of Jno.   11 Jan 1832
    Edmund Baker, sec.

Sparrow, Richard   Zeporah Mears   -- --- 1796

Sparrow, Richard   Esther Wise   6 Oct 1789

Sparrow, Samuel   Mary Jane Marshall   27 Mar 1848
    William T. Marshall, sec.

Speight, Josiah   Hessy Russell   27 Apr 1807
    Elijah Bloxom, sec.

Speight, Josiah   Sally Hickman   28 Jan 1828
                        orphan Dennis
        John Snead, sec.

Speight, Josiah   Sally East   28 Apr 1806
    Elijah Bloxom, sec.

Speirs, William   Nancy Hornsby   26 Jan 1802
    Samuel Coleburn, sec.

Spence, Elijah of Jms.   Betsy Evans of Rich. 18 Jun 1825
    John Lucas, sec.

Spence, Levin ·   Betsy Palmer of John   1 Jan 1850
    John Palmer, sec.

Spence, Thomas R.P.   Margaret D. Thomas   25 Nov 1805
    John Wallop, sec.

Stakes, Johannes   Anne Parker   27 Feb 1799
    William Guy, sec.

Stakes, John   Susan Wright   1 Dec 1841

Stakes, William   Esther Kellam   26 Dec 1808
                        (wid Thomas)
      Bagwell Garrison, sec.

Stakes, William (wdr)   Eliz. Cutler of Rich. 17 Jan 1825
    Samuel Walston, sec.

Stakes, William L.   Priscilla Pritchett   9 Dec 1834
                        of Jabus
        John C. Watson, sec.

Stakes, William   Sally Hogshire of Wm.   4 Apr 1816
    William Hogshire, sec.

Stakes, William   Priscilla Pritchett   9 Dec 1834

Stanford, Jonathan   Polly Thornton   12 Jul 1809
    James Thornton, sec.

```
Stant, Gilbert of Jms.    Sally Miles of Molly    16 Apr 1827
     Parker Miles and John Lewis, sec.

Stant, Henry              Sarah Small              5 Jan 1825
     of James             of James, dec'd.
     David Mears, sec.

Stant, James of Jms.      Nancy Christopher       31 Dec 1816
                          of John
     John Christopher, sec.

Stant, James             Euphamy Wilson           31 Aug 1795

Stant, John              Margaret Ann Bull         5 Nov 1839
                          (wid of Richard)
     Smith Cutler, sec.

Stant, John (wdr)        Polly Woods of Nancy     24 Jul 1854

Stant, John              Sarah Ann McCready        2 Jul 1836
     Ralph Smith, sec.

Stant, John H.           Susan Hinman of Perry    18 Nov 1851

Stant, Robert James      Mary Chase of Robt. Jr.   1 Jan 1851

Stant, Samuel of Jms.    Sally Fisher of Teackle   2 Aug 1822
     Raymond Riley and John Bull, sec.

Stant, William           Sarah A. Hay              1 Aug 1848
     Samuel Taylor of C., sec.

Stant, William of Jms.   Milkah Corbin of Robt.   14 Jan 1829
     Edmund C. Godwin and Edward C. Northam, sec.

Stant, William           Sarah Corbin             23 Dec 1826
     Kendall Silverthorne, sec.

Starling, John           Margaret Nelson           2 Jan 1834
     Levi and Sarah Starling, sec.

Starling, John           Lovey Mason               1 Jan 1806

Starling, Levi           Rachel Ames              23 Sep 1833
                          (wid of Stephen)
     Elijah Floyd, sec.

Starling, Levi           Rachel Ames              18 Oct 1833

Starling, Samuel         Leah Townsend            15 Mar 1834
                          (wid of Southy)
     Purnell O. Taylor and Thomas Gillet, sec.
```

Starling, William   Margaret Hutchinson   4 Feb 1839
                           ward of Major Savage
     Major Savage, sec.

Staten, Joseph (minor)   Catherine Thornton   15 May 1806
     Elisha Fitzgerald, sec.

Staten, Joseph S.   Clarissa Beavans   25 May 1833
                           of Jesse
     Elisha H. Davis, sec.

Staton, Ephriam   Sarah Ann Coard   20 Apr 1841
     Henry Bagwell, sec.

Staton, George   Betsy Taylor   12 Mar 1804
     Nehemiah Broughton, sec.

Staton, George   Sarah Garrett (wid)   15 Aug 1809
     William Smulling, sec.

Staton, Henry   Margaret Whealton   30 Dec 1837
     Noah G. Duncan and Abel R. Thomas, sec.

Staton, Jacob J.   Brunetta Ewell   14 Aug 1839
     William Ewell and James P. Taylor, sec.

Staton, John   Comfort Conquest   30 Dec 1805
     Nathaniel Conquest, sec.

Staton, Joseph   Elizabeth Holt   24 Feb 1808
     John Henderson, sec.

Staton, Joseph S.   Clarissa Beavans   20 May 1833

Staton, Joseph   Cathering Thornton   17 May 1806

Staton, Robert   Betsy Carpenter   15 Nov 1819
     of Thomas   of Aron Holloway
     Sebastian Cropper and Isaac Henderson, sec.

Staton, Thomas   Mary Kelpin   8 Sep 1810
     John Holt, sec

Staton, Warrington   Peggy Davis   30 Jan 1815
     James Collins and Henry S. Copes, sec.

Staton, Warrington Sr.   Sarah Boston of Elijah   30 Sep 1816
     William R. Taylor and Frederick Conner, sec.

Staton, Warrington Jr.   Euphemia Broadwater   29 Jul 1816
     Michael Robins and William Jenkins, sec.

Staton, William   Elizabeth Dix   29 Jul 1816
     Thomas Staton, sec.

Staton, William   Ann B. Ewell   28 Sep 1836
     (wdr)   ward of David Broadwater
     John W. Feddiman and Levin Core, sec.

Staton, William   Eliza Dix   26 Jun 1806

Staton, William (wdr)   Ann B. Ewell   29 Sep 1834

Steelman, David   Elizabeth Mason   29 May 1847

Stephens, Thomas   Elizabeth Carnthers   17 Aug 1831
     John F. Heath, sec.

Stephens, Thomas FN   Betty Francis FN   13 Jul 1804
     Babel Major FN, sec.

Stephens, William   Keziah Sanders   26 Jun 1798

Stephens, William   Leah Tatham   25 Apr 1786
     Ezekiel Tatham, sec.

Stephens, William   Leah Pettitt   9 Sep 1841

Stephenson, Edward   Elizabeth L. Ames   3 Dec 1827
                         of Zorobabel
     Shadrach T. Ames and Samuel Walston, sec.

Sterling, Henry   Euphemia Broadwater   23 Dec 1816
     of Richard   (wid Edward)
     Ralph B. Corbin, sec.

Sterling, John   Lovey Mason   24 Dec 1805
     Jacob Mason, sec.

Sterling, Josiah   Hessy Melson   9 Jun 1820
     of Littleton   of George
     Henry Hall and Samuel Walston, sec.

Sterling, Samuel   Mary Owen   1 Aug 1810
     Thomas Hancock, sec.

Sterling, Shadrack   Betsy Scott   28 Sep 1811
     John B. Warrington, sec.

Stevens, Dr. Thomas   Elizabeth E. Jones   24 Nov 1834
                         of E.H.
     Oliver Logan, sec.

Stevens, Elisha   Sally Holston   25 Apr 1795

Stevens, John   Sukey Badger   29 Dec 1804
     Charles Stevens, sec.

Stevens, Thomas   Elizabeth C. James   24 Nov 1834

Stevens, Williams   Betsy Parks   28 Feb 1798

Stevenson, Isaac K.   Molly A. Bell   20 Dec 1849
                           of Sarah P.
     James H. Caliburn and Joseph G. Feddeman, sec.

Stevenson, Jonathan   Anne Mills   3 Apr 1786
     Presson Snead, sec.

Stevenson, Thomas F.   Ann M. Bell   28 Oct 1839
     John R. Truitt and John P. Taylor, sec.

Stevenson, Thomas   Mary T. Parker   10 Nov 1806
     Robert Parker, sec.

Stewart, Albert   Rachel Phillips   30 Nov 1840
                           (wid of John)
     Thomas Harrison and Thorogood Mears, sec.

Stewart, Edward FN   Molly Webb FN   9 Oct 1811
     John Snead, sec.

Stewart Henry   Hesy Phillips of Jacob   20 Mar 1815
     Shepherd Kellam, sec.

Stewart, Henry   Mary Coleburn   28 Oct 1816
     (wdr)   (wid George)
     George Beach, sec.

Stewart, Henry (wdr)   Sally Nock of Geo.   21 Jan 1820
     Luther Kellam, sec.

Stewart, Henry   Nancy E.   28 May 1834

Stewart, James   Susanna Garrison   4 Mar 1816
                           of Archibald
     Joshua Warrington, sec.

Stewart, James   Tabitha Joynes   20 Mar 1818
     (wdr)   (wid William)
     Elijah A. White, sec.

Stewart, James   Leah Custis   27 Sep 1837
                           (wid of William)
     George F. Snead, sec.

Stewart, James   Sophia Bayly   6 Nov 1798

- 272 -

```
Stewart, Levin C.          Maria Bradford              25 Jan 1815
                           of Thomas A.
        James Stewart, sec.

Stockley, Abram FN         Ann Pool FN                 31 May 1858

Stockley, Charles          Margaret Allen              29 Jun 1784
        John Burton, sec.

Stockley, George FN        Nancy Robins FN             29 Jan 1823
        James Thornton and William Taylor, sec.

Stockley, Isaac, black  Sophia Powell, black           25 May 1809
        Joseph Kew, sec.

Stockley, John             Nancy Bradford               4 Nov 1811
                           (wid Littleton)
        Anthony Bell, sec.

Stockley, Nehemiah         Margaret T. Bolsnard        10 Jul 1813
        William S. Custis, sec.

Stockley, Sylvester        Margaret Downing             2 Nov 1840
        James Hyslop, sec.

Stockley, William          Mahala Matthews             25 Jan 1830
        Elijah Hinman and Michael Robins, sec.

Stockly, Jeremiah          Peggy Ironmonger            11 Aug 1817
        of Peggy               of George
        Abel Bradford, sec.

Stott, Keely               Susanna West                30 Nov 1807
        Tho. Custis of Robt., sec.

Stott, Samuel S.           Margaret Parker             21 Sep 1826
                           (wid William)
        James Doughty, sec.

Stott, Timothy B.          Nancy Shreves               12 Jul 1837
        John S. Robins, sec.

Straham, Alexander         Elizabeth C. Gibb           23 Oct 1819
        Walter R. Finney, sec.

Stratton, Samuel C.        Margaret S. Ker of Geo.      1 Nov 1823
        Edward H. Ker, sec.

Stringer, Arthur           Elizabeth Sturgis            6 Jan 1813
        William Watson, sec.

Stringer, Benjamin         Caroline T. Ames            25 Mar 1833
```

John W. Hyslop and William M. Ames, sec.

Stringer, George W.   Sally Ames of Zodiah   20 Dec 1847
    John J. Nock and Revel West, sec.

Stringer, George W.   Sally Ames   21 Dec 1847

Stringer, Smith   Elizabeth Bell of Wm.   30 Aug 1813
    Agrippa Bell, sec.

Sturgis, Charles T.   Elizabeth Ames   5 Jul 1836
                           ward of William S. Sturgis
    William S. Sturgis, sec.

Sturgis, Charles T.   Mary Custis   30 Jul 1838
    William S. Sturgis, sec.

Sturgis, Daniel   Elizabeth Thornton   27 Dec 1824
                           (wid Kendall)
    David Watts Sr. and William D. Cropper, sec.

Sturgis, George   Susan Hornsby   2 Jan 1838
    John C. Watson and James J. Ailworth, sec.

Sturgis, George   Susan Hornsby   3 Jan 1838

Sturgis, James   Margaret Custis of Revel 14 Jan 1833
    John Sturgis, sec.

Sturgis, James   Margaret Custis   18 Jan 1833

Sturgis, John   Tabitha Royal   15   Jul   1774
    Benjamin Royal, sec.

Sturgis, John Jr.   Mrs. Peggy Richardson (wid) 4 Aug 1801
    Thomas Scarburgh, sec.

Sturgis, John FN   Rachel Phillips   19 Sep 1805

Sturgis, Joshua   Joanna Guy   23 Oct 1787
    George Corbin, sec.

Sturgis, Kendal   Elizabeth Bell   27 Jul 1837
    Gilbert Bell, sec.

Sturgis, Nathaniel   Elizabeth H. Townsend   3 Jan 1827
    of Thomas   of Littleton
    George F. Snead, sec.

Sturgis, Samuel (wdr)   Sally Charnock (wid)   13 Jan 1857

Sturgis, Thomas   Mary Boggs of Arthur   29 Jun 1829

William C. Boggs, sec.

Sturgis, William L.   Demariah Taylor   23 Feb 1835
    Edmund Parker, sec.

Sturgis, William S.   Keziah C. Ames of Jno.   16 Nov 1830
    John W. Sturgis, sec.

Sturgis, Zorobabel   Molly Dowty   7 Mar 1808
    William Pitts, sec.

Sturgis,Joshua   Rachel Philips   19 Sep 1805
    Abraham Williams, sec.

Summers, George   Eveline Wessells   14 Jan 1856
                             of Betsy

Summers, Richard   Elizabeth Ewell   6 May 1804
    Arthur Hickman, sec.

Summers, Richard   Elizabeth Lewis   14 Jul 1836

Summers, Richard   Elizabeth Giddens   29 Dec 1800
    Ephraim Vessels, sec.

Summers, Samuel   Mary J. Justis   22 Apr 1857
    of Elizabeth   of Samuel R.

Taliaferro, William   Anne Hatton   6 Dec 1802
    William Morgan, sec.

Tan, George   Anna Douglass of Jms.   15 Jun 1807
    George Marshall, sec.

Tankard, John   Sally Townsend   18 Jun 1810
    Richard Bayly, sec.

Tankard, Phillip B.   Elizabeth Rodgers   29 Oct 1841

Tarr, David   Mary Ann Gray   24 Mar 1844

Tarr, James (wdr)   Polly Lewis   2 Mar 1820
                           (wid Selby)
    Richard Bull, sec.

Tarr, Peter of Wm.   Sally Claywell of Tho.   28 Jun 1819
    William Sharply and George Clavel, sec.

Tatham, Charles   Elizabeth Wallop   2 Jan 1838
    (wdr)   (wid of Shinner)
    William Parramore, sec.

Tatham, Charles   Mary A.   3 Jan 1837

Tatham, Ezekiel   Cornelia Miles   26 Mar 1833
    William Gardner and J.B. Ailworth, sec.

Tatham, James   Nancy Bull of George   29 Mar 1833
    George Bull, sec.

Tatham, Rickets   Comfort Mears   18 Oct 1792

Tatham, Samuel   Sarah Ann   12 Aug 1830

Tatham, Stephen   Nancy Bloxom of Geo.   22 Dec 1829
    John Groten, sec.

Tatham, Thomas   Keziah Wright of Elijah   21 May 1821
    Elijah Wright and Gilbert M. Leatherbury, sec.

Tatham, William (wdr)   Mary Baker of Elijah   6 Feb 1855

Tatham, William   Molly Miles   16 Jan 1839
    John Miles, sec.

Tatham, William H.   Sarah W. Phillips   31 Jan 1853
                           of Levin

Tatham, Wm. of Michael   Kessy Edwards of Wm.   14 Nov 1816
    Southy W. East, sec.

```
Tathem, William          Peggy Bloxom                    14 Dec 1803
     Ezekiel Bloxom, sec.

Taws, Henry              Elizabeth Hyslop                29 Dec 1854

Taylor, Abel             Elizabeth Mason                 25 Sep 1797

Taylor, Alfred           Mary Johnson                    31 Jan 1854
     of Revel                 of James T.

Taylor, Alfred           Virginia N. Boggs                2 Oct 1857
     of James B.              of Francis

Taylor, Arthur FN        Catherine Bayly FN              25 Dec 1854

Taylor, Asa (wdr)        Mariah Small (wid)              18 May 1841

Taylor, Asa              Critty Baily                    12 Jan 1839
     (wdr)                    of Upshur
     Alexander Land and William Wyatt, sec.

Taylor, Assa             Maria Small                     18 May 1841
                              (wid of Handy)
     Smith and Henry Chesser, sec.

Taylor, Ayres            Rachel Copes                    28 Jul 1791

Taylor, Ayres            Polly Kirby (wid Henry)          5 Jan 1810
     William Walters, sec.

Taylor, Bagwell Jr.      Mary A. Bunting                 28 Dec 1840
                              (wid of John)
     Lewis B. Taylor, sec.

Taylor, Bagwell          Nancy Justice                   16 Oct 1839
     of Tabitha               of Richard
     John Taylor and John J. Blackstone, sec.

Taylor, Bagwell          Lucretia Warner                  3 Nov 1806
     William Warner, sec.

Taylor, Bundick          Nancy Henderson                 29 Jun 1820
                              of Milly
     William H. Taylor and Walter D. Bayne, sec.

Taylor, Bundick          Nancy Marshall                  30 Apr 1839
     William A. Marshall and Elisha J. Whealton, sec.

Taylor, Bundick          Henney Wheatly                  24 Nov 1823
     of Jeremiah              (wid)
     George W. Taylor, sec.
```

```
Taylor, Charles W.          Melina Kellam              3 Sep 1827
   of George                   of Thomas
   Thomas Kellam (SS),  sec.

Taylor, Charles             Tabitha Parks              4 Jun 1806
   William Taylor, sec.

Taylor, Charles             Sally Shipman             31 Dec 1800
   George Parker, sec.

Taylor, Charles             Ann J. Russell            30 Jan 1845

Taylor, Charles             Tabitha Miles             18 Mar 1793

Taylor, Charles Jr.         Peggy Young of Eliz.      12 Jan 1820
   George H. Ewell, sec.

Taylor, Charles Bayley      Betsey Walker             11 Apr 1787
   John Watson, sec.

Taylor, Charles             Catherine Parks            1 Jun 1806

Taylor, Colmore             Elizabeth Broadwater      16 Jan 1821
   of Southy                   (wid Christopher)
   Ralph B. Corbin, sec.

Taylor, David R.            Caroline Ann Prescott     25 Dec 1849
                               of Hester
      David R. Taylor and Russell Chandler, sec.

Taylor, Edward              Leah Tatom                21 Dec 1819
   of Elias                    of John
      David Watts and Richard D. Bayly, sec.

Taylor, Edward of P.        Sarah A. Whealton         22 Jan 1850
                               of John
      Severn H. Hargis and Obed Taylor, sec.

Taylor, Edward              Diadamia Drummond (wid)   23 Sep 1773
   Benjamin Peck, sec.

Taylor, Edward W.           Hetty Dickerson (wid)     19 Jun 1847
   of Bagwell

Taylor, Edward W.           Mary E. Conquest          24 Apr 1844

Taylor, Edward W.           Hetty Dickerson           17 Jun 1847
   (wdr), of B.                (wid of George)
   James J. Ailworth, sec.
```

Taylor, Edward W. (wdr)   Sally White of Thomas   17 May 1849
    Thomas White, sec.

Taylor, Edward of Jno.   Ann Catherine Tindall   2 Feb 1853
                           of John

Taylor, Ephraim   Agnes Wilkerson   19 Dec 1805
    Wilson Taylor, sec.

Taylor, Evans   Wise Morris   19 Jan 1816
    of Jeremiah   of Gilbert
    Charles Whealton and Richard D. Bayly, sec.

Taylor, Ezekiel (wdr)   Sally Wilkerson   16 Apr 1818
    Samuel S. Tunnell and Alexander McCollom, sec.

Taylor, Frederick   Sarah Bull   19 Dec 1854
                           of George, dec'd.

Taylor, George   Nancy Outten   29 Sep 1817
    Thomas West, sec.

Taylor, George K.   Mary C. Smith of Tho.   28 Apr 1828
    William C. Walston and Thomas Smith, sec.

Taylor, Gillet (wdr)   Nancy Fisher of Henry   21 Jan 1850
    Thoroughgood S. Taylor and William T. Bird, sec.

Taylor, Henry   Maria Badger of Ezek.   26 Nov 1838
    William Nocks, sec.

Taylor, Henry W. (wdr)   Elizabeth Coleburn (wid)   27 Jun 1849

Taylor, Henry   Sally Lucas   19 Oct 1820
    of Teackle   of Parker
    Meshack Duncan, sec.

Taylor, Henry   Nancy Addison   7 May 1832
    George Gladding, sec.

Taylor, Henry W. (wdr)   Elizabeth Coleburn   25 Jun 1849
    David Broadwater, sec.

Taylor, Henry   Esther O. Sturgis   12 Nov 1804
    William W.L. Marshall, sec.

Taylor, Henry   Susanna Shield (wid)   28 Nov 1812
    Nathaniel Benson, sec.

Taylor, Henry   Scarborough Henderson   31 Dec 1827
    of Elias   of John

Thomas Russell and Nathaniel Smart, sec.

Taylor, Henry   Nancy Hatfield   24 Jul 1807
    Arthur Whittington, sec.

Taylor, Hezekiah   Sally Adams   15 Jun 1791
Taylor, Jacob   Polly Whealton of Mary   29 May 1812
    James Conner and William Davis, sec.

Taylor, Jacob   Elizabeth Melson   8 Jul 1786
    William Willet, sec.

Taylor, James C.   Caty Bull of Tobias   9 Mar 1824

Taylor, James   Margaret Douglass   19 Feb 1827
    of Horntown   (wid Walter)
    Revell Taylor and Corah Taylor, sec.

Taylor, James H.   Susanna Hall   31 Aug 1820
    of Charles   of Nathaniel, dec'd. and Elizabeth
    David Watts and Parker Lucas, sec.

Taylor, James C.   Nancy Bull   9 Mar 1824

Taylor, James G.   Elizabeth Window   24 Dec 1840

Taylor, James B. (wdr)   Nancy Smith (wid)   26 Nov 1844

Taylor, James   Princess A. Groten   12 Feb 1821
    Galen Conner, sec.

Taylor, James   Peggy Vessels   21 Nov 1810
                         (wid Arthur)
        Major Mason, sec.

Taylor, James A.   Elizabeth Waters   16 Oct 1839

Taylor, James   Henrietta Lucas   3 Feb 1813
    orphan Teackle   orphan Selby
    Parker Lucas, sec.

Taylor, James   Ann Bagwell   25 Feb 1801
    James White, sec.

Taylor, James   Tabitha Bundick   1 Jun 1804
    Daniel Melson, sec.

Taylor, James   Caty Moore   19 Aug 1800
    Teackly Taylor, sec.

Taylor, James   Esther Boggs   13 Feb 1802
    Joseph Boggs, sec.

Taylor, James G.   Elizabeth Window of Geo. 22 Dec 1840
     George Bunting, sec.

Taylor, James   Peggy Marshall   31 Jul 1802
     Ephriam Taylor, sec.

Taylor, Jesse   Eliza Young   16 Apr 1821
     of Jeremiah   ofJohn Young, dec'd. and Mary Rowley
     William H. Taylor, sec.

Taylor, Jesse   Polly Wheatley   22 Jan 1816
     of Jeremiah   of Michael
     Henry Thornton and George Scarburgh, sec.

Taylor, Jestis of Jms.   Eliza Bull of Daniel   24 Dec 1827
     Daniel Bull, sec.

Taylor, John N.   Elizabeth Gardner   11 Dec 1834
                         (wid of William)
     James T. Gibbons, sec.

Taylor, John of Chas.   Catherine Killman   29 Mar 1827
                           of Charles
     Charles Taylor and Charles Killman, sec.

Taylor, John Wesley   Mary W. Waters   11 Nov 1833

Taylor, John B. of Wm.   Elizabeth Benson   29 May 1839

Taylor, John   Mary Collins   23 Jun 1829
     of Nehemiah   of Sally
     Southy Taylor of Southy, sec.

Taylor, John   Milcah Gladding   19 Nov 1827
     of Ezekiel   of John
     Henry Gladding, sec.

Taylor, John D.   Zipporah Crodkett   15 Jan 1846

Taylor, John   Mary Savage   8 Dec 1842

Taylor, John   Margaret Hinman   15 Jan 1835

Taylor, John   Rachel Nock   11 Jan 1799
     Benjamin Nock, sec.

Taylor, John   Sinah W. Hickman   14 Feb 1826
     orphan John   of Elizah
     John Savage of Richard and Elizah Hickman, sec.

Taylor, John   Hester Staton   18 Jan 1802

of Warrington Staton
James Taylor, sec.

Taylor, John James   Susan Taylor   8 Jul 1857
    of Thomas of William   of Betsy

Taylor, John B.   Elizabeth Beavans of Ann 28 May 1839
    William Savage, sec.

Taylor, John   Susanna Simpson   15 Mar 1808
    Smith Melson, sec.

Taylor, Joseph   Rebecca Townsend   29 Nov 1809
    Levi Brittingham, sec.

Taylor, Joseph B.   Elizabeth Phillips   30 Dec 1833
                         of Jacob and ward of Edward
        Edward D. Phillips, sec.

Taylor, Justice of Jms. Elizabeth Bull   26 Dec 1827

Taylor, Levin   Sophia Nelson   25 Jul 1805
    Samuel Mills, sec.

Taylor, Levin   Nancy Taylor of Joseph   19 Jan 1833
    Robert Taylor, sec.

Taylor, Lewis   Elizabeth B. Burton   5 Jan 1839
                         of John
        Peter Shield, sec.

Taylor, Major   Nancy Silverthorne   10 Jan 1816
                         (wid Southy)
        William Taylor, sec.

Taylor, Major   Rachel Addison   6 Oct 1787
    Peter Rodgers, sec.

Taylor, Major FN   Esther Broadwater FN   25 Aug 1834
    David Mears and Spencer Drummond, sec.

Taylor, Major   Elizabeth Turnall   28 Dec 1808
    William Taylor, sec.

Taylor, Matthew   Cassey Annis   19 Aug 1837
        Richard Dix, sec.

Taylor, Mathias   Nancy Hardy   22 Nov 1786
    James Smith, sec.

Taylor, Matthews   Sally Thornton   22 Dec 1798
    Thomas Beavens, sec.

- 282 -

```
Taylor, Nathaniel        Eliza Garrett           15 Nov 1809
     William Northam Jr., sec.

Taylor, Nathaniel        Maria Henderson         27 Jun 1838
     (wdr)               (wid of Joseph)
     William Walston, sec.

Taylor, Nathaniel        Hessey Thornton         12 Jun 1823
     of Alexander
     William Watts and Zadock Selby, sec.
Taylor, Nathaniel        Euphemia Mariner         6 Apr 1816
     of Alexander        of George
     Wm. Matthews Taylor, sec.

Taylor, Parker           Maria Townsend          17 Dec 1833
     John Waterfield, sec.

Taylor, Peter T.         Sarah A. Edwards        29 Dec 1851
                         of Bagwell

Taylor, Preason          Sarah Staton            23 Sep 1828
                         (wid Warrington)
     Jesse Beavans and Peter Blades, sec.

Taylor, Pritson          Harriet Ettes           21 Mar 1849
     James Littiston, sec.

Taylor, Purnell          Sally Holt              28 Dec 1804
     John Madrick, sec.

Taylor Revel             Margaret Gaskins         9 Feb 1849
     (wdr)               (wid of Revel Gaskins)
     James T. Johnson, sec.

Taylor, Revel            Ibba Marshall           16 Dec 1811
     James Taylor, sec.

Taylor,  Richard         Nancy Vessels           30 Nov 1813
                         (wid Custis)
          William Nock, sec.

Taylor, Robert J.        Arinthia S. Wessells    24 Mar 1856
                         of Sally

Taylor, Robert L.        Nancy Dix of Nancy      28 Jan 1831
     David Mears, sec.

Taylor, Robert           Nancy Ewell of Geo.     27 Dec 1813
     Major Taylor Sr., sec.

Taylor, Samuel C.        Lavinia Corbin          29 Nov 1847
                         of Covington
```

John Taylor, sec.

Taylor, Samuel T.   Isabella C. Ames   2 Feb 1834
   John W. Colonna, sec.

Taylor, Samuel (wdr)   Sophia Collins   24 Nov 1831
   Walter Slocomb and Vespasian Ellis, sec.

Taylor, Samuel (wdr)   Mary Dickerson   2 Apr 1839
   James Duncan, sec.

Taylor, Samuel T.   Emily A. Ames   25 Jun 1838
   (wdr)   ward of Richard W. Grant
   John W. Mears and David Watts, sec.

Taylor, Samuel M.   Ann C. Bundick   28 Sep 1822
                           (wid) John A.
   George W. Bundick, sec.

Taylor, Samuel   Polly Morris   26 Feb 1821
   of Alexander   (wid) Gilbert
   William Water and William C. Coard, sec.

Taylor, Samuel E.   Susanna H. Martin   30 Jun 1817
   blacksmith   of Henry
   Thomas Martin, sec.

Taylor, Samuel E.   Elizabeth Ewell   31 Jan 1853
                           of Henry F.

Taylor, Samuel P.   Mary Shreaves   7 Dec 1842

Taylor, Samuel T.   Critty Harmon of John   24 Jan 1827
   Jesse Kelly and John Bird, sec. and John Harmon consent

Taylor, Savage (wdr)   Alice Rogers   7 Sep 1839

Taylor, Savage   Hannah Ball   27 Mar 1826
   (wdr)   (wid) James
   William S. Upshur, sec.

Taylor, Savage   Comfort Taylor   19 Jul 1813
                           (wid Teackle)
   William Lucas, sec.

Taylor, Savage   Sarah Ann Staton   15 Apr 1847
   (wdr)   (wid of Ephriam)
   Samuel N. Mapp and James D. McAllen, sec.

Taylor, Selby   Susanna Evans   27 Oct 1789

```
Taylor, Shadrack          Ritta Fitchette           26 Jan 1789

Taylor, Shadrock          Nancy Chesser of Polly    29 Mar 1847
    James D. Godwin and Thomas H. Parramore, sec.

Taylor, Southy            Susanna Justice           12 Aug 1818
    of Major              of William, dec'd.
    Parker Barnes, sec.

Taylor, Southy            Peggy Rew                 14 Dec 1797

Taylor, Southy            Catherine Justice         28 Apr 1807
    Spencer Lewis, sec.

Taylor, Staton            Susanna Powell of John     6 Jan 1818
    Isaac Henderson, sec.

Taylor, Staton            Comfort Nock              28 Sep 1800
    Crippen Taylor, sec.

Taylor, Stephen           Frances Melson            27 May 1800
    Jonathan Melson, sec.

Taylor, Teackle           Comfort Lucas            *25 Feb 1799
    Southy Lucas, sec.

Taylor, Teackle of Wm.    Rebecca Taylor of Chas.   27 Mar 1823
    Julius Bundick, sec.

Taylor, Teackle           Susanna Bayly             25 Nov 1774
    Elijah Watson, sec.

Taylor, Teackle           Peggy Benston             28 Sep 1790
    James Taylor,sec.

Taylor, Teackle of Jms.   Lany Owens of Taylor      28 Jan 1822
    William Waters, sec.

Taylor, Teackle of Jms.   Keziah Berry of Ebban     10 Dec 1817
    William Davis of Samuel, sec.

Taylor, Thomas B.         Harriet Edwards           21 Jan 1847

Taylor, Thomas Teackle    Mrs. Nancy Williams       27 Dec 1802

Taylor, Thomas            Eliza Snead of Robert     25 Jan 1854

Taylor, Thomas            Nancy Taylor              21 Mar 1834
    of Tabitha            of Charles
    Charles Taylor, sec.

Taylor, Thomas (wdr)      Nancy Chandler (wid)      15 Sep 1857
```

Taylor, Thorogood	Mary Taylor of Teagle	22 Jun 1853
Taylor, William	Mrs. Ede Read (wid)	3 Jun 1806
Taylor, William of Parker, dec'd. William R. Taylor Jr. and James Melson, sec.	Sarah Copes of Severn	26 Feb 1827
Taylor, William William W. Hickman and William Mathews, sec.	Nancy Marriner	22 Jun 1814
Taylor, William George Wilson, sec.	Nancy Wilson	30 Jul 1798
Taylor, William of Elias James Wishart and John B. Walker, sec.	Polly Taylor of Ezekiel	7 Feb 1818
Taylor, William of S.	Sarah Sparrow	8 Aug 1842
Taylor, William carpenter	Sally Copes	25 Jan 1791
Taylor, William	Polly Taylor	nd 1818
Taylor, William M.	Sally A. Chandler	25 Mar 1844
Taylor, William Edward Gunter, sec.	Hulder Smith of Wm.	29 Feb 1808
Taylor, William Henry Davis, sec.	Nancy Boston	10 Feb 1808
Taylor, William John Mears, sec.	Barsheba W. Bundick	10 Dec 1808
Taylor, William Alexander Lang and John Watson, sec.	Rachel Simpson of Geo.	21 Jun 1831
Taylor, William shoemaker Ethel Lyon and Levin Core, sec.	Charlotte Henderson (wid Lemuel)	14 Jan 1825
Taylor, William (wdr) William A. Marshall and John S. Wallop, sec.	Nancy Taylor (wid of Bundick)	12 Nov 1840
Taylor, William	Ruth Smith	18 May 1808
Taylor, William Charles Tyler and Thorogood Dix, sec.	Ann Onions of Wm.	15 Jan 1838

```
Taylor, William          Maria Miles              4 Sep 1827
    of Levin             (wid George)
    Thomas Mathews and Gorah Taylor, sec.

Taylor, William of Chas.  Ann Young of Sally      25 Jan 1841
    David Mears and John Finney, sec.

Taylor, William          Hessy Annis               2 Jul 1814
    James Townsend, sec.

Taylor, William of T.    Mary A. Tyler            29 Dec 1851

Taylor, William R.       Bridget Garrett          27 Feb 1804
    David Watts, sec.

Taylor, William H.       Mary Whealton            12 Apr 1830
    of William C.        of Charles
    Samuel Owen, sec.

Taylor, William (wdr)    Nancy Taylor             12 Nov 1840

Taylor, Willlliam        Tabitha Killman          30 Jun 1800
    Charles Taylor, sec.

Taylor, Wilson           Nancy Marshall           23 Dec 1807
    James Taylor sec.

Taylor, Wm R. Jr.        Nancy Merrill (wid)      12 Jul 1826
    John Matthews of Evans and Josiah Taylor, sec.

Taylor, Zadoch of Jms.   Rachel Riggs of Jos.     25 Dec 1821
    Delighty Christopher, sec.

Taylor, Zadoch of Jms.   Elizabeth Taylor         26 Feb 1817
                         of Ayres
    Nathaniel Taylor, Samuel Walston and Richard D. Bayly, sec.

Teackle, John            Esther Beavans           28 --- 1794
                                              (badly damaged)

Teackle, Thomas          Catherine Stockley        8 Feb 1785
    William Gibb, sec.

Teaguel, George of John  Elisha Mears of Elisha    9 Jan 1821
    James Mears of Elisha, sec.

Thomas, Benjamin         Rachel Bradshaw          28 Jun 1811
    Joseph Crockett, sec.

Thomas, Edward R.        Mary W. Lewis            28 Mar 1853
    of Eliza             of Revel
```

Thomas, George	Tabitha Bloxom	11 Jun 1807
Thomas, George David Davis, sec.	Elizabeth Nock	11 Jan 1806
Thomas, Gillett Thomas P. Lewis and Gillett Taylor, sec.	Comfort Taylor of Tabitha	9 Dec 1847
Thomas, John B. Nathaniel Collins, sec.	Elizabeth Rodger	21 Mar 1807
Thomas, John of Joshua Geo. Crocket and Rich. D. Bayly, sec.	Ann Crocket of Priscilla	29 Dec 1818
Thomas, John of Ben. Thomas Crocket, sec.	Milly Thomas of Joshua	25 Jul 1820
Thomas, John George Croswell, sec.	Eliza Lewis of Revel	20 Aug 1831
Thomas, Joshua	Rachel Evans	10 Sep 1797
Thomas, William John H. Hustly, sec.	Elizabeth Joynes	29 May 1811
Thomas, William James Ewell, sec.	Margaret Young of Catherine	25 May 1848
Thomas, Wingate S.	Julia Drummond	4 Jul 1844
Thorns, Dennis James Ewell of Jms., sec.	Polly Taylor of Charles, Sr.	11 Nov 1826
Thorns, Jacob William R. Custis, sec.	Sally Justice of Thomas, dec'd.	30 Jul 1822
Thornton, Edward	Elizabeth Addison	15 Feb 1838
Thornton, Henry of Mary David Watts and George P., sec.	Euphemia Thornton	27 Jun 1839
Thornton, Henry David Wallop, sec.	Jane Townsend (wid)	20 Feb 1848
Thornton, Henry	Euphemia Thornton	29 Jun 1854

```
Thornton, James Jr.        Sally Mariner of Geo.      22 Oct 1831
     Robert Russell of Joshua, sec.

Thornton, James            Sally Cottingham            9 Feb 1786

Thornton, James            Mary Hickman of Richard      2 Aug 1849
     Richard Hickman, sec.

Thornton, James W.         Jane Killman               30 Aug 1853
     of William            of John

Thornton, John             Hessy Bloxom                9 Feb 1813
     Henry Thornton, sec.

Thornton, John             Eliza Hutson               30 Oct 1809
     William Hinman, sec.

Thornton, John             Grace Trader                6 Oct 1807
     Walter Wessells, sec.
Thornton, John             Eliza Hutson               30 Oct 1809
     William Hinman, sec.

Thornton, John             Grace Trader                6 Oct 1807
     Walter Wessells, sec.

Thornton, John             Margaret Broadwater        27 Nov 1792

Thornton, John             Elizabeth Shay             13 Dec 1822
     of John               of Elias
     Thomas M. Bayly, sec.

Thornton, John             Hessy Bloxom                9 Feb 1813
     Henry Thornton, sec.

Thornton, John .           Rebecca Vernelson          26 Mar 1810
     Thomas Collins and William Watts, sec.

Thornton, Jonathan         Sally Ross                 26 May 1806
     James Thornton, sec.

Thornton, Jonathan         Mary Owen                   5 May 1791

Thornton, Jonathan         Mary Jones                 26 Sep 1808
     James Thornton, sec.

Thornton, Joshua           Polly Delastatius          27 Jul 1807
     Walter Wessells, sec.

Thornton, Kendal           Sarah A. Mason             27 Feb 1852
                           of Randal

Thornton, Kendall          Betsey Read                20 Apr 1796
```

Thornton, Lewis   Dellilah Trader   29 Dec 1852
                               of Henry

Thornton, Parker of Wm.   Elizabeth Ann Burch   17 Dec 1845

Thornton, Robert   Margaret Taylor of John 27 Aug 1856

Thornton, Southy   Polly Vinnalson   8 Dec 1802
     Zadock McMath, sec.

Thornton, Thomas   Mariah Johnson   2 Jun 1856

Thornton, Tunnell   Susanna Taylor   26 Mar 1821
     of William, dec'd   of John
          George Window of Robt. and Adkins Matthews of Elias, sec.

Thornton, William   Eliza Belote   31 Dec 1832

Thornton, William   Polly Rowley   1 May 1821
     of Charles   (wid William)
     William Watts, sec.

Thornton, William Jr.   Elizabeth Mason   19 Jan 1814
     Jesse Clayton, sec.

Thornton, William   Nancy Carpenter   12 Jan 1809
     Henry Hopkins, sec.

Thornton, William of M.   Elizabeth Gaskins of Wm. 10 Sep 1836
     Samuel B. Ewell and Levin Core, sec.

Thornton, William   Elizabeth Gaskins   7 Sep 1842

Thornton, William   Nancy Carpenter   12 Jan 1809
     Henry Hopkins, sec.

Thornton, William   Sarah Hancock   27 Aug 1810
     of Chincoteague Island
     David Watts, sec.

Thornton, William   Margaret Taylor   19 Jul 1791

Thornton, William   Elzay Belote   31 Dec 1832
     ward of William Nock   ward of William Nock
     William Nock and Valentine Trader, sec.

Thornton, William (wdr) Sally Killman of John   25 Apr 1853

Tignal, Charles   Euphamia Phillips   19 May 1827
     George Tigner and Solomon Phillips, sec.

Tignal, Edward   Cassia Fisher   1 Aug 1811
    Augustine Waterfield, sec.

Tignal, James   Nancy Turlington   15 Apr 1786
    Nicholas Shield, sec.

Tignal, William H.   Mary Mister   29 Dec 1834

Tignall, Samuel   Elizabeth Mason   9 Dec 1837
    Edward Poulson, sec.

Tigner, Charles   Euphamia Phillips   19 May 1827
    George Tigner and Solomon Phillips, sec.

Tignor, Phillip   Elizabeth Hancock   9 Jun 1786

Tindal, Levin   Matilda Jones   10 May 1848
    Samuel Henderson, sec.

Tindal, Samuel James   Mary Ann Walters   1 Mar 1853
    of Thomas   of Jesse
Tindall, George   Hester Ann Bunting   20 Dec 1832
    Samuel Taylor and James Broadwater, sec.

Tindall, James   Sarah Miles   21 Jan 1845

Tindall, James   Euphamia Booth   3 Feb 1807
    Micajah Vesey, sec.

Tindall, Levin   Matilda Jones   10 Mar 1848

Tindall, Levin   Sally Birch   25 Feb 1817
    (wdr)   of John Sr., dec'd.
    Littleton Nock and Major Bird, sec.

Tipton, Ephriam   Ann Wright   8 Aug 1841
                        ward of E.L. Bayly
        Edward L. Bayly, sec.

Toby FN   Rachel Nutts FN   30 Jul 1812
    Edmund Nutts FN, sec.

Topping, Bagwell   Jane M. Henderson   15 Dec 1824
                        of Isaac
        James Walker, sec.

Topping, David   Mary T. White of Thomas 2 May 1855

Topping, Garret   Scarburgh Snead   22 Mar 1785
    Tully Snead, sec.

Topping, George   Rosey Bonwell   24 Dec 1795

Topping, Nathaniel   Sally Riley of John   18 Jan 1819
   Dennis Clayton, sec.

Topping, William   Sally Wise   26 Nov 1791

Townsend, Covinton   Nancy Benson   28 May 1799

Townsend, Henry   Sally Lurton (wid)   17 Jun 1786
   William Townsend, sec.

Townsend, Henry F.   Hetty Copes   22 Sep 1838
                ward of John B. Ailworth

Townsend, Jacob   Jane Silverthorn   26 Sep 1836
   of Barshaba
   Peter Delastatius and James Evans, sec.

Townsend, Joseph   Nancy -----cy   2 Jan 1790
                        (badly damaged)

Townsend, Levin   Hepsey Hargis   10 Dec 1798
   John Marshall, sec.
Townsend, Levin FN   Hetty Marshall FN   11 Jan 1819
                (wid James)
   Sebastian Cropper and Jesse Beavans, sec.

Townsend, Levin   Mary A. Sharpley   28 May 1849

Townsend, Littleton   Rose Hornsby   5 Jan 1810
   Elijah Beauchamp, sec.

Townsend, Littleton P.   Ann Blair Henry   29 Jun 1801
   Thomas M. Bayly, sec.

Townsend, Littleton   Tabitha Patterson   24 Jan 1837
   James Brittingham and David D. Abbott, sec.

Townsend, Nathaniel B.   Elizabeth Jacob   5 Aug 1837

Townsend, Robert   Sally Laws   22 Dec 1813
   Littleton Townsend, sec.

Townsend, Southy   Leah Watson of John   29 Aug 1814
   George Showard and William L. Lucas, sec.

Townsend, William H.   Mary Mister   29 Dec 1834
   James K. Savage and Henry Walker, sec.

Townsend, Zadack   Sally Davis   27 Jul 1852
   (wdr)   (wid of Thomas)

Townsend, Zadoch   Polly Roach   11 Jan 1832

David Broadwater and Savage Broadwater, sec.

Trader, Abba   Molly Bayly   3 Mar 1812
    Richard Hart, sec.

Trader, Alfred   Elizabeth Rew   22 Jan 1851
    of Teackle   of John, Jr.

Trader, Archibald Jr.   Elizabet Northam   3 Jul 1806
                    of William
    Teackle Trader, sec.

Trader, Arthur   Katherine Burton   1 Dec 1786
    Samuel Trader, sec.

Trader, Henry   Mary Kelly of John   6 Jan 1841
    Thomas Hack, sec.

Trader, Henry of Hen.   Critty Hutson of Wm.   26 Dec 1829
    William Trader of Henry, sec.

Trader, Henry of Wm.   Mary Belote of Jesse   17 Jun 1839
    William Thornton and Edward Mears, sec.

Trader, Henry   Mary Kelley   7 Jan 1841

Trader, Ishmael   Polly Miles of Comfort   22 Dec 1821
    William Trader, sec.

Trader, Israel   Tabitha Bird of Major   29 Nov 1813
    Edmund Duncan, sec.

Trader, Nathaniel   Rosey Hickman   31 May 1823
    Israel Trader, sec.

Trader, Parker of Henry Nancy Hutson of Wm.   12 May 1823
    James Kelly, sec.

Trader, Samuel   Patience Taylor   19 May 1787
    Arthur Trader, sec.

Trader, Staten   Nancy Smith   21 Apr 1791

Trader, Teackle A.   Rutha Dillestatius   16 Dec 1822
    Thomas Delastatius, sec.

Trader, Teackle   Nancy Powell   15 Jul 1813
                    (wid Joseph)
    Thomas Allen, sec.

Trader, Voluntine   Jane Chace of Robt.   7 Aug 1823
    of Staton

Jms. Chessire and Robt. Chace, sec.

Trader, Whittington   Polly Howard   27 Jun 1816
   William Hinman of Moses, sec.

Trader, William   Comfort Hudson   7 Jan 1829
   Eli Chesser, sec.

Trader, William P.   Margaret A. Knight   25 Jan 1848
                 of Elizabeth
   Stephen Marshall, sec.

Trader, William   Sarah Ann Taylor   22 Mar 1852
                 of Southy

Trader, William   Hannah Wise   17 May 1809
                 (wid Reuben)
   Jacob Wise, sec.

Trader, William of Wm.   Ann Lewis   29 Jan 1827
                 orphan of Isaac, ward of Wm. Taylor
   William Taylor, sec.

Trader, William Sr.   Lucy Baker (wid)   31 Jul 1815
   Purnel Cheshire, sec.

Trehern, James   Sarah Kilman   18 Jul 1809
   Absalom Lewis, sec.

Truett, Justice   Mary Taylor of Southy   27 Feb 1818
   Robert Knoxx and Zadoch Selby, sec.

Truitt, Henry   Mary Ann Thornton   15 May 1847

Truitt, John K.   Reva Hale   8 Jan 1840

Truitt, John K.   Rosa Hall   3 Jan 1840
   Edward U. Powell, sec.

Truitt, William   Caroline Darby   8 Jun 1841
   John D. Wallop, sec.

Tull, George   Polly Merril   11 Apr 1799
   Thomas Slocomb, sec.

Tull, Isaac   Sally Marshall of Wm.   3 Aug 1843

Tull, John S. of Geo.   Elizabeth Dix of Wm. H.   25 Dec 1854

Tull, John N.   Hester A. Marshall   31 Jan 1848
                 ward of Solomon
   Solomon Marshall, sec.

```
Tull, Outten              Harriet Gladding          22 Dec 1847

Tully FN                  Polly Sample FN           14 Apr 1812
     George Case, sec.

Tunnell, Charles          Margaret Walker            5 Aug 1839
     Littleton Walker and William R. Custis, sec.d

Tunnell, Charles Jr.      Maria Snead Topping       15 Feb 1808
     Walter Welsh, sec.

Tunnell, Edmund FN        Mary Outten FN            13 Jan 1858

Tunnell, Isaiah           Sally Onions              23 Nov 1829
                          of William, dec'd.
     William Onions, sec.

Tunnell, Isaiah           Milcha Fisher (wid)       18 Sep 1849
     William Taylor and Richard Young, sec.

Tunnell, Jackson D.       Margaret A.W. Burton      10 Jan 1835
                          of John
     William C. Slocum and John C. Stevenson, sec.

Tunnell, John M.          Rosetta McKeel            15 Jan 1845


Tunnell, John            Elizabeth Ayres            22 Feb 1802
     Zadock Nock, sec.

Tunnell, Robert           Patience LeCato           11 Oct 1836
     William W. Churn, sec.

Tunnell, Robert           Elizabeth Susan Johnson   15 Sep 1840
     (wdr)
     Edward Gunter and William Walston, sec.

Tunnell, Samuel S.        Maris Watts of David      14 Aug 1815
     of Charles
     John H. Watts and James Wishart, sec.

Tunnell, Samuel S.        Susan Riley of John        4 Aug 1821
     James Northam and Samuel Walston, sec.

Tunnell, Warrington       Rachel Clouds             17 Jan 1786
     William Andrews, sec.

Tunnell, William          Caroline Darby            15 Jan 1838

Tunnell, William S.       Polly Mathews of Jos.     28 Apr 1807
     Samuel Henderson, sec.
```

```
Tunnell, William          Henny Leatherbury (wid)   13 Dec 1839
     Thomas Wesssells, sec.

Turlington, Aser          Elizabeth Sturgis          6 Jun 1799
     Robert Rodgers, sec.

Turlington, Charles       Margaret Wimborough        1 May 1800
     Kendall Turlington, sec.

Turlington, Edward        Sarah Ann Heath of Jms.   13 May 1835
     John F. Heath, sec.

Turlington, George W.     Martha A. Kellam of Wm.    5 Jun 1854

Turlington, James         Peggy Mister              31 Mar 1806
     George S. Fisher, sec.

Turlington, John (wdr)    Sally Walker               6 Oct 1823
     Abel Phillips, sec.

Turlington, John S.       Joice Laylor              26 Jan 1835
                          (wid of Levin)
          John M. Fosque, sec.

Turlington, John T.       Rachel S. Jester           7 Jan 1851
                          of Jacob


Turlington, John of Asa  Nancy B. Mears            10 Apr 1826
                          of Hillary
          James W. Twiford, sec.

Turlington, John S.       Joyce Laylor (wid)        18 Jan 1835

Turlington, John          Caty Kellam               15 Jun 1803
     George Taylor, sec.

Turlington, John          Rachel Jester             24 Apr 1826
     of Charles            of John
     William Sharpley, Jr., sec.

Turlington, Jos. of Ed.  Ann C. Savage             12 Jan 1826

Turlington, Joseph (wdr) Elizabeth Fosque of Jno.  22 Sep 1818
     Samuel Parker, sec.

Turlington, Joseph        Ann C. Savage              9 Jan 1826
     of Edmund             of Jacob of Nelson
     Edmund Leatherbury, sec.

Turlington, Joseph        Ann Parker                24 Feb 1806
```

George Fisher, sec.

Turlington, Nathaniel	Polly Lingo	Apr 1851
Turlington, Parker	Mary Jester	4 Jan 1844
Turlington, Peter	Margaret Ann Watson	21 Dec 1836

Turlington, Peter S.(wdr) Catherine Bell of Wm. 9 Aug 1848
    Smith Ames, sec.

Turlington, Peter   Margaret Ann Watson   19 Dec 1835
                       of John
        Peter Turlington and Americus Scarburgh, sec.

Turlington, Samuel   Elizabeth Nock of Edm. 18 Dec 1826
    Edmund Nock, sec.

Turlington, Thomas   Nancy Riggin   30 Aug 1824
    Samuel Nock, sec.

Turlington, William Thos. Sarah East   29 Nov 1852
                       of Makula

Turnal, Elizah of Major Susan Churn of John   3 Jan 1825
    Timothy Kelly and Peter Parks, sec.

Turnal, Major   Sally Parks   5 Apr 1795

Turnall, Thomas   Scarburgh Melson   29 Feb 1812
    Benjamin Prewit, sec.
Turnell, Major   Nancy Hickman   30 Apr 1831
                       (wid Elijah)
        James Melson, sec.

Turnell, Richard   Rosey Watson of Sally 19 Aug 1819
    Charles Booth, sec.

Turner, Andrew   Betsy Mathews   26 Feb 1806
    John Turner, sec.

Turner, Custis S. (wdr) Margaret Mister (wid) 18 Dec 1843

Turner, Custis   Nancy Melson of Isaac 28 Feb 1831
    Benjamin Floyd, sec.

Turner, George   Esther Taylor   13 Jan 1815
    Elias Joynes, sec.

Turner, Hillary   Nanny Mears   10 Sep 1807
                       (wid of Zoro)
        Hillary Mears and John Wise, sec.

Turner, James   Ann Thompson   31 Jan 1853
                            (wid of William)

Turner, James   Sally Smith   14 Jul 1825

Turner, James H.   Margaret D. Custis   17 Apr 1823
                          of John
    Michael Higgins, sec. and John Custis, consent

Turner, James S.   Ann Tomson (wid)   13 Feb 1853

Turner, James S.   Sarah C. Smith of Geo. 6 Jul 1825
    George E. Christian, sec. and George Smith, consent.

Turner, John   Mary A. Kellam   2 May 1836
    Richard Kelly, sec.

Turner, John   Sukey Evams   30 May 1804
    Major Shepherd, sec.

Turner, John   Mary Kellam   27 Aug 1799
    John Bell, sec.

Turner, Joshua   Molly Bell   13 Nov 1832
    George M. Mears, sec.

Turner, Joshua   Ann Mears (wid)   24 Feb 1847

Turner, Morris   Lingoe --(?)--   13 Jan 1800
    Brannon Turner, sec.

Turner, Richard (wdr)   Mary Richardson   2 Nov 1822
    of Andrew   of David
    James L. Darby, sec.

Turner, Richard   Sally Martin of Henry 21 Jul 1815
    James Hornsby, sec.

Turner, Richard   Rachel Joynes   20 Sep 1806
    Stephen Pewsey, sec.

Turner, Richard W.   Margaret Sarah Ames   2 Apr 1851

Turner, Samuel   Sally Downing of John 22 Nov 1830
    John Downing, sec.

Turner, Smith   Abigail Prewit   30 Oct 1797

Turner, Smith   Nancy Kellam   9 Jul 1799
    Arthur Savage, sec.

Turner, Teackle J.   Sarah E. Read   13 Sep 1847
                           (wid) of Richard P.
     T.T. Turner, sec.

Turner, William   Ann Lewis   27 Feb 1832
                           ward of Wm. S. Martin
     William S. Martin, sec.

Turner, Willliam   Caty Abbdill   29 Sep 1800
     James Hornsby, sec.

Turpin, William   Mary Scarburgh   3 Jan 1804
     Robert Twyford, sec.

Twiford, George W.   Margaret Ann Rew   12 Nov 1828
                           of Dennis H.
     Parker Barnes, sec.

Twiford, James   Peggy Hancock of Elijah   26 Jan 1807
     Elijah Hancock, sec.

Twiford, Purnell   Elizabeth Hanniford   17 Apr 1805
     Richard D., Bayly sec.

Twiford, Revell (wdr)   Mary Layfield (wid)   6 Aug 1816
     James W. Twiford and Richard D. Bayly, sec.

Twiford, Revell   Sally Parker   9 Feb 1815
     George C. Revell and James Twiford, sec.

Twiford, Robert   Mrs. Comfort West   14 Mar 1805

Twiford, Robert   Nancy Pitts   11 Dec 1813
     Jonathan Twiford, sec.
Twiford, Zorabable   Agnes Watson   5 Apr 1786
     James Twiford, sec.

Twyford, Edward   Sarah Frances Pusey   18 Oct 1847

Twyford, James   Ann Joynes   10 Aug 1813

Twyford, Julius   Margaret Ann Lewis   11 Jul 1853
     of George W.   of Margaret

Twyford, Obed P.   Charlotte Ann Ailworth   26 Mar 1838
     Joseph N. Bagwell and Stephen Hopkins, sec.

Twyford, Obed P.   Mary L. Edmunds   25 Sep 1849

Twyford, Obed P.   Betsy B. Hornsby   22 Oct 1833
     Samuel Taylor, sec.

Twyford, Thomas W.   Mary E.   1 Nov 1843

Twyford, William B.   Elizabeth J. Mathews   8 Jan 1849
    (wdr)   of William
    James Russell and William Mister, sec.

Twyford, William   Margaret M.   23 Mar 1843

Tyler, David of Jabez   Margaret Simpson of Rev.   6 Aug 1827
    Revell Simpson and Richard D. Bayly, sec.

Tyler, Jabez   Lydia Marshall   10 Jan 1824

Tyler, John D.   Mary R. Hyslop   26 Mar 1838
                               (wid of John)
    Isaiah N. Bagwell and Stephen Hopkins, sec.

Tyler, Nathaniel   Peggy Marshall   21 Jun 1812
    Upshur Bayly, sec.

Tyler, Richard   Margaret Young   6 Aug 1803
    Robert Young, sec.

Tyler, Severn   Sally Bull of Ben.   9 Oct 1812
    John H. Joynes, sec.

Tyler, Severn   Margaret Hopkins   21 Jan 1809
    Major Linton, sec.

Tyler, Thomas   Sally Hopkins   10 Sep 1801

Tyler, William of David Alice Crockett of Zach.   12 Jan 1821
    David Evans and Josiah Crockett, sec.

Upshur, Abel P.   Eliz. Ann Brown Upshur   22 Jun 1824
                         of J.P. Upshur, dec'd.
        William S. Upshur and Richard D. Bayly, sec.

Upshur, Abram FN   Molly Major FN   11 Sep 1816
        David B. Nottingham, sec.

Upshur, Dr. Arthur A.   Esther B.P. Bayly   6 Feb 1835
        Arthur W. Downing and William T. Joynes, sec.

Upshur, James   Susanna Martin   20 Jun 1810
        Nehemiah Stockly, sec.

Upshur, John   Elija Upshur Yerby (wid)   6 Jun 1808
        Thomas M. Bayly, sec.

Upshur, John   Lucy Parker   8 Apr 1818
        Thomas Parker, sec.

Veasey, William H. (wdr)	Margaret A.E. Parker	16 Jan 1856
Vermelson, Willliam Parker Coard, sec.	Sarah Pettitt	17 Apr 1806
Vessells, John	Vice Tull	18 Dec 1789
Vessells, William Jr. George Wilson, sec.	Leah Northam	13 Oct 1798
Vessels, Arthur	Betsy Bundick	8 Jan 1794
Vessels, Ephriam	Nancy Gray	23 Feb 1801
Vessels, Ephriam	Nancy Parks	12 Jan 1789
Vessels, William	Sally Killmon	30 Dec 1799

Waggoman, Joseph   Betsey Scott Lane   6 Jan 1787
    Walter Bayne, sec.

Walker, Elijah   Sally Fisher   11 Jul 1832
    James Davis, sec.

Walker, Henry of Jno.   Sophia Kellam of Howson   25 May 1818
    William Harmon, sec.

Walker, Henry   Peggy Phillips   2 Jun 1807
    John Custis, sec.

Walker, Henry of Southy   Leah Hope of Annabell   28 Feb 1828
    John S. Johnson, sec.

Walker, James K.   Margaret Watson   1 Jun 1843

Walker, John P.   Mary E. Kellam   9 Dec 1834

Walker, John C.   Margaret E. Doughty   28 May 1855
                          of John R.

Walker, John B.   Ann T. Parramore of Wm.   24 Feb 1818
    George D. Wise, sec.

Walker, John P.   Lucinda Parker   8 Aug 1846

Walker, John B.   Ann L. Parramore   20 Feb 1817

Walker, John S.   Susan Nock of Robt.   28 Oct 1822
    George Nock, sec.

Walker, John S. (wdr)   Lydia S. Hyslop of Smith 19 Oct 1857

Walker, John P.   Mary J. Kellam   6 Jan 1834
                          of Bridget
        Napoleon White, sec.

Walker, Levin   Elizabeth Peck   12 Oct 1785
    Isaiah Evans, sec.

Walker, Levin of John   Mary Tull of Wm., dec'd. 28 Jan 1828
    William S. Walker, sec.

Walker, Levin (wdr)   Eliza Melson   7 Jan 1846
                          (wid of Jms.)

Walker, Littleton   Polly Hancock   21 Nov 1832
    Samuel Brimer, sec.

Walker, Southy   Susanna Hutson   9 Feb 1805

Walker, Southy   Lovea Taylor of Wm.   20 Dec 1828
     Samuel Hinman, sec.
Walker, Teackle S.   Margaret Pettit   30 Jan 1838
                               of Nancy
         Teackle and Littleton Walker, sec.

Walker, William   Nancy Trehearn   5 Apr 1858

Walker, William   Betsy Bundick   1 Dec 1801
     Elijah Shoy, sec.

Walker, William B.   Mary Ann Winder   15 Dec 1846

Walker, Wm. Sr.   Sally Taylor   5 Mar 1827
     Wm. S. Matthews, Sr. and Henry Tunnell, sec.

Wallace, George B.   Elizabeth Bradfrod   31 Jan 1853
     of Daniel   of Laban

Wallace, James   Mary Warrington   10 Nov 1785
     James Warrington, sec.

Wallis, Daniel of Dan.   Elizabeth T. Guy   16 Dec 1828
                               orphan of George
         George Guy, sec.

Wallis, Wm. of Dan.   Anseley Elliott of Wm.   16 Dec 1816
     Joshua Burton, Jr., sec.

Wallop, George   Comfort Rowly   1 Dec 1785
     Tully Wise, sec.

Wallop, John D. of John   Sally Holland   11 Feb 1817
                               of Major John
         Peter Roberts and Zadoch Selby, sec.

Wallop, John D.   Susan Cropper   24 Dec 1839
     (wdr)   (wid of William)
     James S. Dunton and James J. Ailworth, sec.

Wallop, John Sr.   Mary Marshall of Geo.   12 Jul 1817
     David S. Watts and Richard D. Bayly, sec.

Wallop, John D. (wdr)   Eliza Walters(wid John) 12 Jun 1828
     James S. Dunton and Levin Core, sec.

Wallop, John S. of John   Harriet Watts of Wm.   6 Nov 1839
     George Marshall, sec.

Wallop, William H.   Mary Davis   17 Apr 1820
     of John   (wid David)

William Silverthorne, sec.

Walston, Samuel   Euphemia Conquest   19 Jun 1828
                         (wid William)
     Richard D. Bayly, sec.

Walston, William   Anna G. Bagwell of Wm.   31 Jan 1832
     William Bagwell, sec.

Walter, James R.   Margaret Tatham   28 Oct 1837

Walter, John T.   Mary A. Mason   26 Oct 1836
     John W. Hutchinson, sec.

Walter, John   Susannah Halloway   24 Sep 1810
     Charles Carpenter, sec.

Walter, John D.   Margaret Beach   3 Dec 1837

Walter, John T.   Mary A. Mason   27 Oct 1836

Walter, John S.   Nancy Downing   7 Jun 1848

Walter, John   Margaret Baker   8 May 1821
     Peter Roberts, sec.

Walter, Richard   Margaret S. Robins   2 Sep 1837
                         of Isaac
     W.A. Thompson, sec.

Walter, Richard   Polly Bentson   26 Jan 1801
     Francis Savage, sec.

Walter, Richard   Juliet Mears   2 Dec 1850

Walter, Solomon   Sally Brinker   9 Dec 1803
     John Sturgis, sec.

Walter, Thomas   Nancy Sturgis of John Sr. 27 Mar 1802
          Jacob Sturgis, sec.

Walter, Thomas (wdr)   Mary Walters of Wm.   31 Apr 1816
     William Walters, sec.

Walters, John (wdr)   Nancy Downing of Frances   6 Jun 1848
     William Harmon, sec.

Walters, Thomas of Tho. Leah Ewell of Solomon   18 May 1826
     John Walter, sec.

Walters, William   Omey Lucas (wid Sy.)   5 Jan 1810
    Ayres Taylor, sec.

Waltham, Teackle   Rosannah Colony   22 Dec 1774
    Littleton Colony, sec.

Waples, Edward D.   Sarah A. Finney of Thos. 24 Nov 1851

Waples, John   Susan Dix   19 Nov 1834
    Dennis Gray, sec.

Waples, Samuel (wdr)   Sabra P. Scarborough   20 Aug 1822
                            (wid)
        Thomas Sturgis and John Bull, sec.

Ward, Charles Henry   Elizabeth Ann Johnson   11 Feb 1850
                            of Samuel
    James T. Johnson, sec.

Ward, Deal   Elizabeth Lewis   8 Jan 1840
    Custis W. Kellam, sec.

Ward, Isaac   Molly Andrews   7 Feb 1786
    William Stran, sec.

Ward, Jackson   Margaret Nottingham   10 Nov 1848

Ward, James of Golden   Margaret A. East   14 Sep 1826
                            of Southy W.
    Joseph Irvin, sec.

Ward, James H.   Tabitha Joynes   19 Nov 1849
    (wdr)   of Sheppard A.
    Sheppard A. Joynes, sec.

Ward, John   Malinda Taylor   7 Jun 1848

Ward, John T.   Hannah L. Ashby   17 Jan 1839
                            (wid of Smith Ashby)
    Custis W. Kellam, sec.

Ward, John T.   Hannah Ashby   17 Jan 1839

Ward, Joseph   Catharine Guy   8 Jan 1823
        Wm. D. Chandler and Levin S. Joynes, sec.

Ward, Joseph   Catherine Gray   8 Jul 1823

Ward, Lancelot Jr.   Margaret A. Mears   6 Nov 1850

Ward, Lancelot   Mary East of James   11 Jan 1816
    James East, sec.

```
Ward, Noah FN              Kesiah Stockley FN      10 Nov 1834
    Esan Boston and Levin Core, sec.

Ward, Noah (FN)            Kesiah Stockly          13 Nov 1834

Ward, Samuel D.            Margaret Turner         24 May 1858

Ward, Samuel               Margaret A. Lewis       24 Nov 1834
                           ward of Samuel
        William Ward, sec.

Ward, Samuel               Margaret Lewis           2 Dec 1834

Ward, Severn G.            Sally Smith             17 Oct 1820
    of Littleton           of George, dec'd.
    Charles Smith, sec.

Ward, Severn G.            Sally Smith             27 Oct 1820

Ward, Southy               Nancy Sparrow            9 Nov 1832

Ward, Southy               Nancy Sparrow            5 Nov 1832
    John Sparrow, sec.

Ward, Thomas of Jos.       Judy Thomas of Wm.      11 Jan 1828
    William Guy, sec.

Ward, Thomas               Judy Thomas                Jun 1825

Ward, William FN           Henny Wise FN           18 Aug 1852

Ward, William              Susan Tatham            29 May 1809

Ward, William              Mary Lewis              26 Jun 1820

Ward, William (wdr)        Susan P. Cutler         19 Feb 1850
    John E. Ames and John J. Blackstone, sec.

Ward, William              Sarah A. Mason          26 Apr 1858
                           of Bagwell C.

Ward, William              Susan Tatham            30 May 1839
    John E. Ames, sec.

Ward, Wm. of Littleton     Margaret Lewis of Tho.  26 Jun 1820
    John Crowson and William R. Custis, sec.

Warner, George Jr.         Elizabeth Coleburn      21 Jan 1811
                           (wid of William)
        Jacob Warner, sec.

Warner, George J.          Emily Core              27 Jul 1842
```

Warner, George   Elizabeth West   28 Dec 1784
    Thomas Coverly, sec.

Warner, Isaac (wdr)   Elizabeth Cole (wid)   20 Jul 1843

Warner, Jacob   Sinar Hickman   30 Aug 1848

Warner, Jacob   Elizabeth Warner   16 Dec 1811
    Elijah Beauchamp, sec.

Warner, Jacob   Elizabeth L. Barnes   26 Dec 1820
                        of George
        Solomon Warner, sec.

Warner, Solomon   Mrs. Lucretia Hickman   13 Aug 1828
                        (wid of George)
Warner, William   Sarah Taylor   3 Nov 1806
    Benjamin Taylor, sec.

Warrington, Abbott   Elizabeth Northam   25 Oct 1824
    John Rew, sec.

Warrington, George (wdr) Catharine Peusey   16 Feb 1822
    James W. Twiford, sec.

Warrington, James   Keziah Richardson   26 Feb 1785
    John Phillips, sec.

Warrington, John   Elizabeth Burton   6 May 1778
    William Gibb, sec.

Warrington, John FN   Eliza A. Sample FN   14 Jun 1853

Warrington, John K.   Sally Hargis   3 Feb 1812
    Parker Copes, sec.

Warrington, John   Susanna Savage   7 Dec 1774
    John Powell, sec.

Warrington, John T.   Margaret C. Ames   29 Jul 1839
    John H. Duncan, sec.

Warrington, John B.   Sally Elliott   16 Nov 1811

Warrington, Joshua   Elizabeth Kelly   16 Feb 1818
    John Wharton, sec.

Warrington, Southy   Euphamia Warrington   18 sep 1805
    Richard Rodgers, sec.

```
Warrington, Staton        Euphemia Broadwater      2 Aug 1816

Warrington, William       Nancy Davis             13 Oct 1803
     John Warrington, sec.

Warson, Arthur            Betsey Finney           31 Jul 1792
     Samuel Wilson, sec.

Waterfield, Isaac         Betsey Addison          16 Mar 1801
     Elijah Hancock, sec.
Waterfield, Jacob of Wm. Mary W. Matthews of Geo. 30 Apr 1821
     James White, sec.

Waterfield, John A.       Betsy Doughty            9 Dec 1823
                          of Josiah
     Isma Bunting and Etheil Lyon, sec.

Waterfield, William       Margaret Ward of Wm.    19 Jun 1849
     William N. Finney, sec.

Waterfield, William       Polly Beavans            4 Mar 1786
     Mathew Taylor, sec.

Waters, Francis           Sally Dennis            27 Oct 1785
     John Teackle, sec.

Waters, John blacksmith  Betsy Ewell of Solomon  30 Jan 1816
     David Watts and John F. Bayne, sec.

Waters, Joseph            Betsy Booth             30 Jul 1814
                          (wid of Covington)
          John Hall, sec.

Waters, William           Sally Taylor             2 Nov 1812
     William Johnson, sec.

Waters, William           Sally Jones             17 Jun 1816
     of John                (wid of George)
     John Waters, sec.

Waters, William Jr.       Elizabeth Parks         28 May 1827
     (wdr)                 orphan of John
     William D. Marshall  and Custis W. Bird, sec.

Waters, William H.        Tabitha C.S. Beavans     1 Feb 1815
     Samuel Downing, sec.

Waters, William C.        Margaret A. Boggs       13 Dec 1843

Watkins, Daniel           Eliza Copes of Major    28 Dec 1814
     Evans Taylor, sec.
```

Watkinson, George   Margaret Rayfield   31 Dec 1849
    (wdr)   (wid of John)
    William Eichelberger, sec.

Watkinson, George   Sally Metcalf   28 Nov 1831
    Susan Metcalf, sec.

Watson, Arthur J.   Lucy Pitts   9 Jan 1832
    James L. Darby, sec.

Watson, Benjamin T.   Peggy Smith Garrett   29 Nov 1785
    Caleb Broadwater, sec.
Watson, Benjamin   Susanna Colony   16 Jun 1812
    Abel Beach, sec.

Watson, Capt. Edmund   Nancy Copes   21 Jan 1824

Watson, Daniel   Hetty Bird   29 Apr 1837

Watson, David   Elizabeth Snead   24 Jun 1828
    (wdr) of John   of Bowdoin
    Americus Scarburgh, sec.

Watson, David S.   Margaret W. Oliver   24 Dec 1839
    John W. Window, sec.

Watson, David (wdr)   Elizabeth Snead   25 Jun 1828

Watson, David   Margaret Oliver   26 Dec 1839

Watson, Dr. Arthur   Mary A. West   7 Dec 1843

Watson, Edmund   Catherine Rayfield   14 May 1822
    of William   of Custis
    Ephraim Mason and Custis Rayfield, sec.

Watson, Edward R.   Elizabeth W. Massey   31 Dec 1830
    Americus Scarburgh, sec.

Watson, Francis A.B.   Emiline Mister   6 Mar 1850

Watson, Henry of Jms.   Ann Melson of Jms.   6 Apr 1822
    James Melson, sec.

Watson, Jacob   Nancy Biggs   27 Apr 1784

Watson, Jacob of Jacob   Susanna Savage of Roland 19 Feb 1819
    James Benson, sec.

Watson, James   Elizabeth Beach   31 Oct 1837
                           (wid of Abel)
        George S. Garrison, sec.

```
Watson, James H.          Emilia Scarburgh          20 Nov 1837

Watson, James             Elizabeth Beach            1 Nov 1837

Watson, James             Elizabeth Beach            1 Nov 1837

Watson, James Tatham      Nancy Bloxom              19 Feb 1796

Watson, James             Mary Emiline Scarburgh    18 Nov 1839
                          of Americus
        Edward R. Watson, sec.


Watson, John R.           Catherine Revell           2 Nov 1835
        Americus Scarburgh, sec.

Watson, John L.           Elizabeth Lingo            2 Apr 1819
                          of Thomas, dec'd.
        James Roberts, sec.

Watson, John              Waters, Rachel            25 Dec 1809
        Elias Taylor, sec.

Watson, John W.           Betsy S. Simpson          29 Jul 1806
        William Tunnell, sec.

Watson, John             Sally Bunting             25 Mar 1799
        Major Hastings, sec.

Watson, John             Elizabeth White           23 Dec 1826
        tailor           (wid of John)
        John Only and Elisha H. Davis, sec.

Watson, John             Mary Lunn                 10 Nov 1847

Watson, John (sailor)    Elizabeth Haley of Ben.   15 Jan 1849
        Benjamin Haley and Edmond Littleton, sec.

Watson, John             Eliza Doughty             25 Nov 1803
        William Doughty, sec.

Watson, John M.          Sarah R. Parker           18 Oct 1820
        of Jesse         of Henry
        John W. Rodgers, sec.

Watson, John L.          Sukey Foster of Sophia     7 Mar 1810
        William Parramore, Jr. , sec.

Watson, John R.          Catherine Revell           4 Nov 1835

Watson, John of Israel   Tabitha Dix               21 Sep 1809
        Hancock Simpson, sec.
```

Watson, Jonathan (wdr)	Nancy Wimbro (wid)	28 Jul 1824
Watson, Joseph	Elizabeth Bull	23 Dec 1846
Watson, Levin Thomas Smith, sec.	Susa Boggs of Wm.	2 Jan 1810

Watson, Littleton
    of Ephrain
    John W. Watson, sec.
	Elizabeth Leatherbury
	of John
		8 Dec 1818

Watson, Purnal David Watts and James J. Ailworth, sec.	Margaret Thornton	18 Apr 1832
Watson, Purnell	Margaret Thornton	10 Feb 1832
Watson, Purnell	Mary Cherricks (wid)	19 Jan 1839
Watson, Robert Arthur Bowden, sec.	Sarah Davis	20 Oct 1806
Watson, Robert		25 Feb 1847
Watson, Thomas P.	Ann P. Ayres	20 Oct 1845

Watson, Thomas
    of John W.
    Samuel C. Abbott and Joseph W. Gibb, sec.
	Sarah Fisher of Riley	15 Jul 1829

Watson, Thomas S. Edmund G. Godwin, sec.	Hetty Godwin of Nicholas J.	7 Apr 1832
Watson, Thomas J.	Fannie Colonna	
Watson, Thomas James T. Palmer, sec.	Fanny Colonna	25 Nov 1837
Watson, William C. (wdr) William Mason, sec.	Fanny Mason	4 Mar 1833
Watson, William C. (wdr)	Fannie Mason	6 Mar 1833
Watts, David Robert Twyford, sec.	Sally Evans	13 July 1803
Watts, Davis John Robins Coard, sec.	Peggy Thomas	c. 1786 (not dated)
Watts, James R.	Margaret Tatham of Martin	28 Dec 1837

John C. Coleburn, sec.

Watts, John H. (wdr)   Margaret Scarburgh   25 Aug 1823
                        of Americus
    Americus Scarburgh, sec.

Watts, John H.   Sally Purnell   13 Aug 1812
                        ward of William Watts
    William Watts, sec.

Watts, John S.   Alatine E.P. Barnes   28 Jul 1851
                        of George P., Jr.

Watts, William   Elizabeth Boston   4 Oct 1840

Watts, William (wdr)   Elizabeth Boston   3 Oct 1840
    David Watts and J.J. Ailworth, sec.

Watts, William S.   Jane W. Mapp   25 Sep 1828
    Samuel Abbott and William Parramore, Jr., sec.

Weaks, Anis FN   Elizabeth Beavans FN 29 Mar 1852
                        of Betsy FN

Weaver, James C.   Sally P. Sturgis   19 Aug 1852

Webb, Gilbert FN   Margaret Jubilee FN   18 Oct 1843

Webb, John FN   Harriet Harmon FN   27 Feb 1854

Welburn, John D. Jr.   Charlotte Melvin   20 Apr 1830
                        of James W.
    Levin Core and Peter Delastatius, sec.

Welburn, John   Coleburn Guy   12 Aug 1785
    William Gibb, sec.

Welburn, John   Kessy White   12 Aug 1840
                        (wid of Levin)
    Samuel Ward, sec.

Welburn, John D. Jr.   Margaret Virginia Ames 30 Mar 1839
                        ward of John D. Mapp
    John T. Johnson, sec.

Welburn, John   Keziah White   12 Aug 1840

Welburn, Peter   Elizabeth Waters of Wm. 28 Oct 1839
    David Wallop and John P. Drummond, sec.

Welburn, Thomas D.   Elizabeth Hickman   30 Dec 1828

John Hope, sec.   (wid of William)

Welburn, William Coleburn Long, sec.	Sabra Corbin	5 Feb 1784
Weldy, William	Rhoda Joynes	15 May 1789
Wescoat, John K.	Elizabeth S. Beach	4 Jun 1843
Wescoat, Joshus G.	Margaret Pitts	3 Jun 1835
Wessells, Arthur James White, sec.	Peggy Pruitt	3 Jun 1803

Wessells, Arthur
   of Arthur
Absalom Lewis and Tho. Wessels, sec.
	Sarah Lewis
	   of Absalom
		23 May 1821

Wessells, Arthur F. Isaac Wessells, sec.	Amey Wessells of Isaac	18 Oct 1826
Wessells, Edward	Betsy Ewell of Ann	12 Mar 1852
Wessells, Ephraim Arthur Wessells, sec.	Molly Savage	14 May 1804
Wessells, Ephraim son of Ephraim Ephraim Wessells of Arthur, sec.	Shady Taylor	20 Dec 1802
Wessells, Ephram of Ephram Thomas Hinman, sec.	Sarah Young of Wm.	1 Mar 1837
Wessells, James William Onions, sec.	Polly Onions	13 Dec 1803
Wessells, John of Jno. John Parks, sec.	Nancy Parks of Jno.	25 Dec 1826
Wessells, Richard	Patty Wessells	24 Feb 1830

Wessells, Richard
   of Arthur
Isaac and Thomas Wessells, sec.
	Polly Wessells
	   of Isaac
		22 Feb 1830

Wessells, Samuel
 	
   Samuel C. Johnson, sec.
	Rachel Dix
	   orphan of Richard
		24 Feb 1832

Wessells, Thomas H.	Elizabeth Davis	11 Jan 1843

```
Wessells, Thomas          Nancy Wessells of Art.   10 Dec 1811
     Arthur Wessells, sec.

Wessells, Thomas W.       Elizabeth Davis           4 Jan 1843

Wessells, Thomas          Ann C. Wessells          28 Dec 1839
     of James             of Thomas
     Joseph Riggs, sec.

Wessells, Walter Jr.      Betsy Bailey             24 Feb 1823
                          orphan of Robert
     Jacob Bird, sec.

Wessells, Walter          Mary Boston               4 Feb 1807
     William Ailworth, sec.

Wessells, Walter          Betsy Riley               6 Mar 1823

Wessells, William W.      Catherine Justice        25 Dec 1854
     of Walter            of Samuel
Wessells, William         Nancy Wessells           22 Jun 1818
     of Ephraim Jr.       of Ephraim Sr.
     Isaac Wessells, sec.

Wessels, Walter           Mary Boston               5 Feb 1807

West, Benjamin            Peggy Russell             7 Jun 1800
     John Custis (B.S.), sec.

West, Benjamin            Mary Ann Vessells         8 Sep 1789

West, Bowman FN           Suckey Baker FN          25 Aug 1824
     William P. Custis, sec.

West, Charles             Maria Parker             27 Dec 1832

West, Charles             Rosey Phillips            3 Dec 1851

West, Charles             Joice Powell              6 Jun 1849

West, Charles B.          Tipporah Topping         11 Nov 1826
     of Thomas            of Garret, dec'd.
     Thomas West and Nathaniel Lang, sec.

West, Charles             Maria Parker             24 Dec 1832
     Bagwell Savage, sec.

West, Dr. Francis         Elizabeth K. Mathews     23 Mar 1848
                          of John K.
     James B. Wright and James D. Groton, sec.

West, Edward              Peggy Bundick of Polly    3 Apr 1849
```

Robert Hickman, sec.

| West, Edward W. | Virginia Lang | 21 Jan 1843 |

| West, Edward W. | Virginia Lang | 21 Jan 1847 |

West, George S.   Margaret Callahan   18 Mar 1847
                         of Trab
     George S. West and John W.A. Elliott, sec.

West, George FN   Maria Walker FN of Mat.   1 Apr 1831
     Harry Walker FN, sec.

West, George R.   Jane Miles   28 Jan 1850
  (wdr)   of William, dec'd.
     John B. Ailworth, sec.

West, George of Jno.   Suckey Melson of David   10 Nov 1813
     McKeel Budd, sec.

West, George   Susan Calahan   24 Mar 1847

West, George R.   Margaret Lang of Nancy   18 Jan 1848
     Henry Melson, sec.

West, Isaac   Patty Hitchins   15 Oct 1813
     Jonathan Young, sec.

West, Isaac (wdr)   Sarah L. Finney   31 May 1837

West, Isaac (wdr)   Sarah S. Finney   29 May 1837
     George W. Bundick and William R. Custis, sec.

West, James FN   Caroline Rone FN   15 Jan 1845

West, James   Tabitha Young of Geo.   14 Jul 1809
     Smith Cutler, sec.

West, James of Ann   Nancy Spiers (wid of Wm) 20 Dec 1813
     Zorobabel Willis, sec.

West, James   Hannah Kelly   8 Jan 1846

West, Jesse   Susan Caruthers   12 Apr 1843

West, John   Rachel Guy (wid)   24 June 1802
     Edmund Bayly, sec.

West, John   Patience Parker   13 Sep 1806
                         (wid of John)
     Thomas M. Bayly, sec.

West, John	Amey Vessells	18 Feb	189
West, John of John Southy Taylor, sec.	Nancy Matthews of Jacob	27 Dec	1816
West, John	Mrs. Polly Powell	27 Dec	1802
West, John	Polly Henderson	8 Sep	1839
West, John John Sherlock, sec.	Tabitha Wise	4 Feb	1785
West, John George Tignall, sec.	Polly Henderson of Rob.	7 Sep	1840

West, John of Ben.
 	
    Southy Grinnalds, sec.
	Euphenica White
	    of Joachim
		14 Oct	1819

West, Jonathan Robinson West, sec.	Susanna Bayly	17 Nov	1806
West, Mitchell	Margaret Ann Smith	6 Jan	1836
West, Mitchell S. William Joynes, Jr., sec.	Margaret Rodgers	30 May	1814

West, Mitchell Wellington
    Levin Rogers and Joseph W. Gibb, sec.
	Margaret Ann Smith
	    of John
		4 Jan	1836

West, Revell P.
 	
    George W. Parker, sec.
	Elizabeth F. Parker
	    of Agnes
		14 Mar	1831

West, Revell of Revell
 	
    Edward A. Revell, sec.
	Mary Ann Coleburn
	    of Samuel
		14 Jun	1824

West, Robinson George West, sec.	Margaret Singleton	28 Jul	1817

West, Salathiel
 	
    Henry Stewart, sec.
	Elizabeth Nock
	    (wid of Samuel)
		3 Jan	1822

West, Solomon Henry Young, sec.	Margaret Dix of Revell	20 Dec	1830
West, Thomas	Mary Bonnewell	5 Feb	1825
West, Thomas (wdr)	Betsy Broadwater	1 Feb	1825

(wid of Robert J.)
Alexander Land, Jr. and Richard Lewis, sec.

West, Thomas (wdr)   Mary Boniwell of Jacob   5 Feb 1825
   Alexander Lang, Jr. and Littleton Bloxom, sec.

West, Toby FN   Keziah Nutts of Edmund   24 Dec 1821
   Samuel Martin FN, sec.

West, William   Emily Lewis   1 Apr 1843

West, Zorobabel   Hetty Savage   13 Jun 1810
   Zorobabel Mason, sec.

Westcoat, Joshus G.   Margaret Pitts   25 May 1835
   Joshua G. Westcoat and Joseph G. Rogers, sec.

Westerhouse, Reuben   Euphamy Merrill   2 Nov 1785
   George Corbin, sec.

Whaley, Henry of Wm.   Mary Matthews of Evans   13 Jan 1821
   William H. Drummond, sec.

Wharton, Bagwell   Esther Tunnel   28 Dec 1791

Wharton, Bagwell   Catharine Custis   15 Jun 1811
   Richard D. Bayly, sec.

Wharton, Charles   Elizabeth Shield   14 Oct 1806
   Samuel Walston, sec.

Wharton, Henry FN   Rachel Stevens FN   30 Jan 1851
                            of Rika FN

Wharton, Jacob FN   Leah Holden FN   29 Dec 1856

Wharton, John   Elizabeth W. Williams   6 Jun 1784
   William Gibb, sec.

Whealor, William   Elizabeth   20 Dec 1837

Whealton, Charles   Polly Taylor   14 Jan 1800
   George Matthews, sec.

Whealton, Eba   Elizabeth Jones of Dan.   9 Apr 1831
   Levin Core, sec.

Whealton, Eba Jr.   Elizabeth Sharpley   14 Sep 1853
   of Eba   of Teackle

Whealton, Elisha   Anne Ewell   7 May 1788

```
Whealton, Elisha          Amey Evans                14 Jan 1799

Whealton, Erastus         Mary Coard                18 May 1842

Whealton, George          Hessy Ayres               14 Jan 1812
     Elisha Whealton, sec.

Whealton, James of Jno.  Sally Thornton of Jon.   14 Feb 1821
     John Massey, sec. and Jonathan Thornton, consent

Whealton, Jeremiah        Sally Marshall            20 Jan 1835
                          (wid of John)
          Delight Christopher and Levin Core, sec.

Whealton, John            Sarah White               14 Jan 1823
     of Arthur            (wid of George)
     James N. Hargis and Edward H. Kerr, sec.

Whealton, Joshua          Nancy Ferguson of Jms.   13 Jul 1853

Whealton, Joshua          Sally Lewis               16 Apr 1808
     Charles Turlington, sec.

Whealton, Michael         Ann Gladding of Jno.      7 Sep 1829
     Oliver Logan and Levin Core, sec.


Whealton, Michael R.      Nancy Matthews           18 Feb 1835
     (wdr)                of Washburn
     George W. Corbin, sec.

Whealton, Smith           Betsey Mason             12 Nov 1801

Whealton, William of John  Polly Jones of Daniel    3 Dec 1834
     Timathy Hill and Levin Core, sec.

Whealton, William (wdr)  Elizabeth Lewis           20 Jun 1839

Whealton, William (wdr)  Tabitha Lewis of Isaac   11 Jan 1839
     Thomas B. Custis, sec.

Wheatley, John            Henny Taylor             20 Jan 1813
     Henry Thornton, sec.

Wheatley, John            Rebecca Addison          26 Feb 1800

Wheatton, Daniel          Sally Bragle(?)           1 Mar 1803
     Davis Watts, sec.

Wheeler, Joseph of Wm.   Ann Massey of Atkinson   28 Dec 1819
     John Porter and Meshanh Fidderman, sec.
```

White, Caleb   Polly Lewis   14 Oct 1805
    John Benson, sec.

White, Elijah   Rose Snead (wid)   25 Dec 1811
    Thomas M. Bayly, sec.

White, Frank   Molly Miles (wid)   1 Feb 1810
    Raymond Lewis and William Annis, sec.

White, George of Geo.   Elizabeth H. Wessells   16 Jun 1828
                        of Ephraim
    John White, sec.

White, George   Nancy Lewis   29 Jul 1799
    Ezekiel Bloxom, sec.

White, George   Henny Belote   26 May 1828
    of William   orphan of Caleb
    Joseph Gunter, sec.

White, George W.   Lovea Bunting of Smith   8 Sep 1839
    John T. Warrington, sec.

White, George W.   Charlotte Badger   18 Oct 1843

White, Henry B.   Hetty Rew (wid of Chas.)   5 Nov 1822
    Jacob White, sec.

White, Henry T.   Elizabeth B. Palmer   26 Feb 1855
                        (wid)

White, Henry of Jno.   Sally Stant of Jms.   29 Dec 1829
    George Cutler and Gilbert Stant, sec.

White, Henry C. of Geo. Sarah Ann Mister   14 Jan 1828
                        of Isaac
    Isaac Mister, sec.

White, Henry   Esther Mathews   30 Nov 1785
    Joseph Mathews, sec.

White, Jacob   Sally Coursey   31 Jan 1797

White, James   Elizabeth Dickerson   30 Nov 1807
    William Ewell, sec.

White, James S.   Margaret White of Wm.   9 Nov 1831
    Samuel B.A. Ewell and Wm. E. Wise, sec.

White, James   Lacy Laws   5 Aug 1801

```
White, James H.          Nancy Dix of W.H.           8 Jan 1851

White, James B.          Sarah Ann Bayly             5 Jun 1853

White, James            Patsy Melson (wid Noah)    11 Aug 1831
    William Walston, sec.

White, James H.          Elizabeth Wallop            6 Dec 1837
    David D. Abbott and James J. Ailworth, sec.

White, John              Elizabeth Ailworth          3 Feb 1817
    of Arthur            (wid of James)
    William White of Wm., sec.

White, John D.           Tabitha Mears              12 Apr 1852
                         (wid of Samuel)

White, John              Tabitha Whealton           30 Jun 1800
    Southy Northam, sec.

White, John C.           Elizabeth (wid)             2 Feb 1817

White, John              Ann W. Edmunds             11 May 1827
    of George            (wid of Thomas J.)
    Raymond Riley, sec.

White, Julius C.         Margaret C. Lewis           4 Apr 1855
    of Henry B.          of William, dec'd.

White, Levin of Wm.      Kessy Belote of Jms.       19 Dec 1822
    Thomas C. Gibb, sec.
White, Levin             Charlotte White            15 Sep 1849

White, Levin             Sophia Drunnond            25 Jan 1836
    Spencer Drummond and Edward A. Revell, sec.

White, Levin             Betsy Ardis                11 Apr 1799

White, Napoleon O.       Eliza S. Walker of Hen.    21 May 1832
    Henry Walker, sec.

White, Napoleon O.       Margaret S. Kelly          14 Jan 1852

White, Napolien O.       Elizabeth Walker           13 Dec 1832

White, Ralph             Elizabeth Wilkerson        25 Mar 1805

White, Richard of Levin  Hennietta R. Prewit         7 Oct 1816
    Charles Lewis, sec.

White, Richard           Frances Baylis of K.B.     31 Aug 1857
```

White, Robert   Mary Wilson   24 Jan 1815
    Henry Gladding, sec.

White, Robert (wdr)   Betsy Delastatius   27 May 1833
    John Fedderman and John Gladding, sec.

White, Samuel C.   Mary E.K. Chandler   20 Dec 1825
    of Jacob   of Mitchel Chandler
    Mitchel Chandler, sec.

White, Solomon   Bridget Hickman   20 Aug 1789
                                                            (badly damaged)

White, Thomas S.   Hester Ann West   28 Oct 1841

White, Thomas   Peggy Watson   24 Feb 1809
    James Hornsby, sec.

White, Thomas   Elizabeth Snead   7 Dec 1820
    of Joachin   (wid of William)
    William A. White, sec.

White, Thomas of Geo.   Polly Bloxom of Wm.   8 Jun 1825
    James W. Twiford, sec.

White, Thomas S.   Hester Ann Bird   13 Oct 1841

White, Thomas J.   Elizabeth Rayfield   3 Sep 1828
                             orphan of William
        Southy Bull and William Laws, sec.

White, William of Jno.   Sally Riggs of Jos.   5 Mar 1827
    Charles Smith and Joseph Riggs, sec.
White, William C.   Sally Bundick of Wm.   30 Dec 1822
    Wm. Justice, Sr., sec. and Wm. Bundick, consent

White, William   Amy Melson   23 Jul 1803
    of Joakim
    John Welburn, sec.

White, William H.   Elizabeth Ann Bayly   26 Oct 1835
                             of John J.
            John J. Bayly, sec.

White, William A. (wdr)   Margaret Crowson   19 Dec 1821
                             of Levin
        Levin Crowson, sec.

White, William (wdr)   Nancy Drummond   11 Feb 1853

White, William   Susanna Guy   24 Nov 1785
    Major Chambers, sec.

```
White, William C.        Elizabeth Blackstone      4 Dec 1829
     (wdr)                    (wid of Wm.)
     Solomon Ewell, Sr. and Littleton P. Henderson, sec.

White, William C.        Henrietta Copes          30 Dec 1833
     (wdr)                    (wid of John)
     George Hickman, sec.

White, William A.        Demoriah Dix             27 Apr 1814
     George Marshall, sec.

White, William          Eveline Powell of Wm.     23 Apr 1855

White, William H.        Elizabeth Ann Bayly      28 Oct 1835

White, William A.        Demoriah Dix             27 Apr 1814

White, Wm.(Metompkin)    Polly Watson              8 Nov 1820
     (wdr)                    (wid of Arthur)
     James White and Richard D. Bayly, sec.

Whitehouse, Nathaniel    Catharine A.W. Johnson   28 Aug 1830
                             of John P.
         John P. Jchnson, sec.

Whittington, John        Elizabeth Drummond       11 Sep 1799
     Colmore Bayne, sec.

Wickham, Daniel          Sarah Savage                 Apr 1851

Wiffin, Henry            Elizabeth Payne           8 Apr 1815

Wilkerson, Arthur FN     Mary Brow FN             28 Nov 1825
     Samuel Henderson, sec.
Wilkerson, Jesse (wdr)   Elizabeth Massey         20 Mar 1832
     William C. Slocomb and Jas J. Ailworth, sec.

Wilkerson, Levin         Sally Collins            11 Mar 1807
     Southy Warrington, sec.

Wilkerson, Samuel T.     Mary Sparrow of Rich.    17 Dec 1831
     George Bell, sec.

Wilkerson, Shadrick      Sarah Willett             6 Jan 1841
     (wdr)

Wilkerson, Shadrock      Catherine Belote         29 Dec 1832

Wilkerson, Shadrock      Catherine Roberts        27 Dec 1832
     Major Mason, sec.

Wilkerson, William       Ann Savage               20 Jan 1845
```

Wilkins, George W.   Elizabeth Bayly of Tho.   30 Jun 1828
    John J. Wise, sec.

Wilkins, James C.   Sally Joynes   29 Aug 1821
    of John   orphan of William
    Stewart Kellam, sec.

Wilkins, John of Jno.   Maria Andrews of Robt.   15 May 1815
    Shepherd Kellam and Abel B. Johnson, sec.

Wilkins, Thomas   Lucy Andrews of Robt.   20 Jan 1819
    of John Sr.
    John C. Wilkins, sec.

Wilkinson, William   Betsy Marshall   9 Jan 1810
                            of Solomon
        James Taylor, sec.

Willet, John   Mrs. Sophia Lewis (wid)   23 Dec 1798

Willett, Charles C.   Mary Turner   12 Mar 1814
    Major Rayfield, sec.

Willett, John Sr.   Sally Hurst of Tho.   16 Jun 1821
    Jacob Warner, sec.

Willett, John   Sirah Crowson   22 Apr 1803
    John Wise, sec.

Willett, John (wdr)   Esther Gardner   17 May 1826
    Robert Lewis, sec.

Willett, Thomas   Tabitha Phillips   17 Jul 1786
    John Phillips, sec.

Willett, Waitman   Sarah White   5 Mar 1806
                            (wid of Levin)
        Daniel Melson, sec.

Willett, Waitman   Betsy White of Wm.   27 Jun 1825
    John Kellam of John, sec.

Willett, Waitman Jr.   Polly Bloxom   27 Jan 1812
    Charles B. Bradford, sec.

Willett, William   Seymour Melson   30 Dec 1813
                            (wid of Jona.)
        Charles Willett, sec.

Willett, William   Elizabeth West of Isaac   7 Oct 1839
    William Kellam, sec.

```
Willett, William          Betsy Stephens          26 May 1806
     Elijah Parks, sec.

Willett, William          Elizabeth Stephens      26 May 1806

Willett, Wm. of Jno.      Mary Gray of Solomon     4 Jan 1827
     William Chandler (SM), sec.

William, freed by         Rachel, freed by         1 Feb 1800
     Richard Drummond          William Layfield
     Thomas Cropper, sec.

William, James            Elizabeth McLain        15 Mar 1851

Williams, Bordoin H.      Leah Baker of Wm.        8 Nov 1825
     of Eli
     John Taylor of John, sec.

Williams, Eli             Rachel Baker             9 Feb 1832
     Vela and John Baker, sec.

Williams, Eli             Polly Baker              5 Aug 1809
     William Baker, sec.

Williams, John            Peggy Beavans           24 Nov 1800
     James J. Abbott, sec.

Williams, John            Sukey Kendall            9 Mar 1803
     William Nock, sec.

Williams, John            Agnes Morgan            20 Sep 1803

Williams, John of Tho.    Elsey Birch of Jno.      6 May 1823
     John Birch and Daniel Jones, sec.


Williams, John            Sally Tindall           24 Apr 1826
     of Litton            (wid of Levin)
     John Turlington and William Sharpley, sec.

Williams, Joshua          Sally Pettit            26 Jun 1824

Williams, Littleton       Elizabeth Birch

Williams, Littleton FN    Sinah Williams FN        2 Jan 1836
     John Miles and James B. Ailworth, sec.

Williams, Obed            Polly Ross               9 Feb 1825
                          alias Polly Taylor
     Geo. Window of Robt., Tho. Matthews, and Sam. Johnson, sec.
```

Williams, Robert W.   Mary Laws of Jno.   2 Sep 1829
     Wm. P. Williams and John Laws, Sr., sec.

Williams, Samuel (FN)   Rachel Wharton   8 Jan 1845

Williams, Wm. P.   Adah C. Laws of Jno. Sr. 28 May 1825
     John Jackson, sec.

Willis, Custis   Sarah Harmon of Jno.   16 Oct 1826
     William Harmon of Jno. and Jeremiah Stockley, sec.

Willis, Edward   Joyce Beach   18 Dec 1844

Willis, James C.   Margaret R. Beach   16 Mar 1848

Willis, Littelton   Sarah W. Coleburn   18 Dec 1830
     William Chance, sec.

Willis, Littleton   Sally Coleburn   22 Dec 1839

Willis, Littleton   Mary Ashby   9 Sep 1826
                             (wid of Wm, Jr.)
          Levin W. Nock, sec.

Willis Zorababel   Ann Rodgers   20 Dec 1798
     Custis Willis, sec.

Willis, Zorobabel   Nancy Spiers   2 Sep 1816
                             of Thomas, dec'd.
          Isaac Coleburn, sec.

Wilmot, Samuel   Belinda Robins   29 Aug 1836
     John S. Robins, sec.

Wilson, George   Rachel Northam   31 Oct 1796

Wilson, Henry P.   Susan E. Savage   16 Jun 1824

Wilson, Henry   Lavina Thomas of Sarah   28 Jun 1821
     Abihea Evans, sec.

Wilson, James Henry   Priscillia A. Godfrey   15 Sep 1847

Wilson, James Henry   Elizabeth Davis   28 Mar 1837

Wilson, Samuel   Tabitha Marshall   24 Apr 1797

Wilson, Severn   Grace Adams   1 Jun 1804
     Samuel Wilson, sec.

Wimbro, Griffin   Elizabeth Sharpley   4 Jul 1839

```
Wimbro, Griffin          Elizabeth Sharpley        29 Jan 1836
    David Watts and Edward P. Pitts, sec.

Wimbro, John (wdr)       Polly Sharply of Wm.        2 Apr 1819
    John Bench, Raymond Taylor, sec.

Wimbrough, George        Nancy Harman              31 Dec 1804

Wimbrough, John D.       Mary Ann Hope              5 Jan 1858
                         ward of Benjamion T. Gunter

Wimbrough, Richard       Santer Hickman            10 Mar 1786
    John Glasby, sec.

Wimbrough, William       Sally Jester              12 Mar 1807
    Thomas Custis, sec.

Winber, John             Nancy Sharpley of Jos.    17 Jan 1816
    Wm. Sharpley and Richard D. Bayly, sec.

Winder, John             Mary Joliff                7 Jun 1843

Winder, Raymond          Mary Ann Churn of John    29 Jul 1840
    John Churn, sec.

Winder, Richard B.       Sally M. Custis           25 Sep 1851

Window, Abel             Anne Fisher               25 Nov 1811
    Phillip Fisher, sec.

Window, George of Robt.  Ann Addison (wid Jno.)    28 May 1822
    John Merrill, sec.

Window, George           Polly Thornton             4 Oct 1813
    James Duncan, Jr., sec.

Window, Henry of Abel    Ann Ames of Churchill      1 Aug 1817
    John A. Edwards, sec.


Window, James            Joice Savage              25 May 1829
                         of John, dec'd.
        Churchill Ames, sec.

Window, Joh D. of Zoro.  Hessy Watson of Jno.      26 Dec 1827
    Americus Scarburgh, sec.

Window, John             Alice Kellam              30 Jan 1826
                         orphan of Zorobabel
        John R. Potter, sec.

Window, John E.          Sarah A. Window           26 Mar 1855
```

of Levin   of John D.

Window, John   Hessy Watson   27 Dec 1827

Window, Levin   Margaret Savage of Jacob 16 Mar 1826
    John B. Bradford, sec.

Window, Raymond   Margaret Ann Churn   30 Jul 1840

Window, Revel   Martha Pitts of John   27 Nov 1837
    William C. Watson and George Turner, sec.

Windsor, James   Nancy Taylor (wid Levin) 6 Sep 1806
    Matthew Dorman, sec.

Winters, John   Margaret Savage   9 Dec 1786
    Andrew Martin, sec.

Wise, Benjamin D.   Harriet J. Scarburgh   13 Sep 1848

Wise, Edward   Mary Guy   10 Jan 1844

Wise, George   B---- Badger   -- Dec 1794
    William Finney, sec.

Wise, Henry of Solomon Eliza. Tigner of Eliza.   24 Dec 1816
    Solomon Wise, sec.

Wise, Isaiah E.   Ann Abbott   25 Apr 1814
    Tommy Abbott, sec.

Wise, John C.   Ann Finney   18 Sep 1833

Wise, John E.   Elizabeth Poulson   21 May 1839
                        of Erastus
    Samuel S. Russell, sec.

Wise, John of Solomon   Leah Cobb   12 Jan 1818
    Henry Wise, sec.

Wise, John R.   Eliza E. Coward   15 Nov 1826
    John W. Custis, sec.
Wise, John J.   Harriet A. Wilkins   14 May 1828
    John W. Custis, sec. and Geo. Scheress (guardian), consent

Wise, John   Leah Cobb   14 Jan 1818

Wise, John E.   Eliza Poulson   22 May 1839

Wise, John C.   Anne Finney of John   17 Sep 1833
    John C. Wise and James H. Addison, sec.

- 328 -

Wise, Joshua FN	Maria Wise FN	26 May 1854
Wise, Lawrence FN	Eveline Scarburgh FN	4 Apr 1856
Wise, Moses S.	Frances Catherine Watson of John, dec'd.	8 Sep 1852
Wise, Peter H. William Salisbury, sec.	Margaret S. Custis of Henry, dec'd.	13 Dec 1823

Wise, Peter H.
    of Reuben
    Smith Hyslop, sec.
	Hessy Savage
	of Charles
		14 Dec 1819

Wise, Solomon Sr. Shadrach Darby, sec.	Ann C. Darby of Benjamin, dec'd.	30 Mar 1820
Wise, Tully R. John R. Wise, sec.	Margaret D.P. Wise	22 Oct 1823
Wise, William E. John A. Bundick, sec.	Sarah J. Core	26 Dec 1810
Wise, William FN	Mary Ann Scarburgh FN	28 Dec 1857
Wise, William E. Alexander McCollum, sec.	Sarah Russell (wid of Robert)	11 Jun 1827
Wise, William	Sarah Scarburgh	15 Nov 1848
Wise, William E. John B. Walker, sec.	Sally Custis of Henry	24 Dec 1816

Wishart, James
    of Joshua
    William W. Burton, sec.
	Elizabeth Coleburn
	of George
		8 Jul 1820

Wisher, James William Onion, sec.	Elizabeth Watts	29 Jan 1812
Wolford, Rev. Stevens	Cassey Waples	22 Dec 1816
Woolbridge, Joseph	Sally Matthews	30 Jul 1839
Wooldridge, James Major Davis, sec.	Mary Beavans	4 Feb 1805
Woolford, Stephen W. Samuel Waples and William Kendall, sec.	Cassey Robinson Waples of Samuel	20 Dec 1816

```
Woolridge, Joseph          Sally Mathews        28 Jul 1840
     (sometimes called Townsend)
     John D. Wilburn and Oliver Logan, sec.

Woolridge, Thomas          Leah Taylor of Mathews  16 Jan 1809
     Nehemiah Taylor, sec.

Wright, Edward             Susanna Littleton    19 Nov 1808
     Savage Crippen, sec.

Wright, Elijah J.          Margaret Snead       28 Dec 1837

Wright, Elijah W.          Margaret Snead of Tully  27 Dec 1836
     John R. Fosque, sec.

Wright, George T.          Elizabeth Laws        9 Dec 1851
                           of Zorobabel

Wright, Henry Jr.          Catherine Bell of Geo.  22 Dec 1825
     George Bell, sec.

Wright, Henry of Isaac     Ann Joynes of Zoro.   20 Dec 1820
     William R. Joynes, sec.

Wright, Henry             Margaret Kellam        9 Dec 1833
     Christopher C. Stachell, sec.

Wright, Henry             Margaret Kellam       18 Dec 1833

Wright, Henry Thomas      Hetty Hannon          21 Dec 1852
     of Henry

Wright, Isaac Jr.         Margaret Kellam       12 Nov 1829
                          (wid of Jesse)
          Peter Shield, sec.

Wright, Isaac             Mary Satchell         27 Dec 1804
     William H. Coxon, sec.

Wright, Isaac             Betsy Wharton         21 Sep 1814
                          (wid of Charles)
          Thomas Chandler, sec.

Wright, Isam              Betsy Wharton         21 Sep 1814

Wright, Jacob             Rachel Pettitt        19 Jun 1788

Wright, James             Mary Ann Finney       14 Apr 1827
                          of Willliam, dec'd.
          William W. Dix, sec.

Wright, James B.          Margaret A. Hope       9 Mar 1846
```

Wright, James B.	Demariah D. Hickman	11 Apr 1847
Wright, James John H. Bayly, sec.	Ann Bundick of Geo.	23 Dec 1816
Wright, Nathaniel W.	Margaret E. Brickhouse	18 Sep 1848
Wright, Thomas	Emilina Mears	15 Jul 1837
Wright, Thomas S. William S. Sturgis, sec.	Emaline S. Mears ward of Shadrock T. Ames	7 Jan 1839
Wright, Thomas	Emenine Mears	13 Feb 1839
Wright, Thomas of Henry Henry Wright, Sr. and Edmund Baker, sec.	Eliza Baker of William, dec'd.	20 Feb 1826
Wright, Walter of Wm. Edmund Baker and George Littleton, sec.	Henny Sparrow of Rich.	5 Aug 1825
Wright, William	Patience Dix	28 Feb 1797
Wyatt, Andrew B. Ephraim Mason and Curtis Rayfield, sec.	Elizabeth Mason of Sarah	14 May 1822
Wyatt, George Nathaniel Badger, sec.	Molly Ironmonger	10 Feb 1836
Wyatt, Isma of Wm. Joseph Gunter, sec.	Polly Gunter of Ben.	26 Aug 1816
Wyatt, John B. Isma Wyatt, sec.	Sally Wyatt of Wm.	27 Sep 1813
Wyatt, Joshua B. of Isma Orseymous Cropper and Wm. B. Seymour, sec.	Sarah Henderson of Wm.	1 Nov 1822
Wyatt, Joshua B. Teackle J. Turner, sec.	Tabitha Turner of Nath.	18 Aug 1825
Wyatt, Littleton Phillip Fisher, sec.	Ebba Fisher	23 Feb 1813
Wyatt, Thomas of Art. William P. Custis, sec.	Elizabeth Churn of Wm.	26 Dec 1816
Wyatt, William James Brittingham and Alexander Lang, sec.	Elizabeth Lang of Alex.	24 Sep 1838

```
Young, Bagwell              Betsy Moore              28 Jul 1800
     Eli Shay, sec.

Young, David                Margaret Wessells        13 Aug 1832
     Robert Hall, sec.

Young, Dr. Edward J.        Sarah E. Parramore       24 Jan 1837
     David D. Abbott and John B. Ailworth, sec.

Young, Ezekiel              Elizabeth A. Smith       15 Oct 1831
                              of Thomas H.
     Thomas Smith, Jr., sec.

Young, Gilbert of Robt.     Catherine Wessells        8 Aug 1822
                              of Robert and Elizabeth
        Art. and Tho. Wessells, sec.

Young, Henry                Ann Wessells             25 Aug 1823
                              of Ephraim, dec'd.
        David Mears, sec.

Young, James of Wm.         Polly Ironmonger         16 Feb 1819
                              of Zadoch
        William Young and George White, sec.

Young, James               Mary Ward                14 Apr 1849

Young, John                Betty Justice            22 Sep 1787
     James Vessels, sec.

Young, John                Susan Clayton            12 Mar 1855
     of Richard               of Thomas R.

Young, Jonathan            Sophia Hargis            10 Mar 1838
     Thomas Hargis, sec.

Young, Jonathan            Catherine Ward           19 Dec 1807
     Abel Phillips, sec.

Young, Littleton (wdr)    Tabitha Scarburgh of Tho.  26 Nov 1838
     Edward C. Thomas, sec.

Young, Richard             Caty Prescott            29 Sep 1823
     George Nelson, sec.

Young, Richard of Wm.     Mary Fisher of Wm.        23 Feb 1830
     John S. Johnson, sec.

Young, Richard            Sally Adams               29 Dec 1805
     John Young, sec.

Young, Richard (wdr)     Nancy Hopkins              28 May 1829
```

```
                         orphan of Henry
Rich. Young and Geo. Christopher (guardian), sec.

Young, Robert            Rachel Rew              22 Jan 1800
   Woney Rew, sec.

Young, Robert A.         Sarah E. Grinalds       25 Jan 1841
   John S. Dix, sec.

Young, Robert            Amelley Wessells        15 Apr 1830
                         of Ephraim
   David C. Taylor, sec.

Young, Samuel            Margaret Lucas of Southy 28 Jan 1828
   James Justice, sec.

Young, Samuel            Rachel Mason            17 Dec 1855
   of Gillet             of Zorobabel

Young, Samuel (wdr)      Mary Bloxom             26 Dec 1855

Young, Samuel of Robert  Sally Wessells of Isaac 15 Feb 1837
   Isaac Wessells, sec.

Young, Severn of Geo.    Sally R. Major of Wm.   12 Jan 1818
   Ezekiel Young and Zoro. Mason, sec. and Wm. Major, consent

Young, Shepherd          Sally Bloxom of Richard 23 Jan 1834
   Thoroghgood Taylor and William P. Custis, sec.

Young, Sheppard          Sally Shreaves          17 Dec 1855
   of Elizabeth Northam     of John T.

Young, Thomas            Elizabeth Parker        27 Nov 1805
                         of John R.
   James Eichelberger, sec.

Young, William of Wm.    Emmy Perry Saunders     29 Dec 1815
                         of Thomas, dec'd.
   David Mears, sec.

Young, William           Susan Bull of Wm.       20 Jan 1851

Young, William Jr.       Elizabeth Crippen       28 Nov 1775
   Thomas Crippen, sec.
```

APPENDIX

The following records were found after the bulk of this volume
had been compiled.

Ames, John   Caroline Gladding   14 May 1804
    Richard Mears, sec.

Brimer, Joseph   Polly Bishop   4 Feb 1803
    Caleb Brimer, sec.

Britches   Betty Nedab   19 Mar 1803
    FN freed by T. Broadwater
    Joshua Broadwater, sec.

Bundick, John A.   Elizabeth Hannaford   13 Sep 1802
    Edmund Bayly, sec.

Crippin, Thomas   Sirrah Crippin   16 Dec 1803
    FN
    Joshua Broadwater, sec.

Henderson, Henry   Elizabeth Massey   31 Jul 1803
    William Slocomb, sec.

Hickman, Isaiah   Mary Long   13 Sep 1803
    William Ardis, sec.

Jester, John   Linda Bull   25 Nov 1803
    Jacob Mason, sec.

Johnson, John P.   Tabitha Ames   4 Oct 1803
    Jesse Ames, sec.

Jones, James   Sally Staton   4 Apr 1803
    Joseph Andrews, sec.

Prewet, Elijah   Arcadia Dies   14 May 1804
    George Prewet, sec.

Sturgis, Joshua   Rachel Phillips   19 Sep 1805
    Abraham Williams, sec.

Wheatton, Daniel   Sally Bragle(?)   1 Mar 1803
    David Watts, sec.

INDEX OF BRIDES

INDEX OF BRIDES

Brides are listed by surname in alphabetical order. An indexed name may appear more than once on a cited page.

ABBOT:
  Sarah 115

ABBOTT:
  Ann 328
  Elizabeth 161
  Leah 1
  Molly 31
  Polly 60, 223

ABDEL
  Mary 72

ABDELL
  Ann 69
  Sarah 183
  Susanna 103

ABDILL
  Caty 299
  Elizabeth 59

ABET
  Mary 72

ADAIR
  Ann 161
  MAry 68

ADAMS
  Elizabeth 234
  Grace 326
  Hetty 148
  Nancy 144
  Polly 22
  Sally 280,332
  Sarah 243

ADDERSON
  Esther 178

ADDISON
  Ann 327
  Betsey 309
  Bridget 155
  Elizabeth 288
  Nancy 279
  Rachel 282
  Rebecca 319
  Suckey 249

AIMES
  Eckey 145

ALEXANDER
  Euphamia 152

ALLEN
  Betsy 106
  Margaret 223, 273
  Mary 145
  Peggy 255
  Sally 75
  Sylvia 161

ALLINE
  Betsy 116

AMES
  Anatha 53
  Ann 191, 327
  Caroline 273
  Catherine 176
  Coty 5
  Eliza 87
  Elizabeth 121, 271, 274
  Emily 284
  Finetta 248
  Isabella 284
  Jane 151, 193
  Joice 2

AMES (Continued)
Juliet Ann 191
Keziah 275
Lavinia 112
Mahala 116
Margaret 6, 308
Margaret Sarah 298
Margaret Virginia 313
Mary 138
Mary Emeline 195
Molly 92
Nancy 147
Nervilla 61
Peggy 78
Rachel 269
Sally 195, 274
Sarah 19
Susan 77
Tabitha 143, 177, 334

ANDREWS
Adah 223
Catherine 102
Caty 104, 131
Elizabeth 146
Joyce 104
Lucy 324
Margaret 67, 78
Maria 328
Molly 306
Patsy 171
Rachel 234

ANNIS
Cassey 282
Demeriah 74
Hessy 287
Maria 148
Mary 205
Polly 42
Ritta 48
Susanna 122

ANTHONY
Rachel 59, 245

ARBUCKLE
Ann 123, 248
Anne 122
Esther 232

ARBUCKLE (Continued)
Margaret 4

ARDIS
Betsy 321

ARLINGTON
Ann 93, 232
Elizabeth 197
Jane 125
Rosey 102
Sally 102

ARMSTRONG
Ann 86

ASHBY
Elizabeth 19, 196, 197
Hannah 306
Margaret 232
Mary 108, 326
Sally 106
Sarah 51

ASHLY
Ann 180
Margaret 85
Mary 133
Susan 226

AYRES
Ann 17, 119, 312
Anne 60
Elizabeth 131, 295
Hessy 319
Letitia 259
Margaret 64, 234
Rachel Ann 124
Sally Ann 55
Sarah 234
Tabitha 198
Tenny 59

BADGER
B--- 328
Charlotte 320
Elizabeth White 156
Louisa 183
Margaret 156, 253

BADGER (Continued)
Maria 279
Mary Ann 183
Sally 93
Sukey 272

BAGG
Ann 10
Elizabeth 105

BAGGE
Anne 10
Charity 107

BAGWELL
Ann 60, 280
Anna 305
Anne 141
Catherine 119, 228
Ellen 3
Elvira 126
Esther 31
Irene 217
Margaret 39, 94, 236
Rosey 9
Sally 176
Sarah 51
Tabitha 124

BAILEY
Betsy 315
Christabella 61

BAILY
Caty 200
Critty 277

BAINES
Nancy 15

BAKER
Ann 11, 58
Eliza 331
Elizabeth 224, 226
Elizabeth Seymour 48
Henney 31
Henny 16
Hepsy 16
Hetty 234
Leah 325

BAKER
Livey 249
Lucy 294
Margaret 195, 305
Mary 276
Molly 47
Polly 325
Rachel 325
Salley 45
Sinah 11
Suckey 315
Tabitha 16

BALEY
Lissa 128
Susanna 50

BALL
Charlotte 144
Hannah 17, 284
Henrietta 130

BANCUM
Elizabeth 120

BANISTER
Anne 260

BARNES
Alatine 313
Ann 129
Anne 259
Bridget 1, 18, 230
Caroline 257
Catharine 148
Comfort 149
Elizabeth 203, 308
Georgianna 245
Jane 257
Leah 36
Margaret 140
Mariah 192
Mary 253, 256
Nancy 179
Polly 131
Rachel 116
Sarah 209

BARRETT
Elizabeth 33

BECKET (Continued)
  Polly 21
  Susan 86

BECKETT
  Eliza 18
  Juliet Ann 250

BELL
  Ann 272
  Anne 246
  Catherine 38, 297, 330
  Caty 38
  Charlotte Ann 26
  Elizabeth 127, 247, 274
  Esther 242
  Kessy 225
  Keziah 243
  Mahala 225
  Margaret 24, 38, 86, 92
  Maria 143
  Mary 82, 199
  May 22
  Molly 272, 298
  Nancy 133, 143, 157
  Rachel 134
  Uphemy 192

BELOTE
  Ann 78, 118, 155
  Catherine 323
  Eliza 290
  Elizabeth 205
  Henny 320
  Hester 186
  Kessy 321
  Margaret 151
  Mary 192, 206, 247, 293
  Mary Eliza 111
  Nanny 33
  Patience 152
  Polly 32
  Sarah 195
  Tabitha 194
  Virginia 240

BENNETT
  Ann 63
  Betty 22

BENNETT (Continued)
  Dinah 53
  Melinda 262

BENSON
  Elizabeth 281
  Joyce 78
  Mary Jane 261
  Nancy 292

BENSTON
  Suzy 235

BENTSON
  Azenith 187
  Molly 63
  Peggy 285
  Polly 41, 305

BERRY
  Anne 156
  Catherine 83
  Keziah 285
  Lucy 190
  Mahala 260
  Maria 189
  Mary 64
  Susan 103

BIGGS
  Nancy 310

BIRCH
  Elizabeth 325
  Elsey 325
  Esther 36
  Hetty 141
  Sally 291

BIRD
  Ann 211
  Anne 135
  Catherine 174
  Damariah 29
  Eliza 140
  Elizabeth 151,212
  Henny 28
  Henrietta 151
  Hessy 104
  Hester Ann 322

BIRD (Continued)
Hetty 77, 310
Ignatia 37
Keziah 103
Margaret 151, 212
Maria 252
Mary 29, 30, 122, 203
Neomy 212
Peggy 157, 220
Rachel Ann 103
Rebecca 191
Sarah 89, 184
Serina 267
Susan 56, 233
Tabitha 293
Vianna 267

BIRTON
Ann 89

BISHOP
Ann 89
Daimey 256
Daney 257
Elizabeth 252
Esther 160
Henrietta 27
Patience 175
Patsy 240
Polly 39, 334
Sinah 16
Tinney 196

BLACKSTONE
Elizabeth 237, 323

BLADES
Hetty 27

BLAKE
Mary 85

BLEN
Elizabeth 20

BLOXOM
Agnes 50, 156
Amey 99
Ann 252
Betsy 180

BLOXOM
Betty 181
Burnetta 32
Caroline 137
Catherine 161
Eliza 187
Elizabeth 14, 37, 61, 115,
    155, 170
Fanny 206
Harriet 145
Henrietta 234
Hessy 289
Hetty 33, 84, 103, 109
Margaret 47
Mary 333
May 140
Nancy 142, 153, 276, 311
Narcissa 32
Peggy 90, 277
Polly 322, 324
Rachel 230
Rebecca 120
Rose Ann 149
Roxanna 160
Sally 54, 82, 103, 200, 203,
    333
Sarah 231
Sinah 211
Sophia 157
Susan 16
Susan Jane 111
Tabitha 15, 34, 136, 149, 150
    184, 288
Tinny Savage 136

BOGG
Achsah 177

BOGGS
Caroline 251
Eliza 239
Elizabeth 76, 186
Esther 280
Jane 206
Leah 34
Lucy 205
Margaret 98, 156, 218, 309
Maria 187
Mary 211, 274
Nancy 211

BOGGS (Continued)
  Rachel 240
  Sally 58
  Sarah Ann 63, 64
  Susa 312
  Virginia 277

BOLENARD
  Margaret 273

BONIWELL
  Ann 265
  Betsy 254
  Mary 318
  Peggy 264

BONNAWELL
  Elizabeth 205, 251

BONNEWELL
  Margaret 264
  Mary 317

BONWELL
  Ann 44
  Betsy 184
  Elizabeth 92, 264
  Hetty 198
  Rosey 291
  Sarah 55
  Zepporah 110

BOONE
  Margaret 195

BOOTH
  Betsy 309
  Euphamia 291
  Hetty 118
  Katherine 266
  Maria 165
  Peggy 78, 155

BOSTON
  Elizabeth 313
  Martha 126
  Mary 315
  Nancy 286
  Sarah 270

BOWDEN
  Christina 265
  Mary Ann 66
  Nancy 192

BOWDOIN
  Elizabeth 37

BOWEN
  Elizabeth 53, 110

BOWLES
  Mary 259
  Rebecca 259
  Sarah 200

BOWMAN
  Catherine
  Euphamia 3

BRACHER
  Matilda 235

BRADFORD
  Alice 95
  Alsey 39
  Ann Maria 154
  Betsy 237
  Elizabeth 136, 182, 220, 304
  Esther 19, 163
BRADFORD (Continued)
  Jenny 233
  Leah 252
  Louisa 39
  Lucinda 189
  Lucretia 189
  Margaret 91, 113, 154, 157,
    239
  Maria 273
  Mary Elln 246
  Nancy 6, 273
  Polly 51, 235
  Rachel 24
  Rosey 156
  Susanna 50, 154

BRADSHAW
  Rachel 287

BRAGLE
Sally 319, 334

BRATCHER
Polly 172

BRICKHOUSE
Margaret 331

BRIMER
Bridget 155, 156
Eliza 188
Elizabeth 246
Nancy 33

BRINKER
Sally 305

BRITTINGHAM
Elizabeth 146
Margaret 58
Narcissa 130
Polly 130, 217, 222

BROADWATER
Atta 41
Betsy 86, 317
Elizabeth 249, 278
Elizabeth Ann 104
Esther 282
Euphamy 188
Euphemia 270, 271, 309
Letita 110
Louisa 105
Margaret 203, 289
Martha 21
Mary 133
Mary Ann 66
Nancy 41, 102
Peggy 210
Rachel 67
Rebecca 67, 141
Rosey Ann 208
Sally 21, 170, 232
Sarah 41
Scarbrough 85

BROW
Mary 323

BROWN
Anna 182
Louisa 103

BRUMBLEY
Leah 96

BUDD
Eliza 134
Mary 22
Nancy 171

BULL
Bridget 35, 197, 200
Catherine 178
Caty 280
Comfort 111
Eliza 281
Elizabeth 128. 274, 282, 312
Harriet 204, 207, 247
Henny 37
Hetty 44
Julia 211
Keziah 161
Linda 334
Lovey 115, 117
Margaret 12
Margaret Ann 269
Mary 109
Mary Susan 9
Nancy 74, 84, 106, 166, 172
184, 208, 265, 276, 280
Peggy 70, 144
Phebe Elizabeth 33
Polly 55, 232, 251
Rosey 32
Sally 205, 300
Sarah 36, 43, 190, 279
Sophia 170
Sukey 45, 46
Susan 135. 333
Tabitha 33, 73

BULLMAN
Margaret 92

BUNDICK
Ann 184, 284, 331
Ann Maria 215
Barsheba 286

BUNDICK (Continued)
  Betsy 246, 302, 304
  Bridget 211
  Catherine 8
  Damy 220
  Elizabeth 30, 31, 129
  Elvina 15
  Esther 111
  Eveline 15
  Henny 208
  Mahala 27
  Margaret 246
  Molly 134, 267
  Nancy 140
  Peggy 315
  Rita 18
  Sally 45, 102, 214
  Tabitha 9, 132, 239, 265, 280

BUNTIN
  Elizabeth 229

BUNTING
  Amey 69
  Amy 201
  Anna 32
  Betsey 177
  Betsy 253
  Charlotte 40
  Elizabeth 90, 114, 255
  Hester Ann 291
  Lovea 320
  Margaret 69
  Maria 49
  Mary 277
  Nancy 127, 189, 260
  Peggy 28, 131
  Rachel 106, 221
  Rosanne 260
  Rosey 17, 263
  Sally 48. 121. 211.311
  Sarah 190
  Seymour 3
  Sukey 50
  Suky 200
  Susan 102
  Susanna 200
  Tabitha 92, 201

BURCH
  Amy 57
  Elizabeth Ann 290
  Polly 168
  Sally 168

BURD
  Catherine 183

BURTON
  Ann 66
  Catherine 183
  Elizabeth 95, 180, 201, 262,
    282, 308
  Katherine 293
  Margaret 140, 295
  Mary 12
  Tabitha 215

BUTLER
  Delany 158
  Sally 57

BYRD
  Eveline 156
  Mary 52
  Melinda 76
  Rachel 156
  Susanna 82
  Thealy Ann 90

CALAHAN
  Susan 316

CALLAHAN
  Margaret 316

CALHAM
Nancy 112

CALLIER
  Mary 128

CARMINE
  Ann 106
  Catherine 252
  Juliet 44
  Tabitha 62

CHERRICKS
Anne 145
Betsy 50
Margaret 267
Mary 312

CHERRIX
Nancy 8

CHESHIRE
Ann 166
Elizabeth 234
Rebecca 259

CHESSER
Eliza 58
Elizabeth 86
Maria 260
Nancy 285
Susan 87

CHOARD
Elizabeth 105

CHRISTOPHER
Nancy 269
Susanna 212

CHURCH
Agnes 31
Caroline 180
Eliza 85
Leah 242
Rebecca 176
Tinny 113

CHURAN
Adah 109

CHURN
Elizabeth 331
Margaret Ann 328
Mary Ann 327
Molly 235
Nancy 163
Susan 297
Tabitha 297

CLARK
Sarah 9, 169

CLARKE
Polly 214

CLAVELL
--- 167

CLAYTON
Elizabeth 9
Susan 332
Tabby 23
Virginia 18

CLAYVILL
Sarah 166

CLAYWELL
Sally 276

CLEGG
Caroline 23

CLEMMONS
Bridget 149
Sinah 70

CLOUDS
Rachel 295

CLUFF
Sarah Ann 258

COAH
Sally 89

COARD
Anna 79
Cassey 90
Hetty 135
Mary 319
Nancy 97
Sarah Ann 270

COBB
Betsy 229
Elizabeth 189
Leah 328
Sally 74

COKE
    Laney 29
    Polly 211

COLBOURN
    Elizabeth 234
    Mary 114

COLE
    Elizabeth 212, 308
    Sally Cropper 191

COLEBURN
    Ann 66, 161
    Eliza 33
    Elizabeth 200, 266, 279, 307
    Elizabeth (Continued) 329
    Louisa 104
    Margaret 76
    Mary 89,115, 272
    Mary Ann 317
    Rachel 38
    Sabra 77
    Sally 326
    Sarah 326

COLLINS
    Betsy 239
    Elizabeth 40
    Fanny 182
    Mahala 1, 181
    Mallie 245
    Margaret 245
    Maria 80
    Mary 60, 69, 281
    Nancy 207, 256
    Patsy 69
    Rachel 182
    Rebecca 179
    Sally 323
    Sophia 130, 284

COLLONEY
    Susanna 43

COLONA
    Polly 166
    Rachel 242

COLONNA
    Elizabeth 35, 64
    Fanny 312
    Joyce 102
    Margaret 12
    Mary 79
    Nancy 172
    Susan 147

COLONNEY
    Catey 168

COLONY
    Margaret 85, 215
    Molly 136
    Nancy 199
    Polly 128
    Rosannah 306
    Susanna 157, 310

CONAWAY
    Betsy 171

CONNAH
    Peggy 217

CONNER
    Ann 68
    Drucilla 238
    Eliza 168
    Elizabeth 247
    Laura 173
    Mary Crippen 28
    Nancy 223
    Sally 87
    Susannah 227

CONQUEST
    Comfort 270
    Eleline 76
    Elizabeth Ann 113
    Euphemia 305
    Hetty 66
    Jane 3
    Keziah 215
    Mary 278
    Sally 148

COPES
    Catherine 160

-348-

COPES (Continued)
  Critty 128
  Eliza 309
  Elizabeth 51, 191
  Esther 230
  Henrietta 323
  Hester Ann 144
  Hetty 292
  Jenny 248
  Margaret 128
  Mary 136
  Nancy 15, 165, 310
  Peggy 16
  Polly 33, 190
  Rachel 277
  Rebecca 179
  Sally 286
  Sarah 115, 286
  Sukey 84

CORBIN
  Ann 119
  Elizabeth 40, 99
  Emiline 217
  Lavinah 283
  Levinia 258
  Mary 101
  Milkah 269
  Polly 141
  Rebecca 89
  Rosey 144
  Sabra 314
  Sally 141
  Sarah 264, 269
  Susanna 73

CORD
  Ann 37
  Hepsey 19

CORE
  Betsey 26
  Betsy 21
  Emily 307
  Sarah 329
  Sarah Ann 125

COTTINGHAM
  Nellie 124
  sally 289

COTTRIL
  Sally 59

COURSEY
  Sally 320

COWAN
  Sally 93

COWARD
  Eliza 328
  Jane 3
  Louise 224

COWLEY
  Elizabeth 69
  Nancy 1

COX
  Nancy 209

CRIPPEN
  Comfort 70
  Elizabeth 333
  Louisa 42
  Narcissa 99
  Sarah 243

CRIPPIN
  Barsheba 41
  Rachel 70
  Sirrah 71, 334

CRIPPTON
  Nelly 80

CROCKET
  Anna 98
  Cathy 71
  Mary 71
  Triffena 97

CROCKETT
  Ann 164, 288
  Ellen 71
  Emiline 71
  Henny 222
  Maria 146
  Mary 72, 203
  Nelly 71

CROCKETT (Continued)
Patty 135
Polly 72
Zipporah 281

CROPPER
Adah Ann 69
Ann 9
Elizabeth 217
Malinda 183
Margaret Pettit 19
Polly 179
Sabra Corbin 118
Sally 47, 50
Sarah 82, 87
Susan 304
Tabitha 201

CROSBY
Mary 245

CROSWELL
Priscilla 221

CROWSON
Agnes 34
Catherine 255
Comfort 105
Elizabeth 255
Hester 111
Margaret 322
Nancy 93
Sirah 324
Susan 157
Susannah 12

CRUMMOND
Tabitha 170

CUNIGAN
Embery 27

CURTIS
Nellie 78

CUSTIS
Adeline 147
Ann 214, 250
Catherine 229, 318

CUSTIS (Continued)
Elizabeth 35, 76, 191, 222, 253
Esther 43
Frances 146
Leah 272
Margaret 107, 227, 274, 298, 329
Mary 4, 49, 274
Matilda 10
Nancy 116
Polly 253
Sally 1, 327, 329
Sarah 75
Sarah Ann 136
Susan 88
Susabba 71, 201
Tabitha 228

CUTLER
Caty 221
Elizabeth 268
Nancy 82, 240
Susan 307

DAISEY
Elizabeth 254

DAIZEY
Mary 158

DALSEY
Nancy 8

DAMBLIN
Fanney 20

DAMERLIN
Nancy 169

DANIEL
Katey 97

DARBY
Ann 329
Anne 65
Betsy 176
Caroline 294, 295
Elizabeth 261

DARBY (Continued)
  Elizabeth Ann 63
  Polly 153
  Sally 17
  Susan 106

DAUZEY
  Polly 129

DAVIS
  Ann 48
  Anne 147
  Betsy 265
  Elizabeth 314, 315, 326
  Leah 53, 207
  Louisa 182
  Love 165
  Mary 304
  Nancy 63, 125, 258, 309
  Peggy 270
  Polly 48, 234
  Sally 178, 215, 292
  Sally Ann 12
  Sarah 57, 312
  Sary 11
  Scarbrough 96
  Sene 31
  Susey 138

DAZY
  Mary 164

DEE
  Nancy 18

DEEBLE
  Jane Hall 135

DEFFERMAN
  Betsy 41

DELASTATIOUS
  Attalanta 89
  Sarah 81

DELASTATIUS
  Ann 89
  Betsy 322
  Margaret 214

DELASTATIUS (Continued)
  Mary 143
  Polly 289

DELATATIUS
  Mary 215
  Nancy 264

DENNIS
  Caty 158, 159
  Esther 179
  Leah 60
  Neily 106
  Sally 309

DERBY
  Susanna 182

DICKERSON
  Betsy 199
  Elizabeth 116, 320
  Hetty 278
  Leah 107
  Mary 82, 284
  Rachel 4
  Sarah 105

DICKINSON
  Sally 100

DIES
  Arcadia 230, 334
  Polly Ann 83

DILLASTRATUS
  Nancy 161

DILLESTATIUS
  Rutha 293

DISON
  Henrietta 119

DIX
  Bridget 127
  Catherine 26, 111
  Demoriah 323
  Elizabeth 135, 271, 294
  Esther 129
  Fannie 244

DIX (Continued)
  Henrietta 259
  Hessy 267
  Hester 96
  Margaret 66, 135, 317
  Mary 244
  May 189
  Nancy 75, 89, 283, 321
  Nany 218
  Patience 331
  Peggy 14, 35
  Polly 199, 229
  Rachel 314
  Rosey 15, 212
  Susan 210, 306
  Tabitha 311

DOE
  Ann 122

DOLBY
  Margaret 158

DOLVY
  Sally 224

DORITY
  Rachel 231

DOUGHTY
  Betsy 309
  Coty 72
  Eliza 311
  Joice 7
  Malinda 106
  Margaret 303
  Susanna 65

DOUGLAS
  Mary Ann 228

DOUGLASS
  Anna 276
  Margaret 280

DOWNING
  Ann 81, 87
  Bridget 86
  Hannah 120

DOWNING (Continued)
  Hetty 99, 182
  Julie 61
  Margaret 34, 273
  Maria 172
  Mary 138
  Nancy 126, 264, 305
  Sally 298

DOWTY
  Margaret 5, 261
  Molly 127, 275
  Susan 87

DREDDON
  Molly 200

DRUMMOND
  Amey 198
  Ann 88
  Betsy 228, 265
  Catherine 88
  Charlotte 86
  Diadamia 278
  Eliza 164
  Elizabeth 32, 87, 104, 113,
    202, 323
  Fanny 53
  Jane 119
  Janet 188
  Julia 288
  Leah 246
  Margaret 264
  Mariah 23
  Mary 233
  Nancy 46, 66, 206, 322
  Patience 180, 205
  Peggy 88
  Sally 68, 141
  Sarah 15, 119
  Sarah A. Parker 126
  Sarah Ann 88
  Sophia 198, 321
  Sukey 197
  Tabitha 166

DRURY
  Susan 244

DUBLE
Elizabeth 262

DUET
Martha 204

DUNCAN
Elizabeth 58
Elizabet Ann 155
Emaline 79
Jane 188
Julia 209
Mary 9
nancy 3
Rachel 183
Sally 113, 212
Sarah 210

DUNSTAN
Euphamy 177
Sarah 126

DUNTON
Catherine Revil 137
Elizabeth 252
Harriet 127
Keziah 25
Margaret 189
Mary 87, 137
Nancy 162
Polly 108
Sally 82
Susanna 258

DURY
Bridget 196

EAST
Alice 219
Ann 114
Elizabeth 226, 246
Leah 122
Leanah 20
Leanna 246
Margaret 92, 184, 217, 306
Mary 306
Molly 124
Nancy 169, 218
Sally 239, 268

EAST (Continued)
Sarah 297
Tabitha 143
Yeardley 242

EDMUNDS
Ann 321
Ann Jane 176
Betsy 20
Elizabeth 79
Margaret 10
Mary 299
Nancy 225
Peggy 191
Polly 210
Sarah Ann 14
Susanna 248
Tabitha 67

EDWARD
Mary 85

EDWARDS
Elizabeth 141
Euphamy 24
Harriet 285
Kessy 276
Margaret 171, 225
Mary 235
Molly 229
Nancy 94, 142
Sally 74, 139
Sarah 283
Susan 142

ELLIOT
Margaret 7

ELIIOTT
Anne 45
Anseley 304
Bridget 186
Catherine 49, 105
Caty 225
Elizabeh 163
Esther 152
Juliet 56
Lorea 50
Margaret 23

ELLIOTT (Continued)
Mary 122, 192
Mary Ann 263
Nancy 163, 165, 195
Peggy 67
Rachel 264
Rosey 228
Sally 179, 190, 308

ELLIS
Nancy 162
Sophia 177

ESHAM/ESHOM
Harriet 75

ETTES
Harriet 283

EVANS
Amey 319
Betsy 268
Deliley 267
Eleanor 178
Elender 244
Elizabeth 2, 99
Euphamia 72
Kepsey 4
Jane 56
Judah 180
Katherine 45
Keziah 204
Levice 91
Levinear 42
Lucretia 31
Mary 21
Mary Ann 72
Mahala 180
Rachel 288
Rose 50
Rutha 267
Sally 230, 231, 312
Sarah 64
Sinah 71
Sukey 298
Susan 21
Susanna 284

EWELL
Ann 271

EWELL (Continued)
Anna 56
Anne 318
Arinthia 229
Betsey 251
Betsy 309, 314
Brunetta 270
Catey 238
Comfort 1
Elizabeth 132. 275. 284
Hetty 97
Leah 305
Margaret 185
Mary 123
Nancy 283
Polley 114
Sakky 140
Sally 19, 107, 142, 171
Serena 66
Seymour 188
Tabitha 244, 259

FASSIT
Mary 28

FEDDERMAN
Martha 188

FELTCHER
Ada 10

FENNY
Susanna 113

FERGUSON
Nancy 319
Polly 28

FETCHER
Elisha 88

FIDDEMAN
Esther 159

FIELDS
Esther 159

FINNEY
Ann 21

FINNEY (Continued)
  Anne 328
  Betsey 309
  Catherine 8, 111
  Elizabeth 240
  Leah 15
  Mary 170
  Mary Ann 330
  Nancy 202
  Sarah 190, 306, 316
  Tabitha 20

FINNY
  Sarah 234

FIRCHETT
  Patsy 26

FISHER
  Anne 327
  Cassia 291
  Comfort 80
  Ebba 331
  Elizabeth 8, 77, 95
  Hetty 52
  Keziah 158
  Margaret 144
  Mary 92, 332
  Milcah 295
  Nancy 8, 279
  Patience 25, 192
  Rachel 226
  Sally 269, 303
  Sarah 137, 312
  Sarah Ann 224
  Susan 81
  Susanna 59
  Tinny 177

FISQUE
  Eliza 233

FITCHET
  Ann Ritta 134

FITCHETT
  Comfort 69
  Elizabeth 232
  Emaline 91
  Jane 210

FITCHETT (Continued)
  Matilda 113
  Nancy 98
  Patsy 158
  Polly 127
  Rose Abb 48, 49
  Sally 246
  Susanna 80

FITCHETTE
  Ritta 285

FITZGERALD
  Juliet Ann 171
  Nancy 43, 198
  Sally 129, 224
  Susanna 45

FLETCHER
  Adah 109
  Betsey 83
  Betsy 75
  Elizabeth 74
  Jinney 33
  Margaret 121, 220
  Nancy 88, 163, 182
  Patty 83
  Sarah 102
  Susan 160
  Susanna 88, 117

FLEWHART
  Jemimah 243

FLOYD
  Judy 132
  Leah 213
  Lizzie 37
  Margaret 27, 47
  Maria 50
  Mary 10
  Molly 5, 6, 91
  Rachel 45
  Sarah 132, 210
  Sarah Ann 93
  Selby 265

FOLIO
  Fanny 192
  Rose 65

FOLLUO
  Margaret 85
  Molly 85

FORTUNE
  Scarburgh 164

FOSQUE
  Charlotte 247
  Elizabeth 55, 233, 296
  Mary 61, 74, 163
  Peggy 252
  Peggy Jones 217
  Rachel 47
  Sarah 234, 248

FOSSET
  Mary 43

FOSTER
  Ann 157
  Betsy 134
  Elizabeth 127
  Nancy 107
  Sukey 311

FOX
  Betsy 50
  Mary 196
  Nancy 35
  Sally 198
  Sarah 207

FRANCIS
  Betty 271

FRANK
  Leah 223

GALT
  Anne 219

GANET
  Nancy 16

GARDENER
  Nancy 54

GARDINER
  Sally 18

GARDNER
  Ann 191
  Betsy 197
  Catherine 281
  Emmie 266
  Esther 324
  Tinny 245

GARETT
  Henrietta 31

GARRET
  Sally 26
  Tabitha 42

GARRETT
  Bridget 287
  Eliza 283
  Nancy 41
  Peggy Smith 310
  Polly 236
  Sally 67, 70
  Sarah 270

GARRISON
  Adah 143
  Ann 263
  Catharine 39
  Charlotte 23
  Cibell 67
  Elizabeth 18, 89, 194
  Esther 209
  Hannah 10
  Jane 10
  Kiturah 112
  Lavinina 95
  Margaret 160, 174
  Peggy 123
  Phillis 6
  Rachel 105
  Sally 262
  Sarah Ann 10
  Susanna 272

GASCOYNES
  Elizabeth 141

GASKIN
  Nancy 263

GASKINS
  Elizabeth 63, 290

GASKINS (Continued)
  Hetty 82
  Margaret 283

GECTRIDGE
  Attalantic 147

GELCHRIST
  Mary 157

GELLETT
  Sarah 72

GIBB
  Elizabeth 273
  Peggy 145

GIBBONS
  Charlotte 171
  Sally 18

GIBSON
  Margaret 197

GIDDENS
  Betsy 33
  Betty 43
  Elizabeth 275

GIDDEONS
  Rosey 125

GILCHRIST
  Rebecca 162

GILLASPEE
  Kesiah 30

GILLESPIE
  Ann 130
  Elizabeth 236
  Leah 141
  Sally 250

GILLETT
  Anna 21
  Betsey 81
  Caroline 181
  Cassey 196

GILLETT (Continud)
  Louisa 175
  Margaret 30, 31
  Mary 80
  mary Ann 173
  Tabitha 75

GILLISPIE
  Esther 32
  Nancy 151
  Tenny 28

GLADDEN
  Ann 173

GLADDING
  Ann 319
  Caroline 53
  Elizabeth 49
  Harriet 295
  Hester 160
  Milcah 281
  Polly 12
  Rebecca 150
  Sally 180. 256, 263
  Tabitha 199

GLASSBY
  mary 20

GLEN
  Sally 107

GLENN
  Katurah 22
  Retuny 22

GODFREE
  Betsy 173

GODFREY
  Lena 113
  Priscilla 326

GODWIN
Hetty 312
Molly 255
Nancy 103
Sarah 101
Susanna 104

GOFFIFON
Sally 152

GOLIAH
Esther 3

GOLLAND
Ann 9

GOOTEE
Elisha 244
Polly 229

GORDON
Margaret 109

GORGON
Mary 125

GRANT
Agnes 116

GRAY
Catherine 306
Elizabeth 198, 242
Lucretia 12
Mary 325
Mary Ann 276
Nancy 302
Sally 193, 200
Tabitha 158

GREEN
Nancy 93
Sarah 22

GRENNALDS
Elizabeth 108

GREY
Nelly 31

GRIFFIN
Harriet 178
Ibby 238
Mariah 65
Nancy 42

GRINALDS
Mary 184
Molly 219
Nancy 14, 118, 186
Sally 86
Sarah 333

GRINNALDS
Ada 75
Hessey 219
Leah 186
Nancy 185
Polly 44, 186
Sarah 222
Tinny 87

GROTEN
Amey 202
Ann 51
Betsy 242
Eliza Levi 93
Elizabeth 109
Maria 154
Nancy 214, 224
Princess 280

GUARDINIR
Caty 216

GUFFIN
Bridget 95

GUNTER
Elizabeth 114, 227, 228
Mahala 256
Polly 126, 331
Sally 193, 194
Sarah 56
Susan 192
Susanna 76

GUNTOR
Susan Jane 12

HARGIS (Continued)
Caty 45
Elizabeth 89
Hepsey 292
Katherine 44
Margaret Ann 255
Nancy 170
Sally 73, 308
Sarah Ann 111
Sophia 332

HARMAN
Ann 247
Leah 86, 120
Nancy 327
HARMAN (Continued)
Sarah 109, 183

HARMON
Anna 203
Barbour 23
Critty 284
Esther 240
Euphanica 156
Harriet 313
Hessy 193
Laney 143
Margaret 183
Mary Ann 253
Nancy 8, 39
Peggy 46
Sally 208
Sarah 71, 326
Tamar 5

HARMONSON
Eliza 19

HAROM
Peggy 125

HARPER
Nancy 34
Sally 81

HARRIS
Elizabeth 192

HARRISON
Ann 123, 132
Leah 5, 176
Mary 193
Mary Ann 261
Nancy 59
Sarah 227
Susan 263

HART
Molly 258
Sarah Ann 169

HATFIELD
Nancy 280

HATHAWAY
Nancy 4

HATTON
Anne 276
Hessy 208
Margaret 197
Sarah 25, 269

HEATH
Ann 5
Aroda 184
Eliza 61
Elizabeth 25, 210
Elvira 38
Kessy 23
Margaret 250
Polly 184
Sarah Ann 296
Susanna 125
Tabitha 87

HEATING
Sarah 70

HELMS
Sally 174

HENDERSON
Ann 92
Catherine 84

HARRISON (Continued)
  Charlotte 190, 286
  Eliza 30
  Elizabeth 58, 112, 190, 244
  Jane 291
  Lucinda 144
  Margaret 85, 180, 247
  Maria 283
  Mary 249
  Nancy 277
  Peggy 142
  Polly 317
  Salley 36
  Sally 9, 177
  Sarah 253, 331
  Scarborough 279

HENRY
  Ann Blair 292

HICKMAN
  Ann 205, 224
  Ann Berry 166
  Anne 37, 208
  Bridget 322
  Catherine 63
  Caty 20
  Comfort 234
  Demariah 331
  Eliza 223
  Elizabeth 46, 131, 171,
    195, 313
  Hester 167
  Lucretia 308
  Margaret 200, 225, 235
  Mary 111, 289
  Milly 46
  Molly 205
  Nancy 48, 66, 297
  Peggy 266
  Rosey 293
  Sally 46, 80, 268
  Santer 327
  Sarah 46
  Santer 327
  Sarah 46
  Seymour 131, 168

HICKMAN (Continued)
  Sinah 281, 308
  Tenny 30
  Tiffany 214

HILL
  Agnes 95
  Ann 28
  Eliza 81
  Esther 41
  Euphany 41
  Lydia 60
  Nan 165
  Nancy 228

HINMAN
  Ann 48, 50
  Caziah 30
  Cretty 190
  Elizabeth 22, 105, 165,
    187, 199
  Margaret 18, 281
  Mary 68
  Mary Ann 192
  Molly 32
  Peggy 240
  Polly 120, 243
  Sally 63, 232
  Susan 269
  Tabitha 199

HINMON
  Keziah 245
  Susanna 174

HITCHENS
  Mary 123
  Rachel 121

HITCHINS
  patty 316

HOFFMAN
  Sally 260
  Sarah Ann 178
  Sinah 138

HOGSHIRE
  Sally 268

HOLDEN
Leah 318
Lydia 41

HOLLAND
Elizabeth 222
Mary 40, 247
Sally 304
Sarah 222

HOLLOWAY
Annmaria 165
Elizabeth 53
Nancy 32
Traney 238

HOLSTEN
Nancy 221
Peggy 93

HOLSTON
Nancy 222
Sally 271
Susanna 241

HOLT
Elizabeth 270
Henny 148
Molly 245
Nancy 62, 88
Polly 40
Rachel 148
Sally 283
Timy 21

HONES
Elizabeth 146

HOOKE
Sarah 201

HOPE
Ann 59
Betsey 32
Betsy 161
Elizabeth 104, 134
Elizabeth Ann 104
Leah 121, 303
Lydia 209

HOPE (Continued)
Margaret 330
Mary 224
Mary Ann 327
Molly 140
Sally 49

HOPKINS
Ellen 218
Margaret 188, 300
Margaret Ann 104
Nancy 332
Sally 300
Sarah 4, 5
Susan 228
Tabitha 107

HOPMAN
Rachel 252

HORNSBY
Ann 6
Betsy 135, 136, 299
Eliza 7
Elizabeth 219
Leah 153
Molly 241
Nancy 268
Polly 136
Rose 292
Sakky 7
Sarah 105
Susan 274

HOWARD
Catherine 85
Elizabeth 131
Polly 294

HOWARTH
Esther 186
Mary 206
Nancy 267

HOWELL
Mary 87

HUDSON
Comfort 294

HUNMAN
  Ann 58

HURST
  Anne 171
  Sally 324

HURT (HURST?)
  Rachel 12

HUSLAY
  Rachel 239

HUTCHINSON
  Dorinde 62
  Elizabeth 227
  Margaret 270
  Nancy 103
  Peggy 67
  Rachel 246

HUTSON
  Betty 83
  Caroline 207
  Critty 293
  Eliza 289
  Fanney 181
  Hannah 4
  Molly 132, 148
  Nancy 293
  Susanna 303

HYSLOP
  Alicia 236
  Ann 152
  Elizabeth 277
  Leah 194
  Lydia 303
  Mary 300
  Nancy 4, 192
  Rosa Ann 151
  Sarah 6

IRONMONGER
  Ann 243
  Elizabeth 185, 265
  Euphemy 68
  Molly 331
  Peggy 273
  Phamey 56

IRONMONGER (Continued)
  Polly 332
  Sally 132
  Sarah 116

IVY
  Catherine 117

JACKSON
  Catherine 101
  Mary 261

JACOB
  Elizabeth 11, 292
  Margaret 99
  Mary 183
  mary Ann 177
  Sally 124

JAMES
  Ann 134
  Ann Eliza 238

JAMES (Continued)
  Betsy 184
  Charlotte 14
  Elizabeth 26, 204, 272
  Emma 199
  Hetty 70, 185
  Lucy 81
  Margaret 5, 6, 220
  Mary 41, 108
  Molly 250
  Nancy 156
  Rachel 102
  Sally 124
  Sarah 57
  Susey 214
  Sussey 3

JAMESON
  Mary Anne 118

JAMOR
  Betsy 245

JAQUES
  Polly 9

JENKINS
  Elizabeth 90
  Peggy 197
  Susan 258

JESTER
  Eliza 115
  Elizabeth 81
  Hetty 79
  Margaret 261
  Mary 297
  Rachel 296
  Sally 327
  Susan 35

JOHNSON
  Arinthia 73
  Betsy 17
  Caroline 135
  Catharine 323
  Charlotte 180
  Eliza 187
  Elizabeth 134, 197, 257
  Elizabeth Ann 306
  Elizabeth Susan 295
  Fanny 14
  Henretta 162
  Hepsey 260
  Leah 122, 123
  Margaret 20, 126, 229
  Margaret Jane 112
  Mariah 290
  mary 205, 210, 253, 277
  Milly 90
  Nancy 19, 103, 254
  Peggy 126
  Polly 84
  Rosey 48
  Sally 18, 155, 197
  Sarah 36, 44
  Tabitha 210

JOLIFF
  Mary 327
  Patsy 155

JONES
  Caty 248
  Eliza 24
  Elizabeth 49, 271, 318

JONES (Continued)
  Harriet 162
  Leah 137
  Mareah 36
  Mary 106, 141, 142, 289
  Matilda 291
  May 141
  Nancy 141, 186
  Patience 101
  Polly 40, 319
  Rebecca 141
  Rebeccah 67
  Sally 27, 309

JOYNES
  Ann 299, 330
  Christiana 96
  Christina 97
  Elizabeth 10, 75, 76, 152,
    288
  Harriet 19
  Margaret 152, 171, 253
  Mary 250
  Polly 67
  Rachel 298
  Rhoda 314
  Sally 115, 324
  Sarah 84, 204
  Susan 264
  Susanna 79
  Tabotha 272, 306
  Virginia 2

JUBILEE
  Margaret 313
  Mary 250
  Peggy 36
  Rachel 54

JUSTICE
  Amey 158
  Amy 257
  Ann 214
  Bernadette 185
  Betty 332
  Catherine 196, 285, 315
  Eliza 252
  Elizabeth 185, 248
  Elizabeth Ann 211
  Emiline 199

KELLY (Continued)
 Susan 51
 Tabitha 198

KELPIN
 Mary 270

KENDALL
 Sukey 325

KENDRICK
 Mary 171

KENNEHORN
 Catherine 182

KER
 Agnes

KEW
 Margaret 273

KICKMAN
 Mary 237
 Nancy 119
 Polly 260
 Susanna 206

KILLMAN
 Eliza 150
 Jane 289
 margaret 222
 Margaret Ann 231
 Sally 290
 Sally Drummond 118
 Tabitha 287

KILLMON
 Frances 18
 Mary 73, 124
 Molly 164
 Sally 302

KILMAN
 Abbe 158
 Elizabeth 205
 Mary 73
 Sally 120, 131
 Sarah 242, 294

KILMON
 Elizabeth 256
 Peggy 222

KIRBY
 Polly 277
KNIGHT
 Margaret 294
 Pamelia 181

KNOX
 Margaret 120, 181

LA---
 Rosey 236

LAMBDEN
 Betsy 201
 Caroline 122

LANDING
 Mary 49
 Sarah 212
LANDING (Continued)
 Sophia 165

LANE
 Betsey Scott 303
 Virginia 140

LANG
 Elizabeth 331
 Frances 165
 Margaret 316
 Matilda 252
 Molly 26, 224
 Virginia 316

LANKFORD
 Mary 206
 Sally 12

LATCHUM
 Sally 144

LAWRENCE
 Betsy 146
 Molly 227
 Susanna 117

LILLISTON (Continued)
  Eleanor 65, 108
  Harriet 66
  Kessy 127
  Leah 44
  Susannah 18
  Tabitha 128

LINGO
  --- 298
  Elizabeth 191, 311
  Margaret 5, 172
  Nancy 144
  Polly 297
  Sally 28, 38

LINTON
  Esther 194
  Mahala 179
  Rachel 172
  Sophia 222

LIPPINCOTT
  Rosanna 70, 73

LITCHFIELD
  Elizabeth 32
  Grace 224

LITTLETON
  Betsy 222
  Linany 214
  Mary 16
  Susanna 330
  Susanna 101

LOGAN
  Mary Ann 101
  Sarah 185
  Susan 127
  Susanna 204

LONG
  Mary 128, 334
  Molly 227

LOYD
  Hester 201

LUCAS
  Ara 86
  Betsy 260
  Catherine 7
  Comfort 285
  Elizabeth 29
  Henrietta 280
  Lucinda 57
  Margaret 333
  Nancy 132
  Omey 306
  Polly 81
  Sally 209, 279

LUKER
  Patsy 255
  Susanna 198

LUMBER
  Elizabeth 223
  Nancy 164
  Petty 200

LUNN
  Mary 311

LURTON
  Betsy 2
  Eleanor 194
  Sally 292

LYON
  Louisa 203

MADDOX
  Lovey 4

MAHORN
  Euphania 161

MAJOR
  Ann 182
  Betsy 245
  Elizabeth 10, 177
  Euphemia 233
  Margaret 218
  Mary 217
  Molly 301
  Sally 333
  Sarah Ann 238

MALONEY
Sarah 160

MAPP
Ann 133
Elizabeth 46, 210
Esther 87
Hester 34
Jane 163, 313
Leah 79
Margaret 23
Margaret Sarah 102
Peggy 80
Polly 45
Sarah 193

MARINER
Elizabeth 255
Esther 200
Euphemia 283
Sally 289

MAROW
Arady 183

MARRINER
Fanny 26
Nancy 286
Polly 206
Rachel 39

MARSHALL
Adah 178
Ann 34, 180
Barbara 159
Betsy 324
Charlotte 96
Eleanor 11
Elisha 167
Elizabeth 102, 138, 159, 189, 214

MARSHALL (Continued)
Emmaline 180
Euphamia 66, 142
Fanney 62
Frances 97
Grace 101
Hester 294
Hetty 292
Ibba 283

MARSHALL (Continued)
Leah 58
Levinah 179
Louisa 173
Lusey 57
Lydia 300
Maria 199, 263
Mariah 58
Mary 40, 209, 304
mary Jane 268
Milly 167
Nancy 4, 277, 287
Patience 160
Peggy 281, 300
Polly 98, 143, 227, 239
Rebecca 157
Rosanna 203
Sally 83, 98, 189, 294, 319
Sarah 98, 241
Tabitha 180, 326
Winney 101
Wise 122

MARTIN
Betsy 24
Catherine 38
Catherine Susan 214
Eliza 250
Elizabeth 119, 125
Margaret 125
Mary 21
Nancy 172
Peggy 78, 153
Sally 14, 298
Susanna 284, 301
Tabitha 252
Thamar 172

MASON
Agnes 218, 221
Ann 200, 209
Betsey 319
Bridget 74
Catherine 123
Elizabeth 240, 271, 277, 290, 291, 331
Ellen 12, 239
Fanny 312
Harriet 113, 197
Juliet 235

MASON (Continued)
Lovea 204
Lovey 269, 271
Margaret 229
Maria 137
Mary 8, 167, 190 305
Matilda 37
Molly 141
Nancy 14, 42, 220
Parmelia 89
Patricia 92
Peggy 57, 93
Polly 45, 71, 144, 239
Rachel 28, 46, 204, 333
Rosey 49
Sarah 289, 307
Susan 30, 218
Susanna 18
Tabitha 9
Tinne 184
Triphany 223

MASSEY
Ann 70, 319
Elizabeth 127, 133, 310, 323, 334
Euphanica 41Henrietta 39
Maria 126
Mary 41, 253
Nancy 70
Peggy 241
Polly 108
Sally 4

MATHEWS
Anne 100
Betsy 297
Elizabeth 101, 258 300, 315
Esther 110, 320
Henrietta 228
Mary 186
Polly 295
Rachel 230
Rebecca 97
Sally 330
Sarah 82, 201
Silvia 42

MATLY
Ann 19

MATTHES
Mahala 273

MATTHEWS
Ann 188
Anna Maria 224
Bridget 251
Cathy 245
Eliza 63, 189
Elizabeth 188, 238
Margaret 94
Mary 132, 135, 188, 309, 318
Nancy 34, 189, 317, 319
Polly 207
Rachel 101
Rebecca 178
Sally 99, 189

MAY
Nancy 41

MAYSON
Leah 50

McCOLLEM
Mary 171

McCREADY
Crity 236
Sally Frances 261
Sarah Ann 269

McKEEL
Catherine 127
Rosetta 295

McLAIN
Elizabeth 325

McMASTER
Elizabeth 140
Elizabeth Ann 101

McMATH
Peggy 33

MEARS
Adah 237, 264
Ann 60, 63, 125, 195, 298
Betsy 157, 249, 258

MEARS (Continued)
  Catherine 26
  Caty 334
  Charlotte 121, 140
  Comfort 258, 276
  Elisha 287
  Eliza 140
  Elizabeth 15, 23, 140 249
  Elizabeth Susan 107
  Emiline 331
  Hessy 30
  Hetty 30, 219
  Jane 153
  Juliet 305
  Keziah 46
  Leah 103
  Margaret 23, 146, 306
  Maria 108
  Mary 25, 29, 46, 86, 123,
    195, 232, 251
  Mary Ann 46, 142
  Molly 149
  Nancy 39, 107, 138, 14, 296
  Nanny 297
  Peggy 191
  Polly 157, 195, 210
  Rachel 25, 207
  Roey 199
  Rosey 195
  Sally 6, 23, 25, 255, 260
  Sarah 204, 246
  Susan 94
  Susanna 199
  Tabby 183
  Tabitha 321
  Virginia 194
  Zeporah 268

MEDAD
  Leah 187
  Sally 223
  Tinny 215

MEHOLLONS
  Susan 198

MELSON
  Amy 322
  Ann 310
  Betsy 99, 208, 226

MELSON (Continued)
  Bridget 167
  Damey 200
  Eliza 303
  Elizabeth 115, 280
  Frances 285
  Hessy 271
  Jane 135
  Kessy 224
  Leah 45, 63, 259
  Mahala 196
  Margaret 43, 92, 110
  Margaret Ann 114
  Mary Ann 167
  Molly 162
  Nancy 74, 130, 246. 297
  Pamelia 214
  Patsy 321
  Ritter 231
  Sally 28
  Sarah 23, 74, 196
  Sarrey 55
  Scarburgh 148, 297
  Seymour 199, 324
  Suckey 316

MELVIN
  Barbara 204
  Charlotte 313
  Elizabeth 78
  Jenney 98
  Sophia 31

MERRIL
  Polly 294
  Sarah 111

MERRILL
  Elizabeth 133, 174, 186, 189
  Esther 62
  Euphamy 318
  Hetty 144
  Margaret 79
  Mary 112
  Nancy 287
  Rebecca 49
  Sally 145, 228
  Shady 136

MERRY
  Mary 243

MERS
  Caty 5

METCALF
  Adeline 185
  Elizabeth 251, 266
  Polly 68, 83
  Salley 67
  Sally 35, 310
  Sarah 68
  Susan 111

METTHEWS
  Peggy 69

MICHAEL
  Nancy 28

MICHOM
  Peggy 25

MIDDLETON
  Laney 111
  Molly 258
  Nancy Ann 218
  Peggy 242

MIGEE
  Sarah 118

MILBURN
  Anna 202
  Elizabeth 262
  Euphamia 4
  Nancy 130
  Peggy 187

MILBY
  Ann 253
  Betsy 87
  Elizabeth 5
  Nancy 3

MILES
  Betsy 59
  Cornelia 276
  Drucilla 46

MILES (Continued)
  Emma 106
  Fanny 110
  Jane 316
  Lucretia 31
  Maria 287
  Mary 115, 276
  Molly 276, 320
  Nancy 39, 42
  Phany 88
  Polly 293
  Rose Ann 149
  Sally 155
  Sarah 291
  Tabitha 278

MILLENNER
  Susannah 136

MILLIGAN
  Charlotte 68
  Critty 90
  Louisa 90
  Tabitha 105
MILLINER
  Eliza 199
  Rachel 116
  Tabitha 104

MILLS
  Anne 272
  Elizabeth 222

MINSON
  Nancy 1

MISTER
  Elizabeth 167, 191, 255
  Emiline 310
  Margaret 26, 297
  Mary 291, 292
  Peggy 296
  Rachel 60
  Sarah 94
  Sarah Ann 320
  Susan 116, 136, 229
  Susanna 204
  Tabitha 233

NORTHAM (Continued)
  Rachel 103, 326
  Rebecca 29
  Sally 119, 130
  Susanna 58

NOTTINGHAM
  Elizabeth 10
  Ester 10
  Margaret 177, 306

NUTT
  Ariena 21

NUTTS
  Keziah 318
  Rachel 291

OLIVER
  Ann 163
  Margaret 310

ONIONS
  Ann 286
  Betsy 15
  Polly 314
  Sally 295
  Serenia 59
  Susan 20

ONLEY
  Ailsey 249
  Margaret 99
  Nancy 48

ONLY
  Betsy 127
  Caty 129
  Margaret 185

OUTTEN
  Ada 218
  Ann 67
  Betsey 263
  Eliza 254
  Elizabeth 84, 256
  Frances 24
  Mary 247, 295
  Nancy 221, 279

OWEN
  Mary 80, 271
  Mary 63
  Rebecca 63

OWENS
  Lany 285
  Sally 81

PAIL
  Sarah 71

PALMER
  Betsy 268
  Elizabeth 320

PANE
  Eliza 115

PARKER
  Ann 102, 116, 185, 296
  Anna 64
  Anne 268
  Annie Wharton 70
  Betsey 43
  Betsy 43
  Caroline 95
  Charlotte 64
  Elizabeth 94, 159, 263, 317,
    333
  Henrietta 263
  Jane 43
  Leah 76, 102
  Lucinda 303
  Lucy 301
  Margaret 273, 302
  Maria 315
  Mariah 249
  Mary 75, 89, 272
  Milly 53
  Molly 125, 154
  Nancy 112, 170
  Patience 316
  Peggy 128
  Rosy 201
  Ruth 261
  Sally 26, 117, 299
  Sarah 311
  Sarah Ann 84
  Tabitha 260

PARKES
    Elishea 124
    Hetty 181
    Leah 151
    Nancy 170

PARKINSON
    Nancy 153

PARKS
    Ann 160
    Betsy 127, 259, 272
    Brunetta 64
    Catherine 278
    Cleo 72
    Comfort 243
    Elisha 136
    Elizabeth 72, 164, 309
    Esther 82
    Jane 43
    Judah 71, 97
    Lucinda 109
    Margaret Ann 169
    Mary 39
    Milcah Ann 2
    Nancy 30, 159, 302, 34
    Polly 48, 158
    Rachel 96, 99
    Rhoda 72
    Sally 97, 297
    Susan 63
    Tabitha 84, 278
    Zeporah 72

PARRAMORE
    Ann 303
    Elizabeth 19
    Harriet 222
    Marianna 130
    Mary 76
    Sally 96
    Sarah 3, 332
    Sophia 146

PATTERSON
    Tabitha 292

PAUL
    Ann 218
    Euphamy 217

PAUL (Continued)
    Mary 163
    Sarah 71

PAYNE
    Anna 130
    Eliza 209
    Elizabeth 323

PEARCE
    Elizabeth 4
    Priscilla 121

PECK
    Elizabeth 303
    Hannah 21
    Maria 73

PENN
    Rachel 17

PENNOCK
    Bridget 76

PETTIT
    Henny 128
    Margaret 304
    Mary 128
    Sally 325

PETTITT
    Leah 271
    Rachel 330
    Sarah 302
    Tippah 129

PEUSEY
    Catherine 308
    ELizabeth 109
    Margaret 12
    Rachel 7

PEWITT
    Bethamia 1

PHILIPS
    Rachel 275

PHILLIPS
Ann 185, 226
Catherine 95
Charlotte 165
Elizabeth 53, 66, 226, 282
Euphamia 290, 291
Harriet 44
Hessy 226
Hesy 272
Jane 44
Louisa 176
Lucy 249
Margaret 55
Mary 192, 197
Molly 61
Nancy 160, 194
Peggy 303
Peggy Burton 55
Prissey 125
Rachel 176, 272, 274, 334
Rosey 315
Sally 26, 219
Sarah 7, 184, 226, 276
Susan 210
Tabitha 324
Taby 62

PICKET
Betsy 227

PICKETT
Tempy 92

PIPER
Mary 126

PITCHET
Margaret 132

PITT
Elizabeth 80

PITTS
Lucy
Margaret 314
Maria 204
Martha 328
Mary 155

PITTS (Continued)
Nancy 299
Sarah 65

PLANTER
Comfort 41

POLK
Patsy 104

POOL
Ann 273
Athelia 162
Cornelia 100, 163

POOLMAN
Eliza
Mary

PORTER
Anne 8
Sally 67
Sukey 78

POTTER
Ann 263
Comfort 207
Elizabeth 235
Susanna 177
Virginia 76

POULSON
Alice 93
Eliza 326
Elizabeth 29, 228, 234, 328
Harriet 155
Hessy 24
Leah 264
Mary 14
Mary Ellen 242
Nancy 203
Sally 10, 183
Susanna 59, 199

POWELL
Agnes 254
Amey 74
Betty 225
Elicia 107
Elizabeth 149, 167, 170, 223

-376-

POWELL (Continued)
  Eveline 323
  Harriet 174
  Hepsey 112
  Jane 98
  Joice 315
  Mahola 262
  Margaret 232
  Mary 1, 63, 105, 264
  Nancy 293
  Polly 96, 317
  Sally 16
  Sarah Ann 257
  Sophia 41, 273
  Susanna 285

PRATT
  Patience 191
  Peggy 81
  Salley 38

PRESCOAT
  Delilah 208

PRESCOT
  Elizabeth 167

PRESCOT
  Nancy 266

PRESCOTT
  Caroline Ann 278
  Caty 332
  Hester 212
  Polly 48

PREWIT
  Abigail 298
  Catey 133
  Henrietta 321

PREWITT
  Ann 164
  Polly 129
  Shady 97

PRICE
  Leah 260

PRITCHETT
  Priscilla 268

PRITILOAE
  Sally 59

PRUITT
  Eleanor 72
  ELizabeth 220
  Hessey 209
  Hessy 11
  Molly 198
  Patsy Ann 98
  Peggy 314

PURNELL
  Belle 5
  Sally 313
  Sally Ann 205

PUSEY
  Eliza 154
  Hester 193
  Sarah Frances 299

PUZEY
  Hester 193

QUINAWAY
  Betsy 114

RAMSEY
  Sally 49

RANGER
  Wooney 164

RAYFIELD
  Ann 184
  Betsy 4
  Catherine 310
  Elizabeth 322
  Margaret 310
  Maria 2
  Mary 230
  Nancy 20
  Susan 2, 84
  Susanna 169

READ
Betsey 289
Ede 286
Leah 165
Mary 254
Nancy 28, 237
Sally 145
Sarah 299
Sarah Finney 174

REID
Elizabeth 65, 239

RESSELL
Margaret 220

✗ **REVELL**
Catherine 311
Margaret 171, 241
Phyllis 2
Rebecca 117
Sally 228

REW
Catherine 27
Elizabeth 69, 256, 293
Emiline 8
Euphamia 37
Hetty 320
Margaret Ann 293
Maria 264
Mary 230
Nancy 51
Peggy 285
Rachel 333
Sally 144
Sarah 221

RICHARDSON
Caroline 196
Elizabeth 206
Hessey 201
Keziah 308
Marcy 63
Mary 105, 189, 298
Peggy 274

RICHISON
Ann 70, 130

RIGGEN
Elizabeth 132
Rhodah 28

RIGGIN
Betty 181
Mamcy 76
Nancy 297

RIGGINS
Hannah 49

✗ **RIGGS**
Betsey 54
Leah 234
Mary 110
Nancy 158, 159
Rachel 287
Sally 322
Sarah 267

RIGHT
Tabitha 65

RILEY
Ann 34, 161
Anne Robinson 89
Betsy 315
Elizabeth 88, 217, 253
Ellen 84
Emily 128
Evaline 211
Henrietta 17
Mary 249
Nancy 237
Sally 292
Susan 295
Susanna 60

ROACH
Polly 292
Rachel 97

ROAN
Eliza 147
Margaret 245
Maria 223

ROANS
  Harriet 21
  Sally 22

ROBERTS
  Ann 202
  Catherine 323
  Elizabeth 22
  Esther 17
  Louisa 106
  Molly 249
  Nancy 191
  Polly 229
  Sally 128
  Sarah 245
  Susan 206

ROBINS
  Ann 170
  Belinda 326
  Eliza 233
  Elizabeth 95, 238
  Leah 96
  Margaret 305
  Mary 14
  Mary Ann 77
  Nancy 273
  Sarah 161, 187

ROBINSON
  Elizabeth 149

RODERS
  Sally 94

RODGER
  Christabel 37
  Elizabeth 288

RODGERS
  Ann 326
  Betsy 110, 151
  Cristobel 137
  Dorothy 259
  Elizabeth 34, 102, 152, 163,
    250, 276
  Esther 109
  Euphamen 94
  Haddasa 147

RODGERS (Continued)
  Hannah 259
  Harriet 137

RODGERS (Continued)
  Jane 217, 246
  Kessy 78
  Margaret 12, 154, 233, 261,
    317
  Mary 246
  Molly 137
  Nanny 49
  Polly 16, 35
  Sally 217
  Sophia 87

ROGERS
  Alice 284

ROLLY
  Margaret 55

RONE
  Caroline 316
  Harriet 21

ROSARY
  Betty 141
  Sabra 82

ROSS
  Bridget 109
  Esther 29
  Mary 108
  Polly 325
  Rachel 164, 168
  Sally 289

ROSSER
  Jane 4

ROWLEY
  Nancy 95
  Polly 290
  Sarah 78

ROWLY
  Ann 51
  Comfort 304

ROYAL
Tabitha 274

RUSSEL
Elizabeth 181, 202
Margaret 36

RUSSELL
Abby 143
Alicia 169
Ann 82, 257, 278
Anna 233
Caroline 144
Catherine 42
Chanty 37
Clarissa 133
Elizabeth 8
Euphemia 141
Hessy 268
Lucretia 242
Margaret 220
Mary 220, 264
Nancy 67
Peggy 315
Polly 168, 244
Rachel 35
Rebecca 81, 130
Rosey 15
Sally 27, 69, 169
Sarah 44, 59, 160, 329
Arah Ann 116
Susan 243
Yearly 220

SALESBURY
Ann 248
Catherine 204
Eliza 43
Kessy 30
Margaret 36

SAMAGE
Rachel 50

SAMPLE
Betsy 182
Candia 21
Charity 21
Eliza 308

SAMPLE (Continued)
Jane 253
Polly 295
Rachel 9
Sally 148
Sarah 147
Susan 16
Susey 18

SANDERS
Keziah 271

SANDFORD
Nancy 259

SASBERY
Martha Ann 206

SATCHELL
Ann Bell 147
Charlotte 147
Hessy 129
Julia 225
Mary 242, 330
Susan 101
Susanna 265

SAUNDERS
Emmy Perry 333
Mary 84
Sarah 232

SAVAGE
Adah 167
Ann 170, 227, 296, 323
Ann Eliza 107
Barbara 208
Betsy 220, 229
Catherine 5, 83
Caty 182
Eliza Ann 107
Elizabeth 61, 162, 210, 240
Esther 182
Euphemia 136
Hanney 218
Henny 218
Henrietta 29
Hessy 329
Hetty 318
Joice 327

SAVAGE (Continued)
Juliet 214
Lacey 73
Leah 218, 225
Lovea 94
Margaret 1, 135, 262, 328
Margaret Ann 245
Mary 73, 241, 281
Mary Ann 1, 73
Mary Jane 14
Molly 227, 246, 314
Nancy 25
Peggy 229
Polly 154
Rachel 111, 260
Rose Ann 243
Rosey 183
Sally 138, 153, 185
Sarah 69, 92, 323
Susan 226, 326
Susanna 92, 308, 310
Susannah 173

SCARBOROUGH
Anne 77
Eliza 81
Margaret 37
Mary Henry 163
Sabra 306

SCARBURGH
Ann 2
Casandra 173
Catharine 83
Demary 94
Elizabeth 55, 76
Emilia 311
Emily 261
Esther 237
Eveline 329
Harriet 328
Jane 153, 232
Lavinia 253
Margaret 313
Mary 163, 299
Mary Ann 329
Mary Emiline 311
Melvina 253
Nancy 86
Sally 83

SCARBURGH (Continued)
Sarah 329
Susan 176
Tabitha 332

SCHERER
Margaret 118

SCHOOLFIELD
Polly 239
Sally 98

SCHREAVES
Julia Ann 202

SCOTT
Ann 107, 146
Betsy 271
Comfort 6
Elizabeth 27, 105, 253
Esther 266
Hennetha 68
Hessy 74
Lavinia 256
Lovey 57
Lovinia 257
Mahala 114
Mary 4, 145, 192, 213
Polly 121
Sally 42, 64, 78
Sophea 17
Sophia 199

SELBY
Amy 113
Eliza 2
Elizabeth 133
Henrietta 111
Nancy 47
Sarah 75, 118

SELVY
Elizabeth 2

SEYMORE
Elizabeth 58

SEYMOUR
Athy 20
Leah 6, 72

SEYMOUR (Continued)
Margaret 120
Rosy 234

SHANKLAND
Polly 20

SHARPLEY
Delilah 141
Elizabeth 318, 326, 327
Henny 3
Mary 31, 292
Matilda 3
Nancy 60, 145, 327
Polly 144
Sally 233

SHARPLY
Elizabeth 38
Polly 327
Sally Ann 120

SHARROD
Rosey 252

SHARWOOD
Nancy 265

SHAY
Elizabeth 289
Molly 136
Nancey 192
Nancy 265

SHEPARD
Elizabeth 122

SHEPHERD
Margaret 65
Sally 72

SHERLOCK
Elizabeth 197

SHIELD
Ann 50, 68
Elizabeth 123, 153, 255, 318
Margaret 176
Polly 11

SHIELD (Continued)
Rachel 123, 231, 235
Susanna 279

SHIELDS
Margaret 152

SHIPMAN
Sally 278
Tabitha 176

SHOARS
Nancy 174

SHORES
Elizabeth 83
Jane 158
Polly 56

SHOUS
Elizabeth 82

SHOWARD
Mary 188
Polly 202

SHREAVES
Esther 259
Mary 284
Sally 333

SHREIVES
Betsy 221
Mary 173

SHREVES
Betsy 221
Nancy 273

SHRIEVES
Polly 8, 143
Elizabeth 197

SHURLOCK
Elizabeth 197

SILVERTHORN
Anne 187
Jane 292

& Joshua on Last page!

TAYLOR (Continued)
Comfort Ann 136
Damy 184
Delina 133
Demariah 275
Edith 233
Eliza 188
Elizabeth 13, 14, 62, 83,
131, 133, 144, 165, 166,
177, 202, 215, 227, 287
Esther 233, 297
Euphamy 189
Euphanica 40
Euphemia 145
Francis 254
Hannah 95
Henny 319
Henrietta 20
Hessy 187
Hetty 8, 28
Jane 47, 158, 159, 186
Julianna 84
Lavinia 112
Leah 330
Leney 61
Levinia 166
Louisa 6
Lovea 304
Malinda 306
Margaret 10, 24, 42, 43, 48
58, 59, 90, 98, 99, 110,
172, 206, 290
Margaret Ann 191
Maria 60
Martha 189
Mary 40, 59, 126, 149, 165
173, 198, 286, 294
Mary Ann 258
Matilda 37
Milcah 178
Milly 148
Molly 141
Nance 134
Nancy 27, 40, 70, 73, 82, 83,
84, 168, 173, 179, 217,
259, 282, 285, 286, 287,
328
Nanny 235
Naomi 174
Narcissa 81

TAYLOR (Continued)
Narissa 180
Patience 293
Peggy 189, 254
Polly 25, 49, 74, 120, 187,
256, 286, 288, 318, 325
Rachel 31, 40, 93
Reba 62
Rebecca 62, 82, 285
Rose 149
Ruth 88
Salley 109
Sally 61, 86, 150, 181, 241,
304, 309
Sarah 198, 308
Sarah Ann 217, 294
Scarburgh 215
Serena 131
Shady 314
Susan 98, 149, 282
Susanna 290
Tabitha 47
Triphany 31

TAYLORE
Sally 309

TEACKEL
Henny 124

TEACKLE
Ann 93, 251, 261
Levinia 113
Margaret 15, 222
Mary 244
Sarah 35
Sarah Upshur 17
Susan 261
Susanna 238

TEAGUE
Nanny 148

THOMAS
Eliza 214
Judy 307
Lavina 326
Margaret 268
Milly 288
Nancy 173

THOMAS (Continued)
  Peggy 312
  Polly 180
  Sally 71, 168
  Sarah 97

THOMPSON
  Ann 298
  Louisa 176
  Nanny 9

THORN
  Sarah 187

THORNS
  Nancy 12

THORNTON
  Betsey 135
  Betsy 217
  Carolina 48
  Catherine 270
  Delia 77
  Delilah 66
  Elizabeth 188, 221, 274
  Euphemia 288
  Hessey 283
  Jane 243
  Margaret 312
  Mary Ann 294
  Phebe 51, 254
  Polly 268, 327
  Rachel 241
  Salley 186
  Sally 62, 112, 186, 282, 319

TIGNAL
  Katherine 194
  Rosey 221, 223

TIGNALL
  Ann 22
  Margaret 184

TIGNER
  Elizabeth 328
  Leah 39

TINDAL
  Matilda 179

TINDELL
  Ann Catherine 279
  Sally 325

TOMSON
  Ann 298

TOPPING
  Maria Snead 295
  Mary 122
  Peggy 36
  Sally 202, 245
  Sarah 218
  Susanna 202
  Tipporah 315

TOWNSEND
  Elizabeth 274
  Fanny 236
  Jane 288
  Leah 269
  Maria 283
  Nancy 229
  Polly 38
  Rebecca 282
  Sabrah 250
  Sally 80, 85, 276

TRADER
  Adeline 232
  Agnes 255
  Ann 95, 121
  Catherine 88
  Comfort 211
  Delilah 290
  Elizabeth 52, 58, 61, 63, 103
  Emeline 235, 241
  Grace 289
  Henrietta 181
  Hetty 79
  Jane 118
  Jernina 255
  Lane 57
  Mary 30, 92
  Nancy 59, 140
  Rachel 110, 142
  Rebecca 120, 149
  Rosey 249
  Rosy 33
  Sally 176

TREHEARN
Elizabeth 8
Leah 208
Nancy 304
Polly 154

TREHEARNE
Nancy 304

TRICKLE
Sinah 98

TUGNAL
Betsy 164

TULL
Esther 40
Mary 303
Vice 302

TUNNALL
Mariah 82

TUNNEL
Elizabeth 60
Esther 313

TUNNELL
Betsy 69
Comfort 145
Eliza 63
Elizabeth 68
Mary 65, 171, 186
Molly 180
Sally 204, 250
Sarah 53
Susan 243
Scarburgh 110

TURLINGTON
Betty 152
catherine 177
Comfort 181
Leah 220, 221
Margaret 118
Maria 248
Mary 60, 124, 142, 250
Nancy 205, 291
Patsy 192

TURLINGTON (Continued)
Peggy 30
Rachel 103
Rosey 192
Sally 227
Sarah 162

TURNALL
Elizabeth 282

TURNEL
Nancy 44

TURNELL
Sally

TURNER
Ann 228
Atha 56
Emiline 261
Margaret 261, 262, 307
Mary 162, 324
Sarah 127
Scarburgh 184
Susan 71, 198
Tabitha 331
Ziliah 85

TURPIN
Nancy 239

TWIFORD
Amey 239
Elizabeth 11, 47
Hennetta 94
Mary 218
Peggy 260
Susanna 115

TWYFORD
Anna 85
Molly 266

TYLER
Ann 203
Comfort 57, 58
Jane 47
Mary 287
Mary Ann 262
Zipporah 96

TYLOR
  Nancy 32

TYNDAL
  Margaret 184

UNDERHILL
  Anna 155
  Elizabeth 34
  Nancy 196
  Sally 14
  Sarah 162
  Susan 34

UPSHUR
  Charlotte 185
  Elizabeth Ann Brown 301
  Leah 176
  Susan 10

VENELSON
  Louisa 260

VERE
  Nancy 7

VERMILLION
  Ann 112

VERNELSON
  Charlotte 226
  Nancy 227
  Rebecca 289

VESSELLS (See also WESSELLS)
  Betsy 111

VESSELS (See also WESSELLS)
  Nancy 84
  Polly 214

VINNALSON
  Polly 209

WALBURN
  Mary 11

WALKER
  Betsey 278
  Eliza 321

WALKER (Continued)
  Elizabeth 137
  Henny 32
  Hester 99
  Margaret 79, 295
  Maria 316
  Martha 209
  Nancy 136
  Sally 296
  Sarah 63

WALLACE
  Elizabeth 191
  Sally 192

WALLIS
  Mary 121

WALLOP
  Elizabeth 105, 121, 276, 321
  Margaret 188
  Mary 79, 111, 265
  Tabitha 51

WALSTON
  Meliah 118

WALTER
  Ann 38
  Louisa 64
  Matilda 106

WALTERS
  Eliza 304
  Elizabeth 163
  Margaret 235
  Mary 305
  Mary Ann 291
  Patty 183
  Sally 125

WAPLES
  Cassey 329
  Mary 238, 239

WARD
  Catherine 332
  Elizabeth 1, 205, 233
  Margaret 75, 262, 309
  Mary 332

WARD (Continued)
Nancy 54
Sally 201
Susa 107

WARINGTON
Elizabeth 35

WARNER
Elizabeth 211, 308
Hessy 129
Lucretia 277
Mary 69
Nancy 88
Peggy 215
Sally 111
Sarah Ann 249

WARRINGTON
Ann 26, 39
Betsey 20
Euphamia 308
Hetty 131
Lovey 251
Margaret 178
Mary 304
Nancy 86, 248
Rosey 182
Sally 25, 251, 262
Sarah 132, 201

WATERFIELD
Ann 227
Elizabeth 49, 97, 129, 190
Margaret 126
Mary 39, 131
May 40
Nancy 196
Sally 251

WATERS
Elizabeth 119, 130, 280, 313
Mary 281
Nancy 97
Rachel 311
Sarah 145
Susan 62

WATSON
Agnes 299
Ann 29
Annis 62
Betsy 37
Catherine 25, 230, 265
Elizabeth 65, 206
Frances 256
Frances Catherine 329
Harriet 88
Hessy 327, 328
Hetty 53
Isea 236
Kessey 223
Leah 27, 78, 292
Lucretia 96
Margaret 83, 219, 303
Margaret Ann 204, 205, 297
Mary 1, 131, 240
Mary Ann 53
Meliah 211
Molly 162
Nancy 101, 220
Peggy 322
Polly 74, 166, 323
Priscilla 134
Rosey 168, 297
Sally 84, 122, 132, 151, 200
Sarah 125
Susan 20, 115
Tabitha 184

WATTS
Ann 89
Elizabeth 329
Harriet 304
Henrietta 179
Jane 237
Margaret 50, 51, 91
Maris 295

WEATLY
Henney 277

WEBB
Magaret 116
Molly 272

WELBORNE
  Hester Ann 179
  Polly 161

WELBURN
  Margaret 215
  Sally 116
  Susan 73

WELBURNE
  Betsy 165

WELCH
  Ann 170
  Elizabeth 153
  Nancy 62

WEOCH
  Margaret 23

WESSELLS
  Adeline 185
  Amanda 22
  Amelley 333
  Amey 314, 317
  Ann 315, 332
  Arinthia 283
  Catherine 242, 332
  Delaney 208
  Elizabeth 52, 98, 236, 267,
    320
  Ellen 8
  Eveline 275
  Laura 134
  Margaret 332
  Mary 33, 206
  Mary Ann 315
  Nancy 156, 221, 283, 315
  Patsy 99, 314
  Peggy 242, 280
  Polly 314
  Sally 52, 142, 333
  Susan 168

WEST
  Ader 115
  Ann 113
  Anna 143
  Anne 45
  Cassey 127

WEST (Continued)
  Clara 132
  Comfort 299
  Elizabeth 230, 266, 308, 324
  Emily 264
  Esther 116
  Euphamia 8
  Fanny 236
  Frances Rearby 75
  Harriet Ann
  Hester Ann
  Indiana Margaret 230
  Jane 224
  Margaret 24, 97, 164, 166
  Maria 164
  Mary 45, 110, 310
  Mary Jane 219
  Nancy 38, 80, 259, 267
  Polly 220
  Priscilla 149
  Sally 133, 236
  Susan 237, 240
  Susanna 170, 240, 273
  Tabitha 75, 198

WHARTON
  Betsy 237, 330
  Peggy 54
  Rachel 326

WHEALTON
  Betsy 57
  Elizabeth 65. 145. 167, 189
    208
  Esther 99, 254
  Leah 233
  Margaret 270
  Maria 51
  Mary 287
  Nancy 81, 174
  Polly 145
  Sally 188
  Sarah 140, 146, 278
  Scarburgh 263
  Tabitha 321

WHEATLEY
  Mary Ann 30
  Patty 134
  Polly 281

WHEATLY
  Hetty 112
  Nancy 260

WHEATON
  Nancy 86

WHEELTON
  Nancy 34

WHITE
  Alicia 22
  Ann 40, 114
  Betsey 32
  Betsy 83, 324
  Catherine 80
  Charlotte 321
  Demeriah 169
  Elizabeth 7, 67, 01, 241, 311
  Euphenica 317
  Henny 248
  Keziah 313
  Lovey 66
  Margaret 264, 320
  Mary 1, 201, 265, 291
  Nancy 42, 174, 313
  Peggy 96, 119, 172
  Polly 26
  Rachel 158, 243
  Rosah 202
  Rosey 114
  Sabra 15
  Sally 111, 173, 279
  Sarah 319, 324
  Sophia 68
  Tabitha 174

WHITTINGTON
  Elizabeth 209

WILDERSON
  Agnes 279
  Sally 279

WILETT
  Elizabeth 156

WILKERSON
  Elizabeth 321
  Euphamy 198

WILKINS
  Eliza 261
  ELizabeth 241
  Harriet 328

WILKINSON
  Nancy 214

WILLET
  Elizabeth 36
  Sarah 222

WILLETT
  Anna 200
  Elizabeth 172
  Kessy 119
  Nancy 93
  Sally 84
  Sarah 323

WILLIAMS
  Betsy 33
  Elizabeth 318
  Fiske 42
  Joyce 177, 178
  Margaret 23, 247, 191
  Mary Ann 191
  Molly 6, 9
  Nancy 207, 285
  Sally 126
  Sarah 42
  Sinah 325

WILLIS
  Ann 238
  Catherine 104
  Elizabeth 90
  Margaret 241
  Susan 247
  Tabitha 209

WILSON
  Bekey 114
  Critty 214
  Elizabeth 256
  Euphamy 269
  Harriet 62
  Leah 59
  Mary 2, 322
  Matilda 264

Nancy 286
Sophia 262

WIMBOROUGH
Margaret 296

WIMBRO
Nancy 312

WIMBROUGH
Sally 32

WINBOROUGH
Susanna 157

WINBROW
Polly 177

WINDER
Margaret 60
Mary 230
Mary Ann 304

WINDON
Elizabeth 64

WINDOW
Ann 121
Elizabeth 137, 280, 281
Rosey 229
Sally 265
Sarah 163, 327

WISE
Ann 225
Betsy 198
Betsy 254
Caroline 243
Charity 202
Charlotte 229
Eliza 151, 152
Elizabeth 7, 25, 70
Esther 268
Hannah 294
Henny 307
Leah 35
Margaret 56, 329
Maria 329
Martha 236
Mary 54, 109, 215
Polly 62

WISE (Continued)
Rebecca 54
Rosey 171
Sally 229, 292
Sarah 15, 19
Sukey 7, 220
Tabitha 246, 317

WITTUS
Ada 218

WOOD
Elizabeth 179
Rosetta 118

WOODS
Anna 157
Polly 269

WOOLDUP
Nancy 80

WOOLRIDGE
Leah 241

WRIGHT
Ann 136, 291
Catherine 110
Elizabeth 19, 85, 135, 212
Henrietta 67
Hester 16
Keziah 276
Louisa 223
Malinda 148
Mary Ann 161
Molly 149
Prudence Jane 103
Rosey 31
Sally 7, 38, 43
Susan 268
Susanna 224
Tabitha 267

WYATT
Bekey 105
Betsy 193
Catharine 193
Elizabeth 194, 195, 196
Margaret 239, 250
Maria 29

WYATT (Continued)
  Mariah Hannah 187
  Peggy Satchell 93
  Polly 108
  Sally 124, 331

YERBY
  Eliza Upshur 301

YOUNG
  Ann 15, 43
  Anne 15
  Betsy 43
  Elia 216
  Eliza 281

YOUNG (Continued)
  Elizabeth 16, 98, 131, 212
  Eveline 202
  Hannah 60
  Leah 140
  Margaret 134, 160, 211, 288,
    300
  Mary 131, 267
  Peggy 278
  Polly 131, 167, 240
  Sally 186
  Sarah 314
  Susan Jane 194
  Tabitha 214, 221, 316
  Tenny 230